SOUTHERN BIOGRAPHY SERIES

SEARGENT S. PRENTISS
Whig Orator of the Old South

SEARGENT S. PRENTISS

FROM A PHOTOGRAPH IN THE OFFICE OF THE PRESIDENT OF BOWDOIN COLLEGE

SEARGENT S. PRENTISS

Whig Orator of the Old South

By

Dallas C. Dickey

Louisiana State University Press

Baton Rouge, Louisiana

1946

324. 2092
D55s
47,582

PRINTED IN THE UNITED STATES OF AMERICA
BY THE VAIL-BALLOU PRESS, INC., BINGHAMTON, N. Y.

To

GERTRUDE AND DOUGLAS

PREFACE

A nation may take pride in her orators as well as her statesmen, poets, and scientists. The power of the spoken word has always made itself felt upon the course of history. While some men employ their oratorical talents to elevate themselves to public office, others care less for this kind of reward. Many choose to be aiders and abettors. Such a man was Seargent S. Prentiss.

Historians and scholarly biographers have not, heretofore, undertaken a systematic account of Prentiss' life. This may be explained on the basis that his period of public office was brief. At the same time, they have made significant references to him as they have chronicled the lives of his contemporaries and depicted the events of his day. Moreover, since Prentiss was a lawyer, so compelling before juries and judges, men of the legal guild have bestowed on him the honor of calling him a great lawyer. Likewise, students of rhetoric (public address) have been aware of his eloquence. But since the historians, lawyers, and rhetoricians have thus far neglected to portray his total career, a biography may be welcomed. Upon the reader devolves the task of deciding how well the author has done his work.

As in all such undertakings, this writer is deeply indebted to many people who have aided him in more ways than he can state. To all he expresses his appreciation, but holds himself responsible for any errors which may be discerned.

Three individuals have been of the most direct assistance. First, the author is profoundly grateful to Professor Wendell Holmes Stephenson of Louisiana State University, who first instilled in him an enthusiasm for southern

history, who suggested this study, who has given unstintingly of his time in counsel and guidance from the inception of the work, and who now considers it worthy of
inclusion in the Southern Biography Series. To as great
an extent, the author is indebted to Professor C. M. Wise,
Head of the Department of Speech, Louisiana State University, for encouragement over the same period of time,
for careful reading of all parts of the manuscript, and for
valuable rhetorical and stylistic criticisms. Also, the author
is indebted to Professor Charles S. Sydnor of Duke University, for a careful reading of the manuscript and for
choice criticisms.

Many others are entitled to an expression of thanks.
Among these are: Mrs. John B. Whittemore, Portland,
Maine; Mrs. Elizabeth Redfield, New York; Miss Janet
Prentiss, Carmel, California; Miss Charlotte R. Prentiss,
Elizabeth, New Jersey; Miss Jeannette W. Payson, Harrison,
Maine; Mr. George K. Prentiss, New Orleans; Mr. Philip
S. Wilder, Alumni Secretary, Bowdoin College; Miss Mae
Gilman, Librarian, Maine Historical Society; Mr. Law-
rence C. Newton, Mr. V. Blaine Russell, Mr. John Bru-
nini, Mr. Mack Moore, and Mrs. David Porterfield, all of
Vicksburg, Mississippi; Mr. Harold L. Leisure, San Fran-
cisco, California; Mr. William D. McCain and Mr. Wil-
liam H. Watkins, Jackson, Mississippi; Mr. Alan Huckle-
berry, Muncie, Indiana; Mr. and Mrs. Orville Miller,
Lafayette, Indiana; Mr. George V. Bohman, Dartmouth
College; Mrs. Lyman A. Cotten, Curator of Manuscripts,
Southern Historical Collection, University of North Carolina; Mr. Edwin Adams Davis, Head of the Department
of Archives, Louisiana State University; Mr. Bernard
Mayo, University of Virginia; Mr. John B. Kaiser, Libra-
rian, Public Library of Newark, New Jersey; Mr. Thomas
P. Martin, Division of Manuscripts, Library of Congress;
Mr. Victor H. Paltsits, Chief of the American History
Division and Keeper of Manuscripts, New York Public

Library; Mrs. Charles G. Blake, Cincinnati, Ohio; Mr. Claude L. Shaver and Miss Ernestine Heard, Baton Rouge, Louisiana. The author is also grateful to Miss Mary Bell White and other members of the staff of the Louisiana State University Press for the care given in preparing the manuscript for publication. Thanks are extended as well to the staffs of the following libraries and repositories: Department of Archives, Louisiana State University; Department of History and Archives, Jackson, Mississippi; New Orleans City Archives; Howard Memorial Library, New Orleans; Library of Congress; State Historical Society, Portland, Maine; Bowdoin College; University of New Hampshire; Chancery Court, as well as the Civil Circuit Court, Warren County, Vicksburg, Mississippi. Appreciation is expressed also to the Macmillan Company for permission to quote from Reginald C. McGrane, *Foreign Bondholders and American State Debts.*

Finally, the author is indebted to his wife, Gertrude E. B. Dickey, without whose encouragement and sense of humor this work might never have been completed.

DALLAS C. DICKEY

Baton Rouge, Louisiana
August 28, 1944

CONTENTS

CONTENTS

ILLUSTRATIONS

Chapter I

EARLY LIFE AND EDUCATION

IN 1839 Seargent S. Prentiss wrote to his brother George, then studying and traveling in Europe: "if it should come in your way, I would like to have you make some inquiry in relation to the two branches of our family. The Prentiss branch is, I believe, English, and the Lewis is, as the name indicates, of Welsh origin. This is the whole amount of my genealogical knowledge." [1]

Seargent was correct in believing that his forebears were English and Welsh. The first member of the Prentiss family to leave England for America was Valentine Prentice, who, with his family, crossed the Atlantic in 1631 and settled in Roxbury, Massachusetts. Several of his cousins came a short time later. Two of these were Captain Thomas Prentice, who located at Newton, Massachusetts, and Robert Prentice, who, like Valentine, established his residence in Roxbury. Another cousin, Henry Prentice, the seventh paternal ancestor of Seargent S. Prentiss, arrived prior to 1640. He settled at Cambridge, Massachusetts, where he became a "member of the first Church in Cambridge, formed in 1636, and of which Rev. Thomas Hooker, who soon removed to Hartford, Conn., was the first pastor." [2] One of his daughters, Mary, married Nathaniel Hancock, great-grandfather of John Hancock.[3]

1 Seargent S. Prentiss to George Prentiss, Vicksburg, June 13, 1839, in [George L. Prentiss (ed.)], *A Memoir of S. S. Prentiss* (New York, 1855), II, 121.

2 *Ibid.*, I, 13. A brief genealogy of the Prentiss family, supplied by Seargent Prentiss Nutt, is available in Joseph D. Shields, *The Life and Times of Seargent Smith Prentiss* (Philadelphia, 1883), appendix, 441-42.

3 *Memoir of S. S. Prentiss*, I, 13.

Henry's great-grandson, Joshua, a minister at Holliston, Massachusetts, is accredited with altering the spelling of the family name from Prentice to Prentiss.[4] His direct descendants followed the alteration, thus distinguishing his branch of the family from the others in America, who have continued to follow the original spelling.

Another of Henry's descendants, a great-great-grandson, Samuel, is of more immediate interest, for he was the grandfather of Seargent S. Prentiss, the subject of this account, and famed in Maine, Mississippi, and Louisiana. Samuel was a graduate of Harvard in the class of 1771.[5] Sometime following the birth of his son, William, who was to be Seargent's father, he moved to Gorham, Maine, where he lived until his death in 1815. Among his nine children was one named Seargent, who died at sea at the age of nineteen. At the turn of the twentieth century, George Prentiss published a sketch of his own life and that of his immediate family for the benefit of his children. In it he referred to the drowning of young Seargent and the resultant preservation of the name, stating: "your uncle Seargent used to deplore the untimely event, as the 'ugly name' was in consequence fastened upon *him*." [6]

The village of Gorham, ten miles west of Portland, was dear to the heart of Prentiss. Here his grandfather had lived, and here his father, William, had been born in 1778, the son of Samuel. Prentiss' mother, Abigail Lewis, was born January 12, 1782.

If the children born to William and Abigail took pride (as they did) in the noble quality of their paternal lineage, there existed sufficient justification for the idolization of their mother. Abigail Lewis, of Welsh extraction, as Seargent wrote, was the daughter of Major George Lewis, who fought in the battle of Bunker Hill and participated in

[4] *Ibid.*

[5] *Ibid.*, 14; George L. Prentiss, *The Bright Side of Life* (Asbury Park, N. J., 1901), I, 1.

[6] Prentiss, *Bright Side of Life*, I, 1.

other Revolutionary events. George Prentiss wrote of his mother: "Through her we go back by four lines to the Mayflower. . . . We are closely allied through mother to all that was best in the ancestral piety, uprightness, patriotism, good understanding and wholesome, affectionate family life of the sturdy yeoman of Cape Cod." [7]

At the time of Abigail's birth, Major Lewis resided at Barnstable on Cape Cod, where he was a neighbor and a friend of James Otis. Following the Revolution, he moved his family to Gorham. [8]

Though William and Abigail met and were married at Gorham, their first years together were spent at Portland. This was occasioned by the fact that William was, by occupation, a shipmaster and operated three ships from Casco Bay. In spite of William's frequent and long voyages away from his family, the home was a happy and religious one. Both husband and wife were members of the Congregational church, and they imbued their children with staunch religious principles.

However, the years just prior to the War of 1812 were anything but ideal ones in which to make a living for an expanding family of children, even though the breadwinner was an enterprising New England shipmaster. The Embargo and Nonimportation Acts of Thomas Jefferson's second administration caused exports to fall from more than 108 million dollars in 1807 to 22 million in 1808, and imports from 138 million to 57 million. This dislocation of commerce brought financial ruin to William Prentiss, as well as to scores of other New England seamen. The commercial consequences were dire in William's case. In the words of his son, George: "Like many others, he was driven into the country by the ruin which had fallen upon commerce." [9]

And so the Prentisses moved to a farm near Gorham close by that of Major Lewis, taking with them the three chil-

[7] *Ibid.*, 2.   [8] *Ibid.*   [9] *Memoir of S. S. Prentiss*, I, 17.

dren who had been born at Portland: [10] Caroline, 1805, who died when five years of age; William, 1807; and Seargent Smith, September 30, 1808. Subsequent to the removal of William and his family to Gorham, six more children were born: Samuel, 1811; Mary Caroline, 1813, who died in infancy; Abby Lewis, 1814; George, 1816; Anna Smith, 1818; and Mary, 1821.[11]

Of the seven children who lived, all but Mary took their places in society, albeit in varying degrees, as leaders and eminent citizens. The plight of Mary was sad enough, though she lived until 1881. Almost the only explanation in the accounts of the Prentiss family as to how she lived out her days is that of George. "At her birth Mary was said to have been a picture of infantine beauty and promise. But when several months old, during her mother's temporary absence from home, she had a fall, as was supposed, which so injured her brain that she became ever after *non compos mentis.*" [12]

The other Prentiss children became people highly regarded. William went into business in New York. Samuel was the roving member of the family. For years he worked for a steamship company and went up and down the Mississippi River from New Orleans to St. Louis. Finally he drifted as far west as California, as one of the numerous Americans who sought riches in the California gold mines. Abby never married. Anna became the wife of a New England clergyman, Jonathan Stearns.

But of all the children, two, George and Seargent, may be said to have been the significantly eminent members of the family. Few more affectionate brothers ever lived. The patterns of their lives were vastly different and in great contrast; yet each contributed mightily to the encouragement and welfare of the other. George, theologian, minister, and religious educator of the nineteenth century, whose

[10] *Ibid.*, 20.   [11] Prentiss, *Bright Side of Life,* I, 2.
[12] *Ibid.*

long life span permitted him to live beyond the turn of the twentieth, was the recipient of gifts from Seargent to the extent that he was deeply his brother's debtor. But with all due respect to the character and worthiness of George, the most notable son of this New England family was Seargent. The first to admit this was George himself.

Seargent, born September 30, 1808, was physically healthy at birth, but in the early months of his life "he was seized with a violent fever, which reduced him to the verge of death, deprived him for several years of the use of his limbs, and was the cause of the defect in one of them, from which he never recovered." For "his partial recovery he was indebted to the unwearied care and devotion of his mother." Without doubt a measure of the high devotion which Seargent exhibited throughout his life for his mother is to be accounted for by gratitude. He knew "she was accustomed to spend an hour or two in rubbing and bathing his torpid limbs; this she continued to do, as far as her own infirm health would allow, year after year, until one by one they became strong enough to perform their appropriate functions: the right leg alone refused to be entirely healed, remaining lame and feeble to the last." [13] Small hope and few aspirations could be held out for this child during the early years of his life. There is a story of his father that while he was on one of his voyages at sea, Mary Caroline, born five years after Seargent, died, and that "by some mistake, the report reached . . . [him] that it was Seargent." In response to this news, "He immediately wrote to the mother, congratulating her that it had pleased Providence to spare Caroline, and to take away the poor cripple, whose prospect for life seemed so hopeless. How little do we know when we are most blessed!" [14]

Thus the beginning of Prentiss' life was scarcely auspicious for the development of an extraordinary personality. Actually he was a near invalid for the first ten

[13] *Memoir of S. S. Prentiss*, I, 15.   [14] *Ibid.*, 20.

years of his life. Though a cane was sufficient (actually essential) to his walking or standing in later life, he walked only by crutches for eight or nine years.[15] In those years scarcely anyone could have predicted that in days hence he would become an enthusiastic angler, hunter, horseback rider, wrestler, and a man fully able to defend himself physically under strenuous circumstances. Constitutionally Prentiss was extremely robust and hence was able, in time, to achieve physical agility of a high order.

If it was his lot to begin life with a bodily handicap, which it must be admitted did mar his happiness to an unfortunate degree, it cannot be said that he suffered in intellectual endowments. Mental alertness and retentiveness were characteristic of his personality. His lameness did not impede his education; very probably it accelerated it. Compelled to remain indoors, he early formed the lifelong habit of reading, with the result that, "Before reaching his tenth year, Seargent was master of every book upon which he could lay his hand. The Bible, in particular, he read and re-read, until his acquaintance with its contents was astonishing. He would repeat large portions from memory. When no one else could 'find the text' on Sabbath evening, he was seldom appealed to in vain. Next to the Bible, his greatest favorite was the *Pilgrim's Progress*." [16]

Nor was his formal schooling long neglected. About one eighth of a mile from the farm upon which Prentiss spent his early boyhood years stood the district schoolhouse. Doubtless the best description of it on record is that from Prentiss himself given years later in one of his finest speeches. "Behold yonder simple building near the crossing of the village roads! It is of small and rude construction, but stands in a pleasant and quiet spot." To it Prentiss could not walk, but rode in a most unusual conveyance. Because he was too lame to walk without his crutches, his brother William

[15] *Ibid.*, 24.   [16] *Ibid.*, 22.

pulled him to and from the school in a small handcart.[17]

As precious as may have been Prentiss' memories of the district school in after years, the education it afforded him was insufficient for a boy of his temperament. For one thing he was a cripple, and hence ill adapted to making his way in life on a farm or by manual labor. Besides, his inclinations were not in the direction of physical endeavor. Both his incapacity and dislike for work on the farm is testified to by his brother, who wrote: "Captain Prentiss brought up his sons to working on the farm; but, in consequence of his infirmity, Seargent was, in great measure, exempt. There were a few things, however, which he was able and accustomed to do; such as, riding the horse to plough and harrow, dropping seeds in planting-time, husking corn, weeding and bunching onions. He loved none of these employments,—but of the last he had a cordial detestation. The only relief he found in it was to get through his stint in season to go a-gunning, or fishing." [18]

But somewhere along the way Prentiss had acquired an intellectual enthusiasm as strong as was his detestation for manual enterprise. Very possibly his forced indoor life stimulated in him zeal for the literary and academic. He was determined to go to college. Parental support of the idea was easily obtained, but finances were not so readily available. The family resources were exceedingly limited in view of the large family, the financial reverses suffered with the collapse of the shipping business, and the relatively small yield of a Maine farm. Nevertheless, Prentiss did not surrender his youthful determination for a good education. He suggested to his mother a means of doing it, saying: "if there were no other way, he would learn a shoemaker's trade, and work at the last, until the means were acquired of accomplishing his purpose." [19]

Some means were found, though just what purse strings

---

[17] *Ibid.,* 23, 24.   [18] *Ibid.,* 26.   [19] *Ibid.,* 26–27.

were opened to him it is difficult to know. He was allowed to escape the abominations of hard labor, and he never became a shoemaker; but notwithstanding, the boy who first traveled to school in a handcart was launched on a splendid educational career. One condition operated to his advantage. In the town of Gorham, two and a half miles from the Prentiss home, there was located one of the numerous New England academies. The exact year when he first attended Gorham Academy, or the length of time he spent there, is hardly discernible from the meager authentic accounts of Prentiss' early life. But the distance from his home to the academy was not so great as to involve a heavy expense to the family. "In the winter he boarded at the village, but the rest of the year at-home, one of his brothers usually conveying him on horseback, and going to meet him on his return in the evening." [20]

The academy was a good one, capably taught and sternly administered. At least the most indispensable asset of any educational institution, good teachers, was not wanting. The principal, the man most clearly identified with the academy, was the Reverend Reuben Nason. One characterization of him is that he was "Puritan in faith, a martinet in discipline, and an encyclopaedia in knowledge." [21] George Prentiss likewise studied at Gorham, some years after Seargent, and wrote comments in high praise of this preceptor. As an old man George looked back upon Nason and declared: "He came nearer to the old-fashioned headmaster in England, of whom we read in books, than any American teacher I ever knew. He was a classical scholar of the first order, well versed also in the higher mathematics, and an enthusiastic lover of good learning." Of the academy George added that "There was at that time no better institution of the kind in Maine, probably not in New England." [22] There were other stern traits of character in Nason.

---

[20] *Ibid.*, 27.   [21] Shields, *Seargent Smith Prentiss,* 5.
[22] Prentiss, *Bright Side of Life,* I, 11.

Though he was not devoid of a sense of humor, and was withal a man of courtesy and fairness, "He has been known (*haud ignota loquor*) to flog a delinquent with the Bible, when no profaner weapon was at hand. He usually prayed with one eye, at least, wide open, on the look-out for transgressors; and often was 'Amen' followed *instanter* by the imperative 'Come up, sir!' and the quick report of birch or ferule." [23]

Assisting Nason was another teacher, William Smythe, a man of fearless and determined characteristics, who later joined the faculty of Bowdoin College. Prentiss came under his influence at Gorham between the time Smythe served in the army during the War of 1812 and his joining the faculty of Bowdoin in 1820. Probably no great or friendly attachment was engendered in Prentiss toward Smythe, at least while at Gorham, if one incident is to be believed. "For some misdemeanor Smythe flogged with the old red cowhide, which was very much in use in those days, twelve scholars, which included but one unknown guilty party." This rashness did not go unchallenged, for Prentiss tried his hand at poetry with the following result:

> Mr. Smythe, I must confess
> You have well proved your foolishness,
> In flogging us poor fellows so
> To find out what you'll never know.
>
> Perhaps you very oft have read
> What God to Abraham hath said;
> He for the righteousness of ten
> Saved two cities full of men,
> But you the contrariwise have done
> And flogged a dozen to find out one.[24]

23 *Memoir of S. S. Prentiss,* I, 27–28.

24 Unidentified clipping in Scrapbook of the Class of 1826, Library, Bowdoin College. A slightly different version of the poem appears in *Memoir of S. S. Prentiss,* I, 29.

But in reality noble influences were brought to bear on Prentiss while at Gorham. Under the classical tutelage of Nason, and with enlarged library facilities afforded by the academy, he achieved greater intellectual stature. The practice of reading which had rooted itself in the nature of the small, crippled child flourished to a greater degree. He was introduced to such works as the *Arabian Nights* and *Don Quixote* and was so stimulated that "He read with extraordinary rapidity, and whatever he read—whether history, biography, poetry, or romance—was ineffaceably impressed upon his memory." Still another work which came in his way, and one which influenced him greatly, was Lempriere's *Classical Dictionary*. "Many years afterwards, he spoke of the perfect delight with which, in the leisure school-hours, he read and re-read this book. He almost knew the whole of it by heart." For a young man destined to exhibit, above all other attributes of his nature, those of the orator, this book had lifelong values. This Prentiss realized, for "Lempriere, he used to say, was an invincible weapon for giving interest and effect to a stump speech; when all other illustrations were powerless, he never knew the shirt of Nessus, the labors of Hercules, or the forge of Vulcan, to fail." [25]

Fortunately, too, Prentiss received, among other advantages afforded at Gorham, some definite training in public address. This was to stand him in good stead in later years. An amusing incident associated with his education there illustrates the emphasis which Nason placed upon public declamation in the training of youth. Each week the students of the academy were individually required to speak some selected "piece." Several times in his early days at the academy, Seargent failed to be prepared for his declamation. The patience of Nason was finally exhausted, so that he refused to accept further excuses and demanded that Prentiss declaim on schedule. "Whereupon the little fellow

[25] *Memoir of S. S. Prentiss*, I, 28.

started out upon the rostrum, and delivered a most ludicrous original poem, full of wit and humor, apologizing for his previous remissness."[26]

The time which Prentiss spent at Gorham contributed to the widening of his mental horizons and the development and cultivation of his own capacities. One picture of him has been given by William T. Hilliard, who wrote: "Our intercourse commenced at the Gorham Academy, under the tuition of the venerable Mr. Nason." Hilliard, who was later a classmate of Prentiss at Bowdoin College, stated that at Gorham, Prentiss "loved sport, and engaged with zest in all our amusements," and that "He had, at this early period, an inexhaustible fund of anecdote, and a most happy mode of telling a story, being peculiarly effective in his embellishments. He was, at times, terribly sarcastic; but he would cut and heal at one and the same moment." Prentiss' reading habits were also observed by Hilliard. "Miscellaneous reading was his delight: he devoured history, fiction, biography, &c., with perfect avidity. I never knew one so young, who would read so rapidly, retain so thoroughly, or so readily reproduce, when occasion called. The *language* he never reproduced,—it was the pith and sentiment which he made his own property." In respect to this trait of Prentiss which so powerfully manifested itself in his later public life and speeches, Hilliard was impressed by the fact that "In reading the dead languages, which he did with much fluency," Prentiss "never troubled himself about a literal translation, but would read off a sentence in the original, and then clothe it in an ample, graceful, yet correct English drapery, seeming all the while, as if by intuition, to seize the intent and meaning of his author." Among still other characteristics which Hilliard noticed in Prentiss in their early lives together was "his coolness and self-possession." This trait Hilliard epitomized by saying of his friend: "One

[26] *Ibid.,* 29.

could scarcely find him unprepared for a reply, prompt and to the purpose." [27]

In the autumn of 1824 Prentiss was sixteen years old. He had acquired a love of reading and learning to such an extent that he sought to continue his formal education beyond Gorham Academy. Almost next door was a splendid New England college, Bowdoin. To Bowdoin Prentiss went.

Bowdoin, established as a Congregational college in Brunswick, Maine, inducted its first president, the Reverend Joseph McKeen, in the autumn of 1802. In the twenty-two years from the date of its opening until Prentiss appeared in 1824, the college had become a recognized educational institution, and had set high standards for admission and graduation. Naturally the curriculum was classical in nature, with electives unheard of. McKeen had looked upon the curriculum of Harvard as a model for his college and had made admission requirements at Bowdoin the same as Harvard's. "These were a knowledge of the principles of Latin and Greek languages, the ability to translate English into Latin, to read the Select Orations of Cicero, the Aeneid of Virgil, and an acquaintance with arithmetic as far as the rule of three." Classical studies formed the bulk of the course for Bowdoin students as they studied to meet the requirements for admission and sought to go from the freshman to the senior class. "Latin, Greek, and mathematics were studied almost continuously during the first three years, Horace, Juvenal, and Cicero being the Latin authors read, while Dalzell's Collectanea Graeca Majora and Webber's Mathematics were the bulky textbooks that supplied material for study in the other two branches." Some attention was given, however, to the functional or more practical phases of education. In the training of Bowdoin men for their places in contemporary civilization, "Rhetoric and elocution were taught by exercises throughout most of the

[27] William T. Hilliard to George L. Prentiss, Bangor, Me., n.d., *ibid.*, 30–32.

course." Moreover, "Geography was a Freshman, logic a Sophomore, and Locke on the Human Understanding, a Junior Study." Religious, philosophical, political, and scientific precepts were not neglected, for "Paley's Evidences of Christianity, Butler's Analogy of Religion, Stewart's Elements of Philosophy of the Mind, Priestley's Lectures on History, Burlamaqui's Natural Law, Enfield's Natural Philosophy, and Chaptal's Chemistry were textbooks used during the Senior year." [28]

Such was the course of study when the college was founded. Few changes had been made by 1824, and the same emphasis on classical education prevailed. The college catalogue for 1825 stated: "*Candidates for admission into the Freshman Class are required to write Latin grammatically, and to be well versed in Geography, Arithmetic, Cicero's Select Orations, the Bucolics, Georgics, and Aeneid of Virgil, Sallust, the Greek Testament, and Collectanea Graeca Minora. An examination in Xenophon's Cyropaedia, or Jacob's Reader, is received as a substitute for that, required in the Acts and Epistles of the New Testament.*" In addition all students were required to "*produce certificates of their good moral character.*" [29]

The academic year at Bowdoin was divided into three terms. Through the successive terms and years the emphasis on the classical was continuous. During the first term of the freshman year the work consisted of "*Graeca Majora (extracts from Xenophon's Anabasis and Herodotus); Livy (2 books); Lacroix's Arithmetic and Euler's Algebra.*" The second term was devoted to "*Graeca Majora (extracts from Thucydides, Lysias, Isocrates, Polyaenus, and Theophrastus); Excerpta Latina (extracts from Paterculus and Pliny's Letters); Murray's English Grammar; Lacroix's Algebra finished.*" [30]

28 Louis C. Hatch, *The History of Bowdoin College* (Portland, 1927), 17–18, 23.

29 *Catalogue of the Officers and Students of Bowdoin College and the Medical School of Maine* (Brunswick, 1825), 14.   30 *Ibid.*

Languages and mathematics were likewise the intellectual diet of the sophomore class, with some attention given to rhetoric and logic. The first term consisted of *"Graeca Majora (extracts from Plato and Homer); Excerpta Latina (Tacitus); Blair's Rhetoric; Cambridge Mathematics (Plane Trigonometry); Legendre's Geometry."* During the second term the studies were *"Graeca Majora; Excerpta Latina; Cam. Mathematics (Heights and Distances, Navigation and Surveying); Geometry finished; Hedge's Logic."* For the third term the catalogue stipulations were *"Graeca Majora; Excerpta Latina; Cam. Mathematics."* [31]

No better reason exists for citing in detail the terms of admission and the course of study for the first two years than to show what high standards must have prevailed at Gorham Academy. Prentiss must have been well prepared else he could never have entered Bowdoin. Since the family finances were limited, and because it was characteristic of Prentiss to move rapidly toward all goals set for himself, he applied in 1824 for admission by oral examination to the junior class. An interesting entry in the Bowdoin catalogue at that time stated: *"Candidates for admission into other classes will be examined also in the books, which have been studied by the class, into which admission is requested."* [32]

Significant testimony exists to show that Prentiss' education at Gorham was the equivalent of the first two years at college and that he passed the oral examination for advanced standing in a commendable manner. One of the examiners was also one of the great Bowdoin teachers, Alpheus S. Packard, Professor of Languages and Classical Literature. [33] On no less than two occasions Professor Packard put into writing his memory of the examination he helped give Prentiss. "I recall with entire vividness the appearance of Seargent when he presented himself for examination for *Junior* standing. He was a rosy cheeked boy," wrote Packard, "lame, and limping with a cane. As was my custom I began

[31] *Ibid.*   [32] *Ibid.*   [33] *Ibid.*

gently with him that I might not embarrass the youth; but he at once showed that he needed no such tolerance and passed very handsomely the long and severe ordeal for one even much older than himself." At another time Packard wrote in a similar vein of the examination. After commenting on his decision to open Prentiss' examination cautiously "on account of his physical infirmity, as also on account of his youth and the severe examination required for one to enter two years in advance, . . . lest he might become embarrassed," Packard stated, "With entire composure, and almost as if in a playful mood, with remarkable readiness, clearness, precision, and fullness, he passed the trial in languages, and in mathematics; for in the condition of the College, at that time, it fell to my lot to have a hand in both branches." Packard expressed the fact, too, that "The testimony of all the examiners to the high promise shown by that examination, was full, and I cannot recall an instance of an examination, which, considering the extent of it— embracing a dozen separate authors and subjects—has, during the many years of my concern in such scenes, been so successful and triumphant." [34]

Having passed the examination which admitted him to the junior class at Bowdoin, Prentiss enrolled. According to the catalogue, "The principal annual expenses are for tuition, $24.00; and for room rent, $10.00. The usual price for boarding is $1.75 a week." [35]

Prentiss' course of study for the two years from 1824 to 1826 is worthy of notice. The curriculum for the junior class continued to emphasize languages and to some extent mathematics, with a great amount of time devoted to philosophy and chemistry. Specifically in the first term were *"Graeca Majora; Excerpta Latina; Cam. Mathematics; Enfield's Natural Philosophy; Locke's Essay."* Mathematics

---

[34] Alpheus S. Packard to Isaac McLellan, Brunswick, Me., November 12, 1879, in Scrapbook of the Class of 1826, Bowdoin College; *id.* to George Prentiss, n.d., in *Memoir of S. S. Prentiss,* I, 33.

[35] *Catalogue of . . . Bowdoin College* (1825), 15.

did not figure during the second term, but language and philosophy did, the requirements calling for "*Graeca Majora; Horace; Enfield's Natural Philosophy; Locke's Essay* concluded." In the third term language requirements had evidently been met, for the course stipulated *Priestley's Lectures on History; Henry's Chemistry; Stewart's Philosophy of the Mind, vol. i.*" [36]

There were no further language courses required for Bowdoin seniors; rather, the major emphasis was placed on philosophy, religion, and literature. This was doubtless more to the liking of Prentiss, as he was inclined all his life to literature, and, to some extent, to philosophy. The work of the first term was "*Henry's Chemistry; Paley's Natural Theology; Stewart's Philosophy of the Mind, vol. i; Paley's Evidences.*" The second term covered "*Astronomy in Enfield; Dialling; Spherical Geometry and Trigonometry; Stewart's Philosophy of the Mind, vol. ii; Burlemaqui on Natural Law; Butler's Analogy.*" For the final term of work Prentiss and his classmates studied "*Natural History; Cleaveland's Mineralogy; Butler's Analogy.*" [37] Advocates of classical education will be able to take great satisfaction in the Bowdoin curriculum.

But Bowdoin did not offer a curriculum without an adequate faculty to teach the prescribed work. One member was Parker Cleaveland, Professor of Mathematics and Natural Philosophy,[38] "one of the greatest teachers that Bowdoin ever had." [39] Another was Samuel P. Newman, "Professor of Rhetoric and Oratory, and Lecturer on Civil Polity and Political Economy," [40] writer, and "systematic reader and thinker." [41] Two others were Alpheus S. Packard, Professor of Languages and Classical Literature, "who

---

[36] *Ibid.* [37] *Ibid.*
[38] *Ibid.;* Hatch, *History of Bowdoin College,* 28.
[39] Hatch, *History of Bowdoin College,* 28.
[40] *Ibid.; Catalogue of . . . Bowdoin College* (1825).
[41] Hatch, *History of Bowdoin College,* 49.

taught at Bowdoin for sixty-five years," [42] and Thomas C. Upham, a Dartmouth graduate and Professor of Metaphysics and Moral Philosophy. [43] Prentiss matured scholastically as he received instruction and inspiration from such capable teachers. Moreover, he gained lasting impressions from reading the poets—Milton, Scott, Byron, and Shakespeare in particular.

Prentiss' career at Bowdoin was a brilliant one, as can be seen in the testimony of both his teachers and his college friends and classmates. Professor Packard wrote to George Prentiss: "Your brother's collegiate course was a brilliant one, and I often said, that it was one of the few instances, in College life, of decided indications of future success and eminence. He exhibited talents, which we used to think would ensure him all he might aspire after, in a Western or Southern career. His remarkable facility in debate, and his wit and humor, were manifested in College scenes." [44] Certain observations of his fellow students are equally illuminating. Hilliard, who knew him both at Gorham and at Bowdoin, says that the students "assigned him a much higher place than his tutors." On the matter of whether Prentiss was compelled to labor much to hold his own scholastically, Hilliard commented: "He felt no anxiety about his standing in his class, and made no extraordinary exertion in any particular branch of study." But Hilliard did not imply that Prentiss was anything short of excellent in his work. "He excelled in metaphysical investigations. I well remember when we were reading *Butler's Analogy,* which to most students is no play, *he* seemed to give it about as much time as an ordinary mind would spend on a book of travels or a novel; but he made both the matter and the mode of reasoning completely his own. The fact is, everything he did was, or at least appeared to be, free from unnatural or violent

[42] *Ibid.; Catalogue of . . . Bowdoin College* (1825).
[43] Hatch, *History of Bowdoin College,* 50, 58.
[44] Packard to George Prentiss, n.d., in *Memoir of S. S. Prentiss,* I, 33.

effort." Hilliard summed up Prentiss' general manner and
demeanor: "He never thrust himself forward, but when
summoned, and the necessity was upon him, like a young
Samson, he felt his strength, and failed not to make others
feel it." Concerning Prentiss' powers of oratory, which were
so readily evident to all who ever knew him, Hilliard observed: "I can now remember two or three instances, perhaps more, in the presence of some six or eight of his classmates, when he gave indications of a fine embryo debater." [45]

For the training of this "embryo debater," Bowdoin
offered certain distinct opportunities outside the college
curriculum proper. As regular school "Exercises During
The Year," the catalogue for 1825 listed "Private Declamations of each Class, and public Declamations of the three
upper Classes, Compositions in English in the two upper
classes, Forensic Disputations of the Seniors, Translations
into Latin and Greek alternately of the two lower classes,
Translations into English of the Sophomore Class, and
Recitations in the Bible every Sunday evening." [46] Besides
these exercises a regular series of "lectures" was scheduled.
In addition to those "On Chemistry, delivered during the
second term to the Junior and Senior Classes, On Natural
Philosophy, delivered during the third term to the Junior
and Senior Classes, and on Mineralogy, delivered to the
Senior Class during the third term," there were others of far
greater significance in the making of the orator. They were
those "On Rhetoric and Oratory, delivered to the Senior
Class once each fortnight during the year." [47]

But of still greater significance were other avenues of
speech training for Prentiss at Bowdoin. Two literary societies flourished in the institution which provided, among
their activities, opportunities for training in debating and
extemporaneous speaking. The two societies were the
Athenaean and the Peucinian. While the Athenaeans took

[45] Hilliard to *id.*, Bangor, Me., n.d., *ibid.*, 34.
[46] *Catalogue of . . . Bowdoin College* (1825), 15.   [47] *Ibid.*

pride in the membership of such men as John P. Hale, William Pitt Fessenden, Franklin Pierce, and Nathaniel Hawthorne, the Peucinians boasted of such members as George Evans, Nathan Lord, Henry W. Longfellow, and Prentiss.[48] Some months went by after Prentiss entered Bowdoin in the fall of 1824 before he affiliated with the Peucinian organization. It was not until February 13, 1825, that the name of "Seargent S. Prentiss of the Junior . . . Class" was "proposed for election to membership of this Society."[49] On March 4 he was elected to membership,[50] and a fortnight later, March 18, was initiated formally.[51]

From an inspection of the records of the fortnightly meetings of the society it is to be inferred that Prentiss participated only moderately in the doings of the organization. Likewise, better programs were planned and announced than were actually presented. Not infrequently various members asked to be excused when it came their turn to deliver what was announced at a previous meeting. Prentiss was no exception. Probably typical of the various subjects for debate that were announced was the one: "Does man enjoy the greater degree of happiness in the barbarous or civilized State?"[52]

It was at the meeting of July 22, 1825, that the program talents of Prentiss were first suggested when it was "Voted to choose an orator and poet this evening, for the next anniversary. [Leonard] Apthorp was chosen Orator and Prentiss Poet."[53] Possibly the Peucinians had not yet recognized Prentiss' oratorical gifts, since he was not chosen orator, and certainly Prentiss felt that they had erred in asking him to be the poet, for at the subsequent meeting he "declined writing a poem for the next anniversary."[54]

[48] Hatch, *History of Bowdoin College,* 309.
[49] Records of the Peucinian Society, February 13, 1825, Bowdoin College Library.
[50] *Ibid.,* March 4, 1825.   [51] *Ibid.,* March 18, 1825.
[52] *Ibid.,* July 22, 1825.   [53] *Ibid.*
[54] *Ibid.,* August 5, 1825.

He was given opportunities more suited to his abilities however and was announced on August 19 as one of four to be prepared to "read forensicks in two weeks on the following question, 'Did the invasion of the northern Barbarians into the South of Europe Contribute to the promoting of literature?' " [55] Not until October 22 did Prentiss seemingly fulfill this assignment, "which had been postponed from last time." [56]

Prentiss was apparently not on any Peucinian program from October, 1825, until March 3, 1826, when he was designated as one of three to engage in disputations in two weeks.[57] At the meeting of March 31, he was assigned to be prepared two weeks later to "read forensicks upon the following question, 'Is an Opposition Party in a Republican Government conducive to the Safety of the State?' " [58] This, it may be inferred, Prentiss never did, for the records of the society state that "Prentiss was excused." [59] Apparently this was the end of his contributions to the Peucinian programs, for on June 30 it was "Voted that the Seniors be not required to attend any further meetings of the Society during this term." [60]

Two years after Prentiss' graduation from college, when he was far from Maine, one of his best college friends, William Appleton, with whom he corresponded for some time, wrote to Prentiss: "I have not heard whether the Peucinian Society has decayed still more, or regained its former standing." [61] The years from 1824 to 1826 evidently were decadent ones in which the society was losing its former standing. A perusal of the records of the organization shows that the members were often not present to perform on schedule and that many asked to be excused. Prentiss seems to have taken little more than a perfunctory interest, though the

[55] *Ibid.*, August 19, 1825. [56] *Ibid.*, October 22, 1825.
[57] *Ibid.*, March 3, 1826. [58] *Ibid.*, March 31, 1826.
[59] *Ibid.*, April 26, 1826. [60] *Ibid.*, June 30, 1826.
[61] William Appleton to Prentiss, Derry, N. H., May 13, 1828, in *Memoir of S. S. Prentiss*, I, 84.

society was an ideal proving ground for youthful debaters and orators. A plausible reason for his disinterest existed, however, as another organization, an unofficial one, competed more successfully for his attention and participation. Evidently the Peucinian society did not meet completely the desires of Prentiss and certain of his friends. This is true, notwithstanding the advantages which both the Peucinian and Athenaean societies presented for the oratorical and literary training of both the brilliant and the more nearly average men, and in spite of the enviable traditions of both organizations at Bowdoin. "The extensive training in debating given by the Athenaean and Peucinian was not enough. In the life of Seargent S. Prentiss there is an account of the 'Spouteroi,' a very informal club of six members of the class of 1826, all Peucinians." [62]

Spouteroi, the name of which represented a jocular compound of Greek and English, had for its distinct purpose the training of its members in impromptu speaking. The six organizers were Prentiss, Charles Lord, Appleton, Apthorp, Isaac McLellan, and William Paine. [63] The best account of this short-lived organization is that of Lord, who said: "It was formed in our junior year," and "it consisted of six classmates, never more, never less: we were brother Peucinians, and that was an additional bond of union. Our first object was, improvement in extemporaneous speaking; we wanted something more frequent, and more familiar, too, than the opportunities presented by the college societies." The organization was quite informal, for, as Lord stated: "We had no constitution, no officers, no by-laws! We met regularly in each other's rooms; the occupant was the presiding officer of the evening: he assigned a subject for present discussion, and literary exercises for the subsequent meeting." One stringent rule was adhered to, however, "that

[62] Hatch, *History of Bowdoin College*, 329. See also, *Memoir of S. S. Prentiss*, I, 35-36; Shields, *Seargent Smith Prentiss*, 7.
[63] *Memoir of S. S. Prentiss*, I, 35-36.

every member, *nolen volens,* should take part in the debate." The basic impromptu purpose of the group was maintained, for since "the topic was not made known till the
moment for discussion, there was, of course, no opportunity
for preparation." Lord justified this practice: "In this respect our forensic exercise was strictly *ex tempore,* and not
like many, now so called, conned by midnight lamp and delivered memoriter." A unique and effective method was
found to ensure the attendance of the members: "The
stimulus, in the absence of fines and penalties, was a cigar,
which the officer, *ex loco,* was expected to provide." [64]

What took place in the weekly meetings of Spouteroi can
probably never be known. What Prentiss contributed to
the life of the organization and how much he learned in the
way of extempore address (or rather, impromptu address)
is only to be surmised, save for one occasion, described by
Lord. At this meeting, Prentiss gave a "burlesque composition . . . descriptive of the explosion of a torpedo." Evidently some sudden disruptive event had happened which
upset the tranquil student-faculty life at Bowdoin, so that
Prentiss produced in Spouteroi a scene in playful imagery
and fancy descriptive of the effect of the torpedo's dis-
turbance upon the college life. "The circumstances of time
and place were detailed with much minuteness,—the state
of the college halls,—the hour, that noon of night when
thought mounts her zenith with the stars!—the relative
position of the heavenly luminaries,—the ominous fore-
bodings of the celestial signs were portrayed in a grandilo-
quent style,—the very elements were described as hushed
in consternation; the heavens were hung in black in antici-
pation of the denouement of the tragedy; the stars, as if
conscious of the plot, watched the progress of the fearful
catastrophe, and ever and anon were seen, here and there,

---

[64] Portland *Express,* June 20, 1925, in Scrapbook of Class of 1826, Bowdoin
College.

peeping out from behind the clouds to witness the consummation and be 'in at the death!' " [65]

In college Prentiss made friends while he gained academic knowledge. He knew, of course, Nathaniel Hawthorne and Henry W. Longfellow, who were seniors during his junior year. His closest friends were very likely those in Spouteroi. One good friend was unquestionably Appleton, who died in 1830, at the age of twenty-two, and who was the son of the Reverend Jesse Appleton, D.D., second president of Bowdoin College.[66] Appleton and Prentiss engaged in much letter writing after they were both out of college and when Prentiss had gone far into the South.[67] Possibly an even closer friend was McLellan. In spite of the physical handicap of lameness, which interfered with outdoor activities, Prentiss developed into a most enthusiastic angler and even woodsman. With McLellan he often "rambled through the woods on Saturday afternoon in pursuit of game." [68] Of his own friends and of these ramblings McLellan recalled at one time "such college associates as Longfellow, Hawthorne, G. B. Cheever, Franklin Pierce, Wm. Pitt Fessenden, John P. Hale, J. S. C. Abbott, Calvin Stowe, and last but not least, the late Hon. Sargeant [sic] S. Prentiss, of Southern celebrity." McLellan noted particularly that "None of these men, with the exception of the last mentioned, found any charm in the sports with rod and gun." [69]

[65] Charles Lord to George Prentiss, Portland, Me., n.d., in *Memoir of S. S. Prentiss*, I, 36–37.

[66] *Ibid.*, 36.

[67] Appleton to Prentiss, Amherst, N. H., February 23, 1827, in *Memoir of S. S. Prentiss*, I, 39–42; *id.* to *id.*, Londonderry, N. H., May 6, 1827, *ibid.*, 42–44; *id.* to *id.*, Londonderry, N. H., June 26, 1827, *ibid.*, 44–46; *id.* to *id.*, Derry, N. H., August 11, 1827, *ibid.*, 77–78; *id.* to *id.*, Derry, N. H., October 14, 1827, *ibid.*, 78–80; *id.* to *id.*, Derry, N. H., February 6, 1828, *ibid.*, 80–83; *id.* to *id.*, Derry, N. H., May 13, 1828, *ibid.*, 83–85; *id.* to *id.*, Derry, N. H., July 30, 1828, *ibid.*, 85–87.

[68] Boston *Herald*, August 22, 1899.

[69] Clipping from *Forest and Stream*, December 31, 1885, in Scrapbook of the Class of 1826, Bowdoin College.

Thus it was Prentiss' high privilege to receive the kind of education which befitted a young man of his talents. What grades or academic marks he received cannot be known, as course records for that period were burned many years ago.[70] Certainly, though, among his friends in the literary societies and in Bowdoin life generally, Prentiss evidently gave much promise of the man he was to be. It has been said that "Practically every one of the traits which distinguished him in later life was evident while he was in college, among them his 'conversational enthusiasm, uniform flow of spirits, wonderful fluency of speech, exuberant fancy of diction, sparkling wit, sarcastic retort as well as humorous repartee.' " [71]

When in September, 1826, Bowdoin College conferred on Prentiss the degree of Bachelor of Arts, his college career was brought to a close. Doubtless the death of his father a short time before impelled him to feel that he should earn his own livelihood as soon as possible. Also, probably while in college, he had decided to make law his profession. Consequently, in less than a month from the time he left college he began reading law in the office of a Bowdoin graduate of the class of 1818, Judge Josiah Pierce, of Gorham.[72] While he approached the study of law most assiduously, fully realizing that he was to make it his life's profession, he did not do so at the expense of continued cultural reading. "In my office, he read law studiously in the former part of the day," Pierce declared, "but in the afternoon perused other works. The writings of Walter Scott, Washington Irving, Cooper, and Byron, afforded him much amusement and pleasant instruction. His favorite author was Shakespeare, and I think a week never passed without his perusing

---

[70] Philip S. Wilder, Alumni Secretary, Bowdoin College, to the writer, Brunswick, Me., September 27, 1937.

[71] Sketch of Prentiss by Dana K. Merrill, in Portland *Express*, June 20, 1923, clipping enclosed in Wilder to the writer, March 13, 1937.

[72] *Memoir of S. S. Prentiss*, I, 38–39; Nehemiah Cleaveland and Alpheus S. Packard, *History of Bowdoin College* (Boston, 1882), 205.

more or less of the productions of the great dramatist." [73]

But Prentiss was not destined to remain with Pierce or in Maine for long. He had made a decision to migrate, for a time at least, either to the West or to the South, having no specific destination in mind. The direction of his migration proved to be southwest. He soon was to identify himself with the life, traditions, and events of the Old South.

[73] Josiah Pierce to George Prentiss, n.d., in *Memoir of S. S. Prentiss*, I, 38-39.

Chapter II

A MISSISSIPPI SCHOOLMASTER

PRENTISS possessed little money but was armed with a degree from Bowdoin College, an eager desire to become a lawyer, and a belief that greater opportunities awaited him beyond the borders of his native state. Thus equipped, he was soon to view new horizons. On August 1, 1827, as a lad of eighteen years, he took leave of his friends and relatives. "Amid the tears and blessings of the little group he mounted the wagon drawn by the old gray horse of the family, and went his way to Portland." [1]

From Portland he journeyed by steamboat to Boston, visiting there for several days. From Boston he went by stage to Providence, then by steamer to New York. [2] He carried with him a letter of introduction from Judge Pierce to Thomas Fessenden, a Dartmouth graduate of the class of 1812, who practiced law in New York from 1817 to 1853. [3] This letter was to begin a chain of events destined to lead Prentiss far from New England.

He resumed his journey August 10, viewing the scenic beauties along the Hudson River as his steamer moved upstream toward Albany. Thence he took the stage west to Buffalo. After an excursion to Niagara Falls, he was again on his "westward way." Going from Buffalo by lake boat to Sandusky, Ohio, and from there by stage, he arrived in Cincinnati on August 15. [4]

[1] Shields, *Seargent Smith Prentiss*, 10.   [2] *Ibid.*
[3] Dorothy C. Bauch, Reference Librarian, New York Historical Society, to the writer, March 10, 1938; Victor E. Palsits, Chief of the American Historical Division and Keeper of Manuscripts, New York Public Library, to the writer, March 10, 1938.
[4] Shields, *Seargent Smith Prentiss*, 11–12.

Another letter of introduction explains his stop in Cincinnati. Before Prentiss left New York, Fessenden had given him a letter to be presented in Cincinnati to Judge Nathaniel Wright, a Dartmouth graduate, who had migrated from New Hampshire.[5] Judge Wright was so favorably impressed by the letter and by the deportment of Prentiss himself that he extended to him the opportunity to read law in his office. Prentiss stood in need of money and was bent upon obtaining a teaching position but was persuaded to abandon his plan in order to remain in Judge Wright's office.[6]

Prentiss was well pleased at first with Cincinnati and may have thought of making it his abode. He was fortunate, too, in the companionship of a former Bowdoin classmate, Samuel S. Boyd, who had emigrated to Cincinnati a short time before.[7] "Cincinnati is a beautiful place. It is considerably larger than Portland," he wrote to his mother, "and is delightfully situated on the right bank of the Ohio. My office is within a few rods of the river, and looks directly upon it, so that I can at any time see the steam and other boats passing and repassing before the city."[8]

But the law office of Judge Wright was no solution to the financial worries besetting him. Being totally without income, he realized that his scant means would soon be depleted. Moreover, he came to feel that Cincinnati did not offer the opportunities he expected to find in the West. The general low ebb of commodity prices impressed him unfavorably. A story from Shields reflects this state of mind. "He was sauntering to the office one day, when seeing an apple-boy, he tossed him a quarter of a dollar, took out a few apples, and walked into the office. When he came out

[5] Information supplied the writer by Ellen Ellis from Mrs. Charles G. Blake of Cincinnati, granddaughter of Judge Wright, Summerville, S. C., March 23, 1938.
[6] Shields, *Seargent Smith Prentiss*, 12.   [7] *Ibid.*
[8] Prentiss to his mother, Cincinnati, August 28, 1827, *Memoir of S. S. Prentiss*, I, 56.

again he saw the little fellow standing still as though waiting for something. 'Well, my little fellow, not gone yet, eh?' said Prentiss. 'No sir; I was waiting for you to tell me where to carry these apples you bought.' Prentiss turned to Boyd, who was standing by, with a look of astonishment, and in a tone of comic drollery said,—'Boyd, I'm bound to go farther,—somewhere. This place is too cheap to thrive in. Phew! I can never make a living where apples are two bits a peck.' " [9]

Ohio's loss was soon to be Mississippi's gain. At the very time when Prentiss felt he should go farther, two wealthy planters from Natchez, Alvarez Fisk and Stephen Duncan, were visiting in Cincinnati. Through Bellamy Storer, a Cincinnati lawyer, Prentiss was introduced to them. Acting upon their assurance that he would experience no difficulty in securing a remunerative teaching position in Mississippi, Prentiss accepted a loan from Judge Wright, and prepared to join Fisk and Duncan on a cruise down the Ohio and Mississippi rivers to Natchez.

If the journey from Cincinnati to Natchez was generally uneventful, one incident occurred which Prentiss was never to forget. Once when it was necessary for the steamer to "lay off" for a short time because of a sandbar, Prentiss took advantage of the stop to go for a duck hunt. Either because the boat was ready to leave earlier than he anticipated, or because he indulged too long in his favorite sport, he returned to find the boat gone. "The owner of a log cabin told him that he might head the boat at the wood-yard below." [10] "I accordingly threw away my ducks," he wrote to his mother, "shouldered my musket and marched on as fast as I could. Upon arriving at the place, I saw the boat had left it, and was nearly a mile on her way. I hailed her as loudly as possible, when she put about, came back and

---

[9] Shields, *Seargent Smith Prentiss*, 12–13.
[10] *Ibid.*, 14.

PRENTISS IN HIS YOUTH

FROM GEORGE L. PRENTISS, "THE BRIGHT SIDE OF LIFE"

took me in. But if I had been one minute later, I should have lost my chance." [11]

It was on November 2, 1827, that Prentiss reached Natchez. Resolved to find a teaching position, probably as a tutor in a private family, he secured letters of introduction and recommendation from Fisk and Duncan. Fisk wrote to Dr. Rush Nutt of Natchez: "This will be handed to you by Mr. S. Prentiss, a young gentleman of high standing both as relates to character and classical attainments. Mr. Prentiss is desirous to obtain a situation as a teacher either in a private family or a neighborhood school where he may obtain a more adequate compensation for instruction either in the higher branches, or those merely elementary, as may be desired. He brings recommendations as to his moral worth and qualifications necessary to enable him to instruct others. I solicit for him your kind aid in this respect, and am, Sincerely, your friend, Alvarez Fisk." [12]

Prentiss had but five dollars, "the last of the loan from his friend Wright and others," when he reached Natchez and registered at the Mansion House Hotel. "Having registered his name and secured a room, he stepped to the bar, laid down the last five dollars he had in the world, and ordered up a bottle of wine and a box of cigars to his room." When the waiter brought them, Prentiss "offered him as a welcome a glass of wine and a cigar." "In after years," related Shields, "when Prentiss was twitted and censured by his friends for his act of improvidence in thus spending his last stiver, he retorted on his censors, 'You don't understand human na-

[11] Prentiss to his mother, Natchez, November 3, 1827, *Memoir of S. S. Prentiss*, I, 62.

[12] Alvarez Fisk to Dr. Rush Nutt, Natchez, January 5, 1828, in possession of Seargent Prentiss Nutt, Washington, D. C., to the writer, September 10, 1937. The fact that this letter is dated January 5, 1828, indicates that Prentiss secured it later, even after he was employed in his first position. The words "where he may obtain a more adequate compensation" might be taken to mean that early in his first position he was searching for a better one.

ture; that five dollars *established* my *credit*, and I never had any trouble with my landlords afterwards.' " [13] He contrived to get along with his landlord in some manner, though it was nearly a month before he obtained his first teaching position.

Since Natchez was now to be the center of Prentiss' life and professional activity for a long period of time, it is well to take some notice of the character and history of the place. It was a romantic and alluring environment which Prentiss discovered when he disembarked at Natchez and climbed the steep hill on his way to the Mansion House. He probably knew little of the colorful history of the land he was adopting as his own. Actually he was some time adjusting himself to his new environment. Moreover, he was only one of the numerous Americans who by one means or another were attracted to this remote outpost, which in a relatively short time was to boast of one of the most unique cultural and economic civilizations in the history of the United States.

Although Natchez had really been founded as a French post as early as 1716, it later developed, in contrast to much of near-by Louisiana, an Anglo-Saxon civilization and culture. The French attempt at the establishment of Natchez had been short-lived, for in 1729 the settlement was destroyed by the Natchez Indians. Early Natchez may be considered more or less French, however, for it did not become a part of the English domain until the treaty of 1763, which terminated the French and Indian War. Being an English settlement, legally at least, it naturally became a part of the American nation upon the close of the Revolution. One irritating factor persisted, though, in that the Spanish claimed Natchez also, and kept a garrison of troops at the Fort. Such an important trading post along the Mississippi was not to be lost without a measure of opposition.

But the American flag was soon to fly over Natchez. During the years of British control, many Englishmen had ac-

[13] Shields, *Seargent Smith Prentiss*, 15.

quired large tracts of land in the vicinity and promoted population growth.[14] Conflicts with the Spanish were inevitable, but in "1795 the Spanish yielded up the area between the latitude of 31° and the mouth of the Yazoo River." [15] The government established for it was essentially that provided for the Northwest Territory in 1787, with the notable exception that slavery was not prohibited.[16]

Thus the Anglo-Saxon control triumphed. Likewise, the Natchez area came increasingly under the influence of New England. In 1798 President John Adams' appointee to the governorship of the Mississippi Territory arrived in Natchez. He was Winthrop Sargent, a native of Massachusetts, and a soldier and officer of the Revolutionary War. As a supporter of Adams, Sargent was naturally a Federalist, "of the race of the Puritans, and with many of the peculiarities of that remarkable people." [17] Sargent was governor until 1801, and during his tenure became established as a southerner, building one of the famous antebellum mansions, "Gloucester," near Natchez. Yet he was none too well accepted by many who had come to Natchez. While the influence of New England settlers was in the ascendancy, the numerically larger groups during this period came from Virginia, Carolina, and Pennsylvania.[18]

When the affairs of the national government passed into the hands of Thomas Jefferson in 1801, Mississippi acquired a new governor. Sargent was relieved, and the new Republican appointee was William C. C. Claiborne. Claiborne was from a Virginia family. He had lived for a time

---

[14] Charles S. Sydnor, *A Gentleman of the Old Natchez Region: Benjamin L. C. Wailes* (Durham, 1938), 3.

[15] James B. Ranck, *Albert Gallatin Brown, Radical Southern Nationalist* (New York, 1937), 2.

[16] Clarence E. Carter (comp. and ed.), *The Territorial Papers of the United States,* V, *The Territory of Mississippi, 1798–1817* (Washington, 1937), 11.

[17] J. F. H. Claiborne, *Mississippi, as a Province, Territory and State, with Biographical Notes of Eminent Citizens* (Jackson, 1880), I, 203.

[18] *Ibid.,* 206.

in Philadelphia, where he studied law. In 1795, when twenty years of age, he migrated to Tennessee, opening a law office in Sullivan County. In Tennessee he rose rapidly. Within a year the territorial legislature made him a trustee of Washington College. In 1796 he was a delegate from Sullivan County as a member of the convention to prepare a constitution for Tennessee, and helped specifically in drafting the constitution and the bill of rights. Other honors followed. The first legislature of Tennessee made him "one of the three judges of the Superior Court of Law and Equity." Then in 1797 he was elected to Congress from Tennessee, and was re-elected two years later, being in Congress when he was made governor of the Mississippi Territory.[19]

Claiborne arrived in Natchez to begin his duties November 23, 1801. One of his first acts was to move the government from Natchez six miles east to the small town of Washington, where a little later, in 1802, was founded Jefferson College. There was thus set up in Mississippi a political and social rivalry between the two towns which was to go on for years. Claiborne continued as governor until 1805, when, upon the completion of all negotiations with France for Louisiana, he was made governor of the Territory of Orleans. His successor in Mississippi was another Republican, Robert Williams of North Carolina.

A growing population and civilization existed in this part of the United States. Natchez was an actual town following 1800, and plantation homes became more numerous on the Natchez side of the Mississippi River. Also, homes were established farther inland. Natchez, as well as all of Mississippi, experienced a vast influx of immigrants during the first thirty years of the nineteenth century. Many, like Prentiss, sought to win their fortunes in this far distant corner of the United States. Even though isolated, there being no other significant settlements closer than Tennessee

[19] *Ibid.*, 250.

to the north and New Orleans to the south, Natchez never developed into a large city. Yet it has had a unique and romantic history. Natchez exemplifies the fact that size is not always the criterion of importance or significance.

In spite of the French and Spanish influences, those who resided in Natchez in 1800 were almost entirely from various parts of the United States. At this time there were 4,444 white persons and 2,995 slaves in Natchez and the area about it.[20] Since Natchez proper was the focal point of trade and culture, the rural settlements were in reality a part of it. Actually there were four times as many people in the Natchez region in 1810 as in 1800, and enough had come, settling in the western part mostly, to enable Mississippi to become a state in 1817. Blacks as well as whites increased, with Negroes gaining in ratio from 38 per cent in 1800 to 42 per cent in 1810 and 43 per cent in 1820.[21]

A basic economic factor explains the rapid growth. This was cotton. Probably no single force was as potent in accelerating the population stream toward the southwest part of the United States as was the invention of the cotton gin in 1793. The efforts to build an economy on tobacco and indigo before 1800 had failed, but cotton, ideally suited to the climate and soil along the Mississippi River, led to a singular opulence of life in this area.

King Cotton meant slaves, large plantations, mansion homes, and then, as a sequence, business places in Natchez, hotels, taverns, churches (Catholic and Protestant), schools, libraries, and in short, diversified cultured and genteel manners and living for a fortunate few. Although it is possible to exaggerate the idea of luxury and gentility in Natchez, it must be admitted that, with slaves doing the actual work on the plantations and in the town and country homes, the whites were free to pursue at will the cultural interests

[20] Sydnor, *Benjamin L. C. Wailes*, 15; Mack Swearingen, *The Early Life of George Poindexter, A Story of the First Southwest* (New Orleans, 1934), 34.

[21] Ranck, *Albert Gallatin Brown*, 2.

and activities that accrue from such a pattern of life.[22]

The size and structure of the houses, gardens, and lawns of the homes about Natchez are evidence of the splendor of Natchez life. After Governor Sargent built Gloucester, others followed by building on even more expansive scales, reaching a climax in the decade of the 1830's. Along with fine homes, nearly always located in a setting of great trees, came gardens and flowers. As one traveler observed when he visited the Natchez region: "Through natural vistas in the wood occasional glimpses could be obtained of white villas, not infrequently large and elegant, half hidden in the centre of plantations, or among the thick woods which crowned the swelling hills on every side." [23] The flowers and gardens impressed him no less. After mentioning the crêpe myrtle "with its pure and delicately formed flower, the oak geranium, the classical ivy, and the fragment snow-drop," he went on to say: "The broad walks were, as usual in southern gardens, bordered by the varnished lauria mundi, occasionally relieved by the cape jessamine, slender althea, and dark green arbor vitae. The splendidly attired amaryllis, the purple magnolia, the Arabian and night-blooming jessamines, the verbenum, or lemon-scented geranium, with the majestic aloe, that hoary monarch of the garden, which blooms but once in a century, the broad-leaved yarra, or caco, . . . and the sweet-scented shrub and oleander, with countless other shrubs and flowers, breathing forth the sweetest fragrance, gratified the senses, and pleased the eye wherever it was turned." [24] With flowers of some kind blooming practically all the year, and most effusively in the spring and summer, the plantation homes, spacious and columned, were colorful in the extreme, and the countryside scarcely less so.

But there were great contrasts also in early Natchez. It is

[22] Wendell H. Stephenson, *Isaac Franklin, Slave Trader and Planter of the Old South* (University, La., 1938), 54.
[23] [Joseph Holt Ingraham], *The South-West* (New York, 1835), II, 79–80.
[24] *Ibid.*, 116–17.

most important to distinguish between Natchez-On-the-Hill and Natchez-Under-the-Hill. It must not be forgotten that Natchez was a river town. In consequence, two societies as distinct as can be imagined lived within a few hundred feet of each other. Natchez-Under-the-Hill was built first; it was all there was to the town as long as Natchez was a French trading post. In time, as settlers came into the region, homes and business houses were built on the hill or the bluffs above the river.

Natchez-Under-the-Hill became identified with all kinds of infamies. Gambling, prostitution, and almost all conceivable vices and crimes prevailed. The river traffic brought to Natchez-Under-the-Hill the worst kind of ruffians and outlaws, which gave the town its evil distinction. "The principal street," wrote Joseph Holt Ingraham, "which terminates at the ascent of the hill, runs parallel with the river, and is lined on either side with a row of old wooden houses; which are alternately gambling-houses, brothels and barrooms: a fair assemblage! As we passed through the street —which we gained with difficulty from the boat, picking our way to it as we could, through a filthy alley—the low, broken, half-sunken side-walks, were blocked up with fashionably-dressed young men smoking or lounging, tawdrily arrayed, highly rouged females, sailors, Kentucky boatmen, negroes, negresses, mulatoes, pigs, dogs, and dirty children. The sounds of profanity and Bacchanalian revels, well harmonizing with the scene, assailed our ears as we passed hastily along, through an atmosphere of tobacco smoke and other equally fragrant odours." [25]

Natchez-On-the-Hill lived by other standards, though gambling and dueling were not uncommon. But men there followed a different code of ethics, which promoted learning, finer tastes, and refinement. Elegant plantation homes, libraries, dancing schools, churches, and academies bespoke the different tone of those who resided apart from the

[25] *Ibid.,* 19-20.

"River scum" below the hill. If churches are indicative of the moral impulses of people, Natchez-On-the-Hill, with Catholic, Presbyterian, Episcopal, and Methodist denominations established before 1830, and the Baptists in 1837,[26] presents a contrast with Natchez-Under-the-Hill that is quite evident.

The interest in, and efforts toward, education may be a truer index of those who lived on-the-Hill and the surrounding area. Public education as established in New England was not institutionalized in Natchez; hence the use in many plantation homes of numerous private tutors such as Prentiss was to become. But schools of cultural and intellectual emphasis were not entirely lacking for the sons and daughters of the more affluent, who could not, or did not, leave home for distant centers of learning. As an example, David Ker established a school for girls in 1801. Another school was the short-lived Elizabeth Female Academy, founded in 1818 by the Methodists at Washington, which graduated its students with the degree of "Domina Scientiarum." [27]

The greatest center of interest in higher education was at Jefferson College, also located at Washington. The history of the college is a story in itself, one of successes and failures, and of persistence in spite of discouragement. The college was incorporated in 1802 by the legislature, and the trustees held their first meeting early the next year. One reason for its location at Washington was the fact that the land was donated. The college did not actually open until 1811,[28] and it operated under great financial difficulties. Yet it did continue to function year after year, so that it was able in time to claim several outstanding alumni, such as Albert G. Brown, Prentiss Ingraham, Jefferson Davis, and John F. H. Claiborne.[29] One significant aspect of the college,

[26] Sydnor, *Benjamin L. C. Wailes*, 78.
[27] Swearingen, *Early Life of George Poindexter*, 47; Sydnor, *Benjamin L. C. Wailes*, 126.
[28] Swearingen, *Early Life of George Poindexter*, 20; Sydnor, *Benjamin L. C. Wailes*, 49.   [29] Sydnor, *Benjamin L. C. Wailes*, 233.

located as it was far from other seats of learning, was the fact that the curriculum emphasized to a considerable degree classical learning and influence.[30]

Thus Natchez had, as suggested earlier, a competitor in Washington. Actually the growth of Washington can be explained politically, and as an aspect of the national Federalist-Republican contest. Just as the Federalists gave way at the rise of Jeffersonian Republicanism, so Natchez surrendered certain points of advantage to Washington. Natchez was the center of conservative aristocracy. Washington in its brief ascendancy symbolized the development of Republican ruralism over Federalistic wealth.[31] As Natchez lost her place to Washington as the territorial capital, and then as the county seat as well, the evidence points to a decline of the Federalists. The location of Jefferson College at Washington is in final analysis to be explained on this basis.

Yet in a larger sense, Natchez retained a distinction which Washington never by any means equaled. Located on the river, Natchez had far superior economic advantages. This enabled her to retain certain political advantages as well. But though Natchez was a center of wealth, certain historic events worked against her, and for that matter, against Washington as well. By the time Prentiss arrived in Mississippi, the capital had been relocated in the central part of the state at Jackson. Moreover, Vicksburg was destined to outstrip Natchez in economic importance as a river town.

Natchez was, nevertheless, the most important city in Mississippi for the first thirty years after 1800. To it had come scores of people whose names are a part of Mississippi history. Planters such as Stephen Duncan, Alvarez Fisk, William Dunbar, Captain James T. Magruder, Levin Wailes, and others made up a notable coterie. Lawyers like William B. Shields, Robert J. Walker, Felix Huston, and John A. Quitman had found their way to Natchez. All these and

[30] *Ibid.*, 51, 208.   [31] *Ibid.*, 24.

many more intellectuals helped to build, prior to and during Prentiss' days in Natchez, the civilization to which he oriented himself when he registered at the Mansion House.

Within a short time after Prentiss reached Natchez, he solved the immediate financial worries besetting him by obtaining a teaching position. Fisk and Duncan had not held out false hopes when they persuaded him he could find opportunity for his talents. By late November he was writing to his mother that he was the tutor in one of the most respectable Natchez families. The home was that of Mrs. Victoria Shields, widow of Judge William B. Shields. Hearing that Mrs. Shields, living "twelve miles northeast of Natchez," was desirous of securing a tutor for her five children, Prentiss rode to her plantation home, "Rokeby," so called after Sir Walter Scott's poem of that name.[32]

The Shields home was one of culture. One of its assets was an extensive library, made up of legal and miscellaneous books. Being favorably impressed with Prentiss, Mrs. Shields called in her eldest son, Thomas Rodney, who had just been graduated from Transylvania University, to examine Prentiss relative to his academic qualifications to become the family tutor. "He began very politely and very gently to catechise him. . . . He had not proceeded far in his examination before he found himself in deep water. The catechumen, in turn," says Shields, "became the catechist, and the examiner at once saw that, in knowledge at least, the candidate was his superior."[33]

Mrs. Shields quickly engaged Prentiss for the position. The agreement provided that "He was to teach her five children for his board and three hundred dollars, with the privilege of getting other scholars from the neighborhood, and, to him, the inestimable privilege of the use of the law library; besides this, whenever he chose, he was to have the

[32] Shields, *Seargent Smith Prentiss*, 16. Mrs. Shields was the mother of Joseph D. Shields, one of the five children instructed by Prentiss and the author of *The Life and Times of Seargent Smith Prentiss*.
[33] *Ibid.*, 17.

use of horse and saddle for recreation." [34] Prentiss was to have a means of livelihood. As happy as he was in this, he was even happier in having at his disposal an exceedingly fine library. To William Prentiss he wrote: "The great advantage of the situation is, that Mrs. Shields has in her home one of the finest libraries in the state . . . so that I shall be in as good a situation for pursuing my studies, as if I were in a lawyer's office." [35]

Prentiss began his instructional duties in a revamped "hewn-log house," once an overseer's cabin. In due time the school was enlarged to include four children of James Dunbar, two sons and two daughters, and two sons of a "retired sea-captain," A. Leonard Magruder. [36] One of the Magruder sons, William H. N., who became Professor of Ancient Languages at Louisiana State University from 1882 to 1893, [37] related hearing his father say when he employed Prentiss, "he's *the smartest man that ever entered this house. If he's not at the head of the bar in Mississippi in ten years I shall be more deceived than I ever was in man.*" [38]

Prentiss estimated that he would augment his year's stipend one hundred dollars by teaching additional children, [39] and that the law library available to him in the Shields home was worth at least another hundred dollars. [40] He consequently spent the winter of 1827–1828 profitably and happily, orienting himself in the atmosphere of culture and leisure in an ante-bellum home. Much of the time was his own. "I am confined about three or four hours a day," he wrote to his mother, "and the rest of the time I have entirely to myself. I spend it in studying law, reading and

[34] *Ibid.*

[35] Prentiss to William Prentiss, Natchez, November 21, 1827, in *Memoir of S. S. Prentiss,* I, 63.

[36] Shields, *Seargent Smith Prentiss,* 18–19.

[37] Walter L. Fleming, *Louisiana State University, 1860–1896* (Baton Rouge, 1936), 383.

[38] Shields, *Seargent Smith Prentiss,* 18.

[39] Prentiss to his mother, Natchez, December 22, 1827, in *Memoir of S. S. Prentiss,* I, 67.

[40] *Id.* to William Prentiss, Natchez, April 20, 1828, *ibid.,* 71.

gunning. I have a horse whenever I wish to ride, and guns and ammunition when I wish to go a hunting, which I do an hour or two almost every day." [41]

But Prentiss was still thinking of his sojourn in Mississippi as more or less temporary. The cold, snowy Maine winters which he had experienced for eighteen years were too much a part of him to allow him to relish completely the mild and balmy winter months of the Deep South. However, it may have been little more than a passing pang of homesickness which led him to write to his mother as the Christmas season approached: "They have no snow in this part of the country; of course no sleigh-riding, a thing I shall miss very much. It is already their winter here, yet a fire is seldom needed, and the roses are blooming every day in the garden. . . . For myself, however, I prefer the cold weather of the North; it is so delightful to sit by a good fire and hear the storm whistling without and beating against the windows, while all is comfortable and pleasant. Still this is a very beautiful climate in the winter, and perhaps I shall like it even better than my own, when I become a little accustomed to it." [42]

The contrast in weather and climate was only one matter to which Prentiss had to adjust himself. He was much impressed with the powerful influence of cotton culture, and observed, "Cotton is the production of this part of the Union, and here they raise nothing else upon their plantations. I have seen thousands of acres of it since I came here. It is picked from the stalks by negroes, and being cleaned of the seed by machines called gins, it is then packed up in bales, nearly as it comes to you." [43] Actually the city of Natchez did not impress Prentiss very favorably. He called "The buildings both publick and private . . . very ordinary in appearance"; but he did observe the economic significance of what cotton meant, and said that because of

---

[41] *Id.* to his mother, Natchez, December 22, 1822, *ibid.*, 67.
[42] *Ibid.*   [43] *Ibid.*

it Natchez "does more business than places of five times its population in some parts of the Union." [44]

But slavery, the concomitant of cotton, was a difficult institution for him to accept. Because of it he said frankly, "I do not like the manner of living here, so well as I do our Northern fashion." His antipathy was so strong that he declared: "Slavery is the great pest of this as well as all the other Southern States. It is considered disgraceful for a white man to do any kind of hand labor—and everything is done by slaves. Of course, things are done in a very poor and slovenly manner." He showed the beginnings of a tolerance of slavery which was to grow on him as time passed, however, when he admitted that the Negroes "appear to enjoy life, and are, for aught I see, as happy as their masters. It is not often that they are treated so cruelly as we are accustomed to suppose, and in general they are better off than they would be if they were free—still it is a hard case for them at best." [45] Tolerance for southern habits increased in Prentiss as he became more adjusted. He saw that slavery gave the whites more leisure, and he did not appear totally disapproving when he said of the people: "They live rather more *freely* than we of the North—and are what perhaps we should call a little dissipated—yet on the whole I think the state of society is more correct & the people more moral than they are usually considered." [46]

Prentiss' states of mind during his first months in Mississippi are interesting to observe. Unless he was expressing moods in his letters home different from those which seemingly engulfed him, he did not intend remaining in the South. He never wavered in his decision to study law. While he hoped to return to Maine, he admitted that opportunities in the legal profession were greater in Mississippi. "Law,

[44] *Id.* to Josiah Pierce, Natchez, April 11, 1828, in the Mrs. John B. Whittemore Collection, Portland, Me.

[45] *Id.* to his mother, Natchez, February 12, 1828, in *Memoir of S. S. Prentiss*, I, 70–71.

[46] *Id.* to Josiah Pierce, Natchez, April 11, 1828, in Whittemore Collection.

here," he wrote to Josiah Pierce, "is a good thing to live by—if a man can keep from dying. Probably the average annual income of lawyers is $2000 or 2500—although I know some who make four, five, & six thousand. . . . Did I wish to make a fortune I should certainly settle myself here." [47] He saw no such opportunities in New England. "I consider the profession of law in New England (where I think I shall settle myself eventually, after all), as one of the very poorest, in point of emolument. In this state, however, the lawyers 'live in clover,' as we say." In spite of this, Prentiss (possibly for no other reason than that he was a homesick lad far from Maine) yearned to return home, and outlined his reasons: "one of the first and most powerful, . . . is that I may be nearer my friends; another is, that I would dislike to live in a slave-holding State; furthermore, I have seen no part of the Union which I think pleasanter . . . than what I left." [48] Besides, he missed the mountains and referred to "the streams and brooks" of Mississippi as only "little muddy puddles." Likewise, his observations cast doubt on the idea that splendor was the sole characteristic of all the plantation homes. "The houses of the planters, notwithstanding their wealth, are not better than those of our common farmers. They are, usually, two or three miles distant from each other, and each one surrounded by some ten, twenty or thirty negro cabins, which are the very pictures of misery and filth." [49]

Certain interesting diversions were his to enjoy, however. One highlight activity during his employment in the Shields household was his participation in a debating society organized by several young men of the community. The society met on Saturdays in what was then known as Union Chapel, where "questions were propounded at each sitting, to be discussed at the next, and speakers were appointed respectively on the affirmative and negative sides. Essayists

---

[47] *Ibid.*

[48] *Id.* to William Prentiss, Natchez, April 20, 1828, in *Memoir of S. S. Prentiss,* I, 72.

[49] *Id.* to *id.,* Natchez, June 23, 1828, *ibid.,* 74–75.

and declaimers were also appointed." [50] Here he found a real forum for the expression of his natural oratorical talents. He matched wits with another school teacher of the community, James Alden,[51] and with other members of the society, beginning an oratorical career in Mississippi which was to lead him to singular fame.

It was in June, 1828, that Prentiss closed his Rokeby school, having paid all his debts to Wright.[52] Besides, "He had fifteen or twenty dollars in his pocket, and was *square with the world*." [53] But his teaching days were not yet entirely behind him. He left Rokeby only because he desired to improve his financial status. After a fruitless eighty-mile horseback ride to St. Francisville, Louisiana, to apply for a college position which he found did not exist,[54] he settled down, apparently as the sole instructor, to the teaching of Dunbarton Academy near the plantation home of Mrs. Martha Dunbar, some ten miles from Natchez.[55]

Prentiss taught at Dunbarton one school session. The academy was larger than the school he had conducted in the Shields home, and his remuneration was likewise greater. But he grew increasingly weary of teaching, longing to pursue his legal studies exclusively. Determined to abandon teaching, but vacillating between returning to Maine and remaining in Mississippi, probably thinking more seriously of the former, he gave expression to his feelings in one of his letters home: "My school is doing well, but I am perfectly disgusted with the business of teaching; it does not suit either my temper or disposition." Still not satisfied to adopt Mississippi permanently as his home, he wrote: "I shall, next fall, either return to Maine, or settle here as a lawyer. . . . Should I settle in this State, I have no doubt I could make a fortune with the greatest ease. . . . In every

50 Shields, *Seargent Smith Prentiss*, 24.   51 *Ibid.*, 24–25.
52 *Ibid.*, 25.
53 *Ibid.*, 26; Prentiss to his mother, Natchez, July 26, 1828, in *Memoir of S. S. Prentiss*, I, 88.
54 *Id.* to *id.*, Natchez, July 26, 1828, *ibid.*
55 *Ibid.*; Shields, *Seargent Smith Prentiss*, 26.

other respect I should far prefer the North to the South. The society is better, the country is more beautiful, and, besides, you have, in the North, no slaves—a strong objection to the South." [56]

Prentiss experienced one event at Dunbarton which is worthy of notice in passing. In later years the name of John F. H. Claiborne was to be linked with that of Prentiss on many occasions. It was during this year at Dunbarton that Prentiss saw his future political rival and foe married to one of the daughters of Mrs. Dunbar.[57]

Soon, too, through another political opponent of the future, Robert J. Walker, the opportunity came for Prentiss to take up the study of law in earnest. He closed his work at the academy January 1, 1829.[58] Following a short excursion through Louisiana to New Orleans, of which he said, "I stayed in New Orleans three or four days, and never was so heartily tired of a place in my life," [59] he was back again in Natchez.

Prentiss entered Walker's law office. In this act he made an important decision, for he was at the same time giving up an ardent desire to return to Maine. The deciding factor was that he felt certain he could be admitted to the Mississippi bar within a few months. He wrote to his relatives: "I should revisit the spot which will always be to me dearer than any other place, yet I think you will agree with me that it is my duty to remain here. . . . By studying this winter, I can be admitted to practice next July—whereas, in Maine, I should be obliged to study more than a year." [60] The die was now cast, and Prentiss was to be a Mississippian for years to come, and a citizen of the South for the remainder of his life.

[56] Prentiss to his mother, Natchez, November 18, 1828, in *Memoir of S. S. Prentiss*, I, 92–93.

[57] Shields, *Seargent Smith Prentiss*, 27.   [58] *Ibid.*, 30.

[59] Prentiss to William Prentiss, Natchez, April 9, 1828, in *Memoir of S. S. Prentiss*, I, 95.

[60] *Id.* to *id.*, Natchez, February 4, 1828, *ibid.*, 94.

Chapter III

LEGAL AND POLITICAL BEGINNINGS

AFTER remaining in Walker's office as a close student of the law for something less than a year, Prentiss wrote to his brother William: "Month after next I shall apply for admission and commence the practice of law." [1] The period spent in Walker's office was not all the time that Prentiss had given to a systematic study of law, however. He had been with Pierce in Portland nearly ten months, and the advantages of the law library in the Shields home had been, as he declared, of "inestimable value." It is almost certain, too, that he continued reading while at Dunbarton. At any rate, though he was less than twenty-one years of age, he determined to gain admission to the Mississippi bar. "I have been studying pretty hard of late," he wrote to Abby Prentiss, "preparing for examination. Candidates for admission are examined at the Supreme Court, which sits next week at Monticello—a town about eighty miles from Natchez, in the interior of the State. I shall go out on horseback a week from next Wednesday; so that, I presume, by the time you read this letter I shall have a lawful right to the title of 'Esquire.' I shall leave Natchez immediately after, and settle, probably, at Port Gibson—a flourishing village some forty miles from this place." [2]

On June 13, 1829, Prentiss mounted his horse and rode to Monticello. Two days later he appeared before Chancel-

[1] Prentiss to William Prentiss, Natchez, April 9, 1829, in *Memoir of S. S. Prentiss*, I, 95.
[2] *Id.* to Abby Prentiss, Natchez, May 31, 1829, *ibid.*, 98–99.

lor Robert H. Buckner, "appointed examiner by the court," [3] and passed the bar examination.

Prentiss' Bowdoin classmate, Boyd, who like himself had come on from Cincinnati to Mississippi, took the examination at the same time. Likewise, other candidates who were to figure in the legal and political history of the South chose that date to present themselves before Buckner. One was Preston W. Farrar, later a member of the Mississippi State Senate, and still later a member of the New Orleans bar. Two others were William C. Harris, who settled in Warren County, and Cyrus W. Buckner, a brother of Chancellor Buckner. [4] The Chancellor commented on the performance of Prentiss and the others in the examination: "Boyd sat with his legs crossed, perfectly self-possessed. When a question was asked he would glance his eye up to the querist and answer briefly, distinctly, and right to the point. Prentiss answered correctly, but amplified and philosophized as he answered. W. C. Harris made no pretention, but went straight to the mark. Boyd, critically speaking, stood the best examination." [5]

Doubtless Prentiss had decided to locate at Port Gibson because he would have less strenuous competition there than at Natchez. The Natchez bar was crowded with able and distinguished practitioners. It required no small amount of courage for a struggling young lawyer to attempt to build a substantial clientele when in that small city such men as Walker, John A. Quitman, John T. McCurran, Aylette Buckner, Eli and Felix Huston, Robert H. Adams, Covington Rawlings, Thomas Armat, George Winchester, and Alexander Montgomery had their own offices of law. [6] But before his Port Gibson plans matured, opportunity opened her doors to Prentiss in Natchez. Felix Huston, who subsequently was to move to Texas and figure in the history of the Lone Star state, offered to take Prentiss into partner-

[3] Shields, *Seargent Smith Prentiss*, 36.
[4] *Ibid.*   [5] Quoted *ibid.*   [6] *Ibid.*, 38.

ship. Prentiss accepted and announced to his mother: "I have made an arrangement of considerable importance, for the ensuing year. . . . I am to have a sufficient portion of the profits of the business to support me handsomely, and defray my expenses of every kind. Next year, in all probability, I shall be able to continue with him on much more favorable terms. But the great advantage of the thing is, that I shall gain more knowledge of business this year, than I should in two or three years, had I started myself." [7]

Proceeding on the assumption that he would learn the intricacies of law and legal pleading more rapidly under the tutelage of an experienced advocate, and that he owed much to the man who had placed confidence in him, Prentiss began in earnest the practice of law. "There is a tradition, for which I shall not vouch, but will tell it as told to me," says Shields, "that Huston remarked when he took Prentiss into partnership he thought he was getting a boy who would *help* him now and then in the drudgery of the practice, but that he soon found Prentiss was the leader and he the assistant." [8]

Prentiss was successful from the start as a lawyer. His status with Huston improved constantly. The partnership began in July, 1829, their announcement in the Natchez *Southern Galaxy* reading "Felix Huston & S. S. Prentiss, Attorneys and Counsellors at Law. Will jointly practice in the Courts heretofore attended by Mr. Huston. Mr. Prentiss will devote himself exclusively to the office and Courts in Natchez." [9] Prentiss' success in the first few months with Huston is indicated by the altered notice in October in the *Southern Galaxy:* "Mr. Prentiss will also attend the Circuit Courts of Jefferson, Franklin and Copiah." [10] In July, 1830, a year after he joined Huston, Prentiss made a new agree-

[7] Prentiss to his mother, Natchez, June 24, 1829, in *Memoir of S. S. Prentiss,* I, 100–101.

[8] Shields, *Seargent Smith Prentiss,* 37.

[9] Natchez *Southern Galaxy,* July 2, 1829.

[10] *Ibid.,* October 1, 1829.

ment with his partner whereby he was to receive one third of the profits.[11] This second arrangement with Huston on more favorable terms meant that Prentiss' earlier idea of returning to Maine to live was becoming more and more remote. He told his mother: "If my success answers my expectations, I shall feel it my duty to continue here for some years—though my inclinations strongly urge me to go home, and settle in my native land." [12]

The sails of Prentiss' life in the South were being set. While torn between a constant desire to return to Maine and the professional advantages of residing in Mississippi, Prentiss found himself a rising lawyer with increasing legal duties. In those days he began riding on horseback to attend various circuit courts. Apologizing to his mother for his infrequent letters because of "two or three weeks" of circuit riding, he laid bare his feelings on the issue of continuing in Mississippi or returning to Maine: "Indeed, so far from becoming reconciled to a residence in the South, or forgetful of my native land, I become every day more tired of the former, and look back with more regret to the latter. Still I feel bound to stay here, though I am sometimes almost sorry that my prospects of success render it my duty to do so—and I do not think I should have at all regretted it, had my ill-fortune compelled me to return to Maine." [13]

The decision to remain in Mississippi was a difficult one for the homesick Prentiss. While he did not allow his desire for home to prevail, his days at Natchez were, nevertheless, numbered. After more than four years of residence there, two and a half of which were in legal practice, he broke his ties, and identified himself with the bar at Vicksburg. This was early in February, 1832. His reasons for leaving Natchez were clear. He saw Natchez to be declining while Vicksburg was "a flourishing town, nearly as large as Natchez,

---

[11] Shields, *Seargent Smith Prentiss*, 39; Prentiss to his mother, Natchez, July 11, 1830, in *Memoir of S. S. Prentiss*, I, 104.

[12] *Id.* to *id.*, July 11, 1830, in *Memoir of S. S. Prentiss*, I, 104.

[13] *Id.* to *id.*, Natchez, November 10, 1830, *ibid.*, 106.

and much superior for business." Prentiss' decision to locate in Vicksburg, where he aspired to a career that would exceed anything he might attain in Natchez, was a most important turning point in his life. Of course, he could not go in quest of opportunities at Vicksburg without, at the same time, relinquishing serious thoughts of leaving Mississippi to return to his home state. What may be considered more nearly a final decision in this regard is stated in the same letter in which he wrote to his mother that he was going to Vicksburg: "I had had serious thoughts of returning to Maine, but competition there, in my profession, is so great, and the prospects of success so small, that I am deterred—at least for the present—from leaving Mississippi." [14]

If legal competition in Maine was so intense that Prentiss declined to encounter it, and if his legal colleagues at Natchez were numerous and able, he could not escape the fact that in Vicksburg also there resided other competent attorneys. In his new location he joined the legal society of such men as John I. Guion, William C. Smedes, Joseph Holt, John M. Chilton, Alexander G. McNutt, William F. Bodley, and Henry S. Foote.[15] Holt, who later moved to Kentucky and subsequently became a member of the cabinet of President James Buchanan, and Foote, afterward governor of Mississippi and later United States senator, came in the course of time to be his most frequent and formidable court opponents. Another member of the Vicksburg bar, Guion, soon ceased to be an opponent, for a year later, in 1833, he and Prentiss formed a partnership which lasted until Guion was elevated to the bench in 1836.[16] Sometime after the dissolution of the partnership with Guion, Prentiss formed another one with Smedes which lasted for the remaining years during which Prentiss re-

[14] *Id.* to *id.*, Natchez, January 6, 1832, *ibid.*, 112–13.

[15] Shields, *Seargent Smith Prentiss*, 44.

[16] *Ibid.*, 59; James D. Lynch, *The Bench and Bar of Mississippi* (New York, 1881), 217–18.

sided in Vicksburg. Relative to the partnership with Guion, Foote has left the statement: "Great as were the abilities of Mr. Prentiss, this . . . partnership was decidedly detrimental to Judge Guion; for it was observed that, owing to his profound deference for his new associate, or from some other cause, he rarely afterwards attempted to take the lead in forensic discussion, and was much more solicitous of building up the fame of Mr. Prentiss than of advancing his own." [17]

In the year and a half that Prentiss was in Vicksburg before joining Guion, his law practice flourished astonishingly. Soon after establishing himself there, he won a case by a two-hour speech for a Vicksburg hotel owner who contested the right of the mayor and city authorities to quarantine the hotel because of the outbreak of smallpox in it. It is very probable that in connection with this case Prentiss made almost his first contact with Foote. Foote was frequently his opponent, but not so in this instance. He had settled in Vicksburg in 1831 and was staying at the hotel at the time the quarantine was imposed. The hotel owner asked him to bring an action for damages. Foote solicited Prentiss' aid. Prentiss agreed to help argue the case, and did so with "such extraordinary force and ingenuity, that he was immediately invited to become a member of a law firm in Vicksburg of the highest rank there." [18] Evidently this early legal appearance had much to do with establishing Prentiss as the exceedingly successful advocate he became. It was, of course, the event leading to his partnership with Guion, and according to Foote, "Thenceforward Mr. Prentiss' forensic career was one of uninterrupted prosperity, and his reputation as an advocate continued to expand and display additional splendor, up to the end of his mortal career." [19]

[17] Henry S. Foote, *The Bench and Bar of the South and Southwest* (St. Louis, 1876), 71–72.
[18] *Ibid.*, 32–33.   [19] *Ibid.*, 33.

A short time after the hotel trial, Prentiss became identified with another case which gave him widespread publicity. This time he proved himself in the role of prosecutor. It was as an opponent of Foote this time that Prentiss obtained a jury vote of hanging for a northern outlaw, Alonzo Phelps, accused of murder. As a young lawyer, and a new one in Vicksburg, Prentiss stood in need of a legal and forensic reputation and he gained both in this colorful trial.

Phelps, like Prentiss, was a New Englander. Like Prentiss, he was very well educated. But unlike Prentiss, who came to Mississippi to build a name for himself, Phelps came to escape the crime of having murdered a rival lover. In Mississippi his criminal career continued until he was guilty of as many as "eight murders and more than sixty robberies, and had some dozen times broken jail and evaded the punishment of the law." [20] Following one of his murders, this one in Yazoo City, he was brought to Vicksburg for trial.

Prentiss, along with Felix Huston and others, constituted the prosecution. Foote was the chief attorney for the defense. Since Foote was defending Phelps, considerable importance may be attached to his observations of Prentiss in the trial. It seems that Prentiss played a very significant part, giving at least one powerful speech. According to Foote, "The speech delivered by Mr. Prentiss would have enhanced the fame of an Erskine, a McIntosh, or a Curran. His delineation of the character of the accused was, indeed, most masterly, in the course of which he bestowed upon him the imperishable cognomen of 'The Rob Roy of the Mississippi.'" [21]

Prentiss obtained a jury verdict of hanging, but a most unusual aftermath seemingly took place. As Shields states, "The subsequent part of his [Phelps'] brief remaining career has a tinge of romance. He actually sent for Prentiss and unbosomed himself; he told him of his early life and of his fall, and that he had taken an assumed name, and would

20 *Ibid.*, 36.   21 *Ibid.*, 36–37.

never let his family know of his tragic end. He told Prentiss
that while he was speaking in the case he intended at one
time to spring on him, crush him, and escape in the *mêlée.*
Prentiss replied to all this, 'I saw it all, and was ready for
you.' " [22]

There must be more than mere fiction in this story, for
Foote, as Phelps's attorney, corroborates it most interestingly. Foote evidently observed the intentions of Phelps as
clearly as did Prentiss. "Prentiss' speech galled and irritated
him greatly. . . . I saw the muscles of this hardened criminal quivver with convulsive agony; and seemingly presently
to grow desperate, he bent forward a little and whispered in
my ear; 'Tell me whether I stand any chance of acquittal,
and tell me frankly; for if my case is hopeless, I will snatch
a gun from the guard nearest me and send Mr. Prentiss to
hell before I shall myself go there.' " Foote was doubtless
honest when he said, "Never was I more embarrassed in
my life." He felt Phelps "was in dead earnest." Prentiss' life
was in danger, and Foote knew it. He wrote: "I may have
been wrong, but frankness constrains me to confess that I
whispered back to Phelps, 'You are not in the least in danger;
we shall have no difficulty whatever in preventing your
conviction, and shall presently introduce a motion for a
new trial, or an arrest of judgment, which will save you
from all further annoyance.' " [23]

Although Phelps was convicted, it is uncertain whether
he was hanged. He is said to have escaped jail, and according to Foote was shot down by a sheriff.[24] Shields agrees that
he broke jail, but says that he was wounded, recaptured,
"and on the appointed day expiated his crimes upon the
gallows." [25]

One measure of the growing reputation of the young
lawyer is the extent to which he appeared before higher

[22] Shields, *Seargent Smith Prentiss,* 48.
[23] Foote, *Bench and Bar of the South and Southwest,* 37–38.
[24] *Ibid.,* 38.
[25] Shields, *Seargent Smith Prentiss,* 48.

courts. Within two years after settling at Vicksburg, Prentiss began a succession of appearances before the Mississippi State Supreme Court. One case in particular seems to have had much to do with giving him a great measure of publicity. It was Byrd *v.* The State.[26]

This case was a sensational one. Details, criminal and political, before and after Prentiss' part in it, are worthy of more than passing attention. Again Prentiss had as his opponent Foote, who many years after made known some unusually interesting angles of the trial.

This Mississippi legal case grew out of circumstances associated with the planting partnership of Alexander G. McNutt and Joel Cameron. McNutt was a Vicksburg lawyer, and Cameron, apparently, was the actual planter in the extensive holdings of the partnership. About 1830, or a little later, Cameron was murdered. The murder occurred, it appears, while he was riding over the plantation. Whoever committed the crime fastened weights to the body and threw it into a lake. A violent thunderstorm caused the body to come to the surface; proofs of murder were evident. Suspicion fell on four Negroes. Foote was appointed to defend them. Although, according to Foote, Cameron was no credit to the community, was cruel to his slaves, and had actually murdered certain of them, the four Negroes were convicted. One of them, whose name was Daniel, seemingly possessed important information concerning which Foote may have learned. McNutt, before Daniel's death, threatened the Negro, telling him that "if he continued to repeat the language which had previously issued from his lips he would cause all his teeth to be drawn by a dentist." [27] This sufficed to keep Daniel quiet until just before his hanging, when he tried to speak to the crowd assembled. He was again prevented from doing so, for "with the direction of McNutt, the drum was most vociferously beaten, so as to

26 Byrd *v.* The State, 1 Howard (Miss.) 247 (1834).
27 Henry S. Foote, *Casket of Reminiscences* (Washington, 1874), 203.

drown the voice of the dying man, and he was thus confusedly hurried into eternity." [28] Daniel had once been the trusted favorite of Cameron, being his actual foreman on the plantation. In time Cameron had taken away Daniel's special privileges, finally compelling him to relinquish his favorite of the two wives he had been allowed to marry. Daniel's hatred of Cameron knew no limit. What he knew and tried to tell, Foote says, was "of a nature to give great umbrage to Mr. McNutt." [29]

The story did not end with the death of Daniel and the other three Negroes. A short time later a watch belonging to Cameron was found in the poultry house of Mercer Byrd, a free man of color. McNutt then instituted proceedings against Byrd through the Circuit Court of Warren County. A change of venue was obtained, however, to hold the trial in Hinds County. At this trial Byrd was found guilty as an accessory to the murder. The case was then carried to the Mississippi State Supreme Court, where in the July term of 1834, the opinion of the lower court was sustained.[30] Then in the January term of 1835 the case was reargued on the grounds that certain of the jurors in the first trial in Hinds were not freeholders or householders, and the decision was reversed.[31] But again the case was argued before the Supreme Court during the July, 1835, term, when the decision was again reversed, causing Byrd to be hanged.[32]

Two questions are of considerable interest in this case. One is: Why did McNutt take such an interest in the prosecution of Byrd? The other is: What part did Prentiss really play in the prosecution of Byrd? If the explanations as given by Foote can be relied upon, a rather complete answer is offered to the first question, and at least a partial answer to the second.

[28] *Ibid.*   [29] *Ibid.*   [30] 1 Howard (Miss.) 163 (1834).
[31] *Ibid.*, 176 (1835).   [32] *Ibid.*, 247 (1835).

As partners in cotton planting, McNutt and Cameron would naturally profit or lose together. Upon the death of one, the assets and liabilities of the venture would fall upon the other. Upon Cameron's death, McNutt came into sole possession of the profitable holdings of the partnership. This was made doubly certain by the fact that McNutt married Cameron's widow within seven months of his death. Foote, as defense attorney for Byrd, stated that following the appeals to save the life of his client, Byrd called him to the jail cell. Prepared to die, Byrd made a confession and statement which, strange as it may seem, had apparently not been made during the successive trials and hearings. He stated to Foote, on the word of Daniel, "that Cameron had been murdered at the instigation of McNutt himself." Foote then put the question, "Mercer Byrd, are you willing to put at hazard your eternal salvation upon the truth of the statements contained in the paper just read?" Byrd replied in the affirmative. Foote then entreated: "Let me suppress this confession; its publication can do no good, and may do much harm. Leave the world, I beseech you, in peace with all mankind—even with those whom you believe to have persecuted you." If McNutt was responsible for instigating the murder through Daniel and his fellow Negroes, and if he knew that Byrd knew the truth, then it follows, possibly, that he was willing to run the risk of being revealed in an effort to get Byrd out of the world as well.

An interesting sequel to the whole affair and its implications was the fact that in a later political campaign McNutt, in making certain severe charges against Foote, caused Foote, in private, to tell McNutt the story Byrd had told him. McNutt, to protect himself from being exposed in public by Foote, refrained from further attacks. The guilt or innocence of McNutt is a mooted question. Foote says he told him, "I do not even now say that I am satisfied of your guilt; for God knows that I have been struggling for years to avoid considering you so bad a man as the dying Byrd charged you with being." [33]

What was Prentiss' role in these events? Foote wrote that McNutt engaged Prentiss to prosecute, paying him a fee of $4,000.[34] Prentiss may have figured considerably more than the records of the Supreme Court show, for in the first two hearings his name does not appear as one of the participating lawyers. At the July, 1835, hearing of the case he did figure as associated with the attorney general. An interesting aspect of this hearing was the fact that the plaintiff charged the prosecutor with having withdrawn, leaving the management to another. In reply to this, the court ruled that it was permissible for Prentiss to assume charge of the case after "preliminaries to the trial have been duly performed." [35] Prentiss evidently prosecuted with severity, for at this time Byrd went to his final doom. Foote has given his reminiscences of Prentiss' part, probably in the earlier stages of the trials of Byrd. "Never shall I forget his terrible delineation, in his concluding speech, of Mercer Byrd on horseback, at the head of an army of infuriated blacks, burning, slaying, and destroying all that they encountered in their fiery and desolating career. Mercer Byrd, being a free man of color, of uncommon intelligence and of most commanding aspect, was a fine subject for the display of Mr. Prentiss' rare powers of delineation." Foote stated also that "The jury almost convicted him in the box, but several of them often told me afterward that they deeply regretted the verdict, for they then thought Byrd innocent, though Mr. Prentiss' irresistible eloquence had driven them to the verdict which had taken away his life." [36] Whatever may have been the thinking of Prentiss in 1835 on the subject of slavery, he had, evidently, learned the power of the white man's prejudice against, and even fear of, the Negro, in persuading juries.

[33] Foote, *Casket of Reminiscences*, 205–10.   [34] *Ibid.*, 204, 435.
[35] 1 Howard (Miss.) 247 (1835).   [36] Foote, *Casket of Reminiscences*, 436.

The cases of Phelps and Byrd indicate that Prentiss was building a legal reputation, and also that he was proving himself adept in prosecution. Yet he never established himself chiefly as a prosecutor. Shields states that actually Prentiss did not like prosecution and referred to his fees earned in this manner as "blood money." [37] Doubtless he defended men accused of murder as often as he prosecuted. Once he wrote to his mother: "For the last week, among other important business, I have been defending a man charged with murder; and after a long and laborious trial, succeeded in acquitting him. Tomorrow I have to start to a court eighty miles in the interior, for the purpose of defending a man in another case of murder. . . . I have been employed, in the last six months, in a good many cases where men were tried for their lives, and so far have been always successful." Prentiss evidently took pride in this, for he went on to say: "This has given me some little reputation in such matters; and now there is hardly a murder or anything of the kind takes place about here (and they occur often) but I am employed on one side or the other." [38] It is true, too, that from the first, and throughout his legal career as well, Prentiss handled his share of civil cases as well as criminal cases.

An interesting aspect of Prentiss' career as a successful lawyer was the fact that he made but one appearance, and that early in his career (1833), before the United States Supreme Court. During his first two years at Vicksburg, and before he joined with Guion, Prentiss journeyed to Washington to plead the case of Sampeyreac & Stewart *v.* United States, a land case which had been in the lower courts for years.[39] He lost the suit, but he must have nevertheless valued the opportunity to plead before Chief Justice John Marshall. He was counsel for the appellants against Attorney General Roger B. Taney for the United States.

[37] Shields, *Seargent Smith Prentiss,* 49.
[38] Prentiss to his mother, Vicksburg, May 22, 1834, in *Memoir of S. S. Prentiss,* I, 139–40.
[39] 7 Peters, 222 (1833); Shields, *Seargent Smith Prentiss,* 56–59.

When three weeks had elapsed, during which time he waited for the case to be called, he argued it, and then wrote to his mother: "I made a speech three or four hours long; and I suppose you will say, I have acquired a great deal of brass since I left home, when I tell you I was not at all abashed or alarmed in addressing so grave a set of men." [40]

That Prentiss' first years of legal practice were flourishing ones cannot be doubted. His letters to relatives in Maine were good evidence of this. Much of his time was spent in circuit riding to courts located at great distances from each other. At one time he wrote: "I have just returned from attending court about forty miles in the interior, and have to start to-morrow to attend another still further distant. We have no stages here, and I go to all these courts on horseback. I think nothing of riding fifty miles a day." [41] Possibly it was on this trip into the interior which led him to write later: "I have been east of Pearl River. I travel entirely on horseback, and have had to swim on my horse, over creeks and bayous that would astonish your northern people, whose roads are all turnpiked. Beyond Pearl River, I had to ride, and repeatedly to swim, through a swamp four miles in extent, in which the water was all the time up to the horse's belly. What do you think of that for a lawyer's life? It would kill your New York cockneys in a week." [42] Soon after he was writing that he could not make a desired visit home: "I start to-morrow to attend the Courts of several counties in the interior of the State. . . . I suppose I shall have to ride altogether at least 250 miles, so you see a lawyer's life in this country is by no means a lazy one." [43]

During 1834 Prentiss found himself so busy that again he had to forgo a visit home. He explained to his mother: "Since I have been in this country, there has not been a

40 Prentiss to his mother, Vicksburg, March 30, 1833, in *Memoir of S. S. Prentiss*, I, 121–22.

41 *Id.* to *id.*, Vicksburg, April 17, 1833, *ibid.*, 122.

42 *Id.* to William Prentiss, Vicksburg, April 30, 1833, *ibid.*, 123.

43 *Id.* to his mother, Vicksburg, August 27, 1833, *ibid.*, 126.

year in which I could have left the State with less sacrifice than during the present. . . . This year I have attended to more business, than all the time I have been practicing before. I have, in particular, engaged in a great many *capital cases,* where men have been tried for murder and other enormous crimes, and I have been very successful." [44] Toward the close of 1834 he apologized to his sister Abby for his infrequent letters. "My business compels me to be absent from Vicksburg at least half my time, and this in periods of a month or two months together." Something of the hectic life he led while on circuit is revealed in this same letter. "Surrounded during the whole time of my absence, by noisy and boisterous people—overwhelmed and perplexed by complicated business—subject every moment to be intruded upon by the calls of clients—I become so vexed and harrassed, that when I return to Vicksburg and find a letter from home . . . it seems as if I had gotten into a new world." That he was earning some money may be inferred from a statement in the letter: "Permit me to act as your banker; and accept the within note to defray such little expenses as you may incur." [45]

That the life of riding the circuit was hectic, exciting, arduous, and reckless can scarcely be doubted. Unquestionably the greatest tragedy of Prentiss' life was that he early became so addicted to strong drink that his life span was considerably shortened. Just when the influence of alcohol was fastened upon him it is difficult to know. Very likely he indulged heavily while in his early court days. Likewise cards and gambling became an excitement and diversion during this period.

Through a miscellany of minor events, the record of which has come down to us, we can piece together something of Prentiss' life during this period. Once in a leisurely

[44] *Id.* to *id.,* Vicksburg, August 31, 1834, *ibid.,* 142.
[45] Prentiss to Abby Prentiss, Vicksburg, December 10, 1834, in *Memoir of S. S. Prentiss,* I, 143–44.

moment, he purchased for five dollars from a woman inn-
keeper a clock which had long ceased to run, repaired it, and
then presented it to her as a gift.[46] At another time he and
a legal opponent are reported to have come to actual blows
during the course of a trial, causing the judge to sentence
both of them to twenty-four hours in the county jail. It is
said that after the judge pronounced the sentence, Prentiss
addressed the court, admitted his guilt "of unintentional
disrespect to the Court, as well as great want of self-respect,"
and then asked the favor in an "affected . . . degree of
naïveté and sincerity," that he not be imprisoned in the same
cell with his opponent. The judge granted the request, and
that night Prentiss' friends gathered at the cell, "where they
spent the night in partaking of a sumptuous supper, and
enjoying the exhaustless good humor of their captive
guest." [47]

Doubtless all of Prentiss' moods and mannerisms revealed
themselves on circuit. A fellow lawyer, John M. Chilton,
recalled: "I remember having once ridden with him to a
neighboring county court, and during the jaunty conversa-
tions usually attending such journeys . . . I would sometimes recite a line from Byron, and he would immediately
take up the stanza and repeat whole successive pages, without hesitation." Another lawyer companion, Edward C.
Wilkinson, recalling his court rides with Prentiss, commented: "I have sometimes known him to push his thoughts,
as it seemed to me, to the outermost verge of human concep-
tion, and then settle for many minutes, into painful and
sickly melancholy, because his intellect could not peer beyond the field of mortal vision. His melancholy never lasted
long, but it was intense while it was upon him. Fortunately
nature had given him such animal spirits as to prevent the
possibility of his becoming a misanthrope, or he, the most

[46] Shields, *Seargent Smith Prentiss*, 60–61.
[47] *Memoir of S. S. Prentiss*, I, 146–47.

joyous being that I ever met, might have sunk into a moody and miserable man." [48]

In October, 1833, Prentiss narrowly escaped death in a duel. Fortunately for Prentiss' state of mind, Foote, his opponent, also survived. Prentiss came near fighting several duels in his life, but actually fought only one, or rather two, both with Foote. It has been mentioned that Foote was one of Prentiss' most frequent and capable legal opponents. They were evidently good personal friends,[49] and were not excessively far apart in political thinking,[50] but the so-called code of honor in the South overrode all other considerations. One of the things Prentiss had to accept when he came south was the code of honor, distasteful to him as it was.

As his legal opponent in a trial, Foote once went beyond the bounds of propriety, using such abusive language in reference to Prentiss that Prentiss impulsively struck him. Instead of striking back, Foote challenged Prentiss to mortal combat on the dueling grounds. Foote later admitted that Prentiss' "language, though sufficiently retaliated by me at the time, induced me to send him a challenge, which I ought never to have thought of doing." [51] The code of honor compelled Prentiss to accept the challenge. Meeting on the Louisiana side of the Mississippi River opposite Vicksburg, they took their positions ten paces apart. Foote fired first, missing Prentiss completely. Prentiss' shot, according to Shields, merely pierced the shoulder of Foote's coat,[52] though Foote says, Prentiss "wounded me very painfully in

[48] *Ibid.*, 145-47.

[49] Foote once wrote that Prentiss was an individual "of whom I am generally supposed to know about as much as any other individual." *Casket of Reminiscences*, 97.

[50] Proof of this is the statement of Foote: "It is gratifying to me to remember that I once voted for S. S. Prentiss when he was a candidate for Congress against the regularly nominated ticket of my own party." *Ibid.*, 431.

[51] *Ibid.*, 188.

[52] Shields, *Seargent Smith Prentiss*, 70.

the left shoulder." [53] Anyway, the honor of both was satisfied, so that they left the field.

But the affair was not ended. Reports were circulated that
Prentiss, by the use of his cane, had the advantage of a
"rest." Angered by these rumors, especially since he was
extremely sensitive about his lameness, Prentiss took the
initiative in challenging Foote to a second duel. Foote accepted, and a second encounter took place where the first
one had occurred. Prentiss threw away his cane and prepared
to fire. But Foote shot first, again missing his aim. Prentiss
pulled the trigger, but the percussion cap was defective, and
the pistol failed to fire. Not willing to consider the battle
settled, since Prentiss did not actually have a chance to make
good his aim, the duelists took their stand for another attempt. Still another shot from Foote left Prentiss unharmed,
but Foote this time was struck and wounded.[54]

Shields relates a story, quite widely circulated, apparently,
that certain boys, seeking the best vantage point for ob-
serving the affair, had climbed into a near-by tree. Prentiss, seeing them as he took his place for the encounter,
called, "Boys, you had better come down. General Foote
shoots wild, you know, and you may get hit up there." [55]
Foote stated he never heard of the ludicrous remark about
his " 'wild shooting,' " until fifteen or sixteen years after it
was supposed to have occurred; and "it would seem to be
hardly in unison with Mr. Prentiss' high-bred refinement
and courtesy; but regarding the joke as told rather too good
a one to be spoiled by contradiction I have not heretofore
given it any serious notice." [56]

The whole incident of the duel must have been extremely
painful to Prentiss and not at all in harmony with his philosophy of living. He knew the news would cause distress be-

[53] Foote, *Casket of Reminiscences*, 188.
[54] For accounts of the duel, see *ibid.*, 187–88; Shields, *Seargent Smith
Prentiss*, 69–73; *Memoir of S. S. Prentiss*, I, 132–34.
[55] Shields, *Seargent Smith Prentiss*, 72.
[56] Foote, *Casket of Reminiscences*, 195.

yond words to his family in Maine. George Prentiss observed: "He well knew that such an act would not only be regarded with severe disapprobation throughout New England, but would pierce with anguish the hearts of those, who were dearer to him than life." [57] Prentiss tried, as best he could, to justify his position to George. His one great request was that his "Mother must on no account hear a word of this." He stated that he regretted the affair, called it a "foolish scrape," but contended that if he had not fought, he would have lost his "own self-respect, and life itself would have had no further objects for me." While he offered this justification, he realized his difficulty in trying to explain: "I know that with your principles, no excuse will be sufficient in such a case." Yet he did not weaken in his contention that he was under moral obligation to fight. The heart of his position he expressed in the words: "I am no advocate of duelling, and always shall from principle avoid such a thing, as much as possible; but when a man is placed in a situation where if he does not fight, life will be rendered valueless to him, both in his own eyes and those of the community, and existence will become a burden to him; then I say he will fight, and by so doing, will select the least of two evils." [58]

The year 1835, like the three preceding years of his early Vicksburg career, was crowned with success. It also afforded Prentiss the pleasure of returning to Maine for the first time since his departure in 1827. He necessarily had to break himself free from a heavy load of professional duties. A contemporary letter to his mother gives a good account of his busy life. "I have just returned to Vicksburg, after an absence of six weeks on business. At least two-thirds of my time is spent from home, in attendance upon courts and other professional engagements. . . . Though I arrived here but yesterday, I am compelled to leave again tomorrow,

[57] *Memoir of S. S. Prentiss*, I, 133.
[58] Prentiss to George L. Prentiss, n.d., *ibid.*, 134.

and shall not be back for several weeks. Indeed, my business pressed me so much that I have hardly time to write the few lines you are reading." [59]

In the summer his plans materialized for the visit to Maine. Telling his mother that the time for his starting must be indefinite because of court sessions, he concluded: "As the time approaches, in which I trust to see you all, I have lost half of my inclination to write; for I am continually thinking how much pleasanter it will be to talk over matters by the fire-side, when I get home." [60]

Prentiss traveled by water from New Orleans to New York. Among his companions was his friend, Edward C. Wilkinson, who later recounted how Prentiss relaxed on the quarter-deck, repeating passages from Milton, Byron, Scott, Shakespeare, and Spenser, and how he "would sometimes wish for a *Storm* as a relief from the dead calm of the sea." Wilkinson remembered particularly an incident when a dolphin was taken and lay dying on the deck, and how Prentiss "gave us those beautiful lines from Byron about 'parting day.'

Parting day
Dies like the dolphin, whom each pang imbues,
    With a new color, as it gasps away,
The last still lovliest, till—'tis gone—and all is gray." [61]

Meeting his sister Abby in New York, Prentiss journeyed on to Maine. "His appearance, at that time," George Prentiss remarked, "was very striking; and arrested the eye of the most casual observer. When animated by conversation, every feature of his countenance glowed with intellectual beauty; his smile was peculiarly radiant; the tones of his voice were clear and persuasive; while the shape of his mouth and the whole carriage of his head gave assurance of an indomitable will." While home he visited with relatives and

[59] Prentiss to his mother, Vicksburg, February 7, 1835, *ibid.*, 157.
[60] *Id.* to *id.*, May 11, 1835, *ibid.*, 159.
[61] Edward Wilkinson to George L. Prentiss, n.d., *ibid.*

old friends, "fished again in the Great Brook," and relived days of his childhood and youth.[62]

After this happy vacation, Prentiss returned to Mississippi in September. Shortly after he arrived in Vicksburg, he stated that "he went immediately into the country to attend court, which had commenced a day or two before. Had I been a few days later it would have caused me considerable injury; for I have got some good fees by being present." [63]

An almost tragic accident occurred to Prentiss shortly after he returned to Mississippi. It is quite well explained by the entry in the diary of a singularly interesting free Negro of Natchez, William T. Johnson, who wrote in his unique and almost illiterate manner: "I herd Mr. Prentice gets some glass in his throat by biting a wine glass. he was then very ill." [64] Evidently the accident was quite serious. In December Prentiss wrote to Anna Prentiss: "I was eating dinner, and by some chance, a small piece of broken glass got into my throat, and in drinking I swallowed it. It lacerated my throat very much and I have been laid up by it till within a day or two." [65] George Prentiss commented on the incident: "This casualty was much more serious than he represents it. For several days his life hung by a single thread: humanly speaking, nothing saved him but his buoyancy of spirit, and the extraordinary vigor of his constitution." [66]

As Prentiss' early years in Vicksburg established him as an able lawyer, so, likewise, these same years marked the beginning of his political career. By the force of various circumstances he found himself allied with the anti-Jackson

[62] *Ibid.*, 160–61.

[63] Prentiss to his mother and sisters, Vicksburg, September 19, 1835, *ibid.*, 161–62.

[64] Diary of William T. Johnson, Department of Archives, Louisiana State University.

[65] Prentiss to Anna Prentiss, Vicksburg, December 10, 1835, in *Memoir of S. S. Prentiss*, I, 163.

[66] *Ibid.*

elements in Mississippi. He played a most significant role in breaking the influence of Jackson and Van Buren in the state, and was a leading figure in the organization of the Whig party in Mississippi.

That Prentiss became a Whig is explained in no small measure by his background. From the days of his childhood when he realized the disastrous effects of Jefferson's embargo on the shipping occupation of his father, he questioned the tenets of the sage of Monticello. Too, during his early years in Maine, he inevitably adopted the federalistic concepts of Alexander Hamilton and John Adams. New England traditions operated on him which he never forsook in spite of the fact that he came to be deeply southernized. Moreover, his advent into public life in Mississippi occurred at the very time Jacksonianism was being challenged. Alert mind that he was, he could not have been ignorant or unconcerned about the causes of disaffection which operated to bring into being a new political party. It was a time for men to make choices. They could choose to be Jacksonian and Van Buren disciples, adhere to John C. Calhoun as state-rights advocates and nullifiers, or move into the ranks of the evolving Whigs, heterogeneous as the party was. In truth, Mississippi was, in 1835, according to John A. Quitman, composed almost equally of these three groups.[67] The nullifiers of the Calhoun school dispersed, in time, into the other two groups. The conflict, then, was between the Democrats and Whigs. Doubtless forces other than his New England background led him into the ranks of the Whigs. They are more difficult to know, however, since Prentiss did not, seemingly, go on record before 1832 as to what his political thinking was and because he made no recorded public speeches outside the courtroom before 1834. The Whigs probably paid no price for his allegiance; rather, his services must have come voluntarily when, if for no other

[67] J. F. H. Claiborne, *Life and Correspondence of John A. Quitman* (New York, 1860), I, 139.

reason, Jackson refused to recharter the national bank. Regardless of what forces contributed to make Prentiss a Whig, the simple fact is that he abhorred the influence of Jackson and Van Buren. He believed their policies ruinous to the nation and certainly to his adopted state.

In time Daniel Webster and, more particularly, Henry Clay became his idols. It is doubtful that Clay ever had a more unqualified supporter or admirer than Prentiss. The two men had much in common. They were both orators of superior merit and power, magnetic in influence, enjoying the same pleasures and vices. While Prentiss seemingly took no part in politics during his first years in Mississippi, he did express as early as 1832 the following antipathy toward Jackson and spirited enthusiasm for Clay: "We are on the tip-toe to hear the results of the Presidential election—but I fear there is no chance of defeating Old Hickory. Louisiana has gone for Jackson. Kentucky, however, has redeemed herself, and gone for Clay by a large majority." [68] Less than a year later when he was in Washington for his appearance before the Supreme Court, he met Jackson for the first time and wrote: "I visited the White House in company with one of the Senators from Mississippi; and was introduced to the President, with whom we chatted about fifteen minutes. I think him about as fit to be President of the United States as I am." He reflected in the same letter that while the men in Congress whom he had the opportunity to meet were mostly "destitute of talent," "There are, however, some truly great men here—among the foremost of whom are Webster, Clay, and Calhoun; I consider these the three most talented men in the nation." [69] Calhoun was one of the very few Democrats to whom Prentiss ever paid tribute or homage. Moreover, Prentiss could not have been unaware of how much in Jackson's disfavor Calhoun was in 1833.

[68] Prentiss to William Prentiss, Vicksburg, November 18, 1832, in *Memoir of S. S. Prentiss*, I, 119.

[69] *Id.* to Abby Prentiss, Washington City, February 3, 1833, *ibid.*, 120–21.

As Prentiss' endeavors at the bar brought him into the public eye in Mississippi, so, likewise, certain other of his public appearances contributed to making him known beyond the confines of Natchez and Vicksburg. One was a speech which he gave in August, 1834, at Jackson. It was a eulogy on the deceased Lafayette. The address is of some significance, as it is one of the very few which Prentiss ever wrote and delivered from manuscript. The speech served to extend his name in Mississippi, but was less able than others which he delivered in later years. Yet it has lived in the sense that it has been one of the specimens of his eloquence most commonly accepted by various editors and compilers.[70] It is really the first available for analysis, and is illustrative, to a considerable extent, of his oratorical style in general. In brief, it is replete with picturesque language, copious in figures, analogies and allusions, and is almost poetic in imagery. One weakness of the speech was expressed by George Prentiss, who stated it was "a hasty effusion, and is said to have been written at a single sitting, a night or two before delivery." [71]

The speech on Lafayette may well be considered to meet many of the requisites of an address of eulogy, however. It was flowery and extravagant but paid high tribute to Lafayette. It contrasted, in particular, Lafayette as "the volunteer of Freedom—the patriot—the philanthropist—the loved of the good and the free," with "Napoleon—the vanquished warrior, ignobly flying from the field of Waterloo: the wild beast, raviging all Europe in his wrath, hunted down by the banded and affrighted nations, and caged far away upon an ocean-girded rock." Other sentiments Pren-

[70] In addition to the text of the speech in *ibid.*, 147–56, see extracts or the speech in full, in Edwin A. Alderman *et al.* (eds.), *Library of Southern Literature* (New Orleans, 1907), X, 4215–18; Thomas B. Reed, *Modern Eloquence* (Philadelphia, 1900), IX, 971–79; William J. Bryan, *The World's Famous Orations* (New York, 1906), VIII, 218–21.

[71] *Memoir of S. S. Prentiss*, I, 147. George Prentiss states that on one occasion when Lafayette visited America, and was in Portland, Seargent met and shook hands with him.

tiss couched in such sentences as "Death, who knocks with equal hand at the door of the cottage and the palace gate, has been busy at his appointed work." "The friend and companion of Washington is no more! He who taught the eagle of our country, while yet unfledged, to plume his young wing, and mate his talons with the lion's strength, has taken his flight far beyond the stars, beneath whose influence he fought so well." "When, hereafter, a gallant people are fighting for freedom against the oppressor, and their cause begins to wane before the mercenary bands of tyranny— then will the name of Lafayette become a watchword, that will strike with terror on the tyrant's ear, and nerve with redoubled vigor the freeman's arm." "He has departed from among us; but he has become again the companion of Washington. He has but left the friends of his old age, to associate with the friends of his youth. Peace be to his ashes! Calm and quiet may they rest upon some vine-clad hill of his own beloved land! And it shall be called the Mount Vernon of France. And let no cunning sculpture, no monumental marble, deface, with its mock dignity, the patriot's grave: but rather let the unpruned vine, the wild flower, and the free song of the uncaged bird—all that speaks of freedom and peace, be gathered in. Lafayette needs no mausoleum. His fame is mingled with a Nation's History. His epitaph is engraved upon the hearts of men."

The speech may have been a "hasty effusion, written at a single sitting," but it is not the handiwork of an ignorant or unlettered man. It may have been extravagant, too much a series of "purple patches," but in those times extravagance was allowable in youth. Prentiss was but twenty-seven years of age, a consideration which should not be overlooked. The elements of sublimity in the address, the manifestations of "words fitly spoken," are evidences of the genius of the Prentiss who was destined to make grander speeches in days to come.

It followed, inevitably, that those who detected the potentialities of young Prentiss put pressure on him to enter the political arena. He mentioned this as early as 1834 in one of his letters to his family in Maine. "I know Anna will laugh at me very heartily," he said, "when I tell her I have been strongly solicited by some of the most influential men in the State, to become a candidate for Congress, and, further, that I believe, if I please, I could be elected. But I have refused without hesitation." [72]

But Prentiss could not refuse the urgency of the anti-Jackson forces in Mississippi, and so assumed political responsibilities. In the autumn of 1835, following his visit to Maine, he consented to become a candidate from Warren County for the state legislature. Successful on election day, he wrote to Anna Prentiss: "I told you in my last letter, that I had the great honor of being elected a member of the Legislature from the notorious town of Vicksburg. In about three weeks the Legislature commences its session, and I shall spend the winter at the seat of Government—making laws instead of expounding them." [73]

From this time forward Prentiss was obliged to divide his time between his professional practice and the cause of the newly organized Whig party. While politics never gained ascendancy over his legal pursuits, he entered upon the political scene in 1835 with considerable abandon. In December, he wrote to his brother George, "We have (the Whigs) gained a great triumph already in the election of a Whig Governor, and a Whig majority in both branches of the Legislature. We hope to finish our victory by the reelection of [George] Poindexter. At any rate, Van Burenism, which heretofore has been all-powerful, is now dead in this State." [74]

[72] Prentiss to his mother and sisters, Vicksburg, August 23, 1834, *ibid.*, 142.
[73] *Id.* to Anna Prentiss, Vicksburg, December 10, 1835, *ibid.*, 163.
[74] *Id.* to George Prentiss, Vicksburg, December 28, 1835, *ibid.*, 164.

Chapter IV

MISSISSIPPI STATE LEGISLATURE

ON record as opposed to Andrew Jackson and the Democratic party, and with his Whig tenets in the process of crystallization, Prentiss went to Jackson in January, 1836, to begin his brief career in the state legislature. Dividing his time between duties in the assembly and court appearances in behalf of clients whose cases he had on appeal at Jackson, he proved himself an able representative of his constituents.

Mississippi was enjoying flush and prosperous times in 1836. The panic conditions subsequent to 1837 were yet to be felt. Reflecting the well-being of the state, Acting Governor John A. Quitman told the two houses assembled to hear his message that the state's revenue was "rapidly increasing beyond the amount required for the necessary expenses of the Government," and urged tax reduction if future surpluses seemed inevitable.[1] Influenced by the seemingly sound financial structure of the state and the nation, Prentiss gave his support to the movement for extended internal improvements, which, overdone, were to be in a measure the cause of less happy and reassuring days in Mississippi.

Soon after Quitman's optimistic message, Charles Lynch was inaugurated governor. Supported by a coalition of Whigs and State-Rights men, he had defeated Hiram G. Runnels, candidate of the Jacksonian Democrats. A fairer test of party strength was recorded in the senatorial election,

[1] Mississippi *House Journal*, 1836, pp. 24–25; quoted also in Vicksburg *Daily Register*, January 14, 1836.

probably the most heated issue of the 1836 session. Three candidates were placed before a joint session of the two houses on January 9: Robert J. Walker, in whose office Prentiss had read law, George Poindexter, and Franklin E. Plummer. Walker was the Jacksonian candidate. Poindexter, long in the service of the state, had broken with Jackson over the Bank question. Plummer was a native New Englander from Massachusetts. As a young man, he had worked his way to New Orleans on a boat and had settled in Copiah County, Mississippi.[2] He represented the small farmers of the eastern part of the state, the piney-woods area, and was particularly antagonistic to the planter class along the Mississippi River. Whigs, rich or poor, were indebted to him for his determined effort to elect Lynch governor.[3] Five ballots were necessary before Walker obtained a majority vote. Prentiss supported Poindexter;[4] despite his indebtedness to Walker for opportunity to read law in his office, Prentiss could not endorse a Jacksonian Democrat.

Recognition of Prentiss, and of his legal attainments as well, came promptly in the initial organization of the house, when he was made chairman of the important Judiciary Committee.[5] Within a few days, January 7, he made his first report from the committee, recommending certain changes in the charter of the Commercial and Rail Road Bank of Vicksburg.[6] On February 1 he made two reports on a subject which must have been of considerable interest to him as a lawyer who had appeared before numerous courts and knew the number and kinds of cases on their dockets. The first pertained to a House resolution directing the committee to study the redistribution of the state into judicial circuits so that all counties would be included.

[2] Claiborne, *Mississippi, as a Province, Territory and State*, I, 423.

[3] Ranck, *Albert Gallatin Brown*, 7–8.

[4] Mississippi *House Journal*, 1836, pp. 77–81; Shields, *Seargent Smith Prentiss*, 91.

[5] Mississippi *House Journal*, 1836, p. 11.

[6] *Ibid.*, 56.

Prentiss reported a bill which amended the law passed for that purpose in 1833.[7]

The second report was an elaborate and eloquent reply to a resolution directing the committee to examine the need for establishing "a criminal court of inferior jurisdiction" for Adams, Claiborne, Jefferson, Warren, and Wilkinson counties. Prentiss reported favorably, and cited advantages both to the counties and the state as a whole. The counties along the river had "become the great thoroughfare of vice and crime, as well as of wealth and enterprise." Consequently, he declared, "Villains of every description, outlaws from other states, refugees from justice, thieves, robbers and bandetti of all sorts are continually floating upon its current, and collect in the towns and villages upon its banks like drifting wood in its eddies." Because these western counties were the scenes of what Prentiss held to be no less than two thirds of all the crimes in the state, he advanced a second reason for the court. The preponderance of criminal cases in the county courts caused delay and inadequate handling of important civil cases. The establishment of a special criminal court for the area would not only eradicate this evil, Prentiss contended; it would also "be a greater terror to evil-doers" and it would "deter many . . . from coming within its reach." The state-wide benefits of the court he emphasized by saying it would act "as a sort of a frontier guard, a barrier against the inroad of vice, a levee against the overflow of crime."[8] The report submitted by Prentiss was cogent and persuasive, characterized by clearness and urgent necessity. Both houses gave approval and, according to Shields, "The court existed for a brief while, but was abolished after having survived long enough to answer the objects of its distinct creation."[9]

An even more extended report from Prentiss as chairman

[7] *Ibid.*, 192.

[8] *Ibid.*, 192–93. The report is given also in Shields, *Seargent Smith Prentiss*, 84–85.

[9] Shields, *Seargent Smith Prentiss*, 85.

of the Judiciary Committee was presented in the 1836 session. Despite the fact that the recommendations were tabled, the report is interesting from the standpoint that a northern man, always a strong advocate of Unionism, should have asserted the theory of state rights as strongly as did Prentiss. It concerned "the right of the State to the *sixteenth sections,* and the five per cent of the sale of the lands embraced in the treaties made by the United States with the Chickasaw Indians." Prentiss stated that the committee had "approached the subject submitted to their consideration with no ordinary degree of anxiety and solicitude. It involves questions of the highest magnitude, such as seldom occur, and which require to be treated with much delicacy. Whether the United States, in their treaty with the Chickasaw Indians, have disregarded the rights of this State, and violated their compact both with this State and Georgia, is indeed a grave question. Equally so is that which will arise in relation to the *remedy,* should we arrive at the conclusion that our rights have been sacrificed."

By way of historical introduction, Prentiss pointed out that Georgia had ceded her western lands to the United States in 1802. Two conditions accompanied this cession: the land was to be the common property of the United States, but it should be retroceded to Georgia if after a year the government assigned "any part of said lands on account of any claim laid thereto, other than those recognized in said articles." On March 3, 1803, Congress set aside every sixteenth section "for the support of schools." Two provisions of the act which admitted Mississippi to statehood were also pertinent, Prentiss observed. Section four obligated the Mississippi convention "to relinquish all right or title to the waste or unappropriated lands in said territory," which should remain at the disposal of the federal government and continue tax exempt for a period of five years following their sale. Section five provided that canals and roads should be constructed from the net proceeds derived from the sale of lands by Congress after December 1, 1817. Prentiss then deduced that these conditions were equally binding upon the United States and Mississippi.

Having disposed of the historical background, Prentiss stated the focal issue: "Upon this point, to wit, that the right of soil in the ceded territory has ever since the cession existed in the United States, and not in the Indian tribes inhabiting the same, depends the question of our legal claim to the sixteenth section in the Chickasaw country." Citing Fletcher *v.* Peck and Johnson *v.* McIntosh, he contended that "wandering tribes of savages are not considered as having any fee or seisin in the lands over which they roam."

But the United States, in making a treaty with the Chickasaw Indians on May 24, 1834, had disposed of some six million acres of choice land "without a single reference to *our claims* upon the school sections." Furthermore, the treaty granted considerable land to the Indians in fee simple and reserved the proceeds from the sale of the remaining portion as a trust fund for their benefit, thus ignoring the compact right of the state to her 5 per cent.

The remedy proposed was a bold one. Specifically Prentiss recommended two things: First, "that *we assert at once our claim by authorizing and directing the trustees of school lands in each township of the Chickasaw territory* to take *immediate possession* of such sixteenth sections as may be vacant, and to *institute suit* forthwith before the proper tribunals for such as may be held adversely to such trustees." The second recommendation, a more difficult one, he thought, had to do with "asserting our claim to the five per cent." The result of the committee deliberations was "that we ought to adopt the course recommended by the Governor, to wit, *taxation* of the Chickasaw land." This he held to be the *"dignified and honorable course."* He pointed out that but two alternatives were open to the state: "one is to take a just, legal, and proper remedy, which is *within our hands;* the other is to *petition for relief* the very power that violated the right." He was in favor of taxation, and opposed to petitioning, because, as he said, "Your Committee cannot recommend *to a free and sovereign State the latter course.* Rights are to be *demanded and enforced,* not *petitioned* for. Besides this, your Committee are informed, application in relation to this matter has already been made in vain to the Federal government." Taxation was his proposed solution. He justified it on the grounds "of international law, as well as on laws of private policy and expediency," which provide "that where there are mutual stipulations and one party is guilty of a violation of a contract, the proper remedy for the other party is a refusal to perform the stipulations on his part." Since the United States had violated her obligations to Mississippi and had shown a willingness to "part with six million acres of the land embraced in the stipulation," Prentiss stated, "surely it is not improper for this State to abandon the contract to the same extent." His final bit of reasoning was that "If the contract is abandoned, then the original right of taxation comes in, not as a *new remedy, but simply as placing the parties in* status quo." [10]

It would be interesting to know just how much Prentiss contributed to the content of the report he penned. His vigorous intellect and commanding leadership could hardly have allowed him to be relegated to the passive role of moderator and amanuensis. If we may assume that he endorsed what he did not contribute, it is a valid conclusion that his constitutional thinking was predicated upon certain strong state-rights concepts. Southern influences were operating upon him. But with Andrew Jackson in the presidential chair such contentions would have carried no more weight than certain assertions in South Carolina a few years before.

Of the internal improvements launched in this period of

[10] Mississippi *House Journal,* 1836, pp. 304–11; Shields, *Seargent Smith Prentiss,* 85–91.

high prosperity in Mississippi, not the least was railroad building. Prentiss cast his vote for one railway project shortly before the legislature adjourned in February. Perceiving the value of a railroad which would connect New Orleans and Nashville, he voted to permit the New Orleans and Nashville Railroad Company to extend a road through Mississippi.[11] In so voting, he was aiding quite directly an area of Mississippi which he did not represent, thus proving his freedom from local selfishness. According to Shields, Prentiss favored locating the railroad east of the Pearl River, inasmuch as Warren County, which he represented, and other western counties in the state were "already provided with transportation by the great river on her border, and that the East was entitled to the *iron river,* which would open her commerce and her vast timber wealth to the markets of the world." [12] The same point of view and explanation is given by George Prentiss who wrote that Seargent "was in favor of locating the New Orleans and Nashville Railroad east of Pearl River, believing it would promote a rapid development of the agricultural and commercial resources of that portion of the State." [13]

Mention has already been made that Prentiss accepted the institution of slavery and adjusted himself to it when he came to Mississippi. Some of his adjustments and justifications have been stated. It is illuminating to note that in his very first public office in the state he found himself involved in legislative discussions concerning the slavery problem. He began his public career in the very decade when Mississippi and other southern states were making the transition from apology for slavery accompanied by expressions of hope for the liberation of their slaves and by the founding of colonization societies, to the point of uttering defenses of slavery, Biblical, social, and economic. That many slaveholding southerners were potential abolitionists

---

11 Shields, *Seargent Smith Prentiss,* 226–27.   12 *Ibid.,* 83.
13 *Memoir of S. S. Prentiss,* I, 167.

in the early years of the nineteenth century cannot be doubted; that in time they felt obliged to defend the institution on account of the activities of northern abolitionists is equally true. Besides, the enormous expansion of cotton culture and the accompanying demand for slave labor caused the southerner to find additional grounds for justifying or rationalizing slavery.[14]

Prentiss apparently made the transition with other Mississippians. By 1836, nine years after coming to Mississippi, he was defending the institution. Certainly he was on record, even in his letters to his family in Maine, as saying that the chief source of friction on the subject was to be laid at the door of the "meddling" abolitionists. The following letter, written in 1835, proves this: "The excitement growing out of the insurrection of the slaves has subsided, and not the slightest danger is now anticipated. During the prevalence of the alarm, there were, throughout the State, six white men and about fifteen negroes hanged. I think the severe measures which were pursued, will prevent a recurrence of similar events—at least for a long period of time. It ought certainly to serve as a warning to the abolitionists, not only of their own danger but the great injury they are doing the slaves themselves, by meddling with them." [15] Yet it should be stated that Prentiss never became a continuous or vigorous defender of slavery. His speeches, taken over the years of his active career, are relatively free from remarks on the subject. Rather, his references to slavery, and his active defense of it, seem sporadic, even opportunistic, as in the 1836 session of the legislature. He introduced the resolution: "That the people of the state of Mississippi look upon the institution of domestic slavery, as it exists among them, not as a curse, but a blessing, as the legitimate condition of

14 For an enlightening treatment of this point of view, see Charles S. Sydnor, *Slavery in Mississippi* (New York, 1933), particularly 239–53.

15 Prentiss to his mother and sisters, Vicksburg, September 19, 1835, in *Memoir of S. S. Prentiss*, I, 162. For a treatment of the insurrection, see Foote, *Casket of Reminiscences*, 250–63.

the African race, as authorized both by the laws of God and the dictates of reason and philanthropy; and that they hope to transmit this institution to their posterity, as the best part of their inheritance. . . . We hold discussion upon this subject as equally impertinent with discussion upon our relations, wives and children, and we will allow no present change, or hope of future alterations in this matter." [16] This resolution produced some action, for a committee on domestic slavery was appointed, with George H. Gordon as chairman. The committee reported, embodying the same resolution as presented by Prentiss.[17] Toward the latter part of February, shortly before the legislature adjourned, Prentiss asked for the committee report and tried to make it a "special order" of the day.[18] The fact that the whole matter was tabled a day or so later prevented any aggressive discussion or action.

As a final contribution to the 1836 session, Prentiss served on a joint committee to reconcile House and Senate on a disagreement.[19] He returned home by the last of February and wrote to George Prentiss: "The Legislature adjourned on Saturday last, after a noisey and laborious session; and, I assure you, I took a full share in the labor and the noise." His opinion of the work of legislation, and his lack of enthusiasm for such endeavors, may be gathered from his statement: "Of all the occupations I have ever tried, I am decidedly of opinion, that making laws is the most obnoxious to comfort and happiness. I am sick of it; and if the people would permit it, would resign forthwith: but as my constituents seem perfectly satisfied with my services, I suppose I shall have to hold on another year—the term for which I was elected." [20]

[16] Woodville Republican, April 21, 1838, quoted in Sydnor, Slavery in Mississippi, 242.

[17] Mississippi House Journal, 1836, pp. 193–97.

[18] Ibid., 441.   [19] Ibid., 418.

[20] Prentiss to George Prentiss, Vicksburg, February 29, 1836, in Memoir of S. S. Prentiss, I, 169–70.

Prentiss was probably sincere in his expressions of detestation of lawmaking. His interests were never in officeholding. From the first to the last in his relatively short
career as a public servant he reiterated these same sentiments. His enthusiasms were elsewhere; officeholding was
with him a side activity. His great interest was in the courtroom. Prentiss could hardly be accused of neglect of duty
while he was a legislator in 1836, yet he had in Jackson a
number of cases on appeal which he conveniently handled
at the same time. One was that of the Vicksburg Commons,
a story in itself.

Prentiss was naturally free to devote more time to his law
practice upon the adjournment of the legislature. He made
a trip to New Orleans in the spring, saw his brother Samuel
there, and announced that he would have all the business he
could attend to. This was doubtless true, in view of the
prestige he was building, together with the fact that his
partner, Guion, was retiring within the year. Guion's retire-
ment and Prentiss' interest in the welfare of his favorite
brother, George, led him to express the hope that George
would come to Mississippi and become his associate in
law.[21] In the late summer Prentiss made a trip to Kentucky;
whether for a vacation, business, or political reasons is not
known. While there he visited Louisville, Harrodsburg
Springs, Lexington, and other parts of the state. Among his
first pleasures on the expedition was a visit with Henry Clay.
He commented on the trip: "While at Lexington, I called
on Mr. Clay, at his residence about a mile from town. . . .
Mr. Clay has a tasteful, but by no means splendid residence
—surrounded, however, by the most highly cultivated
grounds in all Kentucky." [22]

The impression is easily gained that Prentiss was a
prosperous and, for the most part, a happy man in 1836.
Adding joy to his life during the winter of 1836–1837 was a

21 *Id.* to Abby Prentiss, Vicksburg, April 16, 1839, *ibid.*, 172–73.
22 *Id.* to *id.*, Vicksburg, September 3, 1836, *ibid.*, 173.

visit from George, who sojourned with him for months. Prentiss also had expanding business interests and expectations. Without knowing it, he was laying the foundation for less happy and reassuring days. Having won the first suit in the Vicksburg Commons, he ventured, actually plunged. His explanation he gave to William Prentiss. "You ask me about my *speculation,* by which I am to make a fortune." Prentiss assured him it was not in Texas lands, for he had no sympathy with something he thought uncertain, and added: "My speculation consists in having purchased an interest in a portion of land in the town of Vicksburg, which is claimed by the town as Commons, or public property. I purchased of the original proprietors of the town, and the matter is now pending in a suit which will be decided by the Supreme Court of the State, this winter. If I succeed, it will make me wealthy, which I care little about on my own account, but much on account of others." [23] The chances of Prentiss' success were so bright that he may once again have thought of leaving Mississippi as soon as he could gain his financial stakes. At least George Prentiss, visiting him, wrote to the family in Maine of Seargent's plans. "His great suit comes on in a week or two; and should he gain it he will at once retire from practice and sooner or later, leave this country. . . . His intention is to spend a number of years in travel and he has promised to afford me an opportunity of going to Europe, if I choose." [24]

During the fall of 1836 Prentiss watched with some interest the presidential election and expressed the belief that Mississippi would support Hugh White. Now a good Whig, acquainted personally with Henry Clay, Prentiss' political affiliations were to be more clearly known to areas outside Mississippi. In the meantime, he had his second session of the legislature before him. His role in it could not

[23] *Id.* to William Prentiss, Vicksburg, November 16, 1836, *ibid.,* 175–76.
[24] George Prentiss to Abby Prentiss, Vicksburg, January 1, 1837, in Prentiss, *Bright Side of Life,* I, 34.

but extend his name. In the legislature one issue, at least for Prentiss, subordinated all else.

It was early in the 1836 session that action was begun which laid the foundation for Prentiss' most celebrated role in the legislature of 1837. On January 8, Samuel Gholson, an ardent Democrat whose name was to be associated with that of Prentiss in future political events in Mississippi, moved concurrence in a Senate resolution "proposing the appointment of a joint committee upon the subject of organizing into counties the territory in the State acquired from the Chickasaw Indians," [25] an area extending from the Mississippi River in a southeasterly direction to the Tombigbee River. The motion passed, and the committee organized the Chickasaw area into eleven counties to be known as Tunica, Chickasaw, Pontotoc, Bolivar, Marshall, Panola, Lafayette, Tishomingo, De Soto, Tippah, Coahoma, and Itawamba. In addition, the county of Newton, though not a part of the Chickasaw area, was created from parts of Scott and Lauderdale. As a result of the establishment of the new counties, a constitutional problem over their representation in the 1837 session of the legislature created a battle which brought Prentiss to the front.

When the legislature convened the first Monday in January, 1837, Adam Bingaman, of Adams County, moved that the members elected from the new counties present their credentials and take the oath of office.[26] Stormy scenes and exhibitions of parliamentary strategy followed. The fact that the motion to seat the representatives of the new counties came from Bingaman is of considerable significance. He was really a Whig, and in a very real sense the acknowledged leader of the party. It was paradoxical then, that he should have made the motion. Actually, the Democrats stood to gain by the favorable action of the House. The representatives coming from the new counties carved out of

---

[25] Mississippi *House Journal*, 1836, p. 63.
[26] *Ibid.*, 1837, p. 4; Shields, *Seargent Smith Prentiss*, 97.

the Chickasaw area owed their status to the Jacksonian policy of opening the Indian lands to the white man.

The motivation of Bingaman is not altogether clear. He has been alluded to as "a man of rare qualifications for a popular leader—highly gifted by nature in mind and personal appearance, which was most splendid and commanding, with a polished education and fascinating manners, and by nature an orator. Added to these advantages, he was a native of the State, the representative of great wealth, and with extensive family influence." [27] Probably the best explanation for Bingaman's action is that given by John F. H. Claiborne, who knew him intimately. Claiborne once wrote of him: "He has always occupied a high position in the public eye, but with less conscientiousness he would have long since obtained the very highest. Personally he has always been a favorite with the dominant party, and there have been occasions when a very narrow line of demarcation separated them, and he had only to cross it to be placed in power. The present [Chickasaw controversy] was one of them. His convictions induced him to advocate the admission of the new members, and thus to co-operate with the Democratic party in a matter essential to their political ascendency; but he went no farther, although every temptation and every argument was presented to his ambition and his judgment." [28]

Conscience and conviction then, according to Claiborne, explain why Bingaman moved to bring in the new representatives to the detriment of the Whigs and the balance of power. Prentiss may not have been so free from political necessity in opposing representatives who would disrupt Whig prestige, but he probably had as strong personal reasons for feeling that the new representatives had no constitutional right to seats. In any event, two Whigs, Binga-

[27] William H. Sparks, *The Memories of Fifty Years* (Philadelphia, 1870), 351–52.

[28] J. F. H. Claiborne, *Life and Times of Gen. Sam. Dale, The Mississippi Partisan* (New York, 1860), 222–23.

man and Prentiss, found themselves opposing each other. As a result, Prentiss became to the Whigs the "Tecumseh of the Legislature." [29] With him were such men as John T. McMurran and Preston W. Farrar. Against him were some strong Democrats such as Albert G. Brown, Samuel J. Gholson, Buckner Harris, George Gordon, and Morgan McAfee.[30]

In the 1836 session Prentiss registered no opposition to the steps taken to organize the new counties. Likewise, he was not opposed to their eventual representation. But his contention was that the counties had no constitutional right to have representatives seated in the 1837 session. To allow such representation he held to be a gross violation of the constitution. As the leader of the opposition against the seating of the representatives, Prentiss moved to allow them the same privileges extended to him a year later in another situation. They "were unanimously invited to take seats within the bar of the House, during the discussion of the question, whether they be entitled to seats as members." [31] The stage was set for a fight which continued for days.

Even granting that Prentiss and his colleagues were influenced by political considerations, still they had a strong constitutional basis for their stand. The organic act upon which Prentiss took his stand provided that an enumeration should be made of the free white population every four or six years until 1845, and the representation apportioned to the counties accordingly; that elections should be held on the first Monday of November of 1833, and the day following, and triennially thereafter; that members should be elected for two years; that in case of vacancies the governor "or persons exercising his powers, *shall issue writs* of election"; and that vacancies not provided for in the constitution should be filled.[32]

29 *Ibid.*, 218.   30 *Ibid.*, 224.   31 Mississippi *House Journal*, 1837, p. 5.
32 See Francis N. Thorpe (comp.), *The Federal and State Constitutions . . . and Other Organic Laws . . . of the United States . . .* (Washington, 1909), II, 2052–58.

Proceeding upon what he considered ironclad constitutional premises, Prentiss, then but twenty-eight years of age, made his first noteworthy deliberative speech. He at once rebuked Bingaman for taking the attitude "that the resolution is a matter of course, and ought to pass *sub silentio.*" Prentiss announced: "I differ from the gentleman. He cannot so easily introduce this Trojan horse within these walls; I, for one, will hurl a spear against its hollow sides. . . . The gentleman from Adams has lighted the match, and if this House do not extinguish it—if the heel of the majority be not placed upon it—there will be left by its explosion no vestige of the constitution or law." In the beginning, too, Prentiss made clear that he recognized certain other considerations involved in the motion. "I know I labor under many difficulties in opposing it. Popular opinion is in favor of it. The gentleman has the wind full in his sails, while I must row against an adverse current." He sought personal justification of his stand, however. "I know it will be said that I am an enemy of the new counties; that I am hostile to the rights of the people; that I am opposed to democratic principles, and other similar aspersions by which demagogues answer arguments." In reply, he stated: "Sir, I *throw down in advance my denial to such charges*. No man in this State feels a livelier interest in the prosperity of the new counties." Without making any personal mention of the fact that he voted for a railroad in the previous session which would aid portions of the Chickasaw area, Prentiss went on. "No man has watched with greater pleasure their rapid increase in wealth, population, and power, and did not my oath to support the constitution stand in my way, no man would welcome their delegation with a warmer greeting." From this point of departure in which Prentiss attempted to clear the way for his argument, he laid down two issues: "First, that under the constitution the counties embraced in the resolution have not a right as counties to representation in this House at *this session*. Secondly, That even if they have a representative, the persons claiming seats have not been constitutionally elected."

Having learned much of the art of argument in court appeals which he had made, and the necessity of adhering to the issues upon which an advocate builds his case, Prentiss, in a closely knit speech, argued definitely and at length. In defense of his first contention—that the new counties were not entitled to representation in the 1837 session—he based his reasoning on the fact that, according to the constitution, enumeration had been made, and could not be altered until the constitution permitted a further one. His great conclusion, after examining the constitution to show that representation was based upon certain prescribed population enumerations already made, was that the present House represented Mississippi's population, To illustrate, he said: "I see my friend from Washington County in his seat. Whom did he represent at the commencement of this session?" "Every one knows that he represented the whole of the free white inhabitants of that section of the country which now composes the counties of Washington, Bolivar, and Coahoma. Does he represent them still? No one will doubt his capacity to do so. I do not doubt his right. For what period of time was this power delegated to him? The constitution says for two years. Has that time elapsed? It has not!" The basic evil of the motion Prentiss then expressed: "Yet I see in this resolution a proposition to admit another member on this floor to represent the free white inhabitants of Bolivar County." This was the crux of the situation. Prentiss' attitude was: "Now I hold that two men cannot at the same time constitutionally occupy the same office. Either my friend from Washington is no longer the representative of the free white inhabitants living in the county of Bolivar, who sent him here, or the gentleman claiming to represent the same people has no right to represent them." For Prentiss there was no question that his unnamed friend from Washington County was the duly elected representative. His position was that "The electors living in the county of Bolivar have once voted for a representative in this session of the Legislature. He is here, and has not resigned any portion of the power delegated to him. I know of no constitutional right which the people of the county of Bolivar have to resume the power which they have delegated before lapse of two years for which they have delegated it."

Hence Prentiss maintained that there could be no new representatives admitted in 1837 because the full representation had been constitutionally determined by the 1836 elections. The fact that the legislature had adjourned between 1836 and 1837 made no difference. On this point he said: "This adjournment was nothing more than an adjournment from day to day. We met here on the first Monday of January, 1837, the same body precisely in our constitutional organization as we were on the 1st of January, 1836. We have, with those who have been elected to fill vacancies, sixty-four members. Our body is already full, and contains the whole representative power of the government which belongs to a House of Representatives." Several rhetorical questions followed immediately, stressing the implications of his contentions. "How, then, can we admit ten additional persons as members without parting with a portion of the power belonging to us? Have we a right to part with it? Can we give up to others a portion of our delegated power? If so, can we not give up the whole? Can a legislative department of the government act by proxy?"

Prentiss then moved to his second issue, "That the persons claiming seats have not been *constitutionally elected.* No writs of election were issued by the governor." Instead, "These gentlemen, however, claim to be elected by virtue of writs issued by boards of the county police of their respective counties." If Governor Lynch felt he had the power to issue writs during the interim between the 1836 and 1837 sessions, he did not exercise it. Evidently he

evaded the problem. Certainly evasion is suggested by one
Mississippi newspaper in its statement: "In relation to the
admission of the new members into the House he refrains
from giving an opinion upon the question whether 'if their
right of admisssion was acquiesced in by both branches' it
would destroy the constitutional organization of the legislature." Lynch seemed no more positive than that "He
justifies himself for withholding the exercise of his power
to issue writs of election, advises the passage of a bill to take
a census, an adjournment to give time for this purpose, and
concludes by tendering his co-operation, &c." [33] From this
it may be inferred, possibly, that as a Whig, Lynch would
not have favored seating the representatives in the 1837 session.

The failure of Lynch to issue writs and the consequent
doing of it by county police boards, served as a basis for
Prentiss' stand that the representatives were not constitutionally elected. He called attention to the fact that there
were two kinds of elections, one the "General biennial
election, the other to fill vacancies." Since the representatives laid no claim to be elected in the general election, but
to fill vacancies, Prentiss concentrated on this phase of the
constitutional question. In respect to the point advanced by
those favoring the seating of the representatives because
"the moment a county is created the office of representative
is created, and that *whenever an office is without an incumbent a vacancy happens*," Prentiss used the method of
Reductio ad absurdum, combining it with analogy. "For
the sake of argument admit it," he said, "and let us see if
they be constitutionally elected to fill vacancies." He quoted
the constitution, "Whenever vacancies happen in either
house, the governor, or the person exercising the powers of
governor, shall issue writs of election to fill such vacancies."

[33] Vicksburg *Daily Register*, February 1, 1837. It was the opinion of
Shields that Governor Lynch was appealed to by the new counties to issue
writs of election, but refused on the ground that it would be unconstitu-
tional in the case of these counties. Shields, *Seargent Smith Prentiss*, 97.

Since the governor issued no writs, and the mode of electing by police boards was not constitutional, Prentiss illustrated by an analogy in law. A debt, he contended, cannot be collected in court by the creditor who would "loudly demand a judgment." Instead, prescribed rules of law, the obtaining of a judgment, and the securing of a writ from the court authorizing the sheriff to levy on a man's goods who will not pay, are necessary obligations on the one who endeavors to collect. Prescribed modes and procedures in elections, as provided by the constitution, Prentiss held to be equally binding in this issue before the legislature.

Prentiss refuted another aspect of the problem with figurative analogies. To those who knew the constitution was being violated, but who held that "this is but a small irregularity, a slight violation," Prentiss replied: "Sir, a single brick may be stolen from a building without much apparent injury to the edifice, but let the example of the robber be followed by others, and presently the whole fabric will tumble in ruins. . . . A leak no larger than a spear-head will sink the most gallant ship that ever swam the ocean. A crevasse may be made even by a reptile which will let in the waters of the Mississippi till whole counties are inundated." Small violations Prentiss held to be the most dangerous. "When men's liberties are attacked by open force there is but little to fear. They see the danger and meet it boldly. But when, under pretence of a popular measure, under the guise of friendship for the people, a blow is struck at the constitution of the country, then is the time for alarm."

The author of the resolution to seat the representatives came in for an attack as Prentiss closed his remarks. Bingaman had advanced as justification for the motion that "inasmuch as a representative is elected in a county, he is a county officer, and, of course, that a vacancy in the office can be filled by order of the board of county police." He seemingly was not very positive that his position was tenable. Prentiss accused him of sitting "upon the point like a bird upon a rot-

ten twig, ready to fly the moment it gives way beneath him."
Prentiss proceeded to examine the argument and pushed his
refutation to shift all burden of rebuttal to Bingaman. He
maintained that a county officer, such as a sheriff, a judge of
a probate court, and a clerk of a circuit or orphan's court,
was one whose duties were confined to the county. "On the
other hand," Prentiss asserted, "I understand a State officer
to be one whose jurisdiction extends over the State, and the
exercise of the duties of which will operate equally upon all
the citizens of the State. Thus, the governor, the judges of
the High Court of Errors and Appeals and other Circuit
Courts, are all State Officers, because their action is general,
and not confined to any particular county or portion of the
State. . . . The power of a representative is to *pass laws,*
which laws extend all over the State, and affect the people
of all other counties as much as the people of the county in
which he is elected."

With Bingaman answered, Prentiss came to a close. He
emphasized the danger of the measure which "will infuse
into the legislation of the State a poison which no medicine
can cure. *It will part the laws from the constitution and set
them adrift like the broken spars and riggings of a dismasted
vessel, which beat against and destroy the very keel they were
intended to support."* [34]

After the legislature had spent five days on the question
of seating the representatives, the vote was taken. By a narrow majority of 31 to 29, the counties were given representation.[35] But the representatives were, in a sense, seated only
temporarily. The matter was referred to the committee on

[34] For accounts of the speech, see Shields, *Seargent Smith Prentiss,* 98–117;
Memoir of S. S. Prentiss, I, 187–215; Vicksburg *Sentinel and Expositor,*
February 7, 1837. No information is given in Shields or by George L. Prentiss as to how the versions of the speech were obtained. They differ slightly,
that presented in *A Memoir of S. S. Prentiss* being a bit more extensive.
Nothing more than the substance of the speech was supplied in the *Sentinel and Expositor.* At best, the versions are probably only approximations
of what Prentiss actually said, yet reasonably reliable.

[35] Mississippi *House Journal,* 1837, p. 6.

elections for further investigation. Six days later, January 11, John W. King, chairman of the committee, presented a majority report of the committee in favor of seating the representatives, and then moved that it be tabled in order that the minority report might be heard as well.[36]

The minority report is interesting from several standpoints. For one thing, King, chairman of the committee, supported it. The report, to a strong degree, reiterated the same sentiments as those expressed by Prentiss in his long speech. It mentioned the same constitutional provisions that Prentiss had emphasized and defended the same two main contentions which he had affirmed. On the point of actual representation of the counties, the minority report read: "The undersigned affirm that those counties are now, and were, on the first day of January, 1836, constitutionally represented in the present Legislature, to as full an extent as any other portion of the State." On the second issue that Prentiss argued, namely, that the county police boards had no authority to issue writs, the minority reported: "The undersigned believe that there is no warrant to be found in the constitution for the course pursued by the Board of county Police. The 20th section of the third article of the constitution gives to the courts of county Police authority to order all county elections to fill vacancies that may occur in the offices of their respective counties. . . . To make this provision apply to members of the Legislature, would be to make them mere county officers." [37]

Exciting and unexpected events happened after the minority report and resolutions were read. In an effort to prevent possible influences of the minority report, Bingaman moved to table it. As the clerk called the roll to ascertain the yeas and nays on this motion and came to the name of Benjamin Bugg of Chickasaw County, the first name on the roll from the new counties, Prentiss created a sensation. He employed the only means left open to him to prevent a side-

36 *Ibid.*, 84.   37 *Ibid.*, 85–89.

tracking of the minority resolutions. In so doing, he showed considerable knowledge of parliamentary skill and tactics. Rising to a point of order, he appealed to the Chair for a decision on the right of Bugg to vote, since he was in reality voting on his own right to a seat. The Chair ruled that Bugg might vote, and Prentiss appealed from the decision. As the clerk called the roll to determine whether the House would sustain the Chair, he came to the name of Bugg. Again Prentiss rose to a point of order, and demanded of the Chair if Bugg could vote on the appeal. The Chair decided affirmatively, and Prentiss appealed again. The clerk called the roll for another time, coming to Bugg's name. Once more Prentiss appealed to the Chair on Bugg's right to vote. At this point Bingaman moved to withdraw the original motion to lay the minority report on the table and moved to postpone the discussion until the following day. The roll was then called upon the motion to postpone, and as the name of Bugg was called Prentiss was on his feet again and objected to the right of Bugg to vote on this motion. The Speaker ruled that Bugg might vote, and Prentiss made another appeal from the decision. In an effort to stop the siege of appeals, the Chair refused to put Prentiss' last appeal before the House until Bingaman's motion to postpone was acted upon. The motion carried, but when the House gathered for its afternoon meeting, Prentiss protested the action of the Speaker, and appealed to the House for a decision. This the Speaker countered by again refusing to put Prentiss' appeal to the House.[38] Prentiss relented at this point, and on January 16, the new members were voted upon individually, and each seated by a vote of 37 to 28, Prentiss voting against each claimant.[39]

Prentiss had done all he could to prevent what he thought was a dangerous violation of the constitution of Mississippi. The *Mississippi Free Trader* stated: "Mr. Prentiss was at his

---

[38] *Ibid.*, 94–96. See also, Shields, *Seargent Smith Prentiss*, 118–19.
[39] Mississippi *House Journal*, 1837, pp. 116–20; Vicksburg *Daily Register*, February 1, 1837.

post, and left nothing undone that would embarrass the proceedings." [40] Following up other avenues of asserting his disfavor with what the House had done, Prentiss, with twenty-one other senators and representatives, expressed opinions in writing and had spread on the minutes of the *House Journal* their earnest protestations.[41] These were undoubtedly written by Prentiss. His name appears first, and the opinions are those expressed by him in his Chickasaw speech. In a more copious manner, the same group of minority legislators issued an address to the people of Mississippi, in which they outlined the extent to which they considered the constitution violated.[42] Of the protest resolutions the Vicksburg *Register* commented in referring its readers to them: "The course which Mr. Prentiss has taken is we believe a proper and high minded one. The paramount obligations to his oath to support the constitution gave him as he believed no other alternative." [43] Of even more significance was the stand of the Vicksburg *Sentinel,* an ardent Democratic paper, more often in opposition to Prentiss than in support of him: "The session of the late legislature will form an important chapter in the history of the State. . . . The speech of Mr. Prentiss on Mr. Bingaman's resolution inviting the new members to take their seats, settles the question. It is an argument so clear, logical, and conclusive, that sophistry itself cannot affect any of its position. It is a most masterly production; one that will live in the history of Mississippi, and command the admiration of posterity." The newspaper went on to say of Prentiss' speaking: "He used the Club of Hercules, and the Toledo blade with equal power, precision and effect. . . . Mississippi may well be proud of such an intellectual effort. As an argumentative

[40] *Mississippi Free Trader and Natchez Tri-Weekly Gazette,* January 21, 1837.

[41] Mississippi *House Journal,* 1837, pp. 128–29; Vicksburg *Daily Sentinel and Expositor,* January 31, 1837; *Memoir of S. S. Prentiss,* I, 215–17.

[42] Vicksburg *Daily Sentinel and Expositor,* January 31, 1837.

[43] Vicksburg *Daily Register,* February 1, 1837.

debater, it places our representative in the front rank with the intellectual giants of the present age." The *Sentinel* justified Prentiss further: "while the constitution stands as it is at present we do not see how he could consistently with his oath abandon the ground he took and admit the new members." [44]

Prentiss' services in the legislature were actually over. He was, unquestionably, an able member of the House. Even so, he did not devote all his time to legislative matters. During the 1837 session, as in 1836, he appeared in court, particularly in connection with the Vicksburg Commons suit. This meant that he was in and out of the legislative chamber. Shields tells the incident, though upon what authority it is difficult to know, that one of the Chickasaw claimants accused Prentiss of being absent in order to prepare his speeches and chided him: " 'Prentiss, you remind me of the little Tennessee mills in dry time; *you've got to wait for a head* of water every time you grind.' 'Ah, colonel,' replied Prentiss, with a smile, 'I've always got head-water enough to grind the little grist from the Chickasaw counties at any rate.' " [45]

One piece of legislation passed while Prentiss was in the legislature must not be overlooked, the resolution to incorporate the Union Bank, thereby extending banking and credit facilities enormously. Subsequently, when Mississippi had issued bonds and created debts in excess of her willingness to pay them, and when Prentiss opposed the course of the repudiationists in the state, he was chided for having voted, when in the legislature, for the Union Bank. It is probable, however, that he did not vote for it. [46]

---

[44] Vicksburg *Daily Sentinel and Expositor,* January 31, 1837.

[45] Shields, *Seargent Smith Prentiss,* 120.

[46] Shields states: "I do not find in the recorded vote upon the Union Bank bill that Prentiss voted at all, nor can I find in the journals whether or not he opposed it, but presume, as Whigs and Democrats sang truce on the theme, that he too fell beneath the siren song of the hour." *Ibid.,* 83. The writer has, likewise, failed to find the recorded vote of Prentiss on the bank bill.

By February 10, or earlier, he was back in Vicksburg. On February 17, Prentiss wrote to Governor Lynch: "I hereby tender to you my resignation of the office of representative in the Legislature of the State of Mississippi from the county of Warren." [47] He gave no reason for resigning. Possibly his legal interests were too engrossing. By resigning he did escape the necessity of returning to Jackson for a special called session in April to meet certain dire financial problems that Lynch felt to be confronting the state.

When Prentiss resigned from the legislature, he may have considered his political career over; instead, it had just begun. Quite naturally, he returned to his legal pursuits. Also, because he had been so successful in the Vicksburg Commons case, and had made extensive purchases of land in Vicksburg, he began the improvement of his real estate. Among the buildings soon erected by him was a large hotel. He wrote his mother of his legislative activities and of his court successes. Because the court had ruled as it did, his future looked bright indeed. Otherwise he would hardly have told her: "My interest, I have no doubt is worth, and will realize *at least* one hundred thousand dollars." [48]

During the summer of 1837, while political events affecting his life were happening in Mississippi, he made his second visit to Maine.

[47] Prentiss to Governor Charles Lynch, Vicksburg, February 17, 1837, Department of History and Archives, Mississippi State Historical Library, Jackson, Series E., No. 31.

[48] Prentiss to his mother, Vicksburg, February 10, 1837, in *Memoir of S. S. Prentiss,* I, 219.

Chapter V

THE DISPUTED MISSISSIPPI ELECTION

THE short session of the Twenty-fourth Congress came to a close March 4, 1837. Its members prepared at once to witness the induction of Old Hickory's successor, Martin Van Buren, as the eighth president of the United States.

It was the fate of Van Buren to reap the whirlwind of the Jacksonian era of wildcat banking and speculation resulting from the destruction of the United States Bank and the subsequent distribution of vast sums of money to the several states. Whatever economic forces brought on the panic of 1837, it must be admitted that Jackson's bank policy had led to easy credit for canal, road, and railway building, as well as for land speculation. The limit had been reached, and the inevitable reaction had set in as the American Talleyrand took the helm of government.

The new President felt himself duty bound to carry on to completion his predecessor's policies, chief of which was the complete severance of the bank from the state. As a means to this end, Van Buren sought, during the first meeting of Congress in his administration, to establish the Sub-Treasury, where the money of the country would be deposited. This scheme was destined to suffer the severest onslaughts from the Whig press and stump. Not the least of its critics was Seargent Prentiss.

The Van Buren administration had been in power less than a month when ominous signs of hard times were in the skies. The Specie Circular issued by Jackson, July 11, 1836, was considered by many the basic cause of the financial ills besetting the nation. Conditions became acutely alarming when toward the last of April, 1837, New York banks began to fail, causing others to do the same, because they could not redeem in specie.[1]

Toward the end of his second month in office, Van Buren, besieged by demands that he call a special session of Congress, reconsidered his earlier refusals. Consequently, on May 15, he issued a proclamation convening Congress on the first Monday in September. In the interim of more than three months he had time to consider what constructive measures he might lay before Congress. Likewise, Webster, Clay, and other Whigs had time to fan the flames of political hatred toward the financial policies of Jackson and Van Buren.

When Van Buren issued the call for Congress to meet in special session, he was also making history in the states of Arkansas and Mississippi. All the other states had previously chosen their representatives for the Twenty-fifth Congress. These, then, would take their places in the September session. In Arkansas and Mississippi, the elections were not scheduled to occur until November of 1837. These two states were thus faced with the alternative of going unrepresented in the extra session or of calling special elections prior to the September meeting. Constitutionally or not, the governors of both states issued proclamations for special elections. Arkansas suffered no political upheavals as a result. Mississippi was destined to experience a unique, protracted, colorful, and unfortunate series of events. In short, the issue to be fought out was whether Mississippi, in electing representatives for the special session of Congress, was electing for the special session only, or whether she was actually choosing her representatives for the entire Twenty-fifth Congress. In the opinion of Governor Lynch of Mississippi, and, as ultimately demonstrated by a majority of

[1] Denis T. Lynch, *An Epoch and a Man, Martin Van Buren and His Times* (New York, 1929), 404–407.

Mississippians, the midsummer election was valid for the special session only. The early summer proclamation issued by Governor Lynch to the sheriffs of the respective counties of the state called for the election to be held "on the 3rd day following of July next for two Representatives to Congress to *fill said vacancy until superseded* by the *members to be elected* on the first Monday and the day following of *November next*." [2]

A political campaign was begun as a result of the Governor's proclamation. The population of Mississippi in 1837 entitled her to two representatives in Congress to be elected at large. John F. H. Claiborne and General David Dickson had been elected in 1835 for the two-year period. The death of Dickson had resulted in the election of Samuel J. Gholson to serve in his place until 1837. Thus Claiborne and Gholson, who had been in Congress, announced their candidacy for the special election, and found themselves in opposition to Prentiss and A. L. Acee, Whig candidates.

What persuasion was necessary to induce Prentiss to become a candidate, it is difficult to know. Anyway, he was evidently willing to reconsider an earlier refusal. In 1836, at the time of Dickson's death, a notice, signed "A Friend," addressed to Prentiss, had appeared in the Vicksburg *Register*. "A number of your friends both personal and political, desire to know whether or not, if elected, you would be willing to represent the State in Congress." [3] Prentiss had replied: "Though I am proud that any of my fellow citizens should think of my name in connection with so high and honorable a position, yet circumstances render it impossible for me to avail myself of their partiality. Heavy professional engagements, as well as the obligations which I have already assumed, as a member of the State Legislature, imperatively prohibit my absence from the State during any portion of

[2] Quoted in Shields, *Seargent Smith Prentiss*, 129.
[3] Vicksburg *Daily Register*, September 1, 1836.

the ensuing year." [4] But in 1837, with his duties in the legislature behind him, Prentiss signified his willingness to become a candidate.

The contest during May and June was little more than
the semblance of a campaign. Actually Prentiss made no
real canvass. The campaign was of such small significance to
him that he did not abandon his plans for a visit to Maine,
whither he went the latter part of June.[5] He seemingly had
little desire to labor in season and out, sacrificing his personal desires to go to Congress for one extra session. If he had
political aspirations, they could wait until the November
election, when, if successful, he would be assured, he
thought, of a seat for the entire Twenty-fifth Congress.
Moreover, his colleague, Acee, was but little known in the
state, particularly in the southern area.[6] Since Prentiss was
in Maine, he and Acee had little chance of receiving a vote
in excess of Claiborne and Gholson, well-known political
figures who had already been to Washington as representatives of the people. Had Prentiss remained in Mississippi
and worked for the election, it might have been his. In the
opinion of one Mississippian who wrote to the editor of the
Vicksburg *Sentinel and Expositor,* "He could do a good deal
if he was here, for he is a fine speaker, and a clever fellow,
still there are many of the Whigs who will not vote for him,
the old steady and religious ones, on account of his loose
habits." [7]

While Prentiss was delivering a Fourth of July address in
Portland, Maine, the votes in Mississippi were being
counted. Prentiss' mind, as well as presence, may have been
far from Mississippi. Nevertheless, in the oration at Portland
he was expressing Whig sentiments. He was the speaker for
what was termed "a Whig Celebration," in the "Whig Pa-

4 *Ibid.,* September 8, 1836.   5 *Memoir of S. S. Prentiss,* I, 223.
6 Vicksburg *Daily Sentinel and Expositor,* July 6, 1837.
7 Extract from a letter dated June 29, 1837, to *ibid.*

vilion" in Portland, "commanding a view of our magnificent harbor and blue seas with all their hundreds of islands."
He was introduced with the words, "our Guest from Mississippi—a native of Maine, a son of Portland—in whose talents and acquirements we recognize the vigor of the North
united with the fertility and luxuriance of the South."
What Prentiss said in the speech was not preserved, evidently, but his closing words were quoted: *"The Whigs of
'37*—contending for the same principles, may they prove as
successful as the Whigs of '76, whose triumph we this day
celebrate." Following the speech, toasts were drunk, first to
Prentiss himself as "Emphatically the orator of the day";
some of the other toasts were to "The day, our Country,
George Washington, The Union, Constitution of the
United States, State of Maine, William Henry Harrison,
Clay and Webster, and condemnation of the Jackson and
Van Buren administrations." [8] The people in Maine were
aware, too, that Prentiss' name was before the electorate of
Mississippi. The Portland *Daily Advertiser* wished him success in the election, and declared: "If bold and powerful
reasoning—if happy illustration—if generous courtesy—if
indignant sarcasm—if the hearty, frank and fearless bodying
forth of thoughts and opinions, which belong not so much
to a party, as to the principle of free government, everywhere, should be appreciated through the length and
breadth of Mississippi, as we believe they are, then we have a
right to feel sure of his election." [9]

Prentiss returned to Mississippi and wrote to relatives in
Maine: "The election resulted, as I anticipated, in the defeat of the Whig ticket, by a considerable majority, about
3000 votes. I was beaten by 2,800 votes. I had 500 more votes
than the candidate who ran on the same ticket with me,
though he had been electioneering all summer. In the river
counties, where the strength of the whigs principally lies,
they did not give more than half the vote of which they are

[8] Portland *Daily Advertiser*, July 6, 1837.   [9] *Ibid.*

capable—many believing the special election illegal and invalid." [10] Possibly Prentiss could not have won the election had he remained in Mississippi. Moreover, he could not count on Acee to win for him. The Mississippian who wrote to the Vicksburg *Sentinel and Expositor* under the date of June 29, stated that Acee was "a heavy drag for Prentiss to carry in the lower part of the State. It is the intention of the whig party—nine tenths of them—to give Prentiss single shots. . . . The fact is, Mr. Acee is not known in this part of the State, and single-handed, the Claiborne and Gholson ticket would run far ahead of him. As it is, . . . he will fall far behind Prentiss in all the lower counties." [11] This analysis seems to have been relatively accurate.

Claiborne and Gholson found their way back to Washington to participate in the session called by Van Buren to act on his Sub-Treasury Bill as a means of alleviating the panic conditions of the country. There they were declared members of the Twenty-fifth Congress, but only after considerable difficulty.

The fact that Claiborne and Gholson were avowed anti-Bank advocates operated to cause opponents of the Sub-Treasury to take advantage of the irregularity of the Mississippi election to challenge at once their right to be seated.[12] In the initial roll call of the House before it was actually organized and a speaker elected, Representative Charles F. Mercer of Virginia raised the question of the right of the governor of Mississippi to call the special election inasmuch as the time and the manner of elections were determined by legislatures, with the consent of Congress. His inference was that the two Mississippians were not constitutionally elected. This elicited the response from Claiborne that "he would

[10] Prentiss to George Prentiss, Vicksburg, August 14, 1837, in *Memoir of S. S. Prentiss*, I, 226.

[11] Extract from a letter dated June 29, 1837, to the Vicksburg *Daily Sentinel and Expositor*, July 25, 1837.

[12] Franklin L. Riley, "Life of Col. J. F. H. Claiborne," in *Mississippi Historical Society Publications* (Oxford), VII (1903), 226.

not, at that time, suffer himself to be drawn into any argument upon that subject, but he rose to protest . . . that the
gentleman from Virginia had no more right to question his
title to a seat upon that floor, than he had to question the
right of that gentleman or any other." His position was that
until the House was organized and a speaker chosen the appearance of himself and his colleague "was *prima facie* evidence of their right to represent the people of the State
whence they came." He announced further that if objections were persisted in, "he should feel himself compelled to
challenge every member from Maine to Mississippi to produce their credentials, and he should object to any man's
taking his seat there till he and his colleague obtained their
rights." [13] The end result of this skirmish was that though
the clerk was allowed to call the names of Claiborne and
Gholson for the purpose of organizing the House, the matter of their status in the House was referred to the Committee on Elections.

On September 25, Andrew Buchanan of Pennsylvania,
chairman of the Committee on Elections, made a report
expressing the majority views of the committee favoring the
seating of Claiborne and Gholson. Abram Maury of Tennessee, another member of the committee, announced that
the committee was divided in its thinking, and though no
minority report was being made, he favored putting the
problem before the "Committee of the whole on the state of
the Union." [14] Gholson spoke against this idea because the
Committee of the Whole might not be able to settle the issue wisely.

It was truly a constitutional problem facing the House,
influenced of course, by political identifications. Maury
showed the problem to be one of constitutional significance
when on September 27 the House continued to consider

[13] *Cong. Globe and Appendix*, 25 Cong., 1 Sess., 2; *Niles' National Register* (Baltimore, 1811–1849), LIII (1837–1838), 20–21.
[14] *Cong. Globe and Appendix*, 25 Cong., 1 Sess., 69.

the matter, "that by the Constitution of the United States, it was made the duty of the Legislature of Mississippi to prescribe the time, places and manner of holding their elections." Maury held: "It was not in the power of the Governor . . . to determine upon the time, places and manner of holding elections; and even if the Legislature of Mississippi had conferred this power upon the Governor, he could not have exercised it legally, because it would have been in contravention of the Constitution of the United States." This made it clear that the opponents to seating Claiborne and Gholson based their contentions on the issue that Governor Lynch had no authority to call the election in Mississippi. This argument was answered by Isaac Pennypacker, who said that the Mississippi legislature had provided for elections to be held in November but, because of the special session called, the governor had the right to order the election in July under the broader interpretation of the Constitution that "when vacancies happen in the representation of any State, the Executive shall issue writs of election to fill such vacancies." [15]

No new arguments were actually advanced on either side though the discussion continued for several days. The whole question revolved around the right of Governor Lynch to order the special election. In spite of attempts to prevent the seating of Claiborne and Gholson, they were, by a vote of 118 to 101, "declared to have been duly elected members of the twenty-fifth Congress from the State of Mississippi, and, as such entitled to their seats on this floor." [16] The discussion does not appear to have been greatly animated; and, more particularly, both sides avoided any mention of the fact that the seating of Claiborne and Gholson was for the special session only.

But the campaign to decide who should represent Mississippi in the regular session of the Twenty-fifth Congress had

[15] *Ibid.*, 81–82.
[16] *Ibid.*, 99; *Niles' National Register*, LIII (1837–1838), 96.

just begun. Immediately after the July election, the Whigs of the state, as well as many Democrats, taking it for granted that the July election was valid only until superseded by the November election, prepared for the fall contest. While Prentiss was still in Maine, he received notice that he had been nominated by the Whigs as their candidate in the November election. Acee refused to run this time, whereupon Judge T. W. Huling of Marshall County was selected as Prentiss' running mate. To what extent Huling answered the demands of the Vicksburg *Sentinel and Expositor* became evident as the campaign progressed. When Acee declined the nomination, this newspaper made itself clear: "The State Rights party of Mississippi must select another to supply his place on the ticket. We must be cautious in making the choice: we will support no Grimballite, no hybrid politician, no consolidation tory who may creep into the opposition ranks and ostensibly oppose the usurpation of Van Buren and the loco focos, while he goes for the principles on which all the federal usurpations are founded." Its extreme demand was that "Whoever is nominated, must not only call himself a States Rights man, but a Nullifier of the South Carolina school, else we shall oppose him." [17] Prentiss, it must be said, was not exactly that kind of candidate. At first a goodly measure of enthusiasm was expressed for Huling. The Vicksburg *Register* alluded to him as a man "Popular in the northern counties, Judge of the circuit court of the 8th Judicial District of Mississippi, and formerly Speaker of the House in Tennessee." [18] The *Sentinel and Expositor* stated: "Mr. Huling's name will be hailed by every man who wishes success to the cause of the people who are battling for their sacred rights against the encroachments of executive power and executive corruption." [19]

Prentiss accepted the nomination of the Whigs, and was

[17] Vicksburg *Daily Sentinel and Expositor*, September 5, 1837.
[18] Vicksburg *Daily Register*, September 13, 1837.
[19] Vicksburg *Daily Sentinel and Expositor*, September 19, 1837.

back in Mississippi in early August. He found Vicksburg in the throes of hard times, and wrote to his brother George: "There is not a dollar of money in circulation and no business doing." [20] With such conditions prevailing, the time was ripe for him to charge Jackson and Van Buren with the responsibility for the state of affairs, and to make known, as he launched his campaign, that he stood for the re-establishment of the United States Bank, in opposition to the stand of Claiborne, who was an avowed anti-Bank advocate. Prentiss was supplied with ammunition for the contest by Claiborne's declaration: "I am in favor of a specie currency as far as it is practicable, and against the charter of a national bank not only on account of its unconstitutionality, but on the general principle that all monopolies are dangerous to the liberties of the people." [21]

From the outset, Prentiss was determined that the people should know where he stood on the causes of and cures for the financial straits in which the nation found itself. Before beginning his canvass, he issued a message to the voters of Mississippi, in which he declared that the monetary ills of the nation must be "attributed to the derangement of the currency of the country." The remedy he advocated was the restoration of the national bank. In stressing the necessity for the bank, he said: "I believe we cannot have a currency in the United States adequate to carry on the business of the country without such an institution." In his advocacy of the Bank, he was inevitably a foe to the system of state banks. Prentiss opposed them vigorously: "Having their origin under different systems of legislation, . . . these rival and hostile institutions are continually pressing forth their money until public confidence becomes shaken; their issues are returned upon them,—suspension of specie payment is the

[20] Prentiss to George Prentiss, Vicksburg, August 14, 1837, in *Memoir of S. S. Prentiss*, I, 225.

[21] Extract from Claiborne's address to the people of Mississippi when he became a candidate for Congress in 1835, in Columbus (Miss.) *Democrat*, quoted in *Niles' National Register*, LII (1837), 407.

consequence, and seven years of pecuniary famine succeed the seven years of plenty." This was disastrous because "The same course will then be pursued again, and thus the country will alternately be gorged and starved. . . . This is the extent to which State banking can be carried,—furnishing a local, but not a general currency. Experience has shown, and reason demonstrated, the inability of the State banks to carry on the exchange of the country, and their unfitness to act as the fiscal agents of the Government, in the safe keeping and disbursement of the revenues." [22]

Anyone able to read could interpret this clear-cut stand. Prentiss was willing to stake his chances of being elected on the bank issue. Because of this, he told the people: "If, then, I am elected as your Representative, I shall vote for the immediate establishment of a National Bank." [23] The issue was drawn and Prentiss was ready to take the stump. He made it very clear to the people in his address that he was contesting Claiborne and Gholson only because they championed views contrary to his own. Of his opponents he said: "They are both gentlemen whose personal qualifications to represent the people of Mississippi no one can doubt. There is no personal rivalry in this canvas—it is, as it ought to be, a question of principle." [24]

Ten years earlier Prentiss had arrived in Natchez, "A lame and lisping" boy, eager to prove his talents to himself and others. He now chose Natchez, late in August before Claiborne and Gholson began their participation in the special session of Congress, as the place where he should open his campaign. Prentiss' initial bid for votes was made by condemning the financial policies of Jackson and Van Buren. According to the Natchez *Courier*, "He clearly demonstrated that the government never intended to establish a pure metallic currency, but merely held out this golden bait to lure into their toils the numerous *Loco-foco*

---

[22] Message quoted in *Memoir of S. S. Prentiss*, I, 228–30.
[23] *Ibid.*   [24] *Ibid.*, 230.

or *Agrarian* faction, and by means of them to secure the numerical preponderance of the party." [25]

Prentiss campaigned up and down the state, the Democratic newspapers vigorously opposing him, and the Whig papers portraying his eloquent triumphal march from county to county. By October 6, he had visited nearly half of the counties, had made fifty speeches, which were on an average two hours in length.[26] By election time, he had "visited forty-five counties in the State on an election tour of ten weeks," in which "he averaged . . . thirty miles a day on horseback." [27]

In the midst of his speaking tour, upon arriving in Columbus, October 6, Prentiss was informed that Huling had declined to continue in the race. At the same time he learned that the Whigs had chosen Thomas J. Word, a lawyer in Pontotoc, in place of Huling. Prentiss welcomed this change, saying: "We were all mistaken and made a great *faux pas* in the nomination of Judge Huling. . . . We have, however, a candidate in the field, who will answer the purpose as well as Huling. Thomas J. Word, Esq., a member of the bar at Pontatoc [*sic*], has been nominated in that place, and also here. He has taken the field, and will prove an efficient aid to our cause. . . . He is perfectly orthodox in his views, and advocates precisely the doctrines contained in my circular. Mr. Word is popular in the new counties and will be of great service there." [28] Evidently the Whigs were somewhat embarrassed over their earlier selection of Huling. The Vicksburg *Sentinel and Expositor* stated that Word was substituted "as soon as it was ascertained that Mr. Huling was a Van Buren man." [29] Cyrus Buckner was consid-

[25] Natchez *Daily Courier*, August 21, 1837.

[26] Prentiss to George Prentiss, Columbus, Miss., October 6, 1837, in *Memoir of S. S. Prentiss*, I, 240.

[27] *Id.* to *id.*, Vicksburg, November 14, 1837, *ibid.*, 243. See also, Arthur C. Cole, *The Whig Party in the South* (Washington, 1914), 85.

[28] Prentiss to William C. Smedes, Columbus, Miss., October 8, 1837, in *Memoir of S. S. Prentiss*, I, 241–42; Whittemore Collection.

[29] Vicksburg *Daily Sentinel and Expositor*, October 17, 1837.

ered, actually put up in some counties, until general agreement was reached on Word. One opposition newspaper, the
Mississippi Free Trader & Natchez Tri-Weekly Gazette,
even announced that Word had withdrawn and Reuben
Davis was taking his place. It was the indecision and con-
fusion about Prentiss' running mate which led this paper to
say: "Dear Whigs, do pray tell us who your candidates
are." [30]

Word was the permanent choice, and Prentiss was glad to
have him, if for no other reason than that he was popular
in the Chickasaw area. Prentiss' opposition in the state legislature to the seating of the Chickasaw representatives had
not been forgotten. Moreover, the populace of the Chickasaw counties owed much to Andrew Jackson and the Democratic party for the removal of the Indians from that area to
make room for the white settlers. Prentiss canvassed the
Chickasaw counties himself, however, not leaving the full
responsibility to Word. That the Chickasaw counties were a
matter of concern with Prentiss is to be inferred from his
statement: "I have experienced a favorable reception in the
Chickasaw counties, far exceeding my most sanguine expectations, and believe I have succeeded in removing all the
prejudice arising out of my course on the Chickasaw question." Yet Prentiss needed Word's aid in that part of Mississippi. When Word became the candidate, Prentiss announced: "He will confine his canvassing to the Chickasaw
and Choctaw counties, while I shall take the eastern counties. This is the arrangement between us." [31]

The most peculiar aspect of the campaign was the fact
that Prentiss and Word were seeking seats in Congress
which their opponents contended were already theirs. Claiborne and Gholson, having obtained the vote of the House
of Representatives declaring them members of the Twenty-

[30] *Mississippi Free Trader & Natchez Tri-Weekly Gazette,* October 28,
1837.
[31] Prentiss to Smedes, Columbus, Miss., October 7, 1837, in *Memoir of
S. S. Prentiss,* I, 241–42; Whittemore Collection.

fifth Congress, took the position that the November election
was void, and hence did not enter into actual canvass. In
fact, they remained in Washington, their names merely appearing on the ballot along with that of Alexander G.
McNutt, Democratic candidate for governor. This brought
the charge from the Vicksburg *Sentinel and Expositor:*
"We have understood that these worthies do not intend to
return to Mississippi during the interval between the extra
session and the meeting of Congress in December. They
dare not meet their indignant outraged constituency. How
contemptible they must feel, knowing that they hold their
seats thro' a base fraud on the people of Mississippi. . . .
Judging however that they were odious to the people, they
now claim the privilege of holding to the shirts of Mr.
McNutt in order to be dragged into office. Mr. McNutt will
probably have enough to do to save himself, without carrying such dead weights as these two political traitors." [32] In
thus allowing their names on the ballot, they were in a mere
formal manner participating in the election. In case of defeat, they were in a position, through having been declared
members of the Twenty-fifth Congress, to ignore the election results. However, Claiborne and Gholson did not keep
secret their determination to hold their seats under the
July election. They were enough in the open to submit
from Washington a ten-page pamphlet setting forth their
claims according to the following contentions: "1. That
there was a vacancy in the representation from Mississippi
within the meaning of the constitution. 2. That the Governor was bound to exercise the authority conferred on him
by the constitution. 3. That the power has been exercised in
the writ issued; and that the members elected under it are to
fill the vacancy by serving to the termination of the twenty-
fifth Congress." [33]

The intents and purposes of Claiborne and Gholson nat-

[32] Vicksburg *Daily Sentinel and Expositor,* October 31, 1837.
[33] *Ibid.,* October 17, 1837.

urally aroused the Mississippi Whigs, as well as many Democrats, to a state of wrath. The *Sentinel and Expositor,* not
always in support of Prentiss, and differing widely with him
on the bank issue,[34] was most outspoken in condemnation
of the Democratic candidates, particularly Claiborne. One
editorial denounced them severely: "From the course pursued by Mr. Claiborne to secure his election, we were prepared for any expedient by which he might be enabled to
retain the power he gained by treachery and double dealing.
But we confess we did not expect to find Mr. Gholson unit-
ing with him in this flagrant outrage against the rights and
wishes of the people of Mississippi. The masks are at last
torn from these Janus-faced traitors to the great principle of
Republican liberty. We are glad they have exhibited the
cloven hoof. . . . Is it not plain that these men would hold
their seats for life as well as for two years, if they could only
seize a quibble on which to base their pretensions?" Because
of this situation, the *Sentinel and Expositor* issued the challenge: "We hope that the high-minded of all political parties
—those who would sustain the will of the people as the
palladium of our liberties—will march to the polls in November and rebuke the spirit of treachery and usurpation
manifested by Messrs. Claiborne and Gholson. We know
that several Van Buren men have declared their determination to vote against Mr. Claiborne. We now call upon them,
not in the spirit of party, but as freemen who regard principles of liberty and the rights of the people, to vote against
both." [35]

Prentiss and Word carried the November election by
nearly seven thousand votes. Theirs was a decisive victory.

[34] This difference was expressed in the statement: "Though we differ
from Messrs. Prentiss and Word on a very important question, the charter-
ing of a U. S. Bank; yet they ought to receive the votes of the people and
we have no doubt they will get the largest vote ever given to members of
Congress from this State." *Ibid.,* November 7, 1837.

[35] *Ibid.,* October 17, 1837.

Prentiss prepared to go to Washington, answering: "I shall *claim* my seat, and armed with the great 'democracy of numbers,' as the Democrats call it, I have some hopes of procuring a reversal of the outrageous and party-vote in Congress." [36] Mississippi by her November vote of 1837 indicated that the hold of Andrew Jackson on the state had been broken, and was setting the pace to be followed a year later by Georgia, Louisiana, Virginia, North Carolina, and other states in the "reshaping of parties." [37]

The November victors started for Washington about December 10, carrying with them their credentials, dated December 1, 1837.[38] Upon arriving in the Capitol they found their seats occupied by Claiborne and Gholson. A battle was inevitable. Congress, divided evenly between Democrats and Whigs, and including former President John Quincy Adams, Millard Fillmore, Thomas A. Corwin, James K. Polk, John Bell, Caleb Cushing, Henry A. Wise, Rice Garland, William C. Dawson, John Sergeant, and other eminent personages, would have to make a decision. Prentiss analyzed the situation very well in forecasting a strenuous conflict. "There would be no difficulty in the case, were it not that it will be made a party question; the Van Buren party are in too desperate a condition to give up, without a struggle, the two votes of Claiborne and Gholson." [39]

An interesting aspect of the whole struggle is the fact that Gholson at least may have had convictions that he was not the rightful holder of his seat. This may be inferred from Adams' statement that in a conversation with Henry Clay concerning the illegal disputed Mississippi election, Clay

---

36 Prentiss to George Prentiss, Vicksburg, November 14, 1837, in *Memoir of S. S. Prentiss*, I, 243.

37 Cole, *Whig Party in the South*, 52.

38 Quoted in *Memoir of S. S. Prentiss*, I, 249.

39 Prentiss to George Prentiss, Washington, December 27, 1837, *ibid.*, 244-45.

said, "Mr. Gholson himself had told him he thought it is so." [40] Gholson never gave any public impression of this kind, however.

The case of Prentiss and Word versus Claiborne and Gholson was formally brought before the House December 27. On that day, Polk, Speaker of the House, announced that "he had placed in his hands a communication from Messrs. S. S. Prentiss and T. J. Word, claiming seats as Representatives from the State of Mississippi on the floor of the House." In response to this announcement of the Speaker, Bell of Tennessee reminded the House that the case of Mississippi was somewhat analogous to that of Arkansas, and inquired of Archibald Yell, the lone representative from that state, if he had been sworn during the present session. [41]

Probably anticipating embarrassment to himself, Yell, whom Adams called "a shallow, foolish fellow, without principle enough to stand on the point of a needle—fitter for the brawler of a bar-room than for a representative of the people in Congress," [42] rose in defense of himself. He had been elected for the special session but had assured the people of Arkansas that "if he should not be elected again he would resign his seat." Consequently, "Now having submitted his claim to the people a second time, he should have been derelict in his duty and professions to them if he had claimed his seat under the first election, and not qualified over again. He had, therefore, thought it due to the people of Arkansas and to himself, even if he had been legally and constitutionally elected the first time, to claim his seat under the ensuing election. Moreover, he thought it no harm to be sworn over again; for he believed if the House was sworn

[40] Charles F. Adams (ed.), *Memoirs of John Quincy Adams* (Philadelphia, 1876), IX, 445.

[41] *Cong. Globe and Appendix*, 25 Cong., 2 Sess., 56; *Niles' National Register*, LIII (1837–1838), 281.

[42] *Memoirs of John Quincy Adams*, LX, 484.

once a month it would do no harm." [43] Yell was really saying
that had he been opposed and defeated in the November
election he would have resigned his seat.[44] But he was identified with the Democrats, so that his subsequent actions and
vote on the disputed election make the opinion of Adams
quite justified.

With Yell's limping and evasive defense before the
House, the Mississippi case became the pressing issue before
Congress, promising a colorful conflict. Whig friends of
Prentiss, led by John Pope of Kentucky, tried immediately
to persuade Congress to declare Prentiss and Word the representatives from Mississippi, and to rescind the action taken
at the former session. This endeavor was countered by
Churchill Cambreleng of New York, who moved "to refer
the matter to the Committee on Elections because it was
'without precedent, and could not be decided without commitment.' " [45]

The matter lay more or less dormant until January 12,
when Buchanan, chairman of the Committee on Elections,
reported, merely giving a statement of the facts involved,
but making no resolution or recommendation as to what
the committee deemed the advisable course of action for the
House to take.[46]

Four days later, January 16, the House began in earnest
the consideration of what was to be done. The Democratic
opposition to the seating of Prentiss and Word took the
initiative when Isaac H. Bronson of New York moved that
"Messrs. S. S. Prentiss and T. J. Word are not members of
the 25th Congress and are not entitled to seats in this
House." [47] Pending action on this motion, Wise of Virginia,

[43] Cong. Globe and Appendix, 25 Cong., 2 Sess., 56.
[44] Niles' National Register, LIII (1837–1838), 281.
[45] Ibid.; Cong. Globe and Appendix, 25 Cong., 2 Sess., 56.
[46] Cong. Globe and Appendix, 25 Cong., 2 Sess., 97.
[47] Ibid., 104; Washington National Intelligencer, January 18, 1838;
Niles' National Register, LIII (1837–1838), 331.

staunchest advocate for seating the newly elected Mississippians, moved as a preliminary consideration that Prentiss and Word be given permission to take seats within the bar of the House, to state their case, and to speak in their own behalf during the congressional deliberations on the matter. The House voted affirmatively on this motion,[48] paving the way for Prentiss to deliver a chain of speeches which were to make him a nationally recognized figure.

The cause of Claiborne and Gholson was not neglected by the Democrats. Claiborne being ill and unable to appear in the House, Representative Benjamin C. Howard of Maryland presented in Claiborne's behalf a manuscript containing arguments in favor of Gholson and his colleague. When Howard, at the conclusion of his reading, moved that the House print the manuscript, Wise was on his feet. He denounced this request for charity from Claiborne and Gholson, and in substance told them to bear the expense of printing it themselves. The words of Wise "produced a reply from Mr. Gholson, and some remarks of a most painful personal character passed between them." [49] This clash indicated that the Mississippi case was not to admit of quick and easy decision. Wise and Gholson had become more deeply involved than they realized, for both were made to apologize to the House.[50] While they did apologize to the House, they did not withdraw their "offensive language toward each other." Just what offensive language was used between the two men cannot be known for certain. The Vicksburg *Register* quoted an unnamed correspondent in Washington as saying: "By the by, Wise and Gholson had it yesterday roughly enough. Mr. Prentiss had printed at his own expense a statement of facts which was laid on the tables of Members. Mr. Claiborne, who is said to be sick, sent by Mr. Howard of Maryland a sort of argument in answer which Howard wanted to have printed in order to put the parties on an

---

[48] *Cong. Globe and Appendix*, 25 Cong., 2 Sess., 105.   [49] *Ibid.*
[50] *Ibid.*, 107; Washington *National Intelligencer*, January 18, 1838.

equality. Wise in reply stated that Howard was mistaken as to the fact, Mr. Prentiss's statement not having been printed by the House but at his own expense. Gholson said they did not ask for the charity of the House and thought the remark of Wise was unworthy of him and the place he held. Wise rose and said 'Mr. Speaker, if impudence and ignorance can make a *blackguard,* there (pointing to Gholson) stands one.' Gholson said he was a cowardly scoundrel &c. . . . The general impression, indeed I may say universal, was that Gholson could not avoid calling Wise out. He also is said to have been sick and looks badly enough." [51] The interposition of the Chair and the quick adjournment of the House following the scene of words between Wise and Gholson did not serve to settle the matter finally. Wise felt impelled to issue a challenge to Gholson to meet him in a duel. Interestingly enough, Wise asked Prentiss to carry the challenge. This Prentiss refused to do, supposedly "because he said the *onus* was upon Mr. Gholson and not upon Mr. Wise." [52] By the intervention of friends, including John C. Calhoun, the duel was not fought.[53]

The closely drawn battle of this first day left little doubt that the Mississippi case would consume the time of Congress for additional days. The importance of the matter led Bell to move that the disputed Mississippi election be made the special order "on each succeeding day, until the same shall be decided." [54]

On the second day of congressional hearings, Prentiss availed himself of the opportunity granted him and his colleague to speak for themselves, and began an address which continued for three days.[55] He spoke for approximately

---

[51] Vicksburg *Daily Register,* January 29, 1838.

[52] James P. Hambleton, *A Biographical Sketch of Henry A. Wise* . . . (Richmond, 1856), xxvii.

[53] *Ibid.;* Baxter H. Wise, *The Life of Henry A. Wise* (New York, 1899), 41; Dunbar Rowland, *Mississippi* . . . (Atlanta, 1907), I, 788.

[54] *Cong. Globe and Appendix,* 25 Cong., 2 Sess., 107.

[55] *Ibid.,* 113, 119, 121; Washington *National Intelligencer,* January 18, 20, 1838. No account of his day-by-day utterances seems available. The

three hours a day, not only to the House of Representatives, but in time to all who could crowd into the hall. The Senate was virtually adjourned, its members forsaking the duties of that chamber to hear him. Personal friends and political opponents were in close attendance. Without doubt great interest was shown in Prentiss. He had come to know Clay quite intimately, especially as the result of his visit with him in Kentucky two years before. Adams gave space in his diary to the fact that he had been introduced to Prentiss, and that "Prentiss had told him that he came from the Yankee breed." [56]

The twenty-nine-year-old orator from Mississippi began slowly laying his case before the House. Before he attacked and denounced the claims of his opponents, he consumed a copious amount of time in ethical justification of his right to appear in Congress. After thanking the Congress for its courtesies toward him as an individual, he told its members: "I have petitioned this House for nothing; neither have I memorialised it. I have presented myself here as a Representative from a sovereign State of Mississippi to the Con-

Vicksburg *Register*, January 31, 1838, quoted the Baltimore *Chronicle* of January 17, as saying at the end of the first day of speaking: "He left off at that special point in his matchless argument, at which he had taken the ground *that, if the legislature of Mississippi had a right, and had the power by law, to fix the first Monday in November as the day of the annual election of members of Congress, any election under that law must be valid.* To this he will hold the House, fast as a chain of adamant, and let them escape it, if they can." A summary and condensation is provided in Shields, *Seargent Smith Prentiss*, 145–81; *Memoir of S. S. Prentiss*, I, 265–316. "The printed speech is little more than a skeleton. Even the few rhetorical passages that are retained, have lost much of their original form and beauty. The professional stenographers confessed themselves utterly baffled in the attempt to report him." *Memoir of S. S. Prentiss* I, 254. Doubtless the explanation for the form of the speech as printed is that Prentiss himself wrote it for publication following the actual delivery. This he announced as his intention in his words, "In the course of two or three weeks, as soon as the matter is decided, I will draw up the heads or substance of my speech and have it published, though I shall not be able to do myself justice in writing it off." Prentiss to George Prentiss, Washington, January 20, 1838, in *Memoir of S. S. Prentiss*, I, 255. Word did not address the House during the hearings.

[56] *Memoirs of John Quincy Adams*, IX, 472.

gress of the United States, and claim a seat on this floor, not as a matter of *favor*, but as a matter of *right*. I presented my credentials, properly authenticated, showing my due election, according to the laws of that State, and demanded to be sworn."

Prentiss knew that if he was to win the right for himself and Word to occupy the seats held by Claiborne and Gholson, it was incumbent on him to disprove their claims before he could ask Congress to rescind its action in the special session. He had pleaded enough cases in the law courts of Mississippi to know that he had to build a *prima facie* case for himself, and then protect it by refuting the points raised in defense of his opponents. The House was his jury. Before it he intermingled organized logic with persuasive techniques. His strategy was to begin by laying down three basic contentions: that as the July election "was absolutely void— a mere nullity," the Democratic claimants had no legal or constitutional rights to seats in the Twenty-fifth Congress; that if such election had any validity, it terminated with the general November election; and that he and Word had been regularly elected to Congress in November.[57]

Prentiss immediately combined refutation of the contentions of Claiborne and Gholson "that, at the special session . . . *the whole matter became thereby res adjudicata,* . . . incapable of revision," with earnest appeals to Congress to reconsider its past action. Speaking of Claiborne and Gholson as "Dipped Achilles-like, in this judicial Styx, they deem themselves invulnerable," Prentiss carried the battle into the enemy's territory, declaring, "Fast and far I have ridden to meet the gentlemen's high defiance. Ivanhoe has returned from the Holy Land, and the Disinherited Knight dares the proud Templar to Combat."

Prentiss assumed the burden of proof, which required

---

[57] Shields, *Seargent Smith Prentiss*, 149; *Memoir of S. S. Prentiss*, I, 271. For these same contentions, expressed more concisely, see Washington *National Intelligencer*, January 18, 1838; *Niles' National Register*, LIII (1837–1838), 332.

him to show that Congress had erred. He embodied his purpose in the words: "Let us now examine into the character of this *res adjudicata,* which like the seal of Solomon, has closed up the whole matter." A complete review of the facts leading to the two Mississippi elections brought Prentiss to the five contentions upon which he contested the premise: "1st. That it was not a judicial act of this House at all, nor was it adopted by this House acting as a judicature. 2nd. It was not a decision or adjudication upon the election qualification, or return of myself and colleague, our election return having taken place long since pretended adjudication. 3rd. That so far as said pretended adjudication goes to alter or annul the law of Mississippi, fixing the time for the election of her representatives to the 25th Congress, it is void; this House having no power, either legislative or judicial, to alter or annul a constitutional law of a State fixing the time for the general election of her representatives to Congress. 4th. Said pretended adjudication is not conclusive upon the State of Mississippi, because, she was neither a party to the proceeding upon which it was based, nor had any notice thereof, either actual or constructive. 5th. Said pretended adjudication was founded upon palpable mistake, and the House is bound to review it." [58]

Upon these five points Prentiss proceeded to dwell in consecutive order. Just where he left off his first day of speaking is difficult to ascertain. Both the *National Intelligencer* and *Niles' National Register* stated in identical language: "These points were argued with much earnestness and eloquence, and he was about making some remarks upon the general subject, when . . . he gave way to a motion of adjournment." [59] Prentiss attracted no small amount of atten-

---

[58] Shields, *Seargent Smith Prentiss,* 151; *Memoir of S. S. Prentiss,* I, 274. These same five points of the first day of speaking are cited in Washington *National Intelligencer,* January 18, 1838; *Niles' National Register,* LIII (1837–1838), 332.

[59] Washington *National Intelligencer,* January 18, 1838; *Niles' National Register,* LIII (1837–1838), 332.

tion by his efforts. The Vicksburg *Register* watched its chances to quote individuals and other newspapers in respect to Prentiss' speaking in the situation. It referred its readers to the New Orleans *True American* which had printed the observations of a New Orleans citizen who heard Prentiss' January 17 speech: "I have just returned from the House of Representatives, where Mr. Prentiss . . . has been holding a crowded Hall enchanted by one of the happiest exhibitions of oratory I have ever witnessed. . . . Among the Senators who had deserted their seats, and were attentive listeners to the eloquent and argumentative speech of the young orator were Clay, Preston, Crittenden, and the venerable H. L. White." [60] The *Register* also quoted an unnamed member of Congress, who, in a letter to a Vicksburg citizen, wrote: "Mr. Prentiss's speech was not merely clear, forcible, and eloquent, it was a lofty effort of an admirable mind, and characterized equally by brilliant imagery, playful wit and demonstrative argument. . . . There was a manliness too in what he said, and the manner of saying it, properly tempered by courtesy, and yet not flinching from the most painful truth." [61] Two days later the *Register* quoted the Baltimore *Chronicle* as saying of the speech: "It has some excellent figures, is full of demonstrative power, and is praised everywhere as one of the most splendid efforts of oratory which has been in the House for a long time." [62]

Prentiss dwelt most heavily the second day upon the fifth contention he had set forth, that "Said pretended adjudication was founded upon palpable mistake, and the House is bound to review it." It appears from the several versions of the speech that Prentiss moved through the four previous

[60] New Orleans *True American*, January 17, 1838, quoted in Vicksburg *Daily Register*, January 29, 1838.

[61] Quoted *ibid*.

[62] Quoted *ibid*., January 31, 1838. An account of the three-day speech of Prentiss appeared in the Vicksburg *Daily Register*, March 21–26, 1838, and Natchez *Daily Courier*, March 15, 16, 1838.

contentions in fairly rapid fashion. Upon the fifth point he bore down with all the power of which he was capable. In respect to the first four points Prentiss had necessarily spent most of his time in factual delineation. But the fifth one constituted a mighty and vulnerable issue. Prentiss and Word had come to Washington with their credentials properly signed and authenticated. There was method in their procedure, for Prentiss went on to show that Claiborne and Gholson had never presented their rightful credentials, which specifically stated their election for the special session only. Rather, they substituted a statement from the secretary of state of Mississippi that they were duly elected in the July election. It was this wrong done to Mississippi, so Prentiss viewed it, this error of Congress, this treachery of Claiborne and Gholson, that he sought to rectify. He maintained and reiterated the right and duty of Congress to undo its mistake, and thus protect the elective franchise of Mississippi. Prentiss' attack was chiefly against Claiborne in this matter. He showed how Claiborne had admitted in a *"written speech"* that the certificates of election in July reached him, " 'but *perceiving* they contained the *limitation of the term of service* mentioned in the governor's writ to hold the election, *we* applied for and *obtained the Statement* of the Secretary of State *to be used* in their stead.' " This led Prentiss to his indictment for what was done by Claiborne and the congressional Committee on Elections in September. Specifically, he charged that, "Knowing, according to the statement of Mr. Claiborne, that a certificate of election was in existence, but kept back solely on account of its insufficiency to sustain the claim set up by the gentlemen possessing it, the committee, in *palpable violation* of the instructions of the House, neither *compel its production* nor *take notice of its* existence, but make a report favorable to the claimants, based upon partial and secondary evidence avowedly obtained for the *express purpose of avoiding the effect and operation of the certificate* of election."

The burden of Prentiss' second day of speaking was on this point, but again it is not certain at just what point he ceased speaking on January 18. Evidently, though, after he had refuted the rights of Claiborne and Gholson by five contentions, chief of which was the fifth one, he returned to the original three issues which he had laid down. About three o'clock in the afternoon he sat down, and the House adjourned.[63]

On January 19 Prentiss concluded his speech. On that day he talked, in relation to his original three contentions, about the constitutional provisions for elections and analyzed the Mississippi election machinery. He was considerably informative while obviously trying to build a persuasive case. Having stated his basic arguments, he voiced rhetorical and pathetic appeals which made the speech memorable. With his case presented, it was time to appeal. He announced the transition from argument to appeal in the words: "I have now done with my argument in this matter. It is for the grave judges around me to say whether I have established any of my propositions."

As Prentiss moved to his peroration, he made his own attitude clear: "I advance no personal claim; it is the claim of one of the sovereign States of this Confederacy which I advocate,—her claim to the right of choosing her own Representatives according to her own constitutional laws." He asked: "Will you deny her this right? Will you rend the brightest and strongest link in the golden chain of the Union?" This was the basic issue which motivated Prentiss to summon all the eloquence which was to make his speech a classic. Not only did he plead, but he threatened. "Sir, you may think it an easy and trifling matter to deprive Mississippi of her elective franchise; for she is young, and may not, perchance, have the power to resist; but I am much mistaken in the character of her chivalrous citizens, if you

[63] Washington *National Intelligencer*, January 20, 1938; *Niles' National Register*, LIII (1837–1838), 332.

do not find that she not only understands her rights, but has both the will and the power to vindicate them. You may find to your sorrow, that you have grasped a scorpion, where you thought you were only crushing a worm. This House would as soon put its head in a lion's mouth, as to take the course which is threatened, toward the elder and more powerful States. And how happens it, that Representatives of the States which have always been the readiest in the assertion of their own rights should now be most zealous in trampling upon the rights of Mississippi?"

Prentiss was now pleading in earnest. His method became more direct. Turning to the representatives of specific states he inquired: "Come, what says the Bay State—time-honored Massachusetts? . . . Would *Kentucky* submit? Ask her, Mr. Speaker, and her *Mammoth cavern* will find a voice to thunder in your ears her stern response. . . . And what says Virginia, with her high device—her *Sic semper tyrannus* . . . ? How would she brook such usurpation? . . . And where is South Carolina, the Harry Percy of the Union? On which side in this great controversy does she couch her lance and draw her blade?"

Prentiss was nearly finished, but not quite. The part of his speech regarded at the time as the most sublime was still to fall upon the ears of the House. Beseechingly, he implored: "Upon all the States I do most solemnly call for that justice to another which they would expect for themselves. Let this cup pass from Mississippi. Compel her not to drink its bitter ingredients, lest, some day, evenhanded justice should 'command the poisoned chalice' to your own lips. Rescind that resolution, which presses like a foul incubus upon the Constitution. You sit here, twenty-five sovereign States, in judgment upon the most sacred right of a sister State; that which is to a State what chastity is to a woman, or honor to a man. Should you decide against her, you tear from her brow the richest jewel which sparkles there, and forever bow her head in shame and dishonor. But if your determination is taken; if the blow must fall; if the violated Constitution must bleed; I have but one request, on her behalf, to make. When you decide that she cannot choose her own representatives, at that self-same moment blot from the spangled banner of this Union the bright *star* that glitters to the name of Mississippi, but leave the *stripe* behind, a fit emblem of her degradation."

The speech was ended. It was not soon forgotten. Prentiss had gained for himself a national reputation. Fillmore is purported to have exclaimed: "I never can forget it; it was certainly the most brilliant speech I ever heard." [64] Webster is said to have remarked: "Nobody could equal it." [65] Adams wrote in his diary that the speech was "full of spirit and argument, seldom surpassed as a specimen of eloquence in that house." [66] The epitomization of Prentiss and the speech given years later by Wise was: "Prentiss' turn came. He threw himself on the arena at a single bound, but not in the least like a harlequin. He stepped, no stranger, on the boards of high debate—he 'raised the eye to heaven, and trod with giant steps.' . . . I shall never forget the feelings he inspired, and the triumph he won. . . . There is the figure of the *star* and *stripe;* go read it—read it now that the eye is dim and his muscles cease to move the action to the word; then imagine what it was as his tongue spoke it, his eye looked it, his hand gesticulated his thoughts." [67] Fortunately for our own knowledge of the event, Prentiss directed a letter to George Prentiss, giving something of his reaction to the speaking situation in which he found himself. "I have . . . been for three days on my legs; in other words, I have made a three days' speech, and I have no doubt . . . convinced the House that I *ought* to be admitted. At any rate, as I tell them, whether they let me in or not, I have got my share of the session; for if they divide it out, it will

[64] *Memoir of S. S. Prentiss,* I, 253.   [65] *Ibid.*
[66] *Memoirs of John Quincy Adams,* IX, 470–71.
[67] Henry A. Wise to George Prentiss, Richmond, February 21, 1851, in *Memoir of S. S. Prentiss,* II, 53.

hardly afford three days apiece. I suppose you will wonder what I could talk about so long. That's more than I can tell you; though I have no doubt it was a sensible speech, from the fact that I had an attentive house and crowded galleries, from the latter of which I several times received very audible signs of approbation. Could I have put it to a vote in the galleries, especially among the *ladies*, I should have been admitted at once. . . . Many of the most distinguished senators honored me with their presence, such as Webster, Clay, Preston, &c." [68]

Even the eloquence and pleading of a Prentiss could not in one stroke turn such a party conflict. As Adams analyzed the situation: "The decision in October was a dogged party vote; and so it will be now." [69] Nevertheless, the Democratic opposition armed itself full force to offset the possible effects of Prentiss' three days of speaking. Immediately after he concluded, Gholson replied, followed by Henry A. Foster of New York, who spoke until adjournment was called for the day. [70] Adams commented in his diary: "Gholson made a short, feeble, but not indecorous speech, without the attempt to answer the arguments of Prentiss, but holding to his intrenchment behind the decision of the House at the special session. Foster, of New York, began a full-dress speech, but soon after three the House adjourned, leaving him to finish tomorrow." [71] For ten more days the battle was to rage, with such Democrats as Foster and Isaac H. Bronson of New York, Pennypacker of Virginia, and Hugh S. Legaré of South Carolina, defending the action of Congress in the previous session, and attempting to weaken the claims of Prentiss and Word. [72]

[68] Prentiss to *id.*, Washington, January 20, 1838, *ibid.*, I, 254–55.

[69] *Memoirs of John Quincy Adams*, IX, 473.

[70] *Cong. Globe and Appendix*, 25 Cong., 2 Sess., 121; Washington *National Intelligencer*, January 20, 1838; *Niles' National Register*, LIII (1837–1838), 349.   [71] *Memoirs of John Quincy Adams*, IX, 472.

[72] *Cong. Globe and Appendix*, 25 Cong., 2 Sess., 122, 135, 139, 145, 146, 148; Washington *National Intelligencer*, January 22, 25, 26, 27, 29; *Niles' National Register*, LIII (1837–1838), 350–51, 366–67.

On January 30 further events happened. Prentiss resumed the floor once more, and "replied at length to Messrs. Foster, Pennypacker, Bronson, Mason, and Legaré." [73] In fact, he spoke twice on that day, first briefly, relinquishing the floor for a short time, and then speaking until an adjournment was called.[74] On the same day efforts were made to dispose of the matter by bringing it to a vote. Upon request Bell "withdrew the latter part of his modified proposition, and the question was put upon the amendment declaring that the resolution of the last session be rescinded, and that Mr. Claiborne and Mr. Gholson are not entitled to seats in this House." [75] But adjournment precluded actual vote. The following day was consumed in extended debate, Prentiss gaining the floor still another time.[76] After he had given this more or less final refutation of the Democratic spokesmen for Claiborne and Gholson on January 31, the question was put on the first part of the Bell amendment.[77]

The smoke of battle subsided, and the roll was called. By a majority of 119 to 112, the House went on record in favor of rescinding its action in regard to the Democratic claimants.[78] Claiborne and Gholson were thus swept from the scene. The caustic Adams recorded that there was "Wild and ludicrous commotion in the House." [79] By this close vote the House admitted the error of its ways in the special session. Still this vote did not seat Prentiss and Word, the Bell amendment having been divided for purposes of voting. The natural assumption was that "If Gholson and

[73] Washington *National Intelligencer*, February 1, 1838.
[74] *Niles' National Register*, LIII (1837–1838), 367.
[75] Washington *National Intelligencer*, February 1, 1838.
[76] *Cong. Globe and Appendix*, 25 Cong., 2 Sess., 148.
[77] No record of this speech seems available. Doubtless Prentiss never took the pains to reproduce it in writing. In the opinion of George Prentiss, it was equal to his first one and was delivered before a House "still more crowded than on the 18th and 19th of January." *Memoir of S. S. Prentiss*, 256.
[78] *Cong. Globe and Appendix*, 25 Cong., 2 Sess., 150; Washington *National Intelligencer*, February 3, 1838; *Memoirs of John Quincy Adams*, IX, 483.
[79] *Memoirs of John Quincy Adams*, IX, 483.

Claiborne are not entitled to the seats, Prentiss and Word certainly are." [80] But since it was a party contest, the opposition mobilized to prevent the two Whigs from being declared members of the House. The decision of the House to unseat Claiborne and Gholson was observed widely over the country, however, and served to keep Prentiss' name in the forefront. Newspapers made numerous observations. Typical of the anti-Jackson comments was that of the Springfield, Massachusetts, *Republican and Journal:* "This was thunderbolt! A majority of seven on the side of justice! It took the House by surprise; and such consternation was exhibited by the collar men, you never witnessed. . . . I must do the Van Buren men the justice to say that, in all probability, one third of the 112 are rejoiced at the result, though they felt themselves bound by the past decision of the House, and by party consideration, to vote as they did. The eloquence of Mr. Prentiss' appeal in his closing argument had nothing to do with the result. His successful reply may have had some effect upon the vote. That man Prentiss was born to talk—that's certain." [81]

Howard of Maryland, on February 1, made evident the designs of the Democrats to send the matter back to Mississippi for a third election when he moved to modify the Bell amendment to read: "Resolved that Seargent S. Prentiss and Thomas J. Word are not members of the 25th Congress." [82] Aside from the fact that the Democrats were seeking to prevent Prentiss and Word from being seated on purely party grounds, the argument in their defense was that if the July election was illegal and Claiborne and Gholson were seated in the special election, then the November election was no true index to the wishes of the people in Mississippi. Nevertheless, Howard's maneuver

[80] Vicksburg *Daily Register,* February 16, 1838.
[81] Springfield (Mass.) *Weekly Republican and Journal,* February 10, 1838.
[82] *Cong. Globe and Appendix,* 25 Cong., 2 Sess., 150; Washington *National Intelligencer,* February 3, 1838.

brought the impetuous Prentiss to his feet. He spoke the first day of February, and resumed his remarks on the second, scoring the idea of sending the election back to Mississippi. Particularly, Prentiss condemned the House for allowing Yell of Arkansas to retain his seat, his case being analogous to that of Claiborne and Gholson. Earlier Yell had stated that while elected in July, he had submitted himself to the voters again in November. Now he took the position that the November election "amounted to the fact that it was voluntary on his part, for he held his July election to have been a good one, for the whole term of the 25th Congress." [83] Still others on both sides who took the floor compelled Prentiss to wait three more days while Congress discussed the problem. Throughout the long drawn-out contest, he had no better friend than Bell. Along with Wise and others, Bell now rallied against such Democrats as Robert Barnwell Rhett of South Carolina in opposition to sending the election back to Mississippi.

On February 5, the matter was finally brought to a vote. When the roll call was ended, the vote stood tied, 117 to 117. The tie vote was additionally significant because Yell voted against Prentiss and Word. If the vote was in a certain sense tied by the Arkansas representative, it was now to be broken by one man. The decision was completely in the hands of Speaker Polk.[84] He cast his ballot in favor of sending the election back. Prentiss and Word had lost. But a mighty resolution was announced to the House when Prentiss arose once more. He censured the action of Congress as "depriving the people of Mississippi of a representation on this floor," and declared that, "if he was spared life till the next session of Congress, and he saw any prospect of them having justice done to the people of Mississippi, he would again present himself, and see if he could not have this un-

[83] *Cong. Globe and Appendix,* 25 Cong., 2 Sess., 155.
[84] *Ibid.,* 159; Washington *National Intelligencer,* February 6, 1838.

constitutional resolution rescinded, as the one which was adopted in September last." [85] This resolution and declaration meant a return to Mississippi for another campaign.

One incident, almost humorous, but actually adding insult to injury, was yet to occur. Rhett, a leading opponent to the seating of Prentiss and Word, recommended that "Prentiss and Word receive the same compensation per diem and mileage that is allowed to members of Congress." Anticipating this gesture, Prentiss had authorized Wise to tell Congress that he would not accept a "dollar of his pay." In thus speaking for Prentiss, Wise did not hesitate to express his own willingness to vote in favor of the motion of Rhett. Whether or not Prentiss and Word ever accepted the money, payment was approved by a vote of 136 to 41. [86]

This episode in the life of Prentiss did not enhance his meager political aspirations. He had resigned from the state legislature because politics were not to his liking, and now he was definitely convinced that he would never sacrifice his love of the law court for any political attainments which might be his. Writing to relatives in Maine, he gave vent to his feelings: "I am perfectly satisfied with what I have seen of political life, and without having my opinion of myself in any degree raised, I can truly say that my estimation of others is sadly diminished." Disillusioned, he went on to say: "I had no idea of the want of principle as well as the want of sense which characterizes a large portion of the political men of the nation. For my own part, I am heartily sick of the whole matter, and shall feel greatly obliged to the people of Mississippi, if they will allow me to retire. I think, however, that they will send me back here, and if they wish to do so, I feel bound to submit to their wishes." [87]

[85] *Cong. Globe and Appendix*, 25 Cong., 2 Sess., 160.
[86] *Ibid.*, 162–63; Washington *National Intelligencer*, February 8, 1838; *Niles' National Register*, LIII (1837–1838), 379.
[87] Prentiss to Abby Prentiss, Washington, February 14, 1838, in *Memoir of S. S. Prentiss*, I, 263.

Two things remained for Prentiss to do before starting for Mississippi. One was to attend a complimentary dinner given to him and Word. White of Tennessee presided, and with Whig friends of both the House and Senate present, speeches were given, including one by Webster.[88]

The other obligation remaining to Prentiss before leaving Washington was to issue a letter to the people of Mississippi outlining the facts of the disputed election and the action of Congress. He ended the letter: "I shall be in Mississippi in a few days, when I will be able to explain to you, more at large, the outrage which has been committed upon you." [89] Also, Prentiss issued in a more official manner to Governor Lynch a statement of nineteen points covering the controversy in Congress.[90]

Prentiss reached home before the middle of March. Enough enthusiasm was shown him to cause Johnson, the Natchez free Negro barber, to write in his diary: "Mr. Prentiss arrived at vicksburg this afternoon—they gave him very Reseption." [91] Johnson probably had in mind the public barbecue given Prentiss in Vicksburg at which time he addressed the people there in beginning his third race.[92]

With the proclamation of the Governor calling for the third Mississippi election to be held the fourth Monday of April, there was just one month at the disposal of the candidates to repeat their campaign efforts. Gholson refused to run in this election, with the result that General James Davis of Pontotoc, who had migrated from Alabama two years before,[93] was chosen by the Democrats to appear with Claiborne. Actually, Claiborne was in no condition to

---

[88] *Niles' National Register,* LIII (1837–1838), 400; Vicksburg *Daily Register,* February 27, 1838; Shields, *Seargent Smith Prentiss,* 187; *Memoir of S. S. Prentiss,* I, 262.

[89] *Niles' National Register,* LIII (1837–1838), 387; Washington *National Intelligencer,* February 10, 1838; Vicksburg *Daily Register,* March 9, 1838.

[90] Vicksburg *Daily Register,* March 6, 1838.

[91] Diary of William T. Johnson, March 11, 1838.

[92] Vicksburg *Daily Register,* March 19, 1838.

[93] Natchez *Daily Courier,* March 31, 1838.

canvass, being "down with hemorrhage of the lungs." [94]
Other Democrats, particularly Albert G. Brown, did most
of the actual campaigning.

Prentiss spoke at Natchez soon after the barbecue speech
at Vicksburg. The meeting was held in the courthouse yard
to accommodate the crowd.[95] Something of the occasion may
be discerned from the notes of the Negro Johnson: "Mr. S.
S. Prentiss Dellivered a fine Speech at the Court House in
presence of a very Large Congregation—I was Out today." [96]
From Vicksburg and Natchez, Prentiss visited Jackson and
other cities as he moved north and east in the state.

A new angle of the campaign was the charge of the Democrats that Prentiss was not "safe" on southern rights and
that he was at heart an abolitionist. This may have arisen
out of a joint debate at Gallatin on April 4, with Brown
and the new Democratic opponent, Davis. Brown and
Davis charged that Prentiss, coming from the North, was
identified with Clay, whom they indicted as an abolitionist.
The case against Clay was based on the fact that he had defended the abolitionists in their petitions to Congress.[97]
Quite naturally this aroused the press in support of Prentiss,
particularly the Vicksburg *Register*. In one of its articles it
headed the accusations against Prentiss, "Base and Libelious
Denunciation." The paper then rose to a strong defense. It
pointed to Prentiss' past record in the state, printed the
resolutions on slavery attributed to him in the legislature,
and declared: "If we cannot trust our public men who have
uniformly evinced warm southern feeling and always been
foremost in defense of southern rights, then surely we all
have reason to be jealous of each other. . . . They might
as well have denounced the immortal Lafayette, because,
although he had manifested so great an attachment to this
country, he did not happen to be a citizen of it, as to de-

[94] Claiborne, *Mississippi, as a Province, Territory and State* . . . , I, 449.
[95] Vicksburg *Daily Register*, March 24, 1838.
[96] Diary of William T. Johnson, March 21, 1838.
[97] Ranck, *Albert Gallatin Brown*, 13.

nounce S. S. Prentiss because he happened to have been born in another state." [98] Likewise, the Natchez *Courier* played up the fact that Davis had been in the state but two years while Prentiss had been there for thirteen.[99]

By May 3, enough of the election returns were known for Prentiss to announce that he had won by a majority of fifteen hundred votes.[100] Victory assured, Prentiss and Word started to Washington. In Congress on May 30, Rice Garland of Louisiana "announced that the agreeable duty had been confided to him of apprizing the House that the People of Mississippi had affirmed their decision of November last in favor of Messrs. Prentiss and Word, as the Representatives of the twenty-fifth Congress, and that these gentlemen were now in attendance, ready to take their seats." Upon request of Speaker Polk, the Mississippi representatives stepped forward to be sworn. As Polk prepared to administer the oath, Prentiss interrupted him to state: "In taking that oath, sir, . . . I shall take it under the previous election, and not under the recent one, because in our consciences, we do not believe the latter to be constitutional or valid." [101] The fact that they had been elected was sufficient. "The Speaker made no answer, but administered the oath." [102] Prentiss and Word were duly installed. But reverberations of the disputed Mississippi election were to be heard in Congress as long as Prentiss was a member of that body.

[98] Vicksburg *Daily Register,* April 6, 1838. See also, *ibid.,* April 9, 1838.
[99] Natchez *Daily Courier,* March 31, 1838.
[100] Prentiss to Abby Prentiss, Vicksburg, May 31, 1838, in *Memoir of S. S. Prentiss,* I, 339. For other statements of election results, partial and complete, see Washington *National Intelligencer,* May 12, 22, 1838; *Niles' National Register,* LIV (1838), 161.
[101] *Cong. Globe and Appendix,* 25 Cong., 2 Sess., 416; Washington *National Intelligencer,* May 31, 1838; *Niles' National Register,* LIV (1838), 232–33.
[102] *Memoirs of John Quincy Adams,* IX, 548.

Chapter VI

CONGRESSIONAL CAREER

THERE remained but a limited number of days for Prentiss to represent Mississippi in the second session of the Twenty-fifth Congress. Since he was not seated until the last of May, only a short time was available to him to participate in matters of statecraft before adjournment. He had time enough, however, to make a notable speech against Van Buren's Sub-Treasury Bill, which, having been defeated in the special session of Congress, had been reintroduced. Likewise, Prentiss had enough time to make another effort to vindicate his state in regard to the decision of Congress compelling a third Mississippi election.

On June 11, he introduced a body of eight resolutions bearing upon the Mississippi election controversy. The first five outlined the extent to which a state may choose its representatives free from federal supervision. The last three reiterated that the Mississippi election had been held in compliance with the state's sovereign rights, and that the action of Congress in denying seats to the legally elected representatives from Mississippi was a dangerous violation of these rights, which Congress was obligated to rectify.[1]

But Prentiss did not urge the House to take immediate action on the resolutions. He desired merely to get them on record. He could labor for a favorable vote at a more opportune time. Other weightier matters were pressing during the closing days of the session.

[1] Washington *National Intelligencer*, June 14, 1838; Vicksburg *Daily Sentinel*, July 2, 1838; Shields, *Seargent Smith Prentiss*, 202.

One important issue, the Sub-Treasury Bill, challenged Prentiss' interest and elicited from him his one significant deliberative speech before adjournment. While his vote can be found on such other matters as the bill from the Senate to divide the Territory of Wisconsin,[2] the Indian Hostilities Bill,[3] and the Army Bill,[4] his oratorical efforts were expended, as will be seen, on a subject of much greater interest and concern.

Few stormier sessions of Congress have ever been held than during the administration of Van Buren. The Whig party naturally capitalized on the financial state of affairs, fixing the blame on the Democrats, in an effort to lay the groundwork for the 1840 presidential campaign. Van Buren used methods very different from those of Jackson. Old Hickory had ruled by personal force, Van Buren more by political machinations. All the opposition to Van Buren, at least as far as Prentiss was concerned, focused on the accusation of executive corruption and usurpation. The fight over the Sub-Treasury was Prentiss' advent on the scene.

Prentiss had made clear as early as his campaign against Claiborne and Gholson that he stood for the rechartering of the National Bank. Believing in the efficacy and necessity of the institution, Prentiss threw himself into the debate on the Sub-Treasury Bill, helping to defeat it. On June 20, while the House was deliberating in the Committee of the Whole on this Van Buren measure, he spoke in opposition to it until a motion was passed to adjourn.[5] He completed the speech the next day, speaking before and after the "usual recess." [6] According to the National Intelligencer, this was a speech "of great interest and animation in which he [Prentiss] traced the history of the experiments of the currency, and commented with severity on the course of some

2 Washington National Intelligencer, September 1, 1838.
3 Ibid., June 7, 1838.   4 Ibid., July 3, 1838.
5 Cong. Globe and Appendix, 25 Cong., 2 Sess., 463.
6 Ibid., 465.

gentlemen who had changed their political preferences, and were now the advocates of this bill and of the Administration generally." [7] This speech, delivered but a few days before the House vote, evoked a response from Rhett of South Carolina, who "addressed the Committee for about two hours in support of the Bill, and especially in reply to Mr. Prentiss." [8] When the bill came to a vote on June 25, Prentiss, along with his colleague, Word, registered himself in opposition to it, the vote being 111 for to 125 against. [9]

On July 6, one of the late days of the second session, Prentiss spoke once more. "The bill before the House on its third reading was 'to prevent the issuing and circulation of the bills, notes, and other securities of corporations created by act of Congress which have expired.' " [10] More specifically, the bill sought to prevent "the reception for public dues of notes of twenty dollars denomination, and those of any bank that issued notes of less than five dollars." [11] In the rather limited space accorded to Prentiss' speech in the *Congressional Globe* is the sentence: "He then went into a general opposition to the bill." [12] Fortunately, *Niles' National Register* reported the essence of the speech much more completely, and included the humorous in-

[7] Washington *National Intelligencer*, June 23, 1838. The explanation for the speech not being on record is supplied by Prentiss himself. Writing to his sister, he said: "You will, probably, have seen by the papers that I made a speech against the bill. . . . I don't know whether I shall take the trouble to write out my speech. I had rather make ten than write one; and as I am determined to quit political life, I see no reason for putting myself to the trouble." Prentiss to Anna Prentiss, *House of Representatives*, June 26, 1838, in *Memoir of S. S. Prentiss*, I, 346–47. Because the speech was not available for home consumption after delivery, the Natchez *Courier* blamed belatedness of mail from the North and promised to publish it in whole or in part as soon as it arrived. Natchez *Daily Courier*, July 28, 1838.

[8] Washington *National Intelligencer*, June 28, 1838.

[9] *Ibid.; Cong. Globe and Appendix*, 25 Cong., 2 Sess., 478.

[10] *Cong. Globe and Appendix*, 25 Cong., 2 Sess., 499.

[11] Shields, *Sergeant Smith Prentiss*, 203; *Memoir of S. S. Prentiss*, I, 238.

[12] *Cong. Globe and Appendix*, 25 Cong., 2 Sess., 499.

cidents associated with this seemingly impromptu sarcastic attack against the administration.[13]

Actually the bill had for its purpose, since the Sub-Treasury Bill had been defeated, the making of life more difficult for Nicholas Biddle's Pennsylvania institution. By prohibiting the right to accept bank notes of twenty dollars or less, the bill had the purpose of realizing the basic objective of the Sub-Treasury Bill, of centralizing the financial authority in the chief executive, thereby striking a blow at the past policies of the national bank.

The bill was brought up for consideration at the very close of the session, when many members were anxious for adjournment. That Prentiss realized this is shown in the statement of the *Congressional Globe*, which quoted him as saying: "if this were the last day of the political existence of this Government, let alone the last day of the political existence of this nation, he should debate it." [14]

Prentiss had his moment for sarcastic invective. For some time the House had been in the Committee of the Whole discussing the matter. After a time it was moved "to discharge the committee of the whole . . . that it [the bill] might be brought into the house and acted on." This motion was carried by 100 to 93. Virgil Parris of Maine immediately moved the previous question on the bill. Prentiss rose to a "question of order to inquire if the previous question could be moved before the question pending was stated and put to the house." The Chair ruled that it could not, making the motion of Parris out of order, and opening the way for Prentiss to begin speaking.

A most animated speech followed. Prentiss condemned the bill, "commenting with severity on its introduction at this late moment, and [on] the preconcerted movement . . . to force it through the house with a moment's dis-

[13] For a résumé of Prentiss' speech, see *Niles' National Register,* LIV (1838), 330–31.

[14] *Cong. Globe and Appendix,* 25 Cong., 2 Sess., 499; Shields, *Seargent Smith Prentiss,* 203.

cussion." In his denunciation he called the bill "the last
struggle of the sub-treasury scheme, the last hair of its hyde,
the last puppy of the litter, the rump of the sub-treasury
bill." Because "This bill was of the same family," he advised that the House should "let it go down, and be gathered
to its fathers." The absurdity of the bill was that "it was
directed against that which had no longer any existence.
The United States Bank was dead; it now had neither soul
nor body to be punished." Moreover, "if the bill was meant
to punish the Pennsylvania bank, this government had no
jurisdiction in the case." This gave him the opportunity
to make "an earnest appeal, on this point, to the advocates
of state rights doctrine, calling them to the rescue. If the
government could punish one state corporation it might
another, and so no state bank or state institution of any
kind was safe." His language became more severe in respect
to the advocates of the bill. "As to the old bank," Prentiss
"believed there were many around him who would gladly
turn resurrectionists, dig up the dead body, turn the hall
into a dissecting room, and never lay down the scalpel till
every muscle, tendon, artery, vein and nerve had been laid
bare, and neither form nor substance left."

It is possible that his language may have been stronger
even than that recorded by *Niles' National Register*. At
least, Samuel Cushman called him to order. In response,
Prentiss "demanded that his words, to which exception was
taken be taken down." Apparently regarding the language
as not too abusive, Speaker Polk ruled that Prentiss was
not out of order. Prentiss then "proceeded in a still warmer
strain, alluding to the irritability of conscience of gentlemen, which obscured their notion of order." In continuing, he charged that the administration, by demanding
specie, had been "trying to make gold as plenty as paving
stones; but, like the alchymists, it had succeeded only in
causing what the country had to go off in the fumes of its
alembic." Since the Sub-Treasury Bill had been killed, it

was his belief that "The great administration whale had been harpooned to death, and was now in its dying flurry." Thus, "he was for backing the boats a little, and enjoying the spectacle of its flounces and plunges while it kept the whole sea in a foam. This bill was one of the last blows of its tail. As to these five-dollar bills, the people were the best judges whether they were good money or not," and "if not, they would not take them . . . the bank would issue no more of them, and so the bill was needless." On the other hand, "If the bills were good money, and the people liked it and wanted it, then the bill made war on the wishes of the people; and as to the sin of the matter, they did not need that the government should act as chancellor, to take care of their conscience."

As Prentiss continued to speak, Bronson of New York, in an effort to secure the passage of the bill and cut Prentiss off, demanded the yeas and nays. This gave Adams an opportunity to create a humorous situation. He asked the Speaker whether, if the House should refuse to adjourn, 'the gentleman from Mississippi would lose his right to the floor?" Polk ruled "in strictness," yes, and that Prentiss would really have no right under the rules to continue speaking. Adams then made a point of order, but the Chair ruled him out, pending a motion to adjourn. The vote on adjournment was 16 for to 142 against. Adams rose again to a point of order, saying that since "it had been decided by the house that this bill was to be rammed down the throats of the minority without any discussion, and now the gentleman from Mississippi was presuming to discuss it, he wanted to know if the gentleman was in order. [Laughter]." Speaker Polk retaliated by asking Adams "to reduce his question of order to writing." After Adams did so, Polk really reversed himself and declared Prentiss to be in order. Then Adams inquired if "the speaker's decision would be entered on the journal." The Chair replied affirmatively, and Prentiss continued speaking. According to

Niles' National Register, Prentiss "went on with increased animation, expressing his joy that he had roused the game, and called up the hunters, and that the noble hounds stood on every side straining in their slips, and ready to spring." The reporter for the *Register* stated that Prentiss spoke too rapidly to be reported accurately, but emphasized that, as he continued to speak, he "compared the old currency, before the experiment, to the bread of the people; this the administration had taken away, and given them a stone. But not satisfied with this, they now envied them their little gingercakes of these poor five dollar bills . . . and wanted to take this last remnant of the good times away." This led him to allude to Andrew Jackson, because "He could not but fancy that he heard in the language of the bill the last growls of the old Tennessee lion. How would it make his eyes flash and lighten, to witness this last attack on Biddle and Biddle's bank! It would awaken the 'gaudia certaminis,' the old long-loved joys of the fight, and be almost equal to a glance at the field of New Orleans." Prentiss continued invectives on the bill as he drew to a close. His concluding remarks were aimed at Van Buren's trying to carry out Jacksonian financial policies. "This administration had tried to wield his armor, but they might as well take David's course, and put it off, for it was too heavy for them. They wanted to play the part of Sampson, but they seized hold on the strong pillars of the state after their locks were shorn." His very final contention was: "The administration, by this bill, were passing a tacit compliment on the dead bank; the paper even of the dead bank of the U. S. was better than the paper of this living government. The dead Percy was better than the live Falstaff." This idea he illustrated with the words, "It was said when great julep drinkers died, the mint was seen springing on their graves: it seemed so of this bank of the United States; though it was dead, its money still continued to supply the people with their best currency."

Prentiss had his little hour of what must have been exciting fun. Although he had been in the House but a few days more than a month, he had made himself heard and was clearly identified with those in opposition to Van Buren. There were probably few men in Congress more staunch in their support of the National Bank and in opposition to the Sub-Treasury idea than was Prentiss.

Three days later, July 9, Congress adjourned. Combining a series of speaking engagements with a visit to Maine, Prentiss delayed his return to Mississippi for several weeks. With Henry Wise and the youthful and brilliant young orator from Kentucky, Representative Richard H. Menifee, of whom *The Madisonian* said, "He has not the imagination or fertility of Prentiss . . . but has more strength and equal power of analysis," [15] Prentiss journeyed from Washington to Havre de Grace, Maryland, where the trio addressed the citizens of that place. Wise spoke first, then Menifee, with Prentiss concluding.[16]

Arriving in Portland, Prentiss rested briefly. While preparing to go on a fishing excursion to the White Mountains, "He was set upon by a special committee of Mr. Webster's friends and hurried off to Boston, where at a reception given to the great statesman in Faneuil Hall," [17] he was one of the principal speakers.

It was a gala occasion for Boston. "There were 24 tables spread, a part on the floor of the hall, and the residue in the galleries, a temporary extension which was made for the occasion." [18] Directly above the seats provided for the speakers "was inscribed in large letters the following appropriate motto, taken from Daniel Webster's speech on the Sub-Treasury Bill, delivered in the Senate of the United States March 12, 1838: 'I am, where I ever have been, and ever mean to be: Here standing on the platform of the

15 Washington *Madisonian*, May 15, 1839.
16 Shields, *Seargent Smith Prentiss*, 203.
17 Prentiss, *Bright Side of Life*, I, 49. See also, *Memoir of S. S. Prentiss*, I, 355; Shields, *Seargent Smith Prentiss*, 204.
18 Washington *National Intelligencer*, July 31, 1838.

general Constitution—a platform broad enough and firm enough to uphold every interest of the whole country—I shall still be found.' " [19]

Webster arrived from his country home, Marshfield, and "At a quarter past 3 o'clock, every man was in his seat." [20] One speech followed another before Prentiss was introduced. Governor Edward Everett presided and delivered the opening address. Webster responded, the emotion being such that he "wept under it." [21] Speeches were in turn made by the Mayor of Boston, Governor Oliver Ellsworth of Connecticut, Abbot Lawrence, Pelig Sprague, Menifee, and finally, George Blake, who introduced Prentiss with the toast: *"Mississippi and her distinguished Representative in Congress.* We welcome him most cordially to this Hall, consecrated to the cause of our country and independence. He has fought a good fight, and deserves, and will receive, the gratitude and admiration of his country." [22]

Following this introduction, stated the *National Intelligencer,* "Seargent S. Prentiss came forward, amid a loud and warm greeting, such as has seldom been witnessed, even in old Faneuil Hall. He addressed the audience in a speech of more than an hour, during which he was continually interrupted with loud and continued cheering." The *Intelligencer* thought "His address on this occasion was a brilliant effort, replete with invective and sarcasm against the Administration, poetic imagery, and classical illustration. He spoke with exceeding rapidity, and, being at no loss for words or figures, his ideas seemed to gush from him like water from a fountain. Suffice it to say, his address on this occasion was worthy of his reputation, and fully justifies all the eulogiums which have been made upon his oratory." [23]

---

[19] *Ibid.*   [20] *Ibid.*   [21] *Ibid.*

[22] *Ibid.;* Shields, *Seargent Smith Prentiss,* 205.

[23] Washington *National Intelligencer,* July 31, 1838. No complete or exact account of this speech seems available. It was a highly extemporaneous effort which Prentiss doubtless never put in writing. Available accounts

Prentiss strove for what may be termed three objectives in his speech. He eulogized Webster and Massachusetts, condemned the Van Buren administration on several scores, and pleaded the cause of the Union.

Early in the speech Prentiss drew the analogy that "Faneuil Hall may be justly styled the Mecca of Liberty." Because of its patriotic significance, he declared in language of Biblical connotation: "I would recommend those troubled with political maladies to come here. This is a Bethesda in which they may wash and be clean from whatever disease they have. Yes, let the lame, the halt, and the blind and those possessed of Loco-foco devils all come here and be made whole."

Since Van Burenism and locofocoism were always synonymous in his mind, they became the target of his invective. The panic conditions of the country, Jackson's specie circular, the refusal of Jackson and Van Buren to recharter the Bank, and the battles in the preceding session of Congress over the Sub-Treasury were all fresh in the minds of his audience. It was but natural, then, that he should speak in strong language of the government in power. Because of what he held to be evils in Van Burenism, he declared: "I do sincerely believe that never since men have dwelt upon the face of this green earth and had rulers over them was there ever an administration seen in any country of the globe or in any age of time more utterly callous to the sufferings or the wishes of the people. . . . No other people on the face of the earth but the free citizens of this republic would ever have submitted to it. No, sir, not in Turkey it-

are evidently those of reporters then present. The reporter for the *National Intelligencer* was able to furnish only fragments, stating: "We are convinced that no adequate account of the matter will be reported; and the manner, the unique, the fervid, the glowing, living, breathing, burning, and captivating manner will of course be lost." *Ibid*. Of the speech included in the *Memoir of S. S. Prentiss*, I, 359–69, George Prentiss concludes: "This report, the only tolerable one of Mr. P's speech, appeared in the N. Y. *Journal of Commerce*. Several others were published, but they are little better than caricatures." *Memoir of S. S. Prentiss*, I, 359. For another account, differing somewhat, see Shields, *Seargent Smith Prentiss*, 205–12.

self. Had the sultan by his despotic edict suddenly thrown the subjects of his throne as far back from their previous condition, bad as it might have been, as this country has been thrown back by the mad experiments on its currency, he would in the next night have slept in the Bosphorus."

Interweaving references to the disputed Mississippi election with additional charges against the weaknesses of the Van Buren administration, Prentiss moved to the great theme of Unionism. Specifically he indicted Van Buren with attempts at "arraying the local prejudices in mutual hostility —by stirring up a sectional warfare between the North and the South, the West and the East," but at the same time maintained that there were other mightier forces at work which would never permit of disunion. Of these he said: "The laboring population of this country mean to live together as one people, and who shall disannul their purpose? See how they are conquering time and space! See the thousand steamboats that traverse our lakes and rivers; ay, and that Leviathian-like, begin to make the ocean itself *to boil like a pot!* Look at their railroad cars glancing like fiery meteors from one end of the land to the other; blazing centaurs with untiring nerves, with unwasting strength, and who seem to go, too, on the grand *temperance* principle, laboring all day on *water* only! (Laughter and loud cheering.) Think you the American people will suffer their cars to stop, their railroads to be broken in twain, and all their majestic rivers severed or changed in their course because their politicians choose to draw a dividing line between a Northern and a Southern Empire?"

Prentiss, both a northern and a southern man, was never more sincere than when he was speaking in behalf of the Union. Among his concluding remarks were the words: "Yes, we are one people for weal or for woe. When I cannot come from Mississippi and call the men of Boston my fellow-citizens, my kindred, my brethren, I desire no longer to be myself a citizen of the republic." Prentiss ended by offering the toast: "The Commonwealth of this Republic; second to none in the ability, integrity, and patriotism which she has always contributed to sustain it."

Prentiss had spoken in Faneuil Hall. Moreover, he had held the attention of an audience at ten o'clock at night after it had been at the banquet tables since three o'clock in the afternoon. It is doubtful that the speech he gave was one of his greatest, but he did not fail to measure up to what was expected of him. Fortunately there has been preserved the impressions of one who heard the speech, Edward Everett, albeit they were written years after the delivery and even after Prentiss' death. Nevertheless, Everett recounted how Prentiss "rose at a rather late hour, and after a succession of able speakers," and stated: "He was, however, from the outset completely successful. He took possession of the audience from the first sentence, and carried them along with unabated interest, I think for above an hour." The highest praise which Everett gave was: "It seemed to me the most wonderful specimen of a sententious fluency which I had ever witnessed." Everett recorded, too, the reaction of Webster. Everett, sitting beside Webster, "asked him if he had ever heard anything like it?" Webster replied: "Never, except from Mr. Prentiss himself." [24] One other, among the many expressions of praise of the speech, must have made Prentiss happy. A paper from his home town of Portland stated: "Mr. Prentiss said that it was the first time he had heard the echo of his own voice in old Faneuil Hall,—and every man who heard him was anxious that it should not be the last." [25]

When Prentiss returned to Maine he was the recipient of an invitation from his fellow townsmen in Portland to

[24] Edward Everett to George Prentiss, Cambridge, Mass., February 5, 1851, in *Memoir of S. S. Prentiss*, I, 357.
[25] Portland *Evening Advertiser*, July 26, 1838.

be the guest of honor at a public dinner and to speak to the Whigs of that city.[26] He refused, "and to escape further importunity he once more 'fled to the White Mountains.' "[27] With members of his immediate family, he enjoyed a happy vacation. George Prentiss stated: "It would be easy to fill a chapter with pleasant reminiscences of this excursion. He also resorted to the Great Brook, and nothing could exceed the boyish delight with which he sought out the old 'holes,' and abandoned himself to the memories of other days. There was an indescribable sweetness and *bonhomie* in his temper at such times. He was careful, also, to call upon the old neighbors, and have a talk with them about the past and the present."[28]

Another invitation for a speech came to him from the Whigs of Augusta, Maine, but he felt compelled to decline it.[29] At the same time he did respond favorably to a letter from the Mayor and other citizens of New York asking him to speak there in the Masonic Hall. En route to Mississippi, Prentiss appeared in New York on August 17.[30]

Prentiss evidently pleased the Whigs of New York immensely. As recounted by the *National Intelligencer:* "The Whigs of this city last night, in Masonic Hall, gave Mr. Prentiss, of Mississippi, one of the heartiest and proudest tributes it is possible for a great city in a Republic to pay to a public man. It was felt here, that a great deal was due to the State of Mississippi, which, in a very critical time, discharged its high political duty so handsomely, and a great deal due also to Mr. Prentiss, who had been so instrumental in a proper discharge of that duty. . . . Notwithstanding the meeting was summoned for a summer night, the rush was immense; and this great concourse of people Mr. Pren-

[26] Washington *National Intelligencer,* August 16, 1838. For the letter of invitation to Prentiss and his reply, see *Niles' National Register,* LIV (1838), 391.
[27] Shields, *Seargent Smith Prentiss,* 213.
[28] *Memoir of S. S. Prentiss,* I, 371.
[29] Washington *National Intelligencer,* August 4, 1838.
[30] *Ibid.,* August 16, 1838.

tiss had the faculty of keeping in silence over an hour and a half." [31]

In Vicksburg again, it was his obligation to speak to his local constituency and to give account of his stewardship. For a full two hours he spoke to the people. Of his speech the Vicksburg *Register* said: "The argument was convincing, and its effects were visible on every countenance. . . . He commented upon the Sub-Treasury scheme, and handled *Southern agitators* without gloves. His wit amused, his satire stung, and his fertile imagination elucidated his argument in the happiest manner." He did not fail to touch on his familiar theme of preserving the country undivided. "When he alluded to the dissolution of the Union—to the fact that there were 'some things we could not divide' and asked how we could divide the memory of Bunker Hill and Lexington, and what share of the bones of our forefathers who fell in the battles of the Revolution would fall to Mississippi, and what share of that portrait of 'old Washington' which hangs in the Capitol, you might see many a freeman nerved anew, and the patriot tear glittering in many an eye." One part of the speech was heard with regret, though, for "At the close, Mr. Prentiss announced his determination not to become a candidate for re-election." This caused a general cry of "no! no!" [32]

There were reasons why it was time for Prentiss to return to Mississippi and address his constituents. The Democratic papers and Van Buren supporters had been at work undermining his prestige. Prentiss was aware of this, and replied to his attackers: "It is the fashionable slang of the day to denounce the Whig party of the South in the most unqualified terms, as leagued with the abolitionists, traitors to their own interests, enemies to their institutions, and

[31] *Ibid.*, August 18, 1838.

[32] Vicksburg *Register*, quoted *ibid.*, October 31, 1838. See also, *Niles' National Register*, LV (1838–1839), 161; Shields, *Seargent Smith Prentiss*, 216; *Memoir of S. S. Prentiss*, I, 378. For a résumé of the speech, see *Memoir of S. S. Prentiss*, I, 379–80.

other such phrases. Southern Democracy, it seems, consists in general abuse of the rest of the Union, a denial of the existence of any common interest with the North, and a bitter denunciation of every man who has the independence to refuse assent to these strange dogmas." Prentiss could speak from personal experience. "I had occasion myself to travel North," he said, "a few months since, on private business; I was treated with a kindness and hospitality, intended entirely as an expression of good feeling towards the State I represented. Yet have I been most bitterly abused for responding to these courtesies; for daring to break bread and eat salt with our Northern brethren, and especially for so far violating Southern policy as to have wickedly visited the cradle of liberty, and most sacriligiously entered old Faneuil Hall." His answer to these charges was: "I could pity these foolish men, whose patriotism consists in hating everything beyond the limited horizon of their narrow minds; but contempt and scorn will not allow of the more amiable sentiment." On still another score he answered his critics: "It is said against me, that I have Northern feelings. Well, so I have; and Southern, and Eastern, and Western, and I trust that I shall ever, as a citizen of this Republic, have liberality enough to embrace within the scope of my feelings both its cardinal points and its cardinal interests." [33]

Prentiss had no doubt who his friends and enemies were. Of the various Mississippi newspapers, two, the Natchez *Courier* and the Vicksburg *Register* gave him unqualified support. Two others, the Vicksburg *Sentinel* and the *Mississippi Free Trader and Natchez Daily Gazette,* did all in their power to link him with the abolitionists of the North and stamp him an enemy of the slave interests of the South. Prentiss and other southern Whigs were beginning to experience in the late 1830's the difficulties involved in trying to persuade southerners that their institutions were safe

[33] *Memoir of S. S. Prentiss,* I, 379.

while abolitionists of the North were members of the same political party. Nevertheless, he raised his voice in behalf of the Union as he saw a tide of public opinion beginning to move in the opposite direction.

As for support, he certainly enjoyed it in the Natchez *Courier*. About the time he returned from Maine in the summer of 1838, there appeared in the paper the following observations: "Never in the history of our country have we seen an instance, where a man of his age, or of his length of service, as a public man, has received such unusual—such high and proud demonstrations of honor and respect, of warm greeting and admiration, as has Mr. Prentiss received during his present absence from Mississippi. No where but in a newspaper office, where newspapers are received by the hundreds or the bushel, can a person form a tolerable idea of the extensive respect and admiration which his talents command." [34] The *Courier* gave especially praiseworthy comments to the readers of the paper in respect to Prentiss' Faneuil Hall speech. "Mr. S. S. Prentiss, the young and gifted member of Congress from Mississippi, is decidedly the 'Lion' of the North at the present moment. His oratory has passed the severe ordeal of New England's most classic scholarship; and the old Bay State hails with heart-felt pride one of her own sons, who, after an absence of a few years, returns to visit the land of his fathers, covered with the honors which, as the architect of his own fortune, he has gathered in his adopted State." [35]

But all this was in great contrast to the vituperations of certain opposition papers. The other Natchez paper, the *Mississippi Free Trader and Natchez Daily Gazette,* announced his return: "Mr. Prentiss arrived in Vicksburg, preceded and followed by . . . earthquake signals, but without any outrageous outburst of human passion. He boards at Childre's—looks remarkably full-faced and fat

[34] Natchez *Daily Courier*, September 21, 1838.
[35] *Ibid.*, August 28, 1838.

instead of 'travel-worn,' has an excellent appetite, and is about to lay on another streak of fat, by partaking of a dinner to be tendered him by his fellow-citizens, who think that the Yankee Abolitionists must have nearly starved their chivalrous representative to death, in their mock temperance dinners at the North." [36]

The Vicksburg *Sentinel* was equally, if not more, outspoken against him. Though it had aided him in the contest against Claiborne and Gholson, it turned in wrath against him after he went to Congress, because of his opposition to the Sub-Treasury. Prentiss would have had to be an anti-Bank man to keep its support. Of the Vicksburg dinner and speech it had little more to say than that Prentiss spoke for two hours, that he announced he would not be a candidate for re-election, and that "A large number of toasts were drunk; almost entirely of a party character." [37]

Actually this passing reference to the welcome given Prentiss by the people of Vicksburg was complimentary compared with its castigations of him on August 31, when it quoted the Washington *Chronicle* regarding the Faneuil Hall appearance: "If the nullifiers of Mississippi are satisfied with the course of Mr. Prentiss, it will only show that they are not now that which they have been. For a Southern man—a southern Representative—a State Rights Delegate to be found carousing in Faneuil Hall with the thrice dyed disciples of the Federal school—speaking and shouting and extolling Daniel Webster as the 'invincible champion—the Hercules who slew the hydra of Nullification' and gulping down wine by the quart in honor of that 'distinguished Whig' John Q. Adams for his independent and manly defense of the right of free discussion (i. e. Abolition Petitions—) has something surpassingly mysterious and perfectly incomprehensible to us. Such State Rights demonstra-

---

[36] *Mississippi Free Trader and Natchez Daily Gazette,* October 5, 1838.
[37] Vicksburg *Daily Sentinel,* October 8, 1838.

tion may be understood at the 'Mecca of Whigism,' but it has no interpreter here." [38]

The *Sentinel,* throughout the autumn of 1838, continued to denounce Prentiss. Typical of its remarks was a letter to the editor, signed "Forever a Citizen," and published September 12. One expression was: "the Whigs—considering the political situation of our State at least doubtful, they have undertaken to convince the electors of the State of Mississippi what a wonderful, remarkable, extraordinary talented man they have as a representative—a very comet whose tail can be seen as far down east as Maine, when the body itself is in far distant Mississippi." [39] Another comment of "Forever a Citizen," and one extremely interesting in view of the fact that the *Sentinel* had supported Prentiss during the disputed election controversy, was this: "I refer to the deprivation of a certain sovereign State in her might and majesty, by a most unjust, illegal and improper decision, of a representative for a long space of time, to wit, for the space of two long months contrary to the form of the statute in such cases made and provided, and to the very great injury and degradation of said State. This fact appears indelibly imprinted on the mind of the orator, so that time can neither blot out or deface it—indeed it has become his political hobby horse, to which he adheres with the tenacity of an uncle Toby." Consequently, "Should he wish to perform a political campaign, he mounts his hobby. Does he wish to visit his friends of the North? this horse is to be accoutered for the service, or even should circumstances compel him to fight the Moslem Chief with turban on his head and the keen edged scimitar of logic in his hand. No matter where the battle is to be fought or under what circumstances, he must first mount his hobby horse before he can venture to the contest. In short, no matter

[38] Washington *Chronicle,* quoted in Vicksburg *Daily Sentinel,* August 31, 1838.
[39] Vicksburg *Daily Sentinel,* September 12, 1838.

what the time, the occasion or the subject, this Bucephalus is paraded on the carpet." [40]

The third session of the Twenty-fifth Congress found Prentiss in his place. As he arrived in Washington and proceeded in his duties as representative, he made another attempt to revive the disputed Mississippi election controversy by introducing a body of eight resolutions (substantially the same ones he had presented toward the close of the second session) stating the facts of the case, and demanding that the action of Congress in declaring earlier against the election of himself and Word be rescinded. Speaker Polk ruled that his resolutions should "lie over." Prentiss insisted that they should be "considered soon" and moved to fix "a certain day for their consideration." The motion was put to the House, and was opposed by so many "nays" that they were not counted.[41] Prentiss gave up temporarily the attempt to get action, but in January he again asked Congress to take up his resolutions. He succeeded no better this time,[42] with the result that he made no further attempt to ask for this congressional favor or consideration.

As in the second session of the Twenty-fifth Congress when the Sub-Treasury scheme became the chief item of interest to Prentiss, in the third session one single matter, so far as Prentiss was concerned, dominated all else. This was the Samuel Swartwout defalcations. If ever an opposition party found a gratifying fragment it was in this instance when an administrative appointee proved to be a thief of public money. Financial corruption in the Administration was exactly what the Whigs needed to cry out for political

[40] *Ibid.*

[41] *Cong. Globe*, 25 Cong., 3 Sess., 88; *Niles' National Register*, LV (1838–1839), 315.

[42] Washington *National Intelligencer*, January 15, 1839. Shields sums up neatly the efforts of Prentiss on this matter: "He brought them up again on the last day of the year 1838, and again on the 12th of January, 1839, at the third session of the Twenty-fifth Congress. But inasmuch as the substance of the resolutions had been accepted or achieved by his *actual occupancy* of the seat, no further action was taken upon them so far as I can trace." Shields, *Seargent Smith Prentiss*, 202.

purity. To what extent the Whigs were really interested in purity, or in using this incident to advance their own ulterior motive of getting into power, may not be much of a question of speculation. Nevertheless, the Swartwout case was probably Van Buren's greatest single embarrassment. It was another instance of Van Buren's reaping the whirlwind of the Jacksonian era. Jackson appointed men subservient to himself. When one who held office over into Van Buren's period proved unworthy and corrupt, the road was made more difficult for Van Buren. Senators and representatives like Prentiss made maximum capital of the ammunition supplied them.

Swartwout had been appointed collector of customs at New York in 1829, was reappointed in 1834, and served until 1838. According to a report of the Secretary of the Treasury, Levi Woodbury, it was discovered that his misuses of funds dated from 1830, and that after he had gone abroad, his defalcations amounted to $1,374,119. Suits had been instituted, and $30,000 had been recovered.[43] Following an outline of the weaknesses of the custom laws, the Secretary recommended that Congress take steps to increase the clerical force at the port, and to make "more seasonable and thorough examination of the bad accounts." [44]

This instance of flagrant corruption in the Democratic ranks gave Prentiss and others an ideal opportunity to speak out. Prentiss chose to deal with Swartwout somewhat incidentally, but with the party most emphatically. He began his defalcation speech December 26, the House being in Committee of the Whole.[45] Adams noted that Prentiss "commenced an ardent and impetuous speech against the Administration, of which he delivered, however, only the

---

[43] *Niles' National Register*, LV (1838–1839), 275.

[44] *Ibid.*, 276.

[45] *Ibid.*, 285; Washington *National Intelligencer*, December 27, 29, 1838. For texts of the speech, see *Memoir of S. S. Prentiss*, II, 12–41; Shields, *Seargent Smith Prentiss*, 216–36; Washington *National Intelligencer*, February 5, 1839.

introduction. I suppose him charged with a speech of at least three hours." [46] He was so charged, for the next day Adams stated, with none too much enthusiasm for Prentiss' effort: "Prentiss, of Mississippi, concluded, in three hours and a quarter, a speech he had begun yesterday against the President, the Secretary of the Treasury, and the Administration. He did very little more than travel over the ground preoccupied by Wise—recurred to the same acts of malversation in the subordinate officers, the same culpable connivance in the Secretary of the Treasury, and the same documents substantiating the facts. He appeared to be heard, too, with the same indifference and the same dropping off of the administration members from their seats." [47]

Although at a disadvantage in having been preceded by Bell and Wise, as well as by others of his own party, Prentiss did his best to score heavily against the Democratic party. Almost leaving Swartwout out of the picture, and using the incident for a broader attack, he hit at manifold instances of financial corruption. He stated, using ample documentary evidence, that the collectors at Fort Wayne, Indiana, Columbus, Mississippi, and Vandalia, Illinois, were guilty of the same offense as Swartwout, and made it evident that their dishonesty had been kept secret until after the election of 1836 and that they had never been discharged, one or two being allowed merely to resign.

The administration's spoils system and executive patronage bore the brunt of the attack. Actually Prentiss contended that Swartwout's irregularities were used to take the attention of the public from other cases. On this point he asserted: "But our attention is called, particularly, to the case of Swartwout. The Administration has delivered him over to our tender mercies; they have dropped him as the bear, when hotly pursued, drops one of her cubs, for the purpose of distracting the attention of the hunter, and so

---

[46] *Memoirs of John Quincy Adams*, X, 78.   [47] *Ibid.*, 79.

escaping with the rest of her young. I, for one, shall not be thus diverted from my purpose, but will follow the dam to her den, and there, if possible, crush at once the whole brood." Prentiss was thus indicting the sincerity of Van Buren in bringing the Swartwout case to the attention of Congress. Unfair as this may have been, he went on with stinging words. "No, sir, it is a mere *ruse*. Regardless of the maxim that 'there is honor among thieves,' the rest of the office-holders are very willing to turn State's evidence against Swartwout, to gain immunity for themselves, and favor with the commonwealth."

The examination of the other instances of defalcations led Prentiss to include a very considerable amount of documentary evidence. When he had done this, and had accused the Secretary of the Treasury of being just as guilty as the offenders for not removing them, he summarized this particular charge: "Sir, I have given you but two or three cases of defalcations; Would time permit, I could give you a hundred. Like the fair Sultana of the oriental legends, I could go on for a thousand and one nights; and even as in those Eastern stories, so in the chronicles of the office-holders, the tale would ever be of heaps of gold, massive ingots, uncounted riches. Why, sir, Aladdin's lamp was nothing to it. They seem to possess the identical cap of Fortunatus; some wish for $50,000, some for $100,000, some for a million; and behold, it lies in glittering heaps before them."

All this Prentiss laid at the door of Jacksonian and Van Buren spoils. Against such forces it had been most difficult to protest. He illustrated this by eulogizing an earlier senator from Mississippi, George Poindexter, who committed political suicide when he dared to counter Jackson and ask for certain investigations. Poindexter's case was typical, Prentiss felt, of what happened when a senator manifested a measure of independence.

Prentiss' conclusion was that since so much financial corruption had crept into the government, the only solution was a change of rulers. He expected no reform from within, because it was impossible. In answer to his own inquiry as to why the collectors at Fort Wayne, Vandalia, and Columbus had not been removed, he replied: "The administration did not dare to remove them, even had it wished to do so; like pashas, they had become too powerful for the sultan, and would not have hesitated in twisting the bowstring round the neck of the messenger who presented it." In this connection he attacked what Woodbury had proposed as a reform. To make up the losses caused by Swartwout, the Secretary of the Treasury had suggested certain retrenchments. To this feeble effort at reform, wherein the basic evil was in no wise being eradicated, Prentiss asked, "What branches of the public service are to be lopped off on account of the licentious rapacity of the office-holders?" He answered: "Pensions, harbors, and light-houses." Such suggestions offered ideal opportunity for Prentiss to use emotional oratory in replying. "First of all, the scarred veterans of the Revolution are to be deprived of a portion of the scanty pittance doled out to them by the cold charity of the country. How many of them will you have to send forth as beggars upon the very soil which they wrenched from the hand of tyranny, to make up the amount of even one of these splendid robberies?" Continuing, he asked: "How many harbors will it take—those improvements dedicated no less to humanity than to interest; those nests of commerce to which the canvas-winged birds of the ocean flock for safety?" Finally he inquired, "How many light-houses will it take? . . . How many of those faithful sentinels who stand along our rocky coast, and, peering far out in the darkness, give timely warning to the hardy mariner when the lee-shore threatens—how many of these, I ask, are to be discharged from their humane service? Why, the proposition is almost impious. I should as soon wish to put out the stars of heaven."

One other administrative recommendation came in for

attention. In this he saw one more opportunity to attack the principles of the Sub-Treasury while delivering the speech. Since Prentiss saw in Van Buren's designs a gigantic attempt to centralize rigidly all monetary affairs in the executive, he denounced the request of the President and the Secretary of the Treasury for more stringent laws to prevent future recurrences comparable to the Swartwout incident. "But I understand the Executive goes still further," Prentiss declared, "and, pointing to these very defalcations, demands an additional band of officers to watch the rest and prevent them from walking *in the footsteps of their predecessors.*" His contemptuous answer was: "So Pisistratus gashed himself with unseemly wounds, and telling the people that they had been inflicted by his enemies, asked for an additional guard to protect him. His request was granted. Fifty men were given him, with whom he immediately seized upon the citadel and became the tyrant of Athens. Let the lesson not be lost when you are asked to increase the number of office-holders." [48]

Aware of the movement under way to appoint a House committee to investigate the amount of the defalcations, Prentiss made himself clear on this issue, telling the House as he drew his speech to a close: "I shall vote in the House for an investigation, though I do not expect much from it. My hope is in an investigation by a higher authority than this House,—by the people. The evil of the times lies not in particular cases, but in the principles of the party. Legislation cannot reach it. It is a radical evil, and the people alone can cure it. That they will do so, and in the only way it can be done, by a change *of rulers,* I have a high and holy confidence."

This was his chief speech in this session. He was severe, uninhibited, and unrestrained. Much of his knowledge of classical literature and history he used in numerous figures

[48] This passage does not occur in the version of the speech in *Memoir of S. S. Prentiss*, II, but does in Shields, *Seargent Smith Prentiss*, 234.

and analogies. If he was sincere in his determination to seek no further political office, it might be inferred that he was driven by righteous indignation. Yet it must not be forgotten that he was a Whig, and the objective of his party was power too. The day following the speech he wrote to his sister: "Yesterday I made a speech; my text was the corruption and profligacy of the present Administration, and I did not spare the lash, in exposing their folly and wickedness. The recent defalcations of Swartwout and others formed the subject of debate, which was warmly carried on for several days." [49]

In the course of discussion on the general subject of defaulters, Wise, on December 28, moved to print 20,000 extra copies of certain documents pertaining to the subject.[50] These were concerned with more than the Swartwout case and contained the very things which Prentiss had embodied in his speech. In January, as Wise's motion was debated, Prentiss spoke in favor of it: "The great oyster bed had not been disturbed for years . . . and he did not doubt that another grab would bring above water larger and fatter oysters than any which had yet been opened. Yes, there were other fine fish below, which had not yet been hooked up or speared. He was for trying all ways to get them; lines, nets, spears, harpoons; any means and all means he was for trying, so that by some means the fish might be made to appear above water." [51] The resolution passed by a vote of 100 to 82.[52]

During January the House took steps to institute an official inquiry into the Swartwout irregularities by passing a resolution for the appointment of a select committee of investigation.[53] Prentiss helped to carry this resolution in a close vote of 113 to 105 on January 12.[54] The problem of

[49] Prentiss to Anna Prentiss, Washington, December 28, 1838, in *Memoir of S. S. Prentiss*, II, 10.
[50] *Cong. Globe*, 25 Cong., 3 Sess., 70.
[51] *Ibid.*, 74.   [52] *Ibid.*, 114.
[53] *Ibid.*, 128; Washington *National Intelligencer*, January 17, 1839.
[54] Washington *National Intelligencer*, January 19, 1839.

securing a committee proved most difficult, however. The committee chosen on January 17, after repeated ballotings, consisted of James Harlan, Edward Curtis, Henry Wise, William C. Dawson, Francis Smith, Franklin Elmore, Samuel Cushman, George Hopkins, and Edward Hubley.[55] The next day Elmore, Cushman, and Hubley all asked to be excused. Joshua Martin, William Taylor, and David Wagener were designated to take their places.[56] A day later Taylor declined to serve. The reason reported was "that all the gentlemen of the anti-Administration party were distinguished lawyers, while Mr. T. was not a member of that profession." [57]

The repeated requests to be relieved brought Prentiss into action again. He conceived the motives for declining membership on the committee to be a concerted effort of the Democrats to defeat the committee entirely. His sarcastic remark to the excuse offered by Taylor was that he, "as a member of the medical profession, was better qualified to serve on the committee than a lawyer, because they were to examine into the diseases of the body politic, and apply the knife to its corruptions." [58] The request of Taylor was granted, however, and Henry Foster of New York was chosen in his place.[59] The committee as finally organized consisted of Harlan of Kentucky, Wise of Virginia, Dawson of Georgia, Curtis of New York, Smith of Maine, Hopkins of Virginia, Foster of New York, Owens of Georgia, and Wagener of Pennsylvania. The committee went to New York soon afterwards and held its hearings in the Astor House.[60]

The subject of defalcations had interested Prentiss greatly during December and January. In contrast to his feelings after his Sub-Treasury speech in the preceding session, when he had no inclination to write it up, he now set himself,

[55] *Cong. Globe*, 25 Cong., 3 Sess., 132.
[56] *Ibid.*, 133–34; Washington *National Intelligencer*, January 19, 1839.
[57] *Cong. Globe*, 25 Cong., 3 Sess., 134.   [58] *Ibid.*
[59] *Ibid.*, 135.   [60] *Niles' National Register*, LV (1838–1839), 337.

during the last days of January, to putting his defalcation address on paper for publication. On January 31, he wrote to Anna Prentiss: "I have been quite busy the last two or three days in writing out the speech I delivered on the 27th and 28th of December. I had neglected it so long that I should not have written it at all but for the strong solicitations of my political friends, who are kind enough to believe it will do some good." [61] A few days later in a letter to George Prentiss he gave more specific reasons why he wrote it out, as well as his rather low estimate of it: "I overcame my laziness last week sufficiently to write out my speech upon the Defalcations. It came out in the *Intelligencer* yesterday morning, and I have it also printing in pamphlet form for home consumption. It is not a very argumentative speech; indeed, the subject-matter did not well admit of it. . . . The speech, of course, does not contain one-half of what I said; I wrote it more for use than show; and made it short and spicy, to attract the popular taste." [62] An interesting example of how the speech was used at home may be inferred by the announcement of the Natchez *Courier:* "We are indebted to the Hon. Mr. Prentiss, for a valuable Document entitled *'Defaulting Collectors'* forming a ponderous volume of 437 pages. . . . We intend to have it bound as an appendix to the Speeches of Messrs. Wise and Prentiss. The volume to be labelled, *Sub-Treasuryism Illustrated.*" [63]

A reverberation of the defalcations episode brought Prentiss to the floor again in February, this time to lash forth at a fellow congressman. After the incident he wrote to his sister: "I have been very busy lately, as you will have

[61] Prentiss to Anna Prentiss, Washington, January 31, 1839, in *Memoir of S. S. Prentiss*, II, 43.

[62] *Id.* to George Prentiss, Washington, February 3, 1839, *ibid.*, 44. It may be inferred from this statement of Prentiss that the versions of the speech preserved are inadequate accounts of what he actually delivered. This would be true if for no other reason than that an entire month elapsed between the time he delivered the speech and the time he wrote it for publication and home consumption.

[63] Natchez *Daily Courier*, March 14, 1839.

seen by the papers. Among other things, I undertook the very unprofitable task of purifying the House of a great blackguard, by the name of ————. I did not succeed; but I think a lesson was given, which such fellows will not soon forget. It was quite an amusing scene throughout." [64]

The "blackguard" alluded to in this letter was Alexander Duncan, representative from Ohio. On February 21, Prentiss rose to a question of privilege, and presented a resolution: "1. Whether . . . Duncan . . . be the author of a certain publication or publications, under his name, in relation to the proceedings of this House and certain members thereof, published in the Globe newspaper of the 19th inst. 2. Whether by said publication or publications . . . he has not been guilty of a violation of the privileges of this House, of an offense against its peace, dignity, and good order; and of such grossly indecent, ungentlemanly, disgraceful and dishonorable misconduct as renders him unworthy of his seat in this House, and justly liable to expulsion from the same." [65]

The episode had its origin in the debates on the Swartwout case. On January 16 and 17 Duncan spoke on the resolution then before the House to appoint a committee to investigate Swartwout's defalcations. He was followed by Edward Stanly of North Carolina, who insinuated that Duncan was an abolitionist. This charge Duncan answered in the *Globe* on the nineteenth, using such brazen language that Prentiss was led to move that he be expelled. Of Stanly's insinuations, and in justification of his publications in the *Globe,* Duncan stated in the House: "I promptly pronounced the insinuation a base falsehood, and a foul detraction, whether it dwelt upon the lips of the unprincipled calumniator, or floated on the breezes of the corrupt, poisonous, and slanderous Federal sheets of the day. My intention

[64] Prentiss to Anna Prentiss, House of Representatives, March 3, 1839, in *Memoir of S. S. Prentiss,* II, 45.

[65] *Cong. Globe,* 25 Cong., 3 Sess., 209; *Niles' National Register,* LVI (1839), 12.

at the time was to insult the member. So he understood me. So all who heard me understood me. My meaning was that the *member* was a base liar and a foul calumniator; and the only reason that he was *indirectly* thus denounced, was because the rules of the House prohibited me from doing it *directly*, without laying myself liable to its censure." [66]

The whole episode was further complicated by the fact that Stanly had replied to Duncan in the House when Duncan was not present. His speech was subsequently published in the *National Intelligencer* on February 4. Duncan denied that the speech, "purporting to be 'the remarks of Mr. Stanly, in reply to Dr. Duncan,'" was ever actually delivered "except through the polluted columns of the corrupt, Bank bought, servile and degraded sheet, through which it makes its appearances; therefore, its very caption or title contains a base falsehood, and a mean attempt at fraud and imposition upon the public. Its whole body is a tissue of misrepresentations, unmanly insinuations, and low vulgarity, worthy of the man that can be charged with base falsehood and foul detraction with impunity." [67]

Such language seemed too much for the finer sensibilities of Prentiss and others in the House. Prentiss consented to a modification of his resolution to expel Duncan by a motion of Waddy Thompson "That the said Alexander Duncan, has . . . subjected himself to the just censure of the House; and that he be reprimanded therefore by the Speaker in the presence of the House." [68] But Prentiss and his colleagues fought a losing fight against Duncan. By a vote of 117 to 94 the matter was laid on the table. [69]

The third session of Congress was nearly ended. Prentiss had failed to persuade Congress to right the wrong which he maintained had been committed against Mississippi. Moreover, he remembered in particular the deciding vote

[66] *Cong. Globe*, 25 Cong., 3 Sess., 210.   [67] *Ibid.*, 212.
[68] *Ibid.*, 213; *Niles' National Register*, LVI (1839), 12.
[69] *Cong. Globe*, 25 Cong., 3 Sess., 214; *Niles' National Register*, LVI (1839), 12.

of Speaker Polk which sent him back to Mississippi for a third election. He took advantage of one more opportunity to speak his wrath against Polk.

On March 3, as the House disposed of its last duties preparatory to adjournment the day following, Elmore of South Carolina moved the customary resolution that Polk receive the thanks of the House "for the able, impartial, and dignified manner in which he has presided over its deliberations, and performed the arduous and important duties of the Chair." [70] This was too much for Prentiss to swallow. It was common knowledge that he did not intend a further political career. He had little to lose in taking a parting fling at one who had, as he thought and felt, dealt unjustly with him. Prentiss told the House that he could not assent to the resolution, and that Polk had not been impartial. Discerning other motives in the resolution, he admitted that he "had no objections to uttering a courteous farewell to the Speaker as a gentleman, and wishing him a pleasant journey home; *but he believed this vote of thanks was to be used as so much political capital, to do political business upon,* and he for one, was not disposed to furnish it."

Prentiss made no reference to the Mississippi election case. He had other quantities of ammunition which would go far to refute the virtue of impartiality attributed to Polk in the pending resolution. Proceeding to his specific evidence, he pointed out, first, that the House, presumably without adequate confidence in the Speaker, had refused to allow him to appoint the committee to investigate the Swartwout defalcation charges. Second, he examined the political complexion of the major committees appointed by Polk. The Committee on Foreign Affairs, Prentiss reminded the House, had been made to consist of six administration men to three of the opposition. Likewise, the Committee on Ways and Means

[70] *Cong. Globe,* 25 Cong., 3 Sess., 250; Washington *National Intelligencer,* March 5, 1839.

was divided six to three in favor of the Democrats. The Committee on Elections was organized with a Democratic majority of seven to two, as was also the Judiciary Committee. Third, Prentiss contrasted the Democratic majorities on the major committees with the Whig majorities on the unimportant ones. In regard to these he called upon the House to consider that "The Committee on Manufactures contained *eight* Whigs to *one* administration. . . . Then came the Committee on Roads and Canals. . . . It contained seven Whigs. . . . So in the Committee on Revisal and Unfinished Business, seven to two. In the little Committees on Expenditures in the various Departments, it was still larger; some of these were all Whigs."

Moreover, Prentiss discerned that there was a basic political motive back of the Elmore resolution which he could not endorse. He approached this angle of the matter by telling Congress "He was willing to make the Speaker a courteous parting bow; but he would not consent to let him sit there and do all this party work, and then march out with the honors of war. The duties of the Chair were too important for this."

The "honors of war" which would fall upon Polk as a result of this motion Prentiss proceeded to dwell upon. The chief motive of the resolution was the fact that *"The present Speaker was as the House well knew, a candidate at this time for the Chief Magistracy of his own State; and in the canvass there, and throughout all the West, this vote would be referred to as an undeniable proof that he had exercised the utmost impartiality while in that Chair; and yet the House itself had utterly refused to trust him. When that damning fact should be brought by his opponents, what more would he have to do, should this resolution pass, than tear from the records of the House the leaf which contained it, and holding it up to the sun, pronounce all these representations to be unfounded calumnies."* [71]

[71] *Cong. Globe*, 25 Cong., 3 Sess., 251.

Again Prentiss fought against overwhelming odds. The motion passed by a vote of 94 to 57, Prentiss voting in the minority.[72]

Prentiss' congressional career was ended. He had told the people that he would not seek further political office. His love of the courtroom he could not surrender. But in his short term in Congress he acquired a name and fame greatly disproportionate to the time he had spent in Washington. As expressed by the *Madisonian:* "It is to be regretted, that he should find the great political arena of Congress so little suited to his taste, or so hostile to his interests, as to induce him to withdraw from the councils of the nation, and return again to a profession from which he derives more wealth, if not so much fame, as from a career of legislation, which he has just abandoned, and in which he is so well fitted to excel." [73]

Leaving Washington, Prentiss went at once to Harrodsburg, Kentucky, where he defended and obtained acquittal of his Mississippi friend, Judge Edward C. Wilkinson, on a murder charge.[74] By March 23 he was in Vicksburg.[75] Soon busily engaged in law practice, he secured the acquittal of a man charged with murder at Port Gibson, Mississippi, and then attended the Chancery court at Jackson.[76]

Another interlude of politics prevented rest that summer and deferred his close attention to his law office. In early July he was called upon by the Whigs to run against Robert J. Walker for the United States Senate. The Natchez *Courier,* naturally in support of him, stated on July 10: "We are highly gratified with the universal approbation with which our remarks yesterday relative to this gentleman have been received by the Whigs of his city and the unanimity

72 *Ibid.,* 252; Washington *National Intelligencer,* March 5, 1839.

73 Washington *Madisonian,* May 15, 1839.

74 Shields, *Seargent Smith Prentiss,* 254–95, and *Memoir of S. S. Prentiss,* II, 66–113, contain accounts of this trial and Prentiss' speech.

75 Prentiss to Abby Prentiss, Vicksburg, March 24, 1839, in *Memoir of S. S. Prentiss,* II, 114.

76 *Id.* to *id.,* Vicksburg, June 12, 1839, *ibid.,* 120.

with which one and all declare Mr. Prentiss *nolens volens*
must be the candidate for the U. S. Senate." [77] After the
Whigs of Adams and Madison counties had nominated him,
Prentiss, on August 10, issued a letter stating his willingness
to stand for election. The *National Intelligencer* alluded
to it as "an able and eloquent production." [78] The letter reiterated his stand on the issues of the Bank and Sub-
Treasury, and placed the blame for the unfavorable times
upon Jackson and Van Buren. Personally, Prentiss was reluctant to return to the political arena but stated: "On the
other hand, I could not forget the obligations which bind
me to our beloved State—obligations that shall never call
upon me in vain, when they point out a mode by which
I can liquidate my portion of the heavy claim Mississippi
justly holds against me." [79] A few days later, August 16,
Prentiss replied to the Whigs of Adams County, the first
actually to nominate him: "Without hesitation, then, I
will frankly say, that my services are at the command of the
State, though I did not consider them of sufficient importance, ever to have tendered them voluntarily." [80]

Little did Prentiss realize years earlier when he accepted
the offer of Walker to read law in his office at Natchez, that
he would be campaigning against him in 1839 for a seat
in the United States Senate. Prentiss could not, and did not,
underestimate the strength of his opponent. Walker had
earned his place in the Senate by defeating the able Poindexter in the preceding campaign, and had proved himself
to be a capable stump speaker. On issues Prentiss and Walker
were ready to clash. In the Senate Walker had identified
himself with the anti-Bank forces. Prentiss was for the Bank
above all else. This was, then, the logical issue between the
two men in the contest.

Moreover, Prentiss and Walker were two of the most in-

[77] Natchez *Daily Courier*, July 10, 1839.
[78] Washington *National Intelligencer*, September 4, 1839.
[79] Quoted *ibid.*, September 25, 1839; *Memoir of S. S. Prentiss*, II, 126–36.
[80] Quoted in *Memoir of S. S. Prentiss*, II, 124–25.

tellectual men who might have battled each other in the
campaign. Both were college graduates (Walker being an
alumnus of the University of Pennsylvania), both were experienced lawyers, and each undoubtedly respected the
abilities of the other. The Vicksburg *Sentinel* estimated the
capacity of the two opponents in its statement: "The Democrats and Whigs have 'giants in the field.' 'When Greek
meets Greek, then comes the tug of war.'" [81] Although
Walker may not have appeared to be a giant, being small
and stooped and weighing less than a hundred pounds, in-
tellectually he was not insignificant, as his future career
was to prove. Prentiss, on his part, had already proved his
powers on the stump and in Congress. Probably as good a
statement of what motivated each to combat the other was
supplied by a New England newspaper: "Mr. S. S. Prentiss
does not consider himself at liberty to decline an election as
Senator to Congress from Mississippi, in place of Mr.
Walker, if he can get it; and Mr. Walker does not feel at
liberty to give up his seat in the Senate, if he can keep it." [82]

Walker's adherence to Van Buren and Prentiss' support
of Henry Clay became minor factors in the campaign, but it
was really fought out on the bank question. Apparently,
Prentiss opened his brief campaign at Raymond Springs in
Hinds County on August 31. He found his text for the
speech from an earlier statement of Walker: "the whole
banking system . . . is founded in fraud, because a bank
promises to pay more than it is able to do." He "argued that
as no bank can keep specie enough to redeem its issues, and
yet be profitable to a stockholder, their 'promises' are made
in fraud, and the whole system is subversive of the interests
of true religion." Prentiss read this statement to his Raymond Springs audience, and refuted it by an analogy close
at hand: "you have a spring, whose gentle flow supplies the
wants of your whole town. Here yourselves, your wives, and

[81] Vicksburg *Daily Sentinel,* August 16, 1839.
[82] Exeter (N. H.) Weekly *News-Letter,* August 6, 1839.

your little ones are accustomed to drink. True, it is a modest fountain—yet its steady current is more than sufficient for you. You know it—you have confidence in its ability to continue that supply. But suppose some one of your citizens, suspecting the inherent ability of your spring, should recommend a 'run' upon it—and suppose every man of your town, with a bucket in hand, should commence dipping therefrom to hoard up the precious fluid in his private reservoir, would not the spring soon be drained, and, instead of pure water, would you not presently scrape up mud and filth? No, fellow-citizens, you would not permit such madness. You would punish such an experimenter. Let the spring alone, you would say—we have no fears of its exhaustion." The use of such a figurative analogy may well have been observed as an example of effective audience adaptation. Prentiss' answer to Walker, said the *National Intelligencer*, "is as happy an exhibition of an argument in the form of a simile as we recollect ever to have seen." [83]

As on previous occasions, the Vicksburg *Sentinel* was full strength against him. Prentiss' speech at Raymond Springs, it said, "was nothing more than patch work—a reiteration of the stale federal slang with which the whig press has teemed for the last eight years." He attacked state banks and recalled his prediction of evil results when they were established, "but neglected to inform the assembly that he voted for every bank charter which was introduced into the Legislature when he was a member of that body." After further insinuations of inconsistencies in Prentiss' record and logic, the *Sentinel* came to the final conclusion: "The fact is, Mr. Prentiss, although a good stump orator, is no statesman. He is miserably deficient in statistical information, and unpracticed in close thorough and practical reasoning upon the science of Government. He can relate an anecdote with effect, but in the argument of a question of national policy, he must ever fail, until his mind has been trained

[83] Washington *National Intelligencer*, September 25, 1839.

to the rational investigation of numerous subjects to which he is yet a stranger. The 'Solid Simon Pure' can assert roundly, but he can't 'come it' in an argument." [84]

This newspaper did all it could to embarrass Prentiss on the bank issue. On another occasion it criticized a speech in which he "urged as an argument in favor of the establishment of a United States Bank, that it would regulate the issue of the State Banks. He also said that he always acted upon principle, and would always continue to do so." Examining Prentiss' principles and personal conduct, the *Sentinel* inquired: "Does the circumstance of a man being a director in a United States Bank alter his principles, or add to his honesty? Mr. Prentiss says he always acted on principle. How did he act as director of the Water Works Bank of Vicksburg? He said that bank would be authorized to issue $1,000,000 on $69,000 paid in, and the bank did actually issue $169,000,000 on $69,000 paid in, in Brandon money, and not one dollar of specie. According to the same rule, how much would he recommend for Mr. Clay's $50,000,000 bank to issue?" [85]

Prentiss had support, however, from other quarters. The Natchez *Courier,* as usual, praised his campaign. It alluded to an audience at Canton, Madison County, as "a glorious assemblage"; Prentiss spoke "following a dinner for three hours in a strain of deep and impassioned eloquence, which we have never heard surpassed upon any similar occasion. The effect of his speech was tremendous. . . . In short, this effort of Mr. Prentiss, we regard as one of the happiest of his life, and we venture to assert that it will long, long be remembered in Madison as *the great speech.*" [86]

To what extent Prentiss' heart was in the campaign, or to what extent he actually hoped to defeat Walker, it is difficult to know. He seems to have been torn between two

[84] Vicksburg *Daily Sentinel,* September 9, 1839.
[85] *Ibid.,* October 30, 1839.
[86] Natchez *Daily Courier,* September 19, 1839.

desires, one to return to his law practice and forget politics, and the other to reap the personal honor of winning the election. To his mother he stated: "If not elected, I shall feel no disappointment, for I have seen as much of public life as I wish. If elected, it will certainly be a very high honor, and one which seldom falls upon a person of my age." [87] He was challenged to make every effort to win, however. He could hardly have done otherwise when John J. Crittenden of Kentucky wrote him to campaign ardently because, "If the Whigs are defeated, . . . the country will say 'Prentiss could have prevented this'—if they are successful, the country will say 'Prentiss has done this.' " [88] Prentiss worked diligently to meet Crittenden's challenge, but at the same time, he was prepared for defeat. An interesting insight into his mood is revealed in a letter to his sister: "Yet I am now engaged in an exciting political contest, . . . making speeches, and laboring, as for dear life, in a matter in which, personally, I feel no interest whatever. I do not want to go to the Senate; it will break up all my plans of life, and compel me to pursue a vocation which I almost detest." But he went on to say: "The Whig party in this State have called me, with a most unexampled enthusiasm, to assist in the contest, and I could not conscientiously refuse. . . . There is nothing personally unpleasant in the matter, but I am disgusted with politics, and annoyed at the notoriety which has attached to my name." Most revealing of all was his further statement: "Fortunately, there is a very good chance of my being beaten, and though I shall do my utmost to prevent it yet I shall, I believe, feel gratified if it happens." [89]

Prentiss did not go to the Senate. Had the election been one in which a direct vote of the people would have de-

[87] Prentiss to his mother, Vicksburg, August 6, 1839, in *Memoir of S. S. Prentiss*, II, 143.

[88] John J. Crittenden to Prentiss, Frankfort, Ky., September 1, 1839, quoted *ibid.*, 137.

[89] Prentiss to Abby Prentiss, Vicksburg, September 15, 1839, *ibid.*, 144–45.

termined the matter, it might have been a different story. On January 9, the legislature gave Walker a majority of twenty-five votes over Prentiss, and on the same day Alexander G. McNutt, Democrat, was inaugurated governor. When a New Hampshire newspaper, after reporting the election of Walker over Prentiss, went on to say of Mississippi, "The public debt is about seven millions and a half," [90] it was foreshadowing dire financial history in the making, a story in itself.

One incident in which Prentiss participated as the year 1839 drew to a close deserves mention, if for no other reason than to show that he could, after all, forget politics and actually help entertain a supposed enemy. At a public meeting in December a committee was instructed to extend an invitation to Andrew Jackson to visit the State and be present at Jackson, for a public reception. Interestingly enough, Prentiss, Whig and anti-Jackson man that he was, became one of the committee of twenty-five. [91]

For one year Prentiss' time was to be more nearly his own. But he was not to remain inactive politically. The Whigs did not overlook him in 1840 when the cause of William Henry Harrison needed to be presented far and wide over the nation.

[90] Exeter *News-Letter*, February 11, 1840.
[91] Natchez *Daily Courier*, December 4, 1839.

Chapter VII

CAMPAIGN OF 1840

THE newly organized Whig party realized its chances of success in 1840. Though the party was composed of discordant elements and unable to erect a definite platform, the widespread denunciation of Van Buren and locofocoism, north and south, gave the Whigs more than a passing ray of hope, provided they could unite on a candidate generally acceptable to all. The problem for the Whigs was to select the proper standard-bearer. Although Henry Clay possessed many of the qualities needed, he was passed over. In spite of his long career as a public servant, and notwithstanding his magnetic characteristics, the fact that he was a Freemason militated against him in the East, and his strong protective tariff attitudes handicapped him in at least a part of the South. Consequently, he failed to receive the nomination, largely because of the opposition of the New York delegation, and the Whigs in December, 1839, at Harrisburg selected William Henry Harrison as their nominee and John Tyler as his running mate. Harrison was not encumbered with the objections raised to Clay. Moreover, he had been both a military and public servant. He had appealed to many Whigs as the logical choice against Van Buren in 1836. In 1840 the Whigs felt safe with him, when the demand, above all else, was to keep the party united around the personality of their candidate.

The story of the campaign of 1840 has been told often and well. One aspect of it, however, needs elaboration, namely, the role which Prentiss played. Few men did more for Whig victory in this unique and memorable campaign. In a contest demanding a popularization of the candidate's virtues and a depreciation of Van Buren's, Prentiss' oratorical powers in eulogy and invective were at a premium. Because he was considered indispensable to party success, he was called upon to speak at barbecues, log-cabin raisings, and before huge gatherings in many states and cities. In brief, the efforts of Prentiss in 1840 may be divided into three periods. He first labored in Mississippi. Second, he made an extensive tour of the nation. Third, he returned to Mississippi and gave unstintingly of his time and talent.

Prentiss was willing to contribute his services despite the fact that he had personally preferred Clay to Harrison. His explanation for desiring Clay and his statement of reasons why he would work for Whig victory, he expressed in a letter to George Prentiss, then in Europe: "You have, doubtless, heard of Harrison's nomination for the Presidency, instead of Clay. In this I was disappointed and somewhat mortified. However, I am inclined to think, that Harrison has a better chance of election than Clay would have had. Still I think his chance a small one." Such a pessimistic statement needed an explanation. Prentiss gave it in the following analysis: "The spoils-party will, in all probability, succeed. I have lost confidence in the people—not so much in their honesty as in their capacity. The principle of democracy is rapidly destroying and eating out all the principles of the Republic. Indeed, practically, the Republic no longer exists. It ceased under General Jackson. In a Republic, the rights of all are equally protected. In this government, as now administered, the rights of *the majority* alone are protected. We are now living under a *despotic democracy.*" [1]

Although apparently doubtful of Harrison's chances, Prentiss placed principle above personal preference, sacri-

[1] Prentiss to George Prentiss, Vicksburg, January 18, 1840, in *Memoir of S. S. Prentiss,* II, 150–51.

ficed his law practice, and took the stump, delivering his share of votes to Harrison. He asked no political reward, and received none. Rather, he exhausted himself physically and mentally in a campaign which brought him no personal remuneration.

As has been stated, Prentiss' services to the Whigs in 1840 were quite evenly divided between the cause in Mississippi and areas distant from the state. In February he was selected as one of the four Whig electors from Mississippi.[2] By May he was busily engaged in speaking over the state. His first speech was probably at a meeting of the Whigs in Warren County in the courthouse at Vicksburg, preparatory "to opening the campaign." The Vicksburg *Tri-Weekly Whig* commented: "there was a general call for Mr. Prentiss, who responded . . . in a speech complete with sound republican doctrines and adorned with the most forcible and vigorous illustrations. . . . Although the day was excessively warm, yet the audience seemed to have forgotten all mere personal conveniences in the deep and absorbing attention which they paid to the orator, and thus they stood (literally), for there were seats for only a small number, riveted for near two hours listening to a flood of eloquence and wit such as it rarely happens to any man to hear." [3]

A few days later, Prentiss furthered Whig enthusiasm when he spoke to the citizens of Hinds County. Of the meeting and the speech the Vicksburg *Whig* stated: "All accounts from Hinds county concur in representing the meeting of Saturday last as the largest ever held in the county. . . . Hon. S. S. Prentiss addressed the meeting for nearly three hours in a strain of eloquence and argument rarely surpassed. He was constantly interrupted by the applause of the multitude, and when he closed the plaudits were deafening. The spirit of 'Old Hinds' is up, and our

[2] Vicksburg *Daily Whig*, February 20, 1840.
[3] Vicksburg *Tri-Weekly Whig*, May 5, 1840.

friends say she will give Harrison and Tyler a clear majority of one thousand votes." [4]

Not infrequently Prentiss' oratory accompanied log-cabin raisings in the campaign of 1840. On the last of May, the *Whig*, announcing such a jubilee occasion in Vicksburg, issued an appeal: "Let every Whig attend at 8 o'clock this morning to finish it. At 11 o'clock S. S. Prentiss, Esq. will address his fellow citizens on the claims of Gen. Harrison to the Presidency." [5] After the cabin was raised, and Prentiss' speech delivered, the *Whig* declared: "Saturday last was a day long to be remembered in the annals of this good whig city, and one that can never fail to be remembered with pleasure by every one present upon the joyous occasion." The speech must have contributed largely to the significance of the day, for: "Mr. Prentiss' appearance on the stand was greeted with the most deafening and continued cheering. Of this speech, which occupied near two hours in delivery, we need say nothing. Those who heard it will not care to see any report we could make of it, and those who had not that pleasure, would be able to form no adequate idea of its power and eloquence from the meagre sketch which we should make if we were to attempt it. We shall therefore dismiss it with the simple remark, that it was a display of eloquence and oratory every way worthy of its distinguished author." [6]

Late in June Prentiss accepted the Macedonian call, and journeyed to render help in areas outside Mississippi. He went first to Carrollton, Louisiana, where he spoke at a dinner in his honor, and the following day addressed the people of New Orleans in the St. Charles Theater. In announcing Prentiss' speaking in New Orleans, the Vicksburg *Whig* predicted: "The Whigs of the Crescent City will battle with a nobler spirit after listening to the soul stirring appeals which fell from his lips on Wednesday evening.

[4] *Ibid.*, May 19, 1840.   [5] *Ibid.*, May 30, 1840.   [6] *Ibid.*, June 2, 1840.

'One blast from his bugle were worth a thousand men!' " [7]
After the speech was made, the New Orleans *True American* reported: "The St. Charles Theatre was filled last night
by the Whigs of Orleans. Never before has this splendid
edifice been so fully crowded, and seldom has so large a collection of people been seen in New Orleans. The halls and
lobbies, and corners were all filled, and hundreds left because they were unable to gain admittance." Some small
insight into what may have been the thesis or the central
idea of the speech is to be gained from the account in the
True American. "Many Democrats were present, some of
whom we understand, had their eyes opened to see their
political errors, and now have the magnanimity to confess
and to renounce them. We doubt whether the prejudices
of any partisan of the administration could have withstood
the eloquence of Mr. Prentiss without being much shaken."
This assumption was based on Prentiss' "declaration that
the principles which Jackson professed when first inaugurated in office," but from which he and Van Buren so far
departed, "were the principles now contended for by the
Whig party, and that he, as of that party, would be willing
to subscribe to the first Inaugural address of Gen. Jackson,
and adopt it as his political creed and text-book." [8] It might
be inferred that Prentiss knew well enough the popularity
of the name of Jackson in New Orleans to adapt his remarks
and references to Jackson in such a manner as to aid himself.

A month later Prentiss began a series of campaign
speeches for Harrison that took him to many cities, only
some of which he had ever visited before. At the northern-
most point of his tour he delivered an address in behalf of
the Whig cause in his boyhood town of Gorham. His first
major appearance outside of Mississippi and Louisiana was
in St. Louis. His reception there was auspicious, and he
evidently surpassed the expectations of the Whigs of that
city. Reporting the occasion and speech the St. Louis *Re-*

[7] *Ibid.*, June 27, 1840.   [8] Quoted *ibid.*

publican stated: "The Hon. S. S. Prentiss of Mississippi,
arrived in this city on Thursday evening, on his way to the
North, in company with a party of friends. He had taken
passage on board the Detroit, and was to leave at 12, m. of
yesterday. He was waited upon by the Mayor and a large
number of citizens, and was finally prevailed upon to stay
and address the citizens; the boat having agreed to wait until
eleven last night for him." The boat waited eleven hours so
that a night audience could be had. Prentiss prepared a
speech which was most happily received. The following day
the *Republican* stated: "Last night he addressed an immense assemblage from a stage erected in front of the Court
House. Notwithstanding the day had been showery, a large
number of ladies of the city were present. It would be perfectly futile to attempt giving any idea of the force and effect
of his speech. *It was beyond description.* It must have been
heard to have been appreciated." [9] An even more significant
account of the St. Louis speech has been left by John F.
Darby, the man, who, apparently, had most to do with ar-
ranging for the speech and who introduced Prentiss to the
audience. Darby tells how he, with others, met at the *Republican* newspaper office and made plans to call upon Prentiss. Darby and his committee secured the promise of Prentiss to give a speech if the captain of the boat would allow
a delay. The task before the committee was, then, to pro-
ceed to the captain with the request that he stay over twenty-
four hours. Evidently the captain had his price, for "This
he consented to do, if we would pay him one hundred dollars for the delay; to which all most readily assented." The
committee worked fast. "Thereupon large, flaming hand-
bills were struck off and posted over town, announcing that
Sargent [sic] S. Prentiss, of Mississippi, would address the
people, on Fourth Street, that evening, at eight o'clock."
According to Darby, he had the "distinguished honor of
attending to the prominent stranger during his stay . . .

[9] St. Louis *Republican,* quoted *ibid.,* August 1, 1840.

and of introducing him to the vast assemblage of people."
He stated that "Soon after we had appeared upon the stand,
he [Prentiss] took a seat and paused for a few moments, as
if to recover from the fatigue of walking,—a fatigue caused
by his being very lame. When he arose, and I had introduced him, he was received by the people with great applause, and for three hours held that immense crowd spell-
bound." It might be too much to expect Darby to remember
for forty years much or anything of the address that night
in St. Louis, but he never forgot the eloquence of the orator.
"The evening was calm, and the clear, loud-ringing tones
of his voice could be distinctly heard to the very outskirts
of the meeting. . . . He was interrupted occasionally by
great bursts of laughter and tremendous shouts of applause
from his auditors. Perhaps it is not too much to say, that the
great powers of mind and thought, and the great force of
language and eloquence with which he charmed and captivated his hearers have never been equalled by any man who
ever spoke in front of that court-house. . . . His well-
turned periods, modulated cadence, winning accents, and
happy elocution, seemed to fall like music upon the ear,
and to please and charm every one within his hearing." [10]

In due time the boat left, carrying Prentiss. As he journeyed north and east, visiting one center after another, his
political ally in Mississippi, the Vicksburg *Whig,* kept its
readers informed of his successes. Reporting speeches made
in Chicago and Cleveland it commented: "The journey of
this gentleman northward has been a triumphal one." [11]
The *Whig* naturally took pride in the receptions given
Prentiss. "The attention which he has attracted ought to
be a source of high gratification to every Mississippian,
when it is recollected that he is neither in office nor a candidate for office; we must look upon these exhibitions of re-

[10] John F. Darby, *Personal Recollections of Many Prominent People I
Have Known* . . . (St. Louis, 1880), 314–15.
[11] Vicksburg *Tri-Weekly Whig,* August 11, 1840.

spect of the unbought suffrages of an independent people, to the supremacy of genius." [12]

Another of the several more speeches which Prentiss made as he traveled toward his old home was at New York. A Philadelphia paper commented on it: "In all parts of the country we read of great meetings of the Whigs. One was held at New York on Monday evening, at which Mr. Prentiss, of Mississippi, delivered a striking and impressive speech of two hours to a numerous audience." [13]

But this passing complimentary reference was in great contrast to the fulminations of certain enemy papers in Mississippi. Just as the Vicksburg *Whig* followed him on his tour and reported glowing accounts of his oratorical efforts, others, such as the Jackson *Mississippian,* related his journey in the most unsavory manner possible. Of Prentiss and his tour generally, it commented: "This political 'Whig Giraffe' is now figuring at the North, making bacchanalian harangues to his deluded followers. Prentiss is a man of inordinate vanity, and from his having been puffed to death by the 'Reed Birds' of party, he imagines himself a perfect Jupiter Tonans." The *Mississippian* then alluded to his New York address, saying that the account furnished by the New York *Evening Post* "is applicable not merely to that orator, but is good for the whole tribe of Whig Missionaries." The *Mississippian* was delighted to quote the *Evening Post* to the effect that, "As to the matter of the speech, it was as miserable a hoch-poch as one ever heard. It was a gallimaufry, compounded of all sorts of unsavory meats and rejected condiments." Indicting Prentiss personally, it went on to quote: "The speaker seems to have drawn a drag-net through the sewers of political slang, to collect all the garbage and refuse which partisan editors have thrown by in the course of a heated campaign. All that was stale, thread-

[12] *Ibid.*
[13] Philadelphia *Daily National Gazette and Literary Register,* August 6, 1840.

bare, or rotten from long use, was brought together, to be hashed up anew for the especial gratification of his auditory. With true whig veneration for antiquity, he eagerly seized the old. Thus we had old arguments, old figures, old anecdotes, old phrases, old jokes, old falsehoods, and old scraps, shreds, odd ends, and what not." [14]

The climax of this northern tour for Prentiss was Portland and Gorham, Maine, where he had not only the obligations and demands for speeches but the agreeable opportunity to visit his mother and sisters. The Portland *Advertiser,* aware of the political significance of his presence at home, announced his arrival on August 7: "Mr. P. will need the power of ubiquity to meet the demands upon him, coming from different parts of his native State. The Whigs of every county and town are anxious to hear him." [15] The political nature of Prentiss' presence in Portland was undeniable, even though it was justifiable to combine a visit with campaign speeches. Nevertheless, the political reason for his coming was branded by the Portland *Argus* as ulterior. The *Advertiser* came to his rescue with the statement: "Mr. Prentiss is accused of being here on a missionary tour, because he comes to visit with his kith and kin, after a long absence." [16] Whig friends, while not anxious to place Prentiss in the position of visiting in Portland for political reasons primarily, nevertheless proceeded to make arrangements to have him speak. Plans were soon completed, and the *Advertiser* began carrying the announcement of a speech he would make in Portland.[17]

But another speech preceded that at Portland, namely, one at his old home town, Gorham. It was delivered on the fourteenth of August, on a rainy, stormy day. The introduction of Prentiss was fulsome: "Though he now dwells in the far west, though many a broad and mighty river, and many

[14] Jackson *Daily Mississippian,* August 28, 1840.
[15] Portland *Daily Advertiser,* August 7, 1840.
[16] *Ibid.,* August 8, 1840.   [17] *Ibid.,* August 11, 1840.

a high and lofty mountain intervenes between you and his home, his fame which has traversed our continent is your fame, for here, within the bosom of your own town, here with yourselves, he first imbibed those pure democratic principles which he now advocates, which have strengthened with his strength and grown with his growth." The *Advertiser* compared his address to the eloquence "of Burke of modern, and Cicero of ancient times," but did not attempt to give a résumé of what he said because, "To those who were present, this is not necessary; and to such as were not, an opportunity will be offered in this city on Tuesday next, at 6 o'clock, to hear something as good from this able orator of Mississippi." The paper predicted of the Portland speech "that Mr. Prentiss will hold up to . . . view a picture of the times, in which even a child may recognize the likeness of Martin Van Buren, and a sketch of the future, which can pass for no other than a full length portrait of Tippicanoe." [18]

The night for the Portland speech arrived. Prentiss spoke from a platform erected on the steps of the City Hall before what must have been a huge gathering. The immediate setting was described by the *Advertiser:* "The windows of stores, hotel and dwelling houses near the Hall upon Congress and Middle Streets were lined with ladies. The steps in front of the Hall with the adjoining rooms and every accessible doorway and window were occupied with the beauty and fashion of the city of Portland. . . . Lights were scattered all around, and the illumination gave a beautiful and brilliant appearance to the scene."

The *Advertiser* made a fervent effort to report the speech fully and to make it available in numerous copies for the public. The speech (or rather a sketch of it) was prepared at once for publication. "We cannot . . . delay even for a single moment," the *Advertiser* declared, "the pleasant duty we have assigned ourselves of placing before our readers,

18 Portland *Evening Advertiser*, August 15, 1840.

a brief skeleton of the very able, eloquent, and interesting speech of one of the most talented and distinguished orators of the day." After devoting more than five columns of space to the speech in its issue of August 19, it announced: "We give all the room we can spare, to a part of the eloquent speech made by Mr. Prentiss." In addition to announcing that "Our Semi-Weekly paper of to-morrow will contain the whole speech, and extra copies will be furnished if called for before one o'clock," the *Advertiser* on the following day gave four more complete columns to it.

Certain forces operated to make this speech by Prentiss an interesting one for analysis. One is that it was so fully reported. Also, Prentiss certainly felt impelled to rally to the lavish reception given him and was buoyed to do his best in his native city. Moreover, his own mother and sisters were in his audience. Thus, he had to achieve his best.

The usual highly laudatory introduction preceded the speech. It was spoken by John D. Kinsman, who said among other things: "Yes, I thank God, that we are permitted to claim the honor of hailing him as the son of Portland. . . . We come to listen to that voice which has sent forth its note of warning along the majestic shores of the 'Father of Waters' that rolls in the far West—to that voice which has been heard echoing and re-echoing along the cliffs of the Alleghanies—to that voice which has cheered and encouraged the hardy sons that dwell in the vallies [sic] and among the hills of our own New England. Permit me then to have the honor of introducing to your acquaintance, one who was the friend of my youth, the companion of my early years, one who is the pride and the boast of the American people." Prentiss, introduced, began his speech, "continuing for three hours with no diminution of power and interest on the part of the orator, and none of attention or patience on the part of the audience."

Quite naturally, expressions of sentiment constituted the first response of the orator returned home. "A voluntary exile from my old home, returning, in my heart," Prentiss said, "I shake hands with you all. . . . A thousand early associations overpower me. . . . I look back to the thirteen years, in which accident or caprice took me from you in one of the freaks of fortune."

But, as might be assumed, Prentiss stated that the issues of the hour constituted a necessity for him not to linger on matters of sentimental concern. Consequently, he declared: "As one of the humblest of the warriors, I am here from the South West wing of the Union. I come to see whether you of the North East fight with the same weapons that we fight with in the South West. . . . The boldest man will feel stronger, and the weakest man strong, when surrounded by friends. I feel that it is good to be here,—not to instruct you, but to tell you what my opinions are, and, to catch a gleam of your own spirit in your flashing eyes and speaking countenances." Also, before launching into his speech proper, one more point needed his attention. Prentiss knew the charge that he was doing Whig missionary work while ostensibly visiting his relatives. To this he replied: "And though I did come here for other purposes, I will not, in times like these, quarrel with terms, and, in truth, I glory in being called a Political Missionary. I wish, like old Peter, I could lead a crusade against this administration. I wish, like him, I could go forth and fight the good fight for the institutions of my country as he did in behalf of the temple of our holy religion."

Prentiss moved into his subject, telling the audience: "I shall give you my opinions freely as they bubble up from the fountain of the heart." The speech may be said to fall into two parts. For half of his time or more, he denounced Van Buren. In the second part he eulogized Harrison. All that he said in three hours falls as subpoints under the two main headings.

The theme of his first attack was that the record of Van Buren was made up of pretensions, nothing more. He held,

first of all, that the President had accomplished nothing
of positive good. Hence Van Buren "has no claim to confidence or support." Instead, Prentiss declared that the
situation of the country was bad. "A mighty nation of great
energies, in the midst of an abundance, without foreign
invasions, and in a time of profound peace, with the exception of our troubles in Florida, still we are suffering, every
man of us, but the few who prosper do so only as adversity
falls to the lot of others."

The charge made, Prentiss went about to explain and
prove it. To him the chief cause of national suffering was
experimentation with the currency, which had destroyed
credit. Credit he defined as "the child of comfort" and
confidence, "the child of hope." His contention, upon which
he elaborated at length, was that credit had made our commercial and industrial greatness. This was particularly true
in the matter of western and southern development. "Look
at the valley of the Mississippi, famed as the Delta of the
Nile. Who can look upon the six hundred steamboats which
float upon the western waters,—enchanted castles as they
are,—and not have his eyes gladdened with the evidence
and prospect before him, of the blessings of the credit system?" The whole story of western development was inevitably tied up with credit, Prentiss insisted. To illustrate
further, he recounted what he had seen by living far from
Maine. His challenge was: "Go to the West. Ask the first
man you meet what his history is. His response will be that
he went from the North with his plane or his adze or his
spade, and that credit has changed his condition, and made
him a thrifty man." Prentiss could speak from personal experience. "I have seen many such in the South West, and they
have far outstripped me, though blessed with a profession
which is so lucrative in the West. The Western man will tell
you that credit is the poor man's capital." Knowing the criticism that might be leveled against this argument, Prentiss
anticipated the need to say: "I grant you again that the sys-

tem may be abused, and so may eating and drinking—but who is he who will rise up and say eat not and drink not for fear of a surfeit. (Cheers.)"

It followed, then, by Prentiss' thinking, that the suffering of the nation had been caused by interference with the mixed currency. Certain groups were most seriously affected. The first to suffer, Prentiss held, was the laboring man. When business comes to a standstill, labor suffers. He illustrated: "What constitutes the value of labor? It is demand. If there are one hundred mechanics in a town and a single house to be built, it is clear that labor will not have the same demand, or command the same price it would were there twenty houses to build and but ten mechanics. So with other things." Prentiss dwelt at length on this point, and amplified the argument to show that agriculture suffers also when labor cannot buy. Hence, attacking the Administration, he maintained, "It is a poor compliment to Democracy . . . to say to the Poor man you must remain poor in order to be a Democrat. (Laughter and cheers.)"

Again Prentiss felt impelled to safeguard the doctrine of credit as opposed to "hard money" exclusively, by reminding his audience that "The Whigs do not wish a bloated system. They are not in favor of excess." As proof of this he contended that it had been the Whigs who protested in the days of excess credit under Jackson. His challenge was: "But who was the Engineer when credit ran riot? Who stood at the helm when the Pet Bank system was adopted? . . . We told the dominant party when the boat was under way that they were putting on too much steam. Still they continued to pile on the wood and put in the tar and rosin; and when the explosion came, and half the people in the country were scalded to death, they turned round with impudent audacity and said, 'Look here your system has blown us up!'"

With a few passing remarks upon the Sub-Treasury system, Prentiss took up his second charge against Van Buren.

Specifically he said: "I charge home upon the party the creation of local difficulties,—the dissemination of bad principles, and the loss of morals." He decried the effect. "We have reached such a pass, that we are sneered at in exposing the fraud and corruption of the party in power." Because of executive power and patronage, corruption was inevitable. Thus, "The time had come, and now is, when Foreign Ministers and Judges upon the Bench were rewarded for partisan service. . . . The President now rewards those who are cast off as unworthy servants, by the people."

The loss of integrity and the destruction of mutual confidence concerned Prentiss greatly. If it were continued, he saw civil strife and predicted that "The border States would be at war with the inner States, and the stronger would crush the weaker." Moreover, because of a problem which was rearing its head in Mississippi, namely, repudiation of state indebtedness, Prentiss asserted: "There, where the Apples of Sodom were riper than elsewhere, the Loco Foco Governor had declared that the State would not pay the principle or interest on its State Debts."

Prentiss' conclusion relative to Van Buren was that he could not be trusted, that he had done nothing to deserve re-election, and that in contrast with Jackson, Van Buren had neither "boldness [n]or manliness. The skulking propensities of the fox belong to him, but courage he has none."

But if Van Buren was not to be trusted, Harrison was. Thus Prentiss moved to the second half of his speech, declaring: "But as we would scorn the man who crawls into place, by the tortuous movements of the snake, so we should reward the Patriotism of our sons." Three reasons for supporting Harrison were quickly set forth. One was that Harrison was pledged to serve but one term. The second was Harrison's principle that all governmental offices should be given to men of competence. The third was that Harrison had "ever served his country." These points were little more than set forth, Prentiss being desirous of stressing other Whig arguments.

Prentiss capitalized upon the popular emblem of the campaign, the log cabin and hard cider, stating emphatically: "General Harrison was the Father of the Log Cabins of the West." Of the slogan, first used as a term of derision by the Democrats, but taken up by the Whigs as a means to victory, Prentiss said: "The Log Cabin is symbolical of a great and important principle. Shakespeare said there were 'sermons in stones,' and so there is some good in Log Cabins. We have therefore taken the Log Cabin device, although sneeringly put upon us by our enemies, who declared that Gen. Harrison should have a pension of $2000 a year, plenty of hard cider, and then that he would rest content in his log cabin for the remainder of his life." To further stress the significance of the log cabin in the campaign, Prentiss took his eastern audience west. Most of the log cabins, he said, were in the West, symbolic of several things. Harrison belonged to the West and so did the log cabin. Hence Prentiss could say Harrison's character "illustrates the open and frank hospitality displayed in the Log Cabins of the West. . . . The West is dotted with log cabins, and those who dwell in them, for reasons which they could give you, gather and cluster around General Harrison as their early and fast friend." Also, in treating of the symbolic significance of the log cabin in the campaign, Prentiss raised the question of why it was used sneeringly by the Democrats, when they themselves formerly lauded the frontier traits of Jackson. He could only express bewilderment at the Democrats whose "stomachs were not so squeamish when the hickory tree,—having no other charm to them, than the fact that General Jackson once ate hickory nuts—was their rallying cry." Regardless of the inconsistency of the Democrats, the log cabin was a noble and high symbol to the Whigs. "But, and with reverence be it spoken, I ask what is the Cross but an emblem of our

Holy Religion. . . . So of our national flag. . . . But it is symbolical. . . . The man who does not appreciate the Log Cabin, can feel no sympathy with the associations of our national flag."

In the remainder of the speech he predicted Whig victory and built his appeal accordingly. Prentiss held that loco-focoism was dead in the West, using Kentucky as the best illustration, and asked his Portland audience to "Be united then, and let no local difficulties separate you. . . . There never was such a necessity for union as there is now, and I am happy to believe there never was such unanimity as there is now. I have travelled from one end of the Union to the other, and every where I have heard the Whigs using the same arguments, and governed by the same hopes."

The presence of Prentiss' mother and sisters in his audience may, in part, explain some of his closing remarks. As he addressed himself to the ladies present, he said: "In this country we may thank God that female beauty, and female character has a greater value,—a higher reward than in all the earth besides,—But let Loco Focoism prevail, and what will be the result? The war which is going on against Society, destroys that which protects and sustains female character." More pointedly, he stated: "Yes, our revered mothers and grandmothers were as much engaged in olden times in the cause of liberty as were their fathers, their husbands, and their brothers. . . . Our own mothers who, though poor in this world's goods, were not poor in spirit, gave their little all for the cause of liberty."

The hour grew late, and Prentiss drew to a close. He expressed his personal joy in being in Portland again, and closed formally: "I commenced by shaking hands with you all in my heart,—and trusting that we may often be permitted to meet together, I close, by bidding you an affectionate, Good-night." [19]

Two reasons justify extensive reference to this campaign

[19] *Ibid.*, August 19, 20, 1840.

speech. One is that it was reported quite fully, giving some-thing of a clue to the type of campaign speaking he proba-bly did in 1840. A second reason for detailed attention to the speech is that, while the *Advertiser* reported it so en-thusiastically, the Democratic Portland paper, the *Eastern Argus*, did not welcome home with adulation the son of Portland, nor did it report him in any complimentary manner. In fact, some days elapsed before the *Argus* took up the speech itself. When it did, it spared neither the speech nor the speaker.

The technique of the *Argus* was to take the speech, select sentences and passages, often out of context, quote them, and then retort to them. It opened its comments in its issue of August 24: "He speaks an infinite deal of nothing. . . . His reasons are as two grains of wheat hidden in two bushels of chaff; you shall seek all day e'er you find them, and when you have them, they are not worth the search." Of Prentiss' statement, which he had made in his introductory remarks, "I shall give you my opinions freely as they *bubble* up from the *fountain of the heart*," the *Argus* replied: "Was ever language more apt? What word, better than Bubble, could express the true character of the orator's opinions! . . . What a location for the intellectual power of so mighty a mind!" One reference to Prentiss, in particular, hit home. If he thought that his addiction to alcohol was unknown in Portland, the *Argus* exploded the illusion. When Prentiss made the statement, in defense of the institution of credit in the nation, "that the system may be abused, and so may eating and drinking—but *who is he who will rise up and say, eat not and drink not for fear of a surfeit*," he paid his price. The *Argus* very neatly responded: " 'But, who would *rise up, and say, eat not and drink not, for fear of a surfeit?*' Not the *orator*, we suspect! No not he!" Again, as the *Argus* continued its process of retorting to the excerpts from the speech, it alluded to one of Prentiss' statements in regard to the machinations of the Democrats: "There are false prophets now, as there always have been. Men hold out before you the shell, but the meat is poison. They have the *goblet* before your eyes, but the contents are poisonous." The *Argus* struck home with, "But is Mr. Prentiss the man to talk of *goblets* and poisonous liquids therein?"

Many other statements by Prentiss were treated similarly. In respect to the part of his address in which he referred to what was happening in Mississippi where the newly elected *"Loco Foco Governor* had declared that the State would not pay the principle or interest of its State Debts," the *Argus* asserted: "There is a reason for this falsehood and abuse concerning the Governor of Mississippi. The same people who elected that Governor to office, refused to place Mr. Prentiss in the U. S. Senate. He runs down his own State because his own state had independence enough to be Democratic!" Likewise, Prentiss' eulogistic declarations concerning Harrison received much attention. Also, to Prentiss' statement, "I have travelled from one end of the Union to the other, and every where I have heard the whigs using the same arguments, and the enthusiasm is seen every where, where the people are seen," the answer was: "Hard Cider and Log Cabins are 'Whig Arguments' all over the Union, without doubt, but all measures which the Whigs advocate at the South are directly the reverse of those which they advocate at the North. Mr. Prentiss knows this very well."

The attack of the *Argus* was as personal as it could well be. Besides the remarks indicating that Prentiss' alcoholic habits disqualified him to speak of overeating and over-drinking, the *Argus* raised other doubts about his life in the West. Prentiss had complimented the ladies for their presence, and had spoken to them in closing. Of his statement, "In this country we may thank God that female beauty, and female character has a greater value, a higher reward than in all the earth besides," the *Argus* said: "This reckless calumniator resides, we believe in Vicksburg, and

is somewhat popular there; does he wish to save the totter-
ing virtue of Portland females, by introducing here the
customs and habits which characterize the dens of Vicksburg?" Finally, the *Argus* concluded that Prentiss did right
in "thanking" his audience "for he was under great obligation to them. Never did an audience need more of that
cardinal virtue, patience, than did they, on Tuesday evening." [20]

After using this means of refuting Prentiss, occupying
several columns of its paper to do so, the following day the
Argus summarized its total opinion. It pointed out that
though the meeting was held "in the *open air*," the "Exchange Hall would have probably accommodated every
Harrison voter present." It could only conclude that it
was part of "the whig game the present year, to cheat the
people by *show* and *parade*." Prentiss himself bore the
brunt of the attack in the *Argus:* "If there was a great deal
of humbuggery about the *getting up* of Mr. Prentiss's speech,
there was no little of it, certainly, about the speech itself.
When we say that we were altogether disappointed in the
Mississippi Orator, we only express the sincere and honest
convictions of our unbiased judgment." Like other opposition newspapers, the *Argus* admitted, however: "Mr.
Prentiss is a good declaimer, a fluent speaker, and has, generally, an interesting manner; but in all the higher attributes
of a great orator, so far as we could judge . . . he is not
much elevated above the ordinary level of public men."
Moreover, the one most notable characteristic of Prentiss'
oratory came under fire: "Nor has he any of the gorgeous
and magnificent eloquence which his fond admirers have
so often attributed to him! His language is distinguished
neither for originality or great eloquence: and his illustrations are principally borrowed from the columns of the
Federal press; where he seems to have picked up, also, the
most of his facts." The content of the speech the *Argus*

[20] Portland *Daily Eastern Argus,* August 24, 1840.

estimated as exceedingly weak. On this point it said: "Mr, Prentiss spoke for THREE HOURS AND A HALF; but the whole substance of his address might have been easily compressed into the space of one fifth of that time, with manliest advantage." It then proceeded to show that it could have been done by "omitting his long introductory about Himself and His Own Doings and Intentions, his incessant slang about Loco Focoism, and his closing address to the ladies; and the remainder of his discourse would have occupied a very seasonable period." Further, it recommended: "Take out, then, his Log Cabin stories, big predictions concerning the West, and his long disquisition on the advantages of Credit, and his lengthy appeal would be still further reduced; and if you deduct, also, his lamentations over our ruined Country, his fulsome praise of Harrison, and his hypocritical adulation of Jackson, you exhaust nearly the whole matter of his speech." [21]

By the end of August Prentiss had completed his northern swing, and was ready to return to Mississippi. On his journey south he spoke but once—at Newark, New Jersey. A few days following the address, *Niles' National Register* reported that an audience of four thousand people assembled to hear him, and that he held it entranced for three hours.[22] The Governor of New Jersey, William Pennington, sat by Prentiss on the stage, and observed him at close range. He recalled that Prentiss' "main argument was to point out, in connection with the subject of the tariff, the true characteristics of a Republican Government, and to demonstrate that industry has here its reward, and the man of labor his just position in the world." In an industrial city like Newark, it might well be presumed that Prentiss would treat the subject of tariff. Pennington pointed out that "Many of his hearers were our respectable mechanics, men of fortune and of character, and their splendid man-

[21] *Ibid.,* August 25, 1840.
[22] *Niles' National Register,* LIX (1840–1841), 20.

sions surrounded the open air in which he was speaking." [23]
Another who listened to Prentiss at Newark was the Chief
Justice of the State, Joseph C. Hornblower. He was effusive
in his praise of Prentiss: "I had witnessed many exhibitions
of eloquence and mental power in the forum, and on the
political arena, that did honor to the heads and hearts of
the speakers; but I have no hesitation in saying . . . that
I never listened with such intense interest and delight to
any other public speaker." In respect to Prentiss' advocacy
of the protective tariff as an aid to both capital and labor,
Hornblower recalled how, during the speech, Prentiss was
interrupted by a questioner who "loudly asked him, if that
system would not make the rich richer, and the poor poorer."
In response, "The orator, instantly, but courteously, turned
to the interrogator, thanked him for putting the question;
and then slowly turning his gaze, with an appropriate and
corresponding motion of his arm, as if surveying the stately
edifices surrounding the Park, he said: 'My friend, I am
informed that, much to the honor of your city, those elegant
dwellings that adorn this Park, and the glittering equipages
standing before some of their doors, or now rolling through
your streets belong, almost exclusively, to the mechanics,
or to sons of mechanics. It is a splendid testimony to the
enterprise, skill and industry of Newark, and enough to
gladden the heart of every patriot. *But,* let me tell you, that
but for the blessed influence of that protection which the
government has hitherto afforded our manufactures, you
who have worked in your shops, would be doing so now—
and you whose sires, to their honor be it spoken, were black-
smiths and shoemakers, would be mending the old axes
and shoes that they made, instead of occupying the palace-
like dwellings that surround us.' " [24]

While in New York, waiting for the boat to take him

---

[23] William Pennington to George Prentiss, Newark, February 14, 1854,
in *Memoir of S. S. Prentiss*, II, 171–72.
[24] Joseph C. Hornblower to *id.*, Newark, March 6, 1855, *ibid.*, 173–75.

back to Mississippi, Prentiss sent a letter to his brother George, who had gone to Europe for study, in which he told much of what he had been doing, and in which he also reflected a mood typical with him when exhausted physically and mentally. He stated first: "I am now on my return South, and shall leave to-morrow for New Orleans, in a packet-ship. I do this to avoid the fatigue and annoyance of the land route. On my way by the lakes, and since I arrived in the North, I have been continually engaged in the great political contest, until I am worn out and utterly exhausted." As to the extent of his speaking, he wrote further: "I have made speeches at New Orleans, St. Louis, Chicago, Detroit, Cleveland, Buffalo, Syracuse, New York, Newark, Portland, and last, though not least, at *Gorham.* My audiences have varied in number from two to six thousand, and I have usually spoken three hours, generally in the open air. So you see I have been stumping it upon a grand scale. . . . I have, in addition received from fifty to a hundred invitations from different quarters of the country, which I have declined, and I now go by sea for the purpose of avoiding the necessity of addressing the citizens of Philadelphia and Baltimore, who are, I learn, lying in wait for me." All these demands and exertions caused Prentiss to exclaim to George: "Oh! that I were in Germany, quietly studying the history of the past, instead of participating in the history of the present. Indeed, and in good sooth, I am gorged with politics, and surfeited with publicity. I had rather fish in the Great Brook one day, than spend a year amid the senseless hurras of political partisans. It is not reputation one gets—it is only notoriety." [25]

Prentiss reached Vicksburg September 23, 1840.[26] When he had stopped briefly in New Orleans before going on to Vicksburg, his presence was hailed joyously by one of the

[25] Prentiss to *id.,* New York, August 30, 1840, *ibid.,* 175–76.
[26] Vicksburg *Daily Whig,* September 24, 1840.

New Orleans newspapers: "Mr. Prentiss, of Mississippi, arrived in this city yesterday, on his way from the North. This gentleman's friends in New Orleans—and their name is legion—will be happy to congratulate him on his return from his Northern tour." In further complimentary appraisal it stated: "Mr. P. is one of the greatest of the great guns of the Whigs, and few are capable of keeping up a better directed fire against the citadel of Van Burenism. 'He can rule like a wizard the word of the heart. And call up its sunshine or bring down its showers.'" [27] The Vicksburg *Whig*, announcing his return home, commented: "Mr. P. is in good health and fine spirits, and after the grand Convention of the 5th of October, he will commence the canvass of the State." The *Whig* could not forgo saying, too, "Triumphal as has been his greeting wherever he has been, a still warmer reception awaits him from the generous hearts of the people of his own State." [28] But Prentiss was not allowed to rest. Even before October 5, when he began his actual campaign in Mississippi, he was kept speaking. The very night following his arrival, he spoke at a log-cabin raising in Vicksburg. [29]

There was an additional reason why the Vicksburg *Whig* rejoiced upon Prentiss' return. He was needed to meet a challenge. In August, when Prentiss was still in the North, the paper had regretted his absence because of a declaration by Henry S. Foote that he would be willing to have any member of the "bar of Vicksburg individually or collectively to debate with him on the merits of the candidates for the Presidency." The *Whig* remarked particularly, that Foote had said "He was willing to combat with any of them from Mr. Prentiss down." Since Prentiss was out of the state, the *Whig* could not help placing in parentheses, "The General knew as well as the whole of the U. States knew,

27 New Orleans *Daily Picayune*, September 20, 1840.
28 Vicksburg *Daily Whig*, September 24, 1840.
29 *Ibid*.

that Mr. Prentiss was absent or he never would have thought of making that challenge." [30]

But with Prentiss back in Mississippi in the latter part of September, Foote had his chance to meet him in debate. Prentiss and Foote, legal and dueling opponents, met at the Vicksburg courthouse. As might be expected, the *Whig* considered the debate very one-sided. Prentiss opened the debate, dealt with a favorite subject, currency, and spent time, apparently, in attacking the views of Senator Walker on the subject. After commending Prentiss for his "brilliant . . . and conclusive arguments," which "produced the most intense excitement, and repeated and long continued cheering," the *Whig* went on to say: "Gen. Foote attempted a reply to Mr. Prentiss—but such a reply—we cannot describe it. Imagine to yourself a feather attempting to stop in its progress the mighty storm—see it tossed to and fro, and whirled for a few moments in mid air, and then disappear from sight forever. Imagine this, and you have a faint, but imperfect idea of the utter discomfiture of the locofoco orator." [31] In another column of the same issue, the *Whig* continued to dwell upon the significance of the debate and the unequal abilities of the respective debaters: "Some of the most unblushing of the Locofoco party have stated that Gen. Foote completely *used up Prentiss* in their late debate. Oh! ye gods and little fishes! General Foote *use up* Sargeant [*sic*] S. Prentiss. Perfidious! But this proves conclusively, that the Locofoco party are like the *leetle* boy, vot got walloped. *The harder the little fellow was whipped, the louder he cried.*" [32]

Throughout October Prentiss continued to campaign for Harrison, confining his efforts to Mississippi. He really launched his October drive by speaking at the state Whig convention on the fifth of October at Jackson. There he appeared with Balie Peyton and others.[33]

[30] Vicksburg *Tri-Weekly Whig*, August 11, 1840.
[31] Vicksburg *Daily Whig*, September 30, 1840.   [32] *Ibid.*
[33] Vicksburg *Tri-Weekly Whig*, September 10, 1840.

Calls came for him to speak outside Mississippi, but he felt it necessary to refuse. Doubtless the most significant invitation which he declined was that urging him to speak at the state convention of Louisiana Whigs held at Baton Rouge. Numerous Whig groups from Mississippi were invited to be present with the Louisiana delegations, and Prentiss was desired as the chief speaker. The regret of the Louisiana Whigs at Prentiss' absence may be inferred from the welcome speech to the Mississippi Whigs by Thomas Morgan, who said in part: "Led on by the gallant Prentiss, and other noble and kindred spirits, we cannot doubt, that Mississippi, will proclaim to the spoils men, that a free and intelligent people will not submit to dictation, let it come from what source it may." The response of the Mississippi guests to Louisiana was delivered by John M. Chilton of Vicksburg, who stated how much Mississippi was depending on Prentiss: "I wish that the expectations of those whom I now address had been gratified by the presence of Mississippi's favorite Orator. . . . But the Whigs of Mississippi, are too well aware of the necessity of continual preparation and action at home to spare from their ranks, on the eve of a momentous battle, the strong arm and practiced blade of her gallant Prentiss." [34]

Election day approached, and Prentiss had the satisfaction of seeing the Whig cause triumph. Mississippi gave Harrison a majority of nearly three thousand. A few days after the election Prentiss wrote two letters, one to Anna Prentiss in Maine and another to George Prentiss in Europe, in which he revealed the price he had paid in physical and mental exhaustion for Harrison's victory. To Anna he said: "At length 'the wars are all over;' the election has taken place, and we Whigs consider ourselves in some degree paid for our exertions, by the success which has accompanied them. . . . I returned about a week ago, after a most arduous and tiresome canvas, and was literally worn out—so

[34] Baton Rouge *Weekly Gazette*, October 3, 1840.

much so, that this is the earliest moment in which I could muster sufficient energy to write a letter. My health has been good enough, but my faculties of body and mind have been utterly exhausted. . . . I feel as old John Bunyan's Christian did, in *Pilgrim's Progress,* when the burden fell from his back. I will never make the same sacrifices to the public, which I have heretofore done." [35] In a long letter to George Prentiss he stated: "Upon my return from the North, of which you have already heard, I felt it my duty, from every consideration of patriotism and interest, to canvass the State in my capacity for elector. Accordingly, I started out, and for four or five weeks before the election, addressed the people in various portions of the country, exerting myself to the utmost of my ability, mental and physical." He further emphasized the cost in expenditure of energy: "I was exhausted by my previous efforts, on starting, and returned about a week ago, completely worn out. . . . I assure you, however, that on my return, so severely had my powers been taxed, they seemed hardly under the control of volition. In none of my previous political campaigns have my energies been so severely tested." But Harrison had won, and so Prentiss could be exultant: "General Harrison has been elected President, I judge from what we have heard, almost by acclamation; and yet four years ago, the same people, with the same facts as to the characters of the two men before them, rejected him, and chose Mr. Van Buren." What did Prentiss really think of Harrison, however, when he was free to write in confidence to a member of his family? Many of the thousands of listeners to his campaign speeches would not have been too well pleased. They would have expected him to say: "General Harrison is, I doubt not, a good man and a patriot; and, I believe will conduct his Administration so as to restore purity to the Government, and property to the

---

[35] Prentiss to Anna Prentiss, Vicksburg, November 12, 1840, in *Memoir of S. S. Prentiss,* II, 180–81.

people." He would hardly have been expected to add, however: "but he is a very ordinary man." Some might have understood Prentiss' reasoning, though, as he summarized his thinking concerning Harrison: "His election, however, has convinced me that a man of ordinary ability, in a free government, has, in time of peace, a better chance of political success, at least in attaining the chief magistracy, than a man of great and acknowledged talent." [36]

Prentiss had labored to the point of exhaustion and asked no reward but to return unmolested to his law practice in Vicksburg. Possibly a partial explanation of his overindulgence in wines is to be found in his desire for a stimulant in the too strenuous demands which were made upon him. To the question "What office will Prentiss get?" the Vicksburg *Whig* supplied the answer. "Mr. Prentiss, then, will receive *no office*. He desires none, he will receive none." The *Whig* ventured the opinion, "There are many stations upon which his acceptance would confer honor and dignity; but if we know anything of his feelings, there is no office within the gift of the Executive, that he would accept." In reality, because of Prentiss' talents, it recommended that he should "look with indifference, if not contempt, upon the greedy and undignified scramble for office which already manifests itself throughout the country." The basic analysis, reasoning, and advice of the *Whig* was that while "No man of Mr. Prentiss' age has ever assumed so high a stand as the one which that gentleman now occupies by general consent, and . . . without the smiles of Executive favor," certainly "he will not now consent to become a thing which one man can make or unmake by a single dash of the pen." [37]

But if the Whigs were elated by Harrison's victory, they were grieved by his sudden death a month after he became president. The succession of John Tyler to the presidency proved to the party that it was necessary to look into its ranks for a new leader.

[36] *Id.* to George Prentiss, Vicksburg, November 12, 1840, *ibid.*, 182–83.
[37] Vicksburg *Daily Whig*, December 2, 1840.

Chapter VIII

MISSISSIPPI BOND REPUDIATION

THE years between 1841 and 1845 were both happy and gloomy ones for Prentiss: bright and reassuring because of marriage, fatherhood, and domestic tranquillity; dark, because of Whig defeats, panic conditions in the state, and the disgrace of public debts unpaid.

Prentiss, before his marriage, possessed a house but not a home. "Cub-Castle," as he called his bachelor establishment, he once described to his mother as "the prettiest house and the pleasantest situation in the whole State." [1] But Cub-Castle was, as Shields related, "merely his *roosting* place." [2] In spite of friends, fame, and even certain periodic visits from his Maine relatives, Prentiss, notwithstanding a certain morbid sensitivity concerning his lameness which made him shy of women, admitted his desire for marriage.

It is possible, because he was so lame, that Prentiss felt at times that marriage and a home were never to be his lot in life. Although honors and reputation came early to him, marriage was relatively late. In addition to his lameness, which explains, probably more than any other one factor, the fact that he was nearly thirty-four years of age before he married, he had additional anxieties. Prentiss' rise and fall financially is a story in itself; but it does so happen that at the very time of his romance, panic years subsequent to 1837 fell upon the state causing him, like so many other Mississippians, to become the victim of overspeculation.

[1] Prentiss to his mother, Vicksburg, August 28, 1841, in *Memoir of S. S. Prentiss,* II, 204.
[2] Shields, *Seargent Smith Prentiss,* 319.

Nevertheless, Prentiss did not see fit to live all his life alone. He admitted his loneliness and desire for a wife and a home. "I have ever yearned for affection; I believe it is the only thing of which I am avaricious. The necessities of life, business, politics, and the excitements connected with them, have heretofore in some degree occupied my mind and held in suspense," he wrote to Anna Prentiss, "but not satisfied this craving, this hunger of heart." [3]

A happy marriage became a reality for him in 1842. It was his good fortune, probably during 1841 or even earlier, to become acquainted with Mary Williams, daughter of James C. Williams of Natchez. Her father was an extensive planter, the owner of Longwood. On the maternal side, Mary Williams was descended from the Perceys of Northumberland. It is tempting to believe that it was this romance which prompted Johnson, the Natchez free Negro barber, to write in his diary: "Mr. S. S. Prentiss Gets Shaved twice To Day—Something Out I think I know—?" [4] The date of the entry, April 28, 1841, would indicate that the love affair was known in the community a year before the marriage.

The wedding occurred March 3, 1842, at the Williams home, Longwood, a short distance from Natchez.[5] The Vicksburg *Whig* could be expected to announce this happy event as it did all other notable experiences in the life of Prentiss: "Marriage is High Life.—Our distinguished townsman, the Hon. Seargent S. Prentiss, was married in Natchez on Thursday morning, to Miss Mary Jane Williams of that city. The distinguished bridegroom, accom-

[3] Prentiss to Anna Prentiss, Jackson, January 31, 1841, in *Memoir of S. S. Prentiss*, II, 192.

[4] Diary of William T. Johnson, April 28, 1841.

[5] Shields, *Seargent Smith Prentiss*, 317. The Williams home, Longwood, was destroyed by fire some time in the 1850's. Between the time of the fire and the outbreak of the Civil War the building of a new house was begun. The Civil War necessitated a stoppage of the work, many of the workmen being northerners who returned home. The house, a large brick three-story octagonal structure, stands today as it was when the war occurred.

panied by his young and beautiful bride, took passage the same morning for New Orleans, on the steamer Sultana. We understand they leave in a few days for Washington City." [6] Prentiss appeared his best as he began his wedding journey. One observer wrote: "I got on the Sultana at Fort Adams when S. S. Prentiss was aboard on his bridal trip— married that morning at Natchez, and the whole bridal troupe went down to New Orleans. It was my first sight and acquaintance with Prentiss. I was charmed with his manners and appearance. He had the most handsome head, and it sat better on his neck and shoulders than any person I know. That was in 1843 [1842], when his fame was world wide; yet, sir, he was as bashful, timid, and quiet as a boy of 16 in the presence of those ladies." [7]

Following the bridal journey to Washington, Prentiss took his bride to Vicksburg. He built a new home at the corner of what is now Belmont Avenue and Washington Street and named it "Belmont." This house, which was destroyed during the Civil War, was the Prentisses' abode as long as they lived in Mississippi. On April 14, 1843, Jane, the first of the four Prentiss children, was born. [8]

But days of mental disquietude accompanied Prentiss' happy home life because his own financial status was seriously impaired. The financially carefree days for him were over. In certain respects, his monetary worries were but an instance of much wider ills facing Mississippi. Prentiss had speculated, plunged too deeply, and had spent and lived too recklessly. Almost the first evidence that Prentiss was facing straitened financial circumstances he mentioned in a

[6] Vicksburg *Daily Whig*, March 5, 1842.

[7] Dr. A. R. Kilpatrick to J. F. H. Claiborne, Navasota, Grimes County, Texas, n.d., upon request of Claiborne for contributions to *De Bow's Review*, May 2, 1877, in R. M. Jones (ed.), "Some Facts Concerning the Settlement and Early History of Mississippi," in *Mississippi Historical Society Publications*, I (1898), 88–89.

[8] The other Prentiss children were George Lewis, born September 22, 1844; Seargent Smith, born January 5, 1847; and Eunice, born October 21, 1848.

letter to George Prentiss in 1841. He listed first of all the fact that his political campaigns had been costly. Second, he stated: "I find myself largely involved for others, who, prostrated by the storm which has swept over all classes in this country, have left me as security, to bear a very heavy pecuniary burden." In consequence, he continued: "I have already paid very large amounts for others, and within the last three months, have taken up security-debts, by mortgaging my own property, to the amount of at least fifty thousand dollars more. This I have done to obtain time, and afford me an opportunity of availing myself of my professional exertions. Some of my property I have sold, but not to a great extent." After stating, too, that "The best portion I shall be able to save, if my life is spared," he added: "Had it not been for these security-debts, which I hold equally binding with my own, I should have been able to retire from business in the course of the present year." Reassuringly though, he told George: "These things will not make the slightest change in my arrangements with regard to yourself." In short, he told him to continue his European studies and travel, for "The sum I spare you, is not one-twentieth part of what I can make annually at my profession, which will, I doubt not, be worth at least twenty-five thousand dollars a year." [9]

Prentiss was overoptimistic. No panic conditions and general bankruptcy could hit a state like Mississippi without taking a double toll from men like Prentiss, who had been guilty of overspeculation and who now faced increased obligations and reduced professional fees. Otherwise he would hardly have been writing two months after his marriage: "I have hardly ever felt so gloomy. Indeed, a deep gloom seems to pervade the whole country. Times never were known to be in so desperate a condition, and the prospect for a long period does not seem to brighten. For the

[9] Prentiss to George Prentiss, Vicksburg, June 10, 1841, in *Memoir of S. S. Prentiss*, II, 200.

first time in my life, I look with apprehension upon the state of things." [10] The same gloom he re-emphasized a few weeks later in another letter. "There is literally no money in Vicksburg. Not a cent can be collected or borrowed. Such times as we now have here, were never known in the United States; property has no value whatever, and all are equally poor." [11] At almost the same time he was depicting the state of things in another letter. "You can form no idea of the embarrassment, prostration and ruin, which pervade this country. . . . There is no currency at all in this part of the country, and property has no representative. The New Orleans banks, which heretofore furnished this State with the little money that did circulate, have all failed, and now it is utterly impossible to collect debts, or to sell property at any price. Nothing can be more gloomy than the present posture of affairs; and I confess I can see no prospect of speedy relief. In every other country on the face of the globe, property will bring some price; here it will command nothing, and a man may starve in possession of a fortune." [12]

Truly evil days had fallen on Mississippi. While Prentiss was not writing so pessimistically until 1842, he might equally well have done so two or even four years earlier. Mississippi was, in 1842, feeling the deep aftermath of the panic of 1837. This bore on him more personally about 1842; hence, possibly, the extent of his gloom. All this financial depression was in great contrast to the "Flush Times" of the thirties as described by a Mississippian in 1836 just before the panic: "This was the era of banks and discounts, wild speculation, extravagance, and license. Gaming and drinking were carried to excess at Jackson. Men not worth a button would cooly ask for an indorsement for ten thousand dollars, and indorsements in blank to be filled up to suit any trade that might offer. A refusal

[10] *Id.* to Anna Prentiss, Vicksburg, May 10, 1842, *ibid.*, 216.
[11] *Id.* to *id.*, Vicksburg, June 9, 1842, *ibid.*, 217.
[12] *Id.* to George Prentiss, Vicksburg, July 16, 1842, *ibid.*, 218.

to indorse was resented as a reflection on one's integrity; and to suggest a mortgage as security for an indorsement was a matter of great delicacy, and generally offensive. I have seen a man not worth one cent at a gaming-table publicly staking blank paper with the well-known signatures and indorsements of responsible men!" [13]

Prentiss and other residents of Mississippi were not the only ones to observe the dire conditions in the state. The panic of 1837 caused the whole nation to suffer. But quite naturally, where speculation and indiscretion had been most rampant, the suffering, as in Mississippi, was the greatest.

There are always causes for such effects or phenomena. The business cycle, with its inclined curve of prosperity, followed by the decline to depression, is not new in America. To designate the one basic cause for the dire financial straits of Mississippi from 1837 through the first years of the 1840's is not easy. Some effects are often mistaken for causes. For instance, was the state simply feeling the aftermath of the panic of 1837, or was it reaping the whirlwind of certain of its own many indiscretions?

A pertinent question is: To what extent was Mississippi's banking structure and system, lax and uncontrolled through the 1830's, inadequate to withstand the strains and stresses placed upon it in the 1840's? Prior to 1830, the banking policy had been one of conservatism. After that time it was the very opposite. Undue issuance of credit through too many chartered banks not well controlled is, doubtless, one basic explanation for the days of travail in Mississippi.[14]

A brief history of banking in Mississippi is necessary to comprehend the story of inordinate credit. It falls, as one writer has stated, into four periods: "(1) Sound banking

[13] Claiborne, *Life and Times of Gen. Sam. Dale,* 225–26.
[14] For a treatment and substantiation of this point of view, see Reginald C. McGrane, *Foreign Bondholders and American State Debts* (New York, 1935), 193.

and secure issues (1809–1830); (2) State banking and shin plasters (1830–1842); (3) Brokerage and bankruptcy (1842–1865); (4) Private and national banking and cautious conservatism (1865—)." [15] The first period, "Sound banking and secure issue," brings into focus the history of the Bank of Mississippi, established by the territorial legislature on December 23, 1809. The headquarters of the bank were at Natchez, and it had a capital stock of $500,000. It began, really, as a private institution but became virtually a state institution in 1818 by a supplemental charter whereby the state "should subscribe one-fourth of the capital stock and appoint five of the sixteen directors." Also "its notes were made legal tender to all payments to the State and were given a monopoly of circulation until the time fixed for the expiration of the charter, Dec. 30, 1840." [16] The very fact that the bank existed for nine years as a private institution, and was then given new life by the action of 1818, is proof of its genuine worth and function.

But conservatism gave way to the second period, "State banking and shin plasters." By 1830 unprecedented prosperity, bringing in professional men like Prentiss in great numbers, but more especially planters dedicated to cotton and slavery, resulted in pressure for additional banking facilities and credit. Consequently, in 1831 the Planters' Bank was founded, the name indicating its close identification with the agricultural interests of the state. It, also, was located at Natchez, with branches at Vicksburg, Port Gibson, Woodville, Columbus, Monticello, Liberty, Rodney, and, later, at Schula, in Holmes County. [17] The evidence against the Planters' Bank is not at the beginning necessarily damning, for it can be said that such an institution was naturally needed. The capital stock was $3,000,000, and

[15] Charles H. Brough, "The History of Banking in Mississippi," in *Mississippi Historical Society Publications*, III (1900), 317–18.
[16] *Ibid.*, 319.   [17] *Ibid.*, 323.

two thirds of it was assumed by the state upon the issuance of 5 per cent bonds.

But more banks, if not needed, were at least demanded. Political leaders co-operated with planters and merchants in leading a crusade for more banks. Typical of this attitude was the early action of Governor Charles Runnels, who told the legislature in 1835: "The branches of the Planters' Bank, located at different points in the State, with the limited capital assigned them, when taking into view the necessity of the country, are a mere mockery of banking principles. . . . Can it, therefore, with this view of the subject, be thought by the most miserly economist in banking matters, that a State, whose amount of product in a single article of cotton, amounts to $15,000,000, with every probability of an increase ratio of twenty-five per cent per annum for many years to come, can get along with a banking capital of $6,000,000?" [18] With such leadership and endorsement of banking extension, Mississippi legislators ignored the ninth section of the state constitution "forbidding the State to borrow money and to pledge its faith for the redemption of any loan or debt," and began the erection, in rapid succession, of banks, making available vast quantities of easy credit. Possibly as accurate and complete a list of these banks as might be cited was given by *Niles' National Register* in an enumeration of the corporations established from 1833 to 1838. In 1833 there were established two banks, the Western Feliciana Rail Road and Banking Company, with a capitalization of $1,000,000, and the Grand Gulf Rail Road, capitalized at $2,000,000. Then in 1836 a large number of new banks were created. These were the Mississippi Rail Road, the Commercial Bank of Rodney, the Commercial Bank of Columbus, the Tombigbee Rail Road, the Aberdeen and Pontotoc Bank, the Commercial Bank of Manchester, the Agricultural Bank of

[18] Quoted *ibid.*, 324.

Mississippi, the Commercial Bank of Natchez, and the Brandon Bank, all of which enlarged the banking capital of Mississippi by $21,000,000. Still more were established in 1837: the Port Gibson Bank, the Vicksburg Water-Works, the Northern Bank of Mississippi, the Hernando Rail Road, the Bank of Grenada, the Bank of Lexington, and the Benton and Manchester Rail Road, thereby adding $10,500,000 to the banking capital of the state. But the limit was not reached until 1838, when there was incorporated the mammoth Union Bank with a capital of $15,000,000.[19] Obviously the credit of the state had been extended enormously over the approximately $3,000,000 of the Planters' Bank of 1830.

Of the difficulties which Mississippi encountered as a result of the numerous banks which she chartered, the greatest were connected with the Planters' Bank and the Union Bank. The bonds of the Planters' Bank were never actually repudiated, although the default of the state made the consequences practically as dire. The Union Bank, however, because of the size of its capital stock and the methods employed to raise its capital, was the straw that broke the camel's back, and prostrated the state. First of all, to acquire the huge capital stock for the erection of the bank, the state mortgaged itself with 5 per cent bonds for a period of twenty years, the stockholders themselves securing the state. Secondly, the sale of the bonds was undertaken in the midst of the panic conditions. Inasmuch as money was virtually nonexistent in Mississippi, efforts were made to sell the bonds outside the state. At a meeting of the directors in Jackson, May 17, 1838, three commissioners, Colonel James C. Wilkins of Natchez, William M. Pinchard of Vicksburg, and Edward C. Wilkinson of Yazoo City, were designated to endeavor to sell the bonds which the governor had exe-

[19] *Niles' National Register*, LVII (1839–1840), 68. For a similar résumé of the banks created, see Brough, "History of Banking in Mississippi," *loc. cit.*, 325–26. The subject is also treated admirably in McGrane, *Foreign Bondholders and American State Debts*, 193–96.

cuted. They went first to New York, and failing to dispose of them there, went to Philadelphia, where they sold the whole amount to Nicholas Biddle in the month of August.[20] Biddle drove a sharp bargain. As explained by McGrane: "The contract specified that the bonds were to be paid for in five equal installments; but the interest began from the date of the sale. To make them negotiable abroad, they were made payable in England at the rate of four shillings six pence on the dollar. By this transaction Biddle gained two advantages. As the bonds were bought on credit while the interest began immediately, he received the difference of interest during the interval on all that remained unpaid; and by making them payable in England in pound sterling a \$2,000 bond at the current rate of exchange was equivalent to \$2,189.92." [21]

This deal with Biddle, in which the Mississippians were either ignorant of the fact that the bonds were depreciated from the start or were disposed to overlook this contingency, caused much pleasurable excitement at home. Wilkins, Pinchard, and Wilkinson were welcomed home, and in due time the specie and English gold arrived by steamer at New Orleans, was transported up the river to Vicksburg, and then overland to Jackson.[22] At the same time, the English purchasers were kept ignorant of the fact that the bonds had been purchased on credit, and Biddle disposed of the issue gradually and with ease.[23]

Thus, Mississippi approached and entered upon the third phase of her banking history, repudiation. The impetus was certainly given when the bonds were sold as they were to Biddle. Moreover, the bonds passed into the possession of foreign purchasers at the very time when ruinous conditions faced Mississippi, and when a growing deadly hostil-

[20] Brough, "History of Banking in Mississippi," *loc. cit.*, 329; McGrane, *Foreign Bondholders and American State Debts*, 194.
[21] McGrane, *Foreign Bondholders and American State Debts*, 197.
[22] Brough, "History of Banking in Mississippi," *loc. cit.*, 329.
[23] McGrane, *Foreign Bondholders and American State Debts*, 198.

ity was developing toward banks because many financially hard-pressed borrowers were unable to meet their obligations. Quite naturally, many felt no responsibility for conditions as they existed, and looked with increasing reluctance upon shouldering obligations for generations to come. This very point was raised by Governor McNutt before the legislature in 1840 when he "questioned whether one generation had the right to saddle posterity with a heavy debt." [24] The next step, then, for McNutt to take was to argue that if charters may be granted, they may also be taken away. This he asked of the legislature on the grounds that the bonds had been sold below par.

Because of the financial conditions in the state and the Governor's attitude, many members of the legislature were ready to take steps toward actual repudiation. The sentiment for repudiation grew rapidly, especially with certain newspapers fanning the flames. The Vicksburg *Sentinel* was an outspoken advocate, and others, such as the Columbus *Democrat,* the Jackson *Mississippian,* and the *Mississippi Free Trader and Natchez Daily Gazette* followed suit. The Whig papers tended to take the opposite attitude, as did the Whig party generally. The contagion cut across party lines, however. The Whigs, though there were repudiators among them, inclined to oppose repudiation, but the Democrats split quite definitely. Many Democrats, such as Samuel Gholson, Prentiss' former political foe, joined hands with Prentiss to preserve the financial integrity of the state.

Probably no man in Mississippi did more to oppose the course of the repudiationists than Prentiss. One of the truest statements George Prentiss ever made was that "A collection of Mr. Prentiss' principal speeches on the bond question, correctly reported, would be a lasting monument to his legal attainments, the fervor of his patriotism, his dauntless courage, and the nobleness of his political prin-

[24] *Ibid.,* 199.

ciples." [25] Unfortunately his speeches on the question, delivered over a period of time, are among the most difficult
specimens of his public address to find. Nevertheless, at the
very time when he was personally most depressed by his own
financial reverses, as well as those of his fellows, and when
increased taxes to meet the interest on the bonds would
have fallen heavily upon him, he took his stand and delivered speeches over a four-year period, rebuking the repudiators with all his oratorical strength. He justified the severity
of his language "on the ground that, as the evil assaulted the
very being of society, it was entitled to no quarter; that it
was a sort of moral treason to parley with it." [26]

In consequence of the stand taken by Governor McNutt
before the legislature in 1840 and the sentiment for repudiation which was spreading like wildfire, those in opposition to repudiation, regardless of party affiliation, rallied to
prevent it. The first meeting of such a nature was held at
Natchez in 1840. At this occasion, which was "probably,
the first meeting ever held in the United States to denounce
Repudiation," [27] George Poindexter and Prentiss were the
chief speakers. Judge George Winchester presided, and,
after the presentation of a body of resolutions condemning
McNutt for his course of action, Poindexter and Prentiss
spoke.[28]

The issue of repudiation became most heated in 1841 as
Governor McNutt continued to champion it on a whole-
sale basis, and as the state prepared for a gubernatorial campaign. Once the Columbus *Democrat* declared to the
people of Mississippi, "the beds on which your wives and
children sleep, the tables on which you eat your daily bread
will be taken by the excise men for the benefit of those who
sleep in splendid brick palaces, who sleep in mahogany bed-
steads, eat with gold knives and forks, and drink champagne

[25] *Memoir of S. S. Prentiss*, II, 247.   [26] *Ibid.*, 248.
[27] *Ibid.*, 246.
[28] *Conservative and Holly Springs* (Miss.) *Banner*, March 31, 1840.

as the ordinary beverage of the day." [29] An equally typical point of view was once expressed by the *Mississippi Free Trader and Natchez Daily Gazette*. In response to what it called "The State Bonds of Mississippi; What Will Foreigners say," an inquiry "going the rounds of the whig papers," the *Free Trader* said: "The good opinion of foreign nations! ! What did they say of our fathers when they took up arms against the tyrant of the sea? They were denounced as rebels, cutthroats, *'outre barbarians,'* even in the parliament of this 'refined nation,' whose good opinion we are now invoked to obtain at the price of the toil and sweat and slavery of our citizens. The good opinion of foreign nations indeed! Away with such stuff. Is not our declaration of independence a by word and a term of reproach in the mouths of all the royalists and aristocrats in England. . . . We hope to hear no more of 'what will foreigners think of us.' They will think just what they always did think whenever we asserted our rights, should those rights conflict with their interests. Who cares what *they* think or say?" [30] There is no doubt that public opinion was directed in 1841 toward repudiation.

Anticipating the state elections in the autumn of 1841 and certain that the issue of repudiation would be the major item in the campaign, the antirepudiation Whigs and Democrats met in convention at Jackson in February to select their candidates. Prentiss was present as a delegate from Warren County. He "was called for with so much enthusiasm at this moment," stated the Vicksburg *Whig,* regarding the early deliberations of the convention, "that all other business was suspended, and he was conducted to the speakers stand amidst the deafening plaudits of that crowded assemblage when he offered for adoption the following resolutions, which after a speech from him of an hour and a half, were unanimously adopted." The resolu-

[29] Quoted in McGrane, *Foreign Bondholders and American State Debts,* 200.

[30] *Mississippi Free Trader and Natchez Daily Gazette,* December 5, 1841.

tions alluded to by the *Whig* were four in number. The first two expressed gratification over the election of William Henry Harrison. The third was a gesture to the Democrats who differed on national politics, but with whom, said Prentiss, the Whigs "shall not be divided upon the question whether the State of Mississippi shall act honorably and honestly in relation to her pecuniary obligations, and we call upon them to join us in frowning down on all those on either side who are willing to elevate themselves or their party at the expense of the honor and character of the State." The fourth resolution bore directly on the question of repudiation, stating the position, "that the State is *bound by every obligation of honor and justice to pay or cause to be paid,* her bonds issued and sold for the benefit of the *Union* Bank, and for the payment of her stock in the Planters' Bank." [31] The convention adjourned after nominating antirepudiationist David O. Shattuck of Carroll County for governor, and Adam L. Bingaman and William R. Hasley for Congress.[32]

Shortly after the February convention, pressure was put on Prentiss to announce himself for the legislature in order to oppose repudiation in that body. The Vicksburg *Whig* made public the following letter addressed to him: "Many of your fellow-citizens of the county of Warren, regarding the ensuing election for State officers as one involving in its issues, the honor and integrity of our State, and its permanence in correct political principles, are desirous that this county shall be so represented in the next Legislature as to maintain the character and policy of the whig party. Looking to you as in a great measure the founder of that party in this State, and certainly, under every discouragement and defeat, its earnest advocate and supporter, we feel sure, that when that party is for the first time prosperous, your arm will lend its aid to maintain that prosperity. . . .

[31] Vicksburg *Daily Whig*, February 4, 1841.
[32] Natchez *Daily Courier*, February 4, 1841.

We trust you will permit your name to be announced as a candidate for that office." [33]

But Prentiss declined to be a candidate. He told the editor and the public: "While I acknowledge the kindness of my political friends from whom the request emanated, and the flattering terms in which it is couched, I am compelled to decline the honorable distinction tendered." He gave as his explanation: "I had thought of becoming a candidate for the office in question, but I find my personal affairs require for the ensuing year my undivided attention. This consideration, however, would not have prevented a compliance with the wishes of my friends, but that I know other gentlemen, more competent, who are willing to serve the State in the station alluded to." [34]

By early June the Democrats, or antibond party, had held their convention and nominated Tilghiman M. Tucker for governor and Jacob Thompson and William M. Gwin for Congress.[35] Prentiss entered the campaign against the repudiation ticket. Concerning one of his speeches at a Vicksburg mass meeting in which he made a strong defense for bond payment, the *Whig* observed: "Of Mr. Prentiss' speech, we need only say *he was* himself. That is eulogy enough." [36] But in spite of efforts to prevent it, at the end of the spirited campaign, Tucker defeated Shattuck by 2,286 votes, the repudiationists winning the support of the "poor and sparsely settled agricultural districts of the State, while heavy majorities against repudiation were returned from Adams, Hinds, Madison and Warren Counties, that represented the bulk of the State's population and taxable property." [37]

The hour for formal repudiation approached. Tucker took his election as a mandate from the people to usher it

---

[33] Vicksburg *Daily Whig*, March 6, 1841.
[34] *Ibid.*, March 8, 1841.   [35] Natchez *Daily Courier*, June 4, 1841.
[36] Vicksburg *Tri-Weekly Whig*, August 10, 1841. See also, *ibid.*, August 12, 1841.
[37] Brough, "History of Banking in Mississippi," *loc. cit.*, 335–36.

the Natchez address: "It is a masterly speech, and establishes the liability of the State to pay her bonds, we think, beyond contradiction. . . . It has produced some panic among the repudiators of Natchez, and set their organ to growling. But they should have recollected that whenever Mr. P. argues the bond question, he strips repudiation of its humbuggery and holds it up in its naked infamy." [45]

On October 27, the Vicksburg *Whig* announced a meeting of the Anti-Repudiation Club to be held at Vicksburg *"rain or shine,* when the Hon. S. S. Prentiss and others, are expected to address the meeting." [46] Describing the meeting which took place on schedule, the same paper stated that John A. Quitman, "a democrat of the old school, delivered one of the most cogent and logical arguments we have heard upon the question," and advocated payment in spite of the fact that he "now pays a tax of $800 annually," but "would pay still more rather than disgrace the character of the State of his early adoption." The *Whig* stressed that Prentiss in turn paid "an eloquent and just tribute to the speech of Gen. Quitman," as he "launched out in a spirited discussion of the subject, which enchained the attention of his audience for two hours." How effective Prentiss was the *Whig* tried to emphasize: "There is some magic about his speeches; for although we listened to every word, and marked every gesture, we fail in our attempt to describe them. . . . We have heard Mr. Prentiss make many speeches, and such is the impression which they make upon us, that we always fancy that the last is the best." Again a full account of the speech was considered impossible; the only insight to the basic argument of it is the statement: "Mr. Prentiss took a legal view of the question, and discussed its minutiae and details in such a manner as to bring the fallacy of the doctrine within the scope of the most ordinary mind, and stripped it so completely of the mystery

[45] Vicksburg *Daily Whig,* October 30, 1843.
[46] *Ibid.,* October 27, 1843.

and pretexts which demagogues throw around it as to render its enormity more palpable." [47]

But Prentiss' most strategic appeal was his final address made on election day at Vicksburg. The circumstances were unusually interesting because on that occasion Jefferson Davis was defeated for the first public office he ever tried to obtain. Davis, a week before the election, was induced to take the place of a weak Democratic contestant for the legislature from Warren County who had withdrawn from the race.[48] Although the Vicksburg *Whig* had announced a joint debate or discussion between Prentiss and Davis for Saturday, November 4, Davis declined to discuss repudiation in open debate on that date with Prentiss. The fact of the proposal of the debate and of its cancellation is of more than usual interest, in that it makes clear the real position of Davis, who carried in later years the unfair indictment of being a repudiator. The *Whig* knew where Davis stood when it said: "By an agreement entered into on Wednesday, between Hon. S. S. Prentiss and Jefferson Davis, Esq., the nominee of the Vicksburg meeting, the latter gentleman was to have made a speech on the question of repudiation. But we regret to learn that on yesterday the latter gentleman declined making a speech, stating that his party declared they would not attend the meeting." The *Whig* then analyzed and complimented Davis: "Well, we do wonder that repudiators should shrink from a meeting at which they expect to hear the question fairly discussed. But one thing we are certain of, that Mr. Davis will never shrink from the avowal of his opinions upon any subject; but the fact is, the repudiators were unfortunate in their selection of a candidate. Mr. Davis is too candid, too honorable to concentrate on the subterranean votes. That the repudiators have set up a claim to decency in nominating Mr.

---

[47] *Ibid.*, November 2, 1843.
[48] [Mrs. Jefferson Davis], *Jefferson Davis, Ex-President of the Confederacy: A Memoir* (New York, 1890), I, 182.

Davis, we are free to confess, but that there is not the slightest chance for his election, Tuesday will prove." [49]

The significance of this attitude toward Davis can hardly be overemphasized. In fact, it differed scarcely at all in sentiment from that expressed by the *Sentinel,* the outspoken opponent of the *Whig,* and a repudiationist organ, when it announced the nomination of Davis. "Mr. Davis is a sterling Democrat," it declared, "a man of unsullied private character, talents of a superior order, extensive political information, and judging from the structure of his remarks before the convention, a fine public speaker. There may be some in the county to whom Mr. Davis, from the secluded privacy in which he has lived, is unknown, to these we repeat, Mr. Davis is what we have stated, *a man, every inch a man,* of whom the Democracy of Old Warren should be proud. Let us rally around the man of our choice and the victory is ours! To secure it, *action* and *union,* on the part of our friends are alone necessary. Let every democrat, every anti-bonder walk up to the polls on Monday, and cast his vote for the regularly nominated candidates, and we shall be certain to come out triumphantly victorious! !" [50] If both opposing newspapers should so eulogize Davis, the *Sentinel* calling him "a sterling Democrat," and the *Whig* referring to him as "too candid, too intelligent, and too honorable to concentrate on the subterranean votes," some explanation is in order.

While Prentiss and Davis did not meet in debate on Saturday before the election, they did do so shortly thereafter. On election day, as the voters were passing by to the polls in Vicksburg, Prentiss and Davis engaged in a debate which deserves a place in history. For one thing, Davis was thenceforth a public figure; his private and secluded days were over. For ten years, ever since the death of his first wife, he had lived almost as a hermit, and, though a West Point

[49] Vicksburg *Daily Whig,* November 3, 1843.
[50] Vicksburg *Daily Sentinel,* November 1, 1843.

graduate and therefore a military man, had proved his skill
as a planter. But he had improved his time otherwise as
well. From 1827, as he lived on his plantation at Davis Bend
in Warren County, he read history and kept abreast of contemporary events in the United States. Thus he was preparing himself for a conspicuous role in American history, and
was destined to assume the leadership which the South lost
when Davis' mentor, Calhoun, died in 1850. The meeting
with Prentiss, which has been likened to the great debate
between John Randolph and Patrick Henry in Virginia in
1798,[51] brought out the talents of Davis as he matched abilities with a proven orator.

The pertinent question arises: Why should the repudiators in Warren County in 1843 select Davis for the legislature? In truth he was not a repudiator himself. It would be
stretching the point to call him even a mild repudiationist.
Of course, Warren County was a Whig stronghold, and the
antibond forces had little hope of winning. Perhaps it was
best, when a week before the election it became necessary
to present a new candidate, to select a man like Davis,
whom Democrats and Whigs alike could call a sterling
Democrat. Not all Democrats were repudiators; this was
particularly true in the wealthier counties, such as Warren.
Hence, then, the Democrats in that county would be more
certain of sending their nominee to the legislature if he
was a man who, like Davis, appealed to numerous elements
in both parties.

But what was the precise stand of Davis on repudiation?
While not a repudiator, he took a position on the question
which provided an issue upon which he could clash with
Prentiss in the debate. In brief, Davis held that the obligation to pay the bonds was binding until the courts ruled
otherwise. Thus, his was a midway position. Prentiss and
the advocates of bond payment could not concede this, in-

51 William E. Dodd, *Statesmen of the Old South, or From Radicalism to
Conservative Revolt* (New York, 1911), 180.

tually repudiated them, but merely allowed them to go unpaid, they were, in time, met in part. In 1848 the balance of $94,000 in the sinking fund erected by this bank was applied on the first of the coupons which had fallen due.[58] Also, the state in 1848 took steps to sell 500,000 acres of land which had been set aside by the federal government for purposes of "internal improvement," and made acceptable Planters' Bank bonds at par.[59] The matter of these bonds continued to dog the steps of Mississippi, however. Action was taken to refer the matter to the electorate in 1852, with the result that the antibond forces again won.[60]

By a unique circumstance the names of Prentiss and the English poet, William Wordsworth, became linked in the repudiation issue. As George Prentiss studied and journeyed in Europe for four years, it was his good fortune to make the personal acquaintance of various European scholars and men of letters. Among these was Wordsworth, whom he visited in September, 1842, just before returning to America. He gathered directly from Wordsworth some information which he immediately relayed to Prentiss. George had written what he thought would be his last letter to Seargent before sailing for home. But immediately after visiting the poet, he quickly wrote another. He explained: "But I have heard a story to-day which has so grieved me that I cannot help sitting down and writing to you about it." He told of his call on Wordsworth, of how kindly he had been received, of four "delightful hours" spent at Ry-

---

[58] McGrane, *Foreign Bondholders and American State Debts*, 206.

[59] *Ibid.*

[60] *Ibid.*, 212. Secession and Civil War likewise precluded efforts to redeem the bonds, and in 1934, in a case before the United States Supreme Court, Chief Justice Charles Evans Hughes ruled that the Principality of Monaco could not sue the State of Mississippi in an effort to recover payment on Planters' Bank bonds. *Ibid.*, 212–21. An interesting example of the effects of repudiation on Mississippi is the statement in 1845: "The State of Mississippi has a fund of $160,000 secured for the State University, which has been located at Oxford. It lost $95,000 intended for the same object, by investing it in Planters' Bank stock." *Niles' National Register*, LXVIII (1845), 180.

dal Mount, and then added: "And yet hardly have I felt so distressed and mortified as this very afternoon." This he went on to explain was occasioned by the fact that during their conversation Wordsworth had told him of how a sister of his wife had once purchased £3,000 of American stock, over £2,000 being Mississippi bonds, that upon the death of Mrs. Wordsworth's sister some of the bonds were left to a brother and another sister, some to Wordsworth's daughter, and that because all interest on the bonds ceased to be paid they had "abandoned all hope of ever receiving a penny." The story depressed the highly sensitive character of George still more because "The brother and sister and daughter are all in straightened circumstances. The case of the daughter is the most distressing, as she was not long ago married to a gentleman, to whom she was deeply attached, but who was of very limited means. Wordsworth himself is not positively poor, but it is quite out of the question for him to make up either to his sister-in-law, and her brother, or to his daughter, what they have thus shamefully been defrauded of." George had, of course, immediately thought of his lawyer brother in Mississippi and the services he might possibly render. Thus, he told Seargent, "You will perceive, by the enclosed papers, that they were issued before 1835; part are called 'Mississippi Bonds,' part 'New Mississippi Bonds.' " [61]

The fact that the bonds held by members of the Wordsworth family had been issued prior to 1835 meant that they could not have been Union Bank bonds. More likely they were Planters' Bank bonds. This gave Prentiss a ray of hope that Wordsworth might recover their value. Consequently, in ready willingness to be of service, he wrote Wordsworth a few months later. In his letter, after mentioning to the poet how much gratification George had received in his visit, he was generally quite reassuring. He tried to explain

[61] George Prentiss to Prentiss, Ambleside, England, September 4, 1842, in *Bright Side of Life*, I, 291–92.

the different classes of Mississippi bonds, "issued at different periods, and for different purposes." He mentioned that one class, meaning, of course, the Union Bank bonds, had been repudiated by the legislature. The other class, he assured Wordsworth, had not been repudiated, "nor is the validity of them questioned at all." He admitted, however: "It is true no provision has been made during several years for the payment of the interest; but this neglect has arisen from other causes than that of repudiation." But in spite of this, since Wordsworth's bonds were those of the Planters' Bank, Prentiss could say: "Their validity is acknowledged on all hands; nor has any pretence ever been set up of illegality, or irregularity—either in their inception or sale. I have no doubt of *ultimate payment of these bonds; both principal and interest;*—and in this opinion I am sustained by all intelligent men in the country." Prentiss was no prophet; he could only venture an opinion coupled with more advice. "How soon provision will be made for their liquidation, it is difficult to predict with any certainty. I am of opinion that in two or three years, the State will provide for the payment of the interest, and place the ultimate payment of the Principal beyond all cavil. I would, therefore, advise the holders of this class of Mississippi bonds to avoid sacrificing them." [62]

It probably cannot be known to what exent Wordsworth or his relatives ever received the principal and interest of the bonds. George Prentiss told all he knew of later developments. After Seargent moved to New Orleans, George stated that he learned that action by the Mississippi legislature had made most likely the payment of them and that he further acquired information from Governor Brown verifying the fact. The Governor further stated that if Wordsworth would send the bonds to Brown *"he would Personally undertake their sale and remit the proceeds* to

[62] Prentiss to William Wordsworth, Vicksburg, February 5, 1843, in *Memoir of S. S. Prentiss,* II, 261–62.

Mr. W." [63] George Prentiss concluded: "I lost no time in sending the news to Rydal Mount. In a few weeks a touching letter came from the aged poet, informing me that the bonds had been forwarded to Governor Brown, according to my suggestion. Not long after Wordsworth passed away, and I never heard from him again." [64]

This story of bond repudiation in Mississippi, which, at the same time, places Prentiss in the category of the men who struggled for financial integrity, may well be ended with a note of levity. Alexander McNutt must be designated as the first public man in Mississippi to give the movement widespread direction. Also, many Europeans besides Wordsworth suffered and became irate at the Mississippians. Consequently, in 1843, in the very midst of the great struggle in Mississippi, *Niles' National Register* printed a humorous anecdote. It relayed to a wider body of readers a story told in the Mobile *Herald* of how a merchant of Mobile had been on a visit to Liverpool to interview the Scotch head of a branch of his business. A dinner was held for the American, who tried to avoid the subject of repudiation, despite the persistent references to it of those present. "In answer to their assaults, he observed that only one state had repudiated, and that was Mississippi. Inquiry was made how she *happened* to stand alone in this matter?" The answer of the Mobilian was "that they had a very curious man for governor, named McNutt, but that he was not an American. The whole company demanded his birth-place. 'Why,' said the Mobilian, 'he is a most obstinate and cross-grained old Scotchman.' After a *broad look* at each other, the conversation immediately turned upon other subjects." [65]

[63] Prentiss, *Bright Side of Life*, I, 340. For information that Wordsworth received $2,250 for three $1,000 bonds sold by Governor Brown in 1846, see S. F. McCutchen, "The Political Career of Albert Gallatin Brown" (Ph.D. dissertation, University of Chicago, 1929), 65, n. 27, cited by Buford Rowland, "William Wordsworth and Mississippi Bonds," in *Journal of Southern History* (Baton Rouge), I (1935), 507.

[64] Prentiss, *Bright Side of Life*, I, 340.

[65] *Niles' National Register*, LXV (1843–1844), 197.

patriotism which united the Whigs against the Democrats. The differences in party principles, he was quoted as saying, constituted the important considerations. "The Democrats, or at least the demagogues among them, said the people were sovereign—the Whigs contended the laws were sovereign and above the people—only to be altered by a revolution. The former were ever for change—the latter for law and order." He may well have had in mind how he detested the Democrats for destroying the United States Bank and repudiating bonds in Mississippi when "He likened the Democrats to a company of individuals who would charter a steamboat and then resolve that they had a right to do with it as they pleased—who, in pursuance of such resolution, would discharge the pilot and engineer, and take screw after screw from the engine till this would cause the boat to blow up." Whatever else he said was not amplified in the *Picayune* except his eulogy on Clay and his sarcastic opinions of Van Buren. The paper called his eulogy of Clay "eloquently enthusiastic." He represented the Kentuckian "as one who excited an enthusiasm in his party, such as Napoleon did among the youthful conscripts of France, and contrasted him with Martin Van Buren in a manner it may well be presumed was no way flattering to the latter." In early 1844 Van Buren would have been as good a guess as any as a prospective Democratic nominee in the summer. Prentiss must have been willing to predict that a certain South Carolinian would not be selected, or he would likely not have given the press the opportunity to quote him thus: "He took occasion to pass a highly wrought eulogium on John C. Calhoun, saying that a battle between him and Henry Clay would be a battle of giants; with Van Buren for the opponent of Mr. Clay, it was the fox attempting to cope with the lion." [7]

Other speakers were present, among them George Poin-

[7] New Orleans *Daily Picayune,* February 23, 1844. For other newspaper accounts of the Louisiana Convention, see Washington *National Intelligencer,* March 5, 1844; Boston *Daily Advertiser,* March 7, 1844; Baton Rouge *Gazette,* March 2, 1844.

dexter. Prentiss was quite evidently the prime orator of the occasion, however, judging from the publicity given him. On the second day he was used again. Clay was called upon at the St. Charles Exchange for a speech. He appeared and spoke but briefly, saying, "He did not intend to make a speech, and would *not* make a speech; but he would congratulate them on the glorious prospect which the Whig cause everywhere presented." If Clay would not speak, Prentiss would desist also. The *Picayune* explained Prentiss' action in deference to Clay and quoted his brief remarks: "He excused himself from making a speech by saying— 'Fellow citizens, men are not apt to turn to crumbs after having feasted on costly viands. The owl, the bat or other inferior birds do not expose their limited power of flight while the eagle is soaring in the sky above them. You will excuse me, after having heard Henry Clay for not making a speech.'" Probably, however, Prentiss was thinking of another speech he was to give that night. This circumstance explains the "P.S." attached to the account: "Since writing the above, we learn that the Hon. S. S. Prentiss is to address the Whigs at Bank's Arcade this evening, and that the galleries will be appropriated to the ladies.—The place, immense as it is, will not be half large enough for the throngs that will assemble to hear the great and popular orator." [8] The following day the *Picayune* reported: "As we anticipated, Bank's Arcade was thronged with our citizens last evening, all anxious to hear the address of Mr. Prentiss. The galleries, too, were graced with a large number of ladies, and some even occupied places on the lower floor— hundreds of the other sex were obliged to leave, unable to get near enough to hear, among which number we must include ourselves." [9]

Almost immediately after the New Orleans occasion, Prentiss made a business and political trip north, going as

[8] New Orleans *Daily Picayune*, February 24, 1844.
[9] *Ibid.*, February 25, 1844.

far as Maine. At the same time, he took advantage of the opportunity to speak repeatedly for Clay. His first speech was at Montgomery, Alabama.[10] What he said of his champion that night caused a reporter to write with enthusiasm: "In conclusion, Mr. Prentiss alluded to Henry Clay, in strains of fervent eloquence, which made his hearers' hearts exult within them—of his great services to the cause of his country, of his love and abiding faith in its honor, its glory and the success of institutions—of him, as the ever present, ever sleepless advanced Sentinel on the ramparts of freedom." As if these extravagant words were not enough, he was quoted as saying of Clay: "success could not add a cubit to his stature, and yet tho a leader, towering by the head and shoulders above other men, he was not like Saul, sought and armed for the purpose, but was there present, ready in proof mail clad, with lance in rest and visor down, to whom at once all turned and at whose cry all rallied as at the spirit-stirring tones of a bugle call." [11]

Going north, Prentiss stopped in New York, and then went on to Boston, where he delivered a speech to the No. 1 Clay Club of the city. He spoke in the Odeon. The Boston *Daily Advertiser* said: "Although no notice of the meeting was given until this morning, the house was crowded, and Mr. Prentiss spoke for two hours and a half with unflagging eloquence." [12] The Portland *Advertiser* covered the speech more fully by quoting the Boston *Atlas*. It passed on to its readers in Prentiss' home city an extended commentary: "At half past seven, every place in the large Hall of the Odeon—floor, boxes, orchestras, and every position in which a person could be placed, was filled. . . . He was listened to by the vast audience, with a profound and rapt attention, interrupted only by applause, which the orator seemed to disregard in the intense pursuit of his object.

10 Prentiss to his wife, Montgomery, Ala., March 16, 1844, in *Memoir of S. S. Prentiss*, II, 297.
11 *Alabama Times*, quoted in Vicksburg *Daily Whig*, April 1, 1844.
12 Boston *Daily Advertiser*, April 6, 1844.

. . . It was a noble, enthusiastic and patriotic speech. The thanks of the Whigs of Boston are due to Mr. Prentiss, for the highly acceptable service which he has thus rendered to them and their cause. After the Orator had finished his Speech . . . three hearty cheers were given for Mr. Prentiss, and three for Henry Clay." [13]

Several other speeches were also required of him. One was at Newburyport, Connecticut.[14] And again, while at home, he spoke in Portland. Soon he was on his way south, but he delivered at least two addresses en route, one at Philadelphia, and one at Louisville. His Philadelphia appearance was given high appraisal: "In pursuance of the notice given, the Whigs of the city and county of Philadelphia met yesterday evening at half past 7 o'clock at the Whig Reading Room; but the opinion being general that it would not hold half the number of Whigs who would desire to hear and welcome the Hon. S. S. Prentiss to Philadelphia, they determined to adjourn and meet in front of the State House." Prentiss was reported as speaking "upwards of two hours and twenty minutes, in a strain of the most argumentative, powerful, and impressive eloquence, on all the great and important subjects which have agitated the country, particularly since the memorable defeat of Mr. Van Buren, by the Whig Harrison Party in 1840." [15]

By April 25, Prentiss was back in Vicksburg.[16] Five days later, on April 30, it was announced that he was in New Orleans.[17] Whatever had been his specific mission to New Orleans, politics were relegated to the background as he

13 Boston *Atlas*, quoted in Portland *Daily Advertiser*, April 5, 1844.

14 *Memoir of S. S. Prentiss*, II, 299; New Orleans *Daily Picayune*, April 10, 1844. It was on this occasion when he unsuccessfully tried to decline speaking that George Prentiss said: "On returning to the breakfast-room, he remarked playfully, but with a care-worn look: 'They seem to think it as easy for me to make speeches as it is for a juggler to pull ribands out of his mouth.'" *Memoir of S. S. Prentiss*, II, 299.

15 Philadelphia *North American*, quoted in Boston *Daily Advertiser*, April 16, 1844.

16 Vicksburg *Daily Whig*, April 25, 1844.

17 New Orleans *Daily Picayune*, April 30, 1844.

engaged in an oratorical effort of an altogether different nature. In brief, a movement was under way in New Orleans to raise funds for the erection of a statue of Benjamin Franklin. A preliminary meeting had been held on May 24 to lay plans for a large mass gathering on April 29 in the church of the Reverend Theodore Clapp. Prentiss was not announced in advance as scheduled to speak; [18] very likely he did not know he would participate. It seems, rather, that he was in the audience and was called upon quite suddenly. Judge Theodore McCaleb presided, and the chief speaker, then a resident in New Orleans, was Richard Henry Wilde. Prentiss spoke after Wilde, and since the *Picayune* reporter left to prepare his notes of the meeting and Wilde's address, he actually missed Prentiss' speech.[19] Whoever reported the occasion for the New Orleans *Tropic* stayed until the meeting adjourned and stated that the "people were beginning to move off, when a gentleman announced to the President the presence of the favorite orator of the Southwest. The announcement was electrical; the name of Prentiss had scarcely been pronounced when every voice and hand in the Church was brought into requisition in calling him out." The speech is of no small significance in revealing one aspect of Prentiss' power in public address. In an impromptu situation, with law and politics foremost in his mind, he delivered a nonpolitical speech so well that he scarcely ever received higher newspaper acclaim. For forty-five minutes he spoke with the effect that "Flowers and gems, the rarest and richest, were thrown out by him with prodigal profusion, until every heart throbbed and every eye glistened in obedience to his magic touch." Most significantly, indeed, the speech was alluded to as "an off-hand, extemporaneous effort, but one eminently worthy of the distinguished reputation of Seargent S. Prentiss. His allusion to the statue of the dying Gladiator stirred the hearts of all present from their inmost recesses. It was palpably

18 *Ibid*   19 *Ibid.*, May 1, 1844.

before their eyes, even to 'his rude hut which by the Danube lay!' " [20] An orator must speak from some background of knowledge and interest to receive such praise. To have risen to the occasion as Prentiss did bespeaks ability.

There was little time, however, for the pursuance of the arts in the summer of 1844. Henry Clay was candidate for the presidency, and, to Prentiss' mind, the country needed Clay. One interesting situation called for attention as soon as Prentiss returned from the North to Mississippi. During his absence, the Jackson *Mississippian* endeavored to show that he had ventured to interpret Clay's stand on the question of Texas annexation. Prentiss denied this immediately upon returning, and asked the Vicksburg *Whig* to announce: "The Hon. S. S. Prentiss requests us to state upon his authority, that the charges of the *Mississippian* in regard to his having stated the opinions of Mr. Clay in relation to the annexation of Texas, are utterly without foundation; for he never made such an assertion to anyone." [21]

The Texas question suggests, of course, the basic problem before the candidates aspiring to office. Prentiss' denial of ever attempting to explain Clay's stand on the issue was made but a few days before the Whigs met in Baltimore, on May 1, and in one day selected their candidates and wrote their platform. No voice dissented to the nomination of Clay, and there was but little opposition to Theodore Frelinghuysen of New York, who was chosen on the third ballot for vice-president. The outlook for the Whigs was bright indeed. Clay was the leader, the party was supposedly united, and several months of time was at the disposal of party orators to solidify an overwhelming vote. Almost the only thorn in the flesh was the Texas question, but its complete seriousness was not then so apparent. The problem was avoided in the party platform, as was also

[20] New Orleans *Daily Tropic*, quoted in Vicksburg *Daily Whig*, May 11, 1844; Baton Rouge *Weekly Gazette*, May 4, 1844.
[21] Vicksburg *Daily Whig*, April 25, 1844.

the National Bank question. More emphasis was placed on what the Whigs called "A well regulated currency," and a protective tariff. With or without much of a platform the Whigs were exultant in being able to say "That the name of Henry Clay needs no eulogy. The history of the country since his first appearance in public life is his history."

Another reason for the high hopes of the Whigs was that the Democrats seemed hopelessly divided on a leader. Van Buren was at first the thought and hope of many. But he lacked sufficient popularity generally, and his anti-Texas letter ruled him out for southerners at least. Tyler was another possibility, but he had been anti-Jackson and bore the stigma of having been a Whig as well. Moreover, his administration was no safe recommendation. Calhoun was another candidate, but his chances were too much limited to the South. The Boston *Advertiser* capitalized upon this Democratic predicament and gave Prentiss the credit for humorous analysis: "Prentiss thinks the locofoco party may have the same excuse for having half a dozen candidates for the Presidency, as the Irishman advanced who was brought before the magistrate for marrying six wives. The magistrate asked him how he could be so hardened a villain? 'Plase your worthip,' said Pat, 'I was trying to get a good one.' " [22]

Paradoxically, however, the Democrats settled on a better man than did the Whigs so far as getting votes in the campaign was concerned. On the third day of their convention in Baltimore, May 29, seeing that they could not agree on Van Buren, Calhoun, or James Buchanan, they nominated James K. Polk. Polk was the friend of Jackson (a recommendation in itself), an avowed proponent of the annexation of Texas, and was, moreover, equally certain that the Oregon question should be settled to the advantage of the United States. This indicated to both the South and the North that he was an exponent of Manifest Destiny,

[22] Boston *Daily Advertiser*, May 29, 1844.

and all knew him to be as staunch a Democratic partyman as could be named. George M. Dallas, from the doubtful and pivotal state of Pennsylvania, was selected as Polk's running mate. James G. Birney, the nominee of the Abolitionists, would get some votes, but none in the South. The contest was, then, between Clay and Polk.

Polk was thought to be handicapped, however, in being a "dark horse," really the first in American party history. The Whigs exclaimed: "Who is James K. Polk?" "Polk the Mediocre!" and "Polk the Mendacious!" Such innuendo would, they thought, enhance their chances, especially as they could boast of the universally known Clay as their leader. But with Jackson's blessing and with a record of having been a staunch, regular party man, of having served in Congress and as speaker of the House and then as governor of Tennessee, Polk was stronger than at first supposed. Probably no one more than Clay himself knew how successfully the Democrats had presented him with a formidable opponent. Very likely, too, the immediate stand of Polk for the annexation of Texas, concerning which Clay vacillated, had more to do with the election results than any other factor. The United States was ready to begin her imperialistic advances.

The charge that Prentiss had tried to explain Clay's position in regard to Texas is interesting in view of Clay's uncertain stand. Even though Prentiss denied having interpreted it, almost anything he might have said on the subject in the early months of 1844 could have been used against him. While Prentiss was on his northern tour, pressure was being put on Clay, as well as on Van Buren, who then was thought the most likely Democratic candidate, to answer inquiries on the subject. Opportunist that he was, when he thought Van Buren would stand opposed to annexation, Clay, in his famous Raleigh Letter of April 17, came out in opposition also. But this he found to be too unpopular in the South, and so in the first Alabama Letter on July 1, he made a gesture to southerners by saying he would not oppose annexation if it could be accomplished without harm to the Union. This suited southerners no better; Clay's anxieties were increased. There then followed his second Alabama Letter, in which he crossed the Rubicon. On July 27 he made a statement which received wide publicity through the channels of the *National Intelligencer, Niles' National Register,* and other publications. If Texas could be annexed "without national dishonor, without war, with the general consent of the States of the Union, and upon fair and reasonable terms, I should be glad to see it," he said. This letter called for more and more statements of clarification and amplification to satisfy inquiries north and south, and also served as the best ammunition for Democrats and Abolitionists. Clay's saying "I should be glad to see it," was a commitment which damaged him heavily among those opposed to annexation, and at the same time did not make him noticeably secure in the South.

Regardless of how much Clay's manifestoes hurt him with the people, they did not weaken him with Prentiss. The Texas question was to Prentiss entirely incidental. While he did not go to the Baltimore convention, he rejoiced as few men did when Clay was placed before the people. Yet the earlier attempt of the Democratic press to accuse Prentiss of interpreting Clay on the Texas question was followed by more rumors and press notices in midsummer to the effect that Clay and Prentiss had parted ways, separating on the issue. It was actually charged that Prentiss had turned Democratic. The New Orleans *Bee* was one paper that knew better. It came to his rescue: "Among the fanciful figments for which the Locofoco press is remarkable, not the least bold and dashing was the story circulated . . . of the Hon. Sargent [sic] S. Prentiss' conversion to Locofocoism." [23]

[23] New Orleans *Daily Bee,* quoted in Washington *National Intelligencer,* July 9, 1844.

Such a conversion would have been a political miracle. Prentiss had just been on a long speaking tour for Clay. It was widely known that they were the best of personal friends. Moreover, the disputed Mississippi election was remembered too, in connection with which Polk had incurred the eternal wrath of Prentiss for his deciding vote as speaker of the House, compelling the third Mississippi election. The charge that Prentiss had become a turncoat was absurd, and Prentiss proceeded forthwith to smash it. He needed, first of all, to correct its evil effects in Mississippi. He turned, very naturally, to the Vicksburg *Whig* to clarify matters, knowing that this paper would broadcast the news far and wide to Whig papers which would copy his remarks. Consequently, he sent a long letter to the *Whig*, in which he gave an emphatic and unequivocal declaration. "I have with surprise and mortification, seen it reported in several public prints," he wrote, "that I had withdrawn from the support of Mr. Clay on account of his course in relation to the annexation of Texas. It is not with the view of obtruding my humble opinion upon the public, nor for the fashionable purpose of defining my position on the Texas question, that I ask the favor of a very small space in your columns; but for the purpose of relieving myself from the obloquy of the report alluded to, and of asserting that it is unfounded and untrue in every particular." This introduction laid the basis for Prentiss to assert himself fundamentally. "I look upon the Whig cause as far more important than the Texas question, and would rather see the cause triumphant, and Mr. Clay elected, than to witness the annexation to the United States of all the territory between here and Patagonia. I believe the question of Annexation, as now presented, to be a mere party question, brought forward expressly to operate upon the Presidential election, and that it ought not to have the slightest influence upon the course, or action, of any member of the Whig party." Coming still closer home to Mississippians and southerners, he further declared: "Indeed, the ground taken upon it in this quarter, that those who support Mr. Clay are unfavorable to the Southern institutions, and opposed to Southern interests, is as insulting as it is false, and should arouse an honest indignation in the breast of every true Whig." To scotch the rumor of his own disloyalty to the Whigs, Prentiss must have felt that still more needed to be said: "I am proud of the Whig party and its noble leader"; for "they are worthy of each other, and of the glorious triumph that awaits them both. I would rather vote for Henry Clay for the Presidency than any other man now living, and most assuredly shall do so in November next, unless, in the meantime, he turns Locofoco; and, but for the pressure of my private business, I would not hesitate to devote the time between now and the election in persuading others to do likewise. I have not deserted the Whig cause in the time of its adversity, and certainly shall not now do so upon the eve of victory." Notwithstanding this seriousness of purpose and declaration, Prentiss knew that a little double-edged levity would be welcomed. "In conclusion, I will say, if ever I join the Mormons, I shall attach myself to Joe Smith, the founder of the sect, and not to one of his rival disciples. And should I ever turn Locofoco on the question of *the immediate annexation* of Texas, I will support John Tyler, not James K. Polk." [24] This was enough to stop any further rumors.

As ambitious as Prentiss was to see Clay defeat Polk and become president, and as willing as he was to work to that end, he doubtless dreaded the exhaustion which he knew would accompany a series of strenuous campaign speeches. Having made one long speaking tour at a time when he was beset by financial worries, he seemed a tired man by the time Clay was nominated and the campaign was to start in earnest. "Indeed, I am quite worn out," he wrote, "and

[24] Vicksburg *Daily Whig*, June 20, 1844; Washington *National Intelligencer*, July 9, 1844; *Memoir of S. S. Prentiss*, II, 315–16.

would give anything to spend a month or two in perfect seclusion." Financially he was so depressed that a decision was in the making. "I have made no progress in the settlement of my affairs, and very much fear that I shall not be able to extricate myself from my embarrassments. I have almost fully determined to wind up here during the next year, and then go to New Orleans to live. I think I should succeed in my profession there; and I am utterly disgusted with this State, especially this portion of it. Vicksburg is becoming every day more vulgar and despicable." [25]

But with his unequivocal reaffirmation of faith in Clay on record, Prentiss gave a fair portion of his time toward making the election a Whig victory. It was from August onward that he made his chief contributions. In that month he made his one excursion outside the state after returning from the North. Upon invitation, he, along with a great battalion of other outsiders, invaded Polk's state of Tennessee to participate in a great Whig festival at Nashville. While he was but one of the numerous speakers for the two-day affair, he was reckoned as one of the choicest. In announcing the event, the Vicksburg *Whig* listed the celebrities: "Virginia sends Leigh and Rives, South Carolina, W. C. Preston, Georgia, A. H. Stevens [sic], Kentucky, J. J. Crittenden, Mississippi, S. S. Prentiss, Illinois, J. J. Hardin, whilst Tennessee has at home Gov. J. C. Jones, E. H. Foster, John Bell, and others." [26] Prentiss received his invitation from a body of ladies to whom he replied that he would be present: "this mark of your kind consideration will always be cherished by me as one of the proudest occurrences of my life. I need not say," he added, "that nothing but imperative necessity could prevent my compliance with your wishes. As such a necessity will not, I trust intervene, I

[25] Prentiss to George Prentiss, Belmont, May 19, 1844, in *Memoir of S. S. Prentiss*, II, 312.
[26] Vicksburg *Tri-Weekly Whig*, August 8, 1844.

only express my ardent inclination in promising a ready obedience to your request." [27]

Prentiss reached Nashville on August 19. He headed the Mississippi delegation, as did Randall Hunt of New Orleans the Louisiana one, both groups traveling together on the same boat. Their arrival was heralded by the Nashville *Whig* with "Prentiss is Here! And at 9 o'clock, this distinguished son of the South and his colleagues were warmly and enthusiastically received by the *Straight Outs* and a large number of citizens at the upper wharf, the boat having run up, according to previous arrangement." The delegations were conducted from the boat to the City Hotel, "where Mr. Prentiss and Mr. Hunt were both loudly called for by the crowd, after they had alighted from their carriage, and briefly, though promptly and eloquently responded from the steps of the Hotel." [28] The next day there began the two-day mass convention, the Nashville *Whig* exclaiming: "Lo! the People are here!" Delegations appeared from different counties and different organizations representing Tennessee, carrying banners, mottoes, and pictures of Clay. Banners and slogans accompanied the delegations from other states, Mississippi's appropriately being "Mississippi's democracy is repudiation, we repudiate *such* Democracy." [29]

The Nashville meeting was signally important. It followed a similar Democratic gathering held there the week before when no less a personage than Stephen A. Douglas had been one of the speakers. The Whigs were determined, in Polk's own state, to stage a grander show. To overshadow the Democrats and their candidate, the widest kind of publicity had been given the Whig convention. Interestingly enough, both the *National Intelligencer* and *Niles' Na-*

[27] Letter quoted in Washington *National Intelligencer*, August 13, 1844; *Niles' National Register*, LXVI (1844), 403.
[28] Nashville *Daily Whig*, August 20, 1844.
[29] *Ibid.*, August 22, 1844.

tional Register quoted the same item from the Vicksburg *Whig,* making its sentiments their own: "We wish that Nashville were not so far off, that we might be present at the glorious gatherings of the freemen of the West. . . . Crittenden, the generous, eloquent, the favorite Kentucky orator . . . will be there; and Prentiss, than whom this broad land does not boast, among all its statesmen and orators, a more polished and effective popular speaker or a more whole-souled devoted Whig, will be there; and other speakers of scarcely less note, both far and near, will come up to the help of the good cause, and contribute their distinguished abilities to swell the universal joy and triumphant success of this great occasion." [30] Some papers in distant parts of the country waited until the meeting had taken place and then capitalized upon its political significance. Such a one was the Boston *Advertiser,* which copied the New York *Express:* "This was all that was anticipated by the most sanguine. The city was decorated from one end to the other with Whig insignia,—the gathering of the delegates was continually going on for more than twenty hours before the moving of the procession,—the military and uniformed Whig associations acted as escort to the line which was thus arranged." The procession in particular received attention: "On the extreme right were twenty-six open carriages, filled with ladies, dressed in white with blue sashes, bearing the banners of the twenty-six States, and escorted by the Nashville Straight Out. The extreme left consisted of the Cavalry companies and associations on horseback. On the arrival of the procession at a certain point, a beautiful procession of ladies on foot, took the right of the column, escorted by the Harrison guards. In front of the ladies was borne the prize banner." Additional features of the procession, as described in the *Advertiser,* were most spectacular: "Then came the committee and invited

---

[30] Washington *National Intelligencer,* August 15, 1844; *Niles' National Register,* LXVI (1844), 403.

guests, and hosts of banners and mottoes of every device and pithy allusion. Then the different delegations in their order, mounted and on foot. Alabama, Louisiana, Mississippi, Kentucky, Arkansas, North Carolina, Iowa, Missouri, and Illinois were all represented." [31] The *National Intelligencer* considered the procession most significant also. Gleaning its information from the Nashville *Whig,* it reported: "The most attractive part of the procession was composed chiefly of the military companies and uniformed Whig associations, to the number of about six thousand; and when it was joined on the Convention ground by the delegates in citizen dress . . . the immense concourse swelled up, according to the most moderate rule of computation, to Twenty Thousand—or, says the Whig, if estimated by the rule adopted by the Locofocos in reference to their Convention of the preceding week, to seventy-five or a hundred thousand." [32] Since the Democratic meeting the previous week fell behind the Whigs in colorful pageantry, the reference to the methods of computation of numbers by the Democrats is interesting. Certainly one Democratic paper in Nashville, the *Union,* could not count such a concourse of people. It called the Whig attempt at "pomp, pride, and circumstance" a "total failure—a failure without the credit of being splendid." It said that after the first day, "as soon as the Barbecue was eaten, the people began to leave bag and baggage, in great numbers." It was the same on the second day for those who remained over night; they left by the hundreds, causing the *Union* to ponder "Whether this had been owing to the paucity of good speaking and speakers—to the dying condition and cause of whiggery in the country—or to what other cause, this 'deponent saith not.' " [33]

[31] Boston *Daily Advertiser,* September 2, 1844. For other notices which this paper gave to the convention in advance and immediately after, see issues of July 25, August 24, 1844.
[32] Washington *National Intelligencer,* August 31, 1844.
[33] Nashville *Daily Union,* August 23, 1844.

Whigs exaggerated and Democrats depreciated. Nevertheless, every effort was made to make the Whig gathering in Nashville a great occasion. Prentiss helped to make it so as one of the favored participants. On the first day, August 21, he appeared early on the speaking roster. John Bell, his very good friend of congressional days, was president of the convention. As presiding officer, he made a "very forcible and eloquent address," [34] and then introduced Prentiss. Typical of the estimate placed on Prentiss as compared with the other speakers on the first day was the high compliment paid him by the Nashville *Whig:* "Mr. Prentiss of Mississippi, . . . made . . . *the speech* of the occasion, an effort of the highest degree of warm and effective eloquence, of glowing language, of splendid imagery. It was an able and thorough argument withal upon the great principles that distinguish the Whig party as compared with the disorganizing tendencies of locofocoism." Prentiss' speech of the first day was so good that the *Whig* concluded: "Judging from the high compliments we have heard bestowed upon it by men not given to hasty opinions, we should say Mr. Prentiss met the most extravagant expectations of the large assembly." [35]

A night meeting with speaking took place, and on the second day the oratory continued on an elaborate scale. Prentiss appeared again, but instead of speaking first, he served as the concluding orator. The *National Intelligencer* admitted the events of the second day were "less exciting than the first, on account of the absence of any imposing pageant," but insisted that they were "nevertheless highly interesting." It alluded to speeches by Hunt of Louisiana, Albert Pike of Arkansas, Governor James C. Jones of Tennessee, William J. Graves of Kentucky, and others, adding: "Mr. Prentiss, of Mississippi, made the concluding speech,

34 Washington *National Intelligencer*, August 31, 1844.
35 Nashville *Daily Whig*, August 22, 1844; quoted also in Washington *National Intelligencer*, August 31, 1844.

of whom the *Whig* says he spoke as never man spoke from
that stand before, though Mr. Crittenden's speech in 1840
may have excited more general applause." [36] Exactly what
Prentiss said in the speech is not easy to ascertain since the
published reports consisted mostly of eulogy, rather than
quotation.

Prentiss paid a really great price for the commendation
which he received for his Nashville speeches, as well as for
all his strenuous exertions of the preceding years. An incident occurred during the convention which indicated all
was not well with his health. In one of his two speaking efforts, he was seized with "a stricture of the chest," and was
compelled to inform his audience that he could not go on.
Cries from the assembly indicated that he should rest, that
his listeners would wait. After a short while he was able to
continue. The attack was probably nothing less than a
fainting spell which occurred in consequence of "over-
exertion in speaking." Possibly the best explanation of
the strain upon Prentiss is supplied by Governor Jones.
He was with Prentiss from the time of his arrival. He observed that Prentiss showed much anxiety for his responsibilities and that "His whole demeanor indicated a deep and
solemn feeling of the fiery ordeal he was called to pass." [37]
Evidently the physical man was not able to sustain the emotional strains and stresses placed upon him, and for the first
time Prentiss gave way. The attack was not of long dura-
tion, however, and Jones noted that after his rest "he arose
and continued his address with undiminished interest to the
close." A story that appeared in print in more than one
paper recounts that as Prentiss fell fainting at a high moment of his speaking, someone shouted: "Die, Prentiss *die!*
you will never have a more glorious opportunity." [38] Of
the attack, as well as the convention, Prentiss wrote to

[36] Washington *National Intelligencer,* September 3, 1844.
[37] James C. Jones to George Prentiss, Memphis, February 12, 1851, in
Memoir of S. S. Prentiss, II, 321–24.
[38] *Ibid.,* 323–24.

George Prentiss: "I have been here just a week, and you are, doubtless, surprised that I have not written you before. But, in truth, I have not been able. I broke myself down by speaking, and can now barely drag a pen over paper. I shall give you but a little account of our Whig doings here, as you will see it all in the papers. We have had a most glorious Convention; far exceeding in numbers and enthusiasm anything I ever saw. My opinion is, that there were 40,000 people present. It is admitted that this Convention exceeded in number by one-third, at least, the greatest one of 1840, and to the same extent, exceeded the Democratic Convention of the 15th." As to his own participation he appraised himself: "I made the opening speech, and another the next day. I think they were both good speeches— I mean, as compared with my other efforts. I do not think I have ever spoken better, taking into consideration the object and circumstances. As far as public estimation is concerned, I have no cause to complain." [39]

The next significant oratorical endeavor which Prentiss made for "Harry of the West" was at Natchez on September 5. An imposing assembly, estimated at from seven to ten thousand, gathered in a grove near the city. "The barbecue alone was gotten up at a cost of six thousand dollars." [40] Prentiss was again one of several speakers, but was given credit for being the chief one. Some others were William and George Yerger, Patrick Tompkins, and James M. Smilie. It was a gala Whig day in Natchez. The free Negro barber, Johnson, wrote in his peculiar manner: "This has been a Beautifull and very pleasent and agreable day and the whole City was on the walk. Everything Look brisk to day. I was as buisy as I could well be a part of the forenoon, and after the Long procession passed Out. and got Out to the Ground Some time I started Out myself and Looked at them a while, there was Some four or five thousand Persons

[39] Prentiss to George Prentiss, Nashville, August 26, 1844, *ibid.*, 324–25.
[40] Shields, *Seargent Smith Prentiss*, 342.

On the ground I have butt little [doubt], I allowed the
Boys to close the Shop for a Short time in order for them
to hear the Speaking. . . . I herd a part of Mr. Mathew-
sons Speech and a part of Mr. Yergers. and a part of Mr.
Smilies and in the Afternoon a part of Mr. Prentess." [41]

The events of the day happened much as Johnson described them. After an eloquent appeal to the "Giver of
all good," an address by William Yerger, and a dinner,
Prentiss plunged into an exultation over the Whig cause
and continued with one of his most withering abuses of
the Democrats and Polk. One of the statements attributed
to Prentiss during the campaign was his reference to Polk as
"a blighted burr that has fallen from the mane of the War
Horse of the Hermitage." [42] Shields, his biographer, was
present and alluded to the same incident, saying that Prentiss referred to Polk as "An ordinary man who owed his
notoriety to the fact of his being attaché of General Jackson." He quoted Prentiss as saying specifically, " 'The old
war-horse had dashed through the crowd of common men,
and when he emerged James K. Polk was found, like a
cockle-bur, sticking to his mane.' " [43]

There can be no doubt that Prentiss was exceedingly
severe toward Polk, judging from the newspaper controversy that followed. He very likely went beyond the bounds
of good taste in his onslaughts. At least the *Mississippi Free
Trader and Natchez Gazette* contended that he did so, and
the Vicksburg *Whig* as well as the Natchez *Courier* felt
themselves obliged to say a word in his defense. The *Free
Trader* was equally critical of Prentiss as it described the
speech and his insinuations against Polk. It first described

---

[41] Diary of William T. Johnson, September 5, 1844.

[42] He is so quoted, for example, in George F. Milton, *The Eve of Conflict, Stephen A. Douglas and The Needless War* (New York, 1934), 28. The
origin and widespread use of this statement may have arisen from T. B.
Thorpe, "Reminiscences of Seargent S. Prentiss," in *American Whig Review* (New York), XIV (1851), 245; cited also in *Memoir of S. S. Prentiss*, II,
332.

[43] Shields, *Seargent Smith Prentiss*, 345.

his speaking: "The Vicksburg portion of this travelling *managerie,* Mr. Prentiss, exhibited himself along side of the embodiments of piety and religion, representing the Church and morality. Thus pillard [*sic*] and supported, he took the stand in the afternoon, and for three mortal hours, in a tempest of almost unearthly passion, . . . foaming at the mouth, convulsed in every limb, flushed almost to apoplexy, and, at times, quite black in the face, looking more like a demon than a man, he poured out the vials of his wrath on the democratic party, sparing neither age, nor sex, or condition." Prentiss' caustic attack on Polk undoubtedly prompted the further condemnation of his speech: "Bitter and brutal as Prentiss was, while speaking of the democratic party, it was nothing when compared with the concentrated hate and malignity he evinced, in his allusions to Gov. Polk. He looked like a savage in the act of butchering his victim. He felt like a famished wolf on the scent of blood. He poured out upon this distinguished and exemplary man, a flood of fierce invective and ribaldry, but hate, deadly *personal hate* of the man, envy of his high position, his pure character and probable glorious destiny, rankled in the bosom of Mr. Prentiss." [44]

One Democratic charge against Prentiss in this speech was that he used the term "dogs" in reference to his opponents, and this, true or false, called forth Whig denials. The Vicksburg *Whig,* deriving its defense largely from an article in the Natchez *Courier* of September 12, entitled "Mr. Prentiss and the Extremely Sensitive Locofocos," said: "Mr. Prentiss never used any other language than that of polished invective on this occasion." It then proceeded to quote the *Courier:* "On the evening of the day on which the speech was delivered, we were asked by several democrats if Mr. Prentiss had said so and so, if he had called the whole 'democratic' thieves, liars, robbers, &c. . . . Mr. Prentiss only used the word 'dogs' once in the whole

[44] *Mississippi Free Trader and Natchez Daily Gazette,* September 12, 1844.

in 1840, from being present for a Louisiana Whig rally. In
one issue it thanked the Baton Rouge ladies: "To them we
shall be indebted for a visit of the Hon. S. S. Prentiss, they
wrote to him and he could not refuse them." [53] But one of
his canceled engagements was that at Baton Rouge. When
the meeting took place, a letter was read from Prentiss stating the reasons why he could not be present.[54]

Prentiss did not completely cease speaking after the
occasion at Natchez, however. He appeared at Rodney, Mississippi, where again, in the midst of impassioned speaking, he fell in another faint. This time he revived his energies while the assembled Whigs took time for dinner and
then finished the speech in the afternoon.[55] "On that day,
at Rodney," Shields stated, "he spoke three hours. I met
him in the evening, and found him utterly jaded and worn
down. Even during the address, his physical frame was so
exhausted that he was frequently overcome and compelled
to stop; but the buoyancy of his spirit triumphed over
bodily weakness. After every rest, he took a yet higher
bound. Referring to his speech, he said to me, 'I am like a
weak horse running down hill—when I start I cannot
stop.' " [56]

Shields also indicated what Prentiss talked about that day.
Prentiss did not, seemingly, have much to say in the campaign about specific issues, such as the annexation of Texas.
Rather, he discussed what he called bigger matters, such as
the philosophy of government and the relative merits of
Clay and Polk as candidates. The Rodney speech may have
been something of an exception, even though he attacked
a political enemy in Mississippi. In this speech it was Robert J. Walker who suffered his onslaughts.

Early in 1844, Walker had been asked, in connection

[53] Baton Rouge *Weekly Gazette*, October 5, 1844.
[54] *Ibid.*, October 12, 1844.
[55] Shields, *Seargent Smith Prentiss*, 345.
[56] Shields to George Prentiss, Natchez, n.d., in *Memoir of S. S. Prentiss*,
II, 336.

with a movement in Mississippi to nominate him for vice-president, for a statement of his position on the annexation of Texas. There resulted Walker's "Texas Letters," in which, though a southern slaveholder himself at that time, he advocated bringing Texas in as a free state "as a safety valve for the disposal of negroes, who could then work their way over the line into Mexico, where their color would be no bar to their success in life." [57] This should be interpreted as an attempt to appease both the North and the South. Prentiss knew this, and at Rodney he came before the mass gathering with two Walker letters in his hands, showing that one had been written for the benefit of the North, in which it was emphasized that Texas should enter free, and another for the South, in which this particular stand was more lightly touched. The story is that Prentiss, after reading the letters and castigating the man and his motives, "dashed them together, calling them 'the acid and alkali vanishing into frosty nothingness.' " [58] That Prentiss was emotionally overwrought may be inferred from his fainting again. Doubtless one of the highest tributes to his effectiveness that day is the account of a shrewd observer of people and events in Mississippi, Horace S. Fulkerson: "As he warmed up in his masterly discussion of the political topics of the day and issues of the canvass, the audience began to move in the direction of the stand. I was myself a good way off, but moved up with the others, *insensibly* (so absorbed was I in his great thought,) . . . and stood entranced with the rest of the crowd, then hanging about the stand—as I have seen bees about the mouth of a hive eager for every drop of the distilled nectar—shouting and weeping by turns; and when at the close, I gradually began to realize my individuality, I turned . . . to say something

[57] Walmsley, "Presidential Campaign of 1844 in Mississippi," *loc. cit.,* 192–93.

[58] *Ibid.,* 193. Shields, *Seargent Smith Prentiss,* 348, quotes him as saying: "I wonder that, . . . like the acid and alkali, they do not effervesce when they come into contact."

to whomsoever might be nearest me, when I found right at my side a devout and pious Methodist lady, the wife of a leading *Democrat* of the town, whose first utterance, as my eyes met hers, then streaming with tears, was, with uplifted hands, 'Oh that he were a preacher.' " [59]

In spite of exhausted energies, Prentiss made two more noteworthy speeches in the 1844 campaign, one at Vicksburg and the other at Jackson. The Vicksburg address occurred the latter part of September. In this speech, almost the only one in the campaign which has been preserved, and that only in skeleton form,[60] Prentiss selected a theme closely related to the interests of his sponsors. Championing one tenet of Clay's American System, the protective tariff, he spoke before the Vicksburg Manufacturers Association, known as the Straight-Out Clay Club. The text of the speech was *"that a tariff for the purpose of raising revenue, but carefully and skillfully discriminating in the articles upon which the duty is laid, and the amount of duty, for the protection of American manufactures, while it is a cardinal Whig doctrine, is essential to the true prosperity and independence of our great Union."*

This was a different kind of speech from Prentiss. It is to be wondered at that he should have spoken so extensively on such a theme in the South, and in a center no more industrialized than Vicksburg. He realized he was attempting an unfamiliar type of mass address, and warned his audience

[59] Horace S. Fulkerson, *Random Recollections of Early Days in Mississippi* (Vicksburg, 1885), 108; quoted also in Walmsley, "Presidential Campaign of 1844 in Mississippi," *loc. cit.*, 193.

[60] This speech was supplied George Prentiss by Smedes who stated: "I was one of his auditors, seated on a bench without a back, and surrounded by a miscellaneous crowd of people. It was a long speech, made manifestly without preparation; and struck me so much that I went home and, *calamo currente*, wrote it out, as well as I could, that night and early the following morning, *from memory*. On reading it to your brother, the next day, he highly commended my *diligence;* but remarked, that it was not *such* a speech as he would have made on the subject to a different audience, which I very well knew." Smedes to George Prentiss, n.d., in *Memoir of S. S. Prentiss*, II, 341. Smedes' version of the speech is included *ibid.*, 342–53; Shields, *Seargent Smith Prentiss*, 351–65.

that it might be disappointed. He stated frankly: "At this time I shall mingle neither salt, pepper, spice, or vinegar, with what I may have to offer you."

If on other occasions Prentiss indulged in too much bitterness toward his opponents, he did not do so in this speech. This address is unique, in that Prentiss, according to his qualifications, argued the economics of tariff. His allusions to Polk and the Democrats were subordinated. His great charge was that the Democrats were inconsistent, appearing to favor free trade in the South, but afraid to do so in the North, particularly in Pennsylvania, where the cry was "Polk and Protection," "Polk and the tariff of 1842." The Whigs, in contrast, he maintained, were consistent in declaring that a discriminating tariff was basically necessary for the prosperity of all. Prentiss found it convenient to trace the tariff history of the United States, whereby industries were established until England was no longer any great financial competitor.

Prentiss knew he faced the responsibility of showing how the agricultural and slaveholding South benefited equally with the industrial North and East by a tariff. He tried to do this constructively, meeting one by one the arguments commonly used against the tariff. His premise was "that even the cotton-planter is benefited by a protective policy in the increased consumption of, and consequently the increased demand for, his staple." If the cotton planter could expect increasingly better prices for his product, he could then champion the tariff and meet the arguments against it just as Prentiss sought to do.

Several stock objections were set forth. One was that tariffs raise the price of commodities. Prentiss admitted this might be true temporarily, but insisted that in the long run prices would be diminished by greater opportunities for competition. Another objection which he advanced and met, one particularly widespread in "the mouth of the partisan demagogue," was that "the manufacturers are

Crittenden: "The election of Polk has terribly shaken my confidence in the virtue of the people and the stability of the government. Were I somewhat younger and had not a wife and two children to provide for, I think I should endeavor to improve my condition and associations by turning pirate, which I think would be as respectable & quite in the same line of business as being a citizen of this state. . . . Polk was elected by a union of factions. He has neither the honesty or capacity to be the President even of his party. He will become at once the tool of one of these factions. The Whig party is united in all great principles—is filled with a noble and genuine indignation at the villainous defeat of a beloved . . . leader." [64]

Mississippi, like the nation, preferred Polk and his avowed determination to annex Texas, to the vacillating position of Clay. The United States was ready to begin her imperialistic ventures in Texas as well as in the Oregon boundary dispute. Some factors in Mississippi are important, however. While Prentiss could state the case for Clay most cogently and persuasively, the Democrats had orators and leaders as well. When Prentiss allowed himself to be the debating opponent of Jefferson Davis in 1843, he was, at the same time, giving experience to the man who did for Polk what he tried to do for Clay. Also, Henry S. Foote, later to part way with Davis, joined the latter in a thorough canvass of the state in behalf of the Democratic ticket.[65]

Among the various causes contributing to Polk's victory, the fact that Mississippi was Democratic in its history cannot be ignored. Not since the election of Lynch to the governorship had the Whigs been victorious. McNutt and Brown became governors in turn. The rich river counties were compelled to surrender control to the piney woods

64 Prentiss to John J. Crittenden, Vicksburg, December 22, 1844, in Crittenden Papers, Manuscripts Division, Library of Congress, Washington, D. C.
65 For a discussion of the roles of Davis and Foote in the campaign, see Reuben Davis, *Recollections of Mississippi and Mississippians* (Boston, 1891), 192–93.

and hill country more and more. The hold of Andrew Jackson in Mississippi was difficult to break. In 1844, with Polk as his choice, it is not surprising that Mississippi's six electoral votes were destined for him as the state gave him nearly 6,000 majority. It was a hard-fought campaign rather than a close one, with Prentiss first on the Whig firing line.

Chapter X

THE VICK CASE

SEVERAL years before Prentiss arrived in Mississippi, a series of events occurred there, the tangled and complicated consequences of which were to elevate him to wealth, and then at a single stroke to make him a pauper for the rest of his life. Specifically, in the 1830's Prentiss was reaping from his services as attorney in the celebrated Vick case such sudden and increased financial rewards that he could with ease buy his mother and sisters a choice home in Maine and send George Prentiss abroad to achieve his coveted desire to study in European universities. Then in 1845 there came a reversal of fortunes which by comparison made Prentiss' earlier financial anxieties seem small. With the coming of calamity, he was called upon to maintain more than a normal amount of personal equanimity.

Sometime in the latter part of Mississippi's territorial days, a sturdy pioneer Methodist minister by the name of Newit Vick, after whom the city of Vicksburg is named, found his way from Virginia to Mississippi, and settled near Natchez. A few years later he was attracted to a particular spot known as the "Open Woods," an area of land denuded by the Indians, located about five miles east of what came to be the site of Vicksburg.[1] This land he acquired. Subsequently, he purchased two additional tracts along the Mississippi: one embracing two hundred, the other several

---

[1] Vicksburg *Evening Post*, August 23, 1913; Shields, *Seargent Smith Prentiss*, 63; Claiborne, *Mississippi, as a Province, Territory and State . . . .* I, 534–35; Lee Richardson, *In and About Vicksburg . . . Its History: Its Appearances: Its Business Houses . . .* (Vicksburg, 1890), 28–33.

hundred acres.[2] Exercising prophetic foresight, Vick envisioned that a city might logically be founded on his land, and about 1819 he began to lay off lots.[3]

But Vick did not live to see the building of his city. In the same year, 1819, he died of what was probably yellow fever, and his wife likewise, just twenty minutes after him.[4] As heirs to claim the estate, there were thirteen children, several of whom were minors at the time of their father's death. In successive years, the best lawyers of Mississippi argued before the State Supreme Court in opposite interpretations of the will left by Vick. When the decision was handed down by the State Court, it was appealed to the Supreme Court of the United States, where it was argued by two famous Kentucky lawyers, Ben Hardin and John J. Crittenden.

Vick's will revealed that Mrs. Vick had been designated executrix, along with one of his sons, Hartwell, and a nephew, Willis B. Vick, as executors. The death of Mrs. Vick left Hartwell and Willis as sole administrators. Hartwell immediately asked to be relieved from duty, and the Probate Court, granting the request, assigned Willis the task of closing the estate.

The will also provided, in essence, that all his personal property should be divided equally among his wife and children, and that his sons were to receive certain parts of his real estate. A final statement read: "I wish my executors furthermore to remember that the *town lots laid off, or hereafter to be laid off on the aforementioned two hundred acres* of land, should be sold to pay my just debts or other engagements in preference to any other of my property,

---

[2] Shields, *Seargent Smith Prentiss*, 63. The account of the Vick case as given *ibid.*, 63–68, 368–72, is doubtless the most adequate on record. Intimately acquainted with Prentiss and the history of Mississippi, and himself a capable lawyer and judge, Shields was able to relate what is apparently an accurate account of the facts involved in the celebrated case.

[3] *Ibid.*, 64.   [4] *Ibid.*

for the use and benefit of all my heirs." [5] The last feature of the will became increasingly significant in court proceedings because the words "for the use and benefit of all my heirs" were underscored, or as designated in the terminology of the day, were "interlined."

By 1821, Willis Vick had made no progress in closing the estate, and asked to be relieved from further service. This request was at first refused by the Probate Court in Vicksburg, but when John Lane, who had married one of the Vick daughters, appealed to the Supreme Court to have Willis discharged, the request was granted, and Lane was designated by the court as executor. Willis died a short time later, and in view of his death and because of Lane's appointment, Hartwell Vick tried unsuccessfully to regain his executorship on the grounds that he had never relinquished his right, but merely conferred it upon Willis.

Considering himself the legal executor, Lane proceeded to carry out the provisions of the will, and completed his supposed duties by 1829, about the time Prentiss was establishing himself in Mississippi. By far the most important action taken by Lane was the sale of sixty or seventy town lots to meet the encumbrances of the estate, setting aside those not sold as "Commons" for the city of Vicksburg, located on what came to be known as Levee Street.[6]

But more complications developed. For one thing, two Vick sons, William and J. W. Wesley, did not come of age until 1827 and 1828 respectively, and the youngest heir, Newit, was still an infant in the eyes of the law when the Lane settlement was made.[7] Another complication was the fact that one Rappleye had by some means purchased a por-

---

[5] Will quoted, *ibid.* See also, 3 Howard (U. S.) 463 (1837); Will Book (1818–1823), 42–44, in Chancery Court, Warren County, Vicksburg, Mississippi. Also, in the records of the Probate Court, Vicksburg, Box 147, there are numerous papers of John Lane and Willis Vick.

[6] Shields, *Seargent Smith Prentiss*, 66.

[7] *Ibid.*; 1 Howard (Miss.) 379 (1837).

tion of the property claimed by the city of Vicksburg as the Commons. Consequently, by 1837, or earlier, as the additional Vick heirs began protests against the settlement made by Lane, as Rappleye saw the necessity of securing title to the property claimed by the city, and as the municipality wanted to establish its rights not only against Rappleye but to all the Commons, Prentiss and other Mississippi lawyers were retained and appeared before the State Supreme Court in an effort to arrive at a final adjudication of the whole matter.

While the case did not receive a hearing before the State Supreme Court until 1837, Prentiss became identified with it as early as 1834. In March of that year he wrote to his mother: "I have some business placed in my hands here by which I feel almost certain of making three or four thousand dollars and perhaps more." He went on to explain, "The business is this— Some gentlemen of this place have a claim to a portion of this town and the property to which they lay claim is of very great value." He was confident of succeeding, having "examined the matter fully," and he added, "It will be worth to me from three to five thousand dollars at least—if I do not—I lose only my labor." [8] The letter is significant in that it gives evidence of the time of Prentiss' identification with the case, shows that he represented the parties in opposition to the claims of the Mayor and Aldermen of Vicksburg, and explains that he took it upon a contingent basis.

A battle of legal giants began when the case of the Mayor and Aldermen v. Rappleye was called in the Chancery Court in Vicksburg. Prentiss and Guion, together with William Bodley and James J. Harrison represented Rappleye; the very able Joseph Holt and Spence M. Grayson were attorneys for the city. Henry S. Foote wrote: "Mr. Prentiss and Mr. Holt were, of course, the Achilles and

---

[8] Prentiss to his mother, Vicksburg, March 23, 1834, in Whittemore Collection.

Hector of the scene, though several other attorneys participated to some extent in a manner highly creditable to them." [9] The decision was adverse to Prentiss at first, however, for before the Chancery Court in Vicksburg the city won the suit in respect to the Commons.[10]

The case was appealed to the State Supreme Court, where it was tried in 1837. The Court was at that time composed of three judges, Coatesworth P. Smith, William Sharkey, and Daniel Wright. However, Wright and Sharkey declined to sit in judgment, because they were both "interested in the incipient stages of the case." As a result the Governor appointed special judges to serve with Smith, viz., Thomas J. Jenning, and Prentiss' old Bowdoin friend, Boyd.[11]

Prentiss and his colleagues, in arguing that the claimants, the Mayor and Aldermen of Vicksburg, had no right to the Commons, based their contentions on four points. These were that the City of Vicksburg had not used the property for a sufficient length of time to lay any permanent claim to it; that there had been no actual dedication of the land to the city; that John Lane was never the legal administrator of the estate, and hence his proceedings were void; and finally, that the only source of power resided in the Vick heirs themselves.[12] They hardly more than stated the first contention, but they argued the other three at length. Their elaborate arguments boiled down to maintaining that there had been no actual dedication to the city, because any such dedication "must be open and public"; that the mere laying off of lots by Vick before his death did not constitute any dedication; and that in actuality Vick's "plan at the time of his death was inchoate and incomplete." Moreover, they asserted that Lane was never the rightful executor, since the will of Vick specified two others, one of whom,

9 Foote, *Bench and Bar in the South and Southwest*, 43.
10 Shields, *Seargent Smith Prentiss*, 67.   11 *Ibid.*
12 1 Howard (Miss.) 379 (1837).

Hartwell Vick, was still alive and had never been relieved. Hence it followed that "Lane had exceeded his powers." Finally, they concluded that only the Vick heirs could make any disposition of the land; and, since Newit was still under age, the land and the heirs were protected by his minority.[13]

The case of Holt and Grayson, in brief, rested upon two points. They maintained first that Vick, by laying off lots and by the provisions of his will, had actually dedicated the land to the city. In the second place, they contended that Lane was the duly installed administrator.[14]

In a unanimous decision of the court, the contentions of Prentiss were upheld. Boyd read the decision, and admitted that Lane was in no sense the administrator. But, more important, the court put stress on a point little emphasized by the lawyers: that the daughters of Vick had received no rights to the property, as they had been given their inheritances from Vick's personal property rather than his real estate. The court ruled, too, that inasmuch as certain of the Vick heirs had but recently come of age, and that one, Newit, was still an infant in the eyes of the law, no dedication had been made to the city of Vicksburg. In consequence, then, neither the city of Vicksburg nor the daughters of Vick could lay claim to the Commons. Instead, the Commons were the property of the male heirs, to be disposed of as they saw fit.[15]

This significant court decision brightened the future for Prentiss. For one thing, he naturally received a good fee for his services. Moreover, in this period Prentiss began to purchase a considerable quantity of the land in question. He naturally felt, as a result of the court decision, that he had a secure title to all that he bought. While it seems impossible to know the exact extent of his holdings at any one time, especially as he continued over a period of years to buy additional town lots in Vicksburg, we have at least the

[13] *Ibid.*   [14] *Ibid.*   [15] *Ibid.*

statement of George Prentiss, who visited in Vicksburg in 1837, that Seargent's claim to the Commons amounted to "one-half and . . . [was] very valuable."[16] The Deed Books in the Chancery Court at Vicksburg refer to a vast number of lots as originally "laid off by S. S. Prentiss and others," and old maps of Vicksburg show lots as laid off by him and others to be from lots "A to N from Winn's Landing at the Mouth of Glass Bayou to South Street."[17]

To what extent Prentiss disposed of the land which became town lots, it is also difficult to know, but he seemingly retained a goodly portion of it. Also, quite naturally, he placed improvements upon land to which he thought he had secure claim. On one portion of the property, Square L, at the foot of Crawford Street, he built an expensive and elaborate hotel, which became known as the Prentiss House. The hotel, a three-story brick building overlooking the river, was probably erected in the early 1840's. The entrance was on Levee Street, and columns or pillars extended from the top of the first floor to the cornice of the third, making a balcony in the center of the building.[18] Unquestionably the hotel was Vicksburg's finest in those days. The business part of the city was close to the river below the bluff, with the river traffic stopping near by. The Vicksburg *Whig* gave it good press notices. Once the *Whig* commented that "it was inferior to no Hotel in the South. The table is neatly furnished and elegantly supplied." After visiting it the reporter observed further: "we found the chambers handsomely furnished, and the whole establishment presenting a neatness and comfort worthy of a first rate Southern Hotel." In an elated manner he concluded, "We rejoice to see that our City now presents to the stranger and travel-

[16] George Prentiss to his mother, Vicksburg, February 6, 1837, in *Bright Side of Life*, I, 41.

[17] An example of such a map is in the office of the City Engineer at Vicksburg.

[18] A description of the hotel was given the writer June 7, 1943, by Mack Moore of Vicksburg, who retains vivid memories of it. In the late years before it was torn down about 1890, it was used as a warehouse.

ler what she had long needed, (a comfortable Hotel,) and we feel no hesitation in saying that this establishment will be found in every respect worthy the patronage of the travelling community." [19]

A year later the *Whig* commented more significantly on it. Again it mentioned how excellently the proprietor, H. J. Childres, operated it, particularly the dining room where the bill of fare was all anyone would "desire to sit down to, comprised of red fish, oysters, turkey, venison, roast beef, &c., with a choice assortment of vegetables." This was more of an advertisement than a news item, for the concern of the *Whig* was that the hotel was not receiving the patronage it deserved. "In a dining room, large enough to dine two hundred persons," it declared, "there were about forty at the table, and at least thirty of these transient visitors." To stress its real point, the *Whig* urged: "We understand, that among the large number of Merchants and their young men, who reside in Vicksburg, there are only *six* or *eight* who board at this Hotel. This should not be the case, for although it may cost two or three dollars per month more than boarding at private houses, it seems to us, that every merchant should feel an interest in this Hotel, which is the only good one Vicksburg could boast of." In another vein, the *Whig* appealed to civic pride. "Before this Hotel went into operation, it was the cry of persons travelling up and down the river, that they could not stop at Vicksburg because it had not a hotel fit to stop at. But transient custom alone will not support a hotel in a place the size of Vicksburg, and we respectfully think the merchants would find it to their interest to support the one they have got, and not suffer it to stop, for want of that patronage which they are scattering in other places." [20] The appearance of this type of appeal is important in view of subsequent financial events in Prentiss' life.

[19] Vicksburg *Daily Whig*, March 5, 1844.
[20] *Ibid.*, January 24, 1845.

The year 1845 may be considered to mark Prentiss' financial doom. For years he had expressed financial anxieties, but the basic causes he had implied, or asserted, to be the mad doings of the Democratic party. He did not admit that avoidance of his own indiscretions and speculations would have saved him. Whatever hopes he had of saving his holdings were blasted in that year when he discovered that he was not only penniless, but hopelessly involved in debts. This circumstance came about through a revival of the Vick case.

In December, 1844, John Lane and his wife Sarah, together with their daughter, Elizabeth Irion, then residents of Louisiana, appealed to the United States Supreme Court from the decision of the Mississippi State Supreme Court in 1837, which had been sustained in 1842 by the Federal Court of Southern Mississippi, in an effort to secure rights to the Vicksburg Commons for the daughters of Vick. John W. Vick, Seargent S. Prentiss, *et al.,* were named as defendants. Hardin of Kentucky represented the appellants, and Crittenden, likewise of Kentucky, was retained by Vick and Prentiss. Clearly Prentiss had been in touch with Crittenden relative to the case for a long time. As early as 1841, Prentiss mentioned in a letter to Crittenden that he was sending him the brief he used in arguing the case in 1837.[21] In 1843, when Prentiss was certain that the case would receive a hearing before the high court, he wrote to Crittenden again, reminding him that he had sent the brief earlier, and enclosed $500 from himself and others, notwithstanding Crittenden's "refusal to charge . . . any fee." [22] The case was heard early in 1845, and Justice John McLean delivered the decision of the court.[23]

The basis of the appeal undertaken by the appellants, and the line of argument advanced by Hardin, was that if

21 Prentiss to Crittenden, Vicksburg, January 27, 1841, in Crittenden Papers.
22 *Id.* to *id.,* December 8, 1843, *ibid.*
23 3 Howard (U. S.) 463 (1845).

the Commons did not belong to the municipality of Vicksburg, then the property belonged to all the Vick heirs, and not to the sons alone. In refutation of the contentions of Crittenden that all the land belonged to the Vick male heirs, since the daughters were provided for from the personal property of the testator, Hardin put emphasis upon the "interlined" words in the latter part of the will, which stated that the land was to be sold "for the use and benefit of all my heirs." [24] Hardin's deduction was, then, that the daughters of Vick had been denied what was rightfully theirs. If this was true, it followed that Prentiss and others did not have clear title to the property. In further consequence, the improvements on the land, such as the hotel, estimated to be worth $100,000,[25] could be claimed by the Vick heirs if the court should uphold Hardin's argument.

Justice McLean, in delivering the decision (from which Chief Justice Roger B. Taney and Justice John McKinley dissented), stated that the chief task before the court was to determine the genuine intent of Vick when he made the will. The court held that Vick purposely interlined the words "for the use and benefit of all my heirs," in order to divide the property equally among all his children. This decision reversed that of the Federal Court of Southern Mississippi and established the claims of the daughters to the Commons along with the sons.[26] The irony of the whole case was that whereas Prentiss in the first place had secured the Commons for the Vick male heirs, the daughters, in 1845, took from him what he had acquired by his original efforts.

A thunderbolt had fallen on Prentiss. "In fact," he declared, "I am entirely used up, and do not expect my property to liquidate my debts. . . . The consequence has been, that the largest portion of my property, including the

24 *Ibid.*

25 Shields, *Seargent Smith Prentiss*, 368.

26 3 Howard (U. S.) 463 (1845). See also, the complete decision in the Vicksburg *Daily Whig*, February 20, 1845.

hotel, has been sacrificed, under execution, for comparatively nothing. I hope still to be able to work out even, if I can realize some debts due me. Indeed, I shall be very well satisfied to begin the world anew, providing I can begin free from old debts." [27] Prentiss' great hope was that larger opportunities would present themselves in New Orleans.

But a mighty question, and one virtually defying answer, is: To what extent was Prentiss ruined by the high decision, and to what extent was it his own fault? The financial transactions of Prentiss were complicated, and remain shrouded in mystery. Undoubtedly he lost heavily when the Vick daughters won their suit. The property thus taken from him was rendered useless to help him meet his many obligations. But the fact that he had on his shoulders so many other debts raises the question: What had he been doing with the earnings from his practice over a period of years? The general answer seems to be that he had been speculating in land. Prentiss appears to have been little short of a financial fool. A glance at his financial records indicates that in this respect he hardly challenges imitation.

Prentiss' feeling in the flush 1830's evidently had been that Vicksburg had a future as a growing city. His interest in the Commons and his subsequent purchase of a great portion of the two hundred acres probably constituted his first landholdings. The land along the river front would be increasingly valuable as the city grew and as demands for building sites mounted. In time Vicksburg began to climb the bluffs above the river, but in the 1830's the business part of the town was largely on Levee Street.

Quite naturally, however, a great part of the residences of Vicksburg were already on the hill. Thus, what was apparently Prentiss' second land purchase was the site of his home, Belmont, high on the bluffs. He purchased it in 1839 from Arent S. Van Rensselaer for $12,000. The amount of land was designated in the deed as "Containing one acre

[27] Prentiss to William Prentiss, n.d., in *Memoir of S. S. Prentiss*, II, 355.

more or less," and as "lots number *thirteen* and *fourteen* in Square Seven." [28] On the land was a modest house which he called Cub-Castle and in which he lived until he built Belmont on the same site in 1842.

Evidence is abundant that Prentiss was to a considerable extent the breadwinner for his mother and sisters in Maine. Also, he was sending his brother George much or all of the money the latter spent in European study and travel from 1839 to 1842. One of the very interesting instances of generosity on the part of Prentiss was his deeding in 1841 of two lots in Vicksburg, "with all singular appurtenances and improvements belonging to the same," to his mother and sisters, Abby and Anna, "in consideration of the natural love and affection" which he had for them. John Guion was appointed trustee as he assigned the property to them "forever in fee simple." [29]

It would be a near impossibility to trace just what plots of land Prentiss owned in Vicksburg, where they were all located, what sums of money were involved, how he disposed of certain tracts from time to time, and to what extent they were free from encumbrances or were mortgaged. One thing is quite clear, however. In addition to his interest in the Commons and his home, he frequently bought lots and property sold by the sheriff for delinquent taxes. Over and over again, he was the highest bidder at such auctions. These purchases appear to have been made chiefly in the period from 1841 to 1843. The dire financial condition of the state in those and previous years resulted in many tax sales. Prentiss may have figured that such purchases would be valuable investments when times improved. Early in 1841 he bought eleven lots in various separated squares for slightly less than $900.[30] Later in 1841 he bought at least one other lot at a sheriff's sale for $80.[31] During 1842 he

---

[28] Deed Book Q, Chancery Court, Warren County, Vicksburg, October 1, 1839.

[29] *Ibid.*, August 1, 1841.   [30] *Ibid.*, S, March 1, 1841.

[31] *Ibid.*, R, August 16, 1841.

VICKSBURG ABOUT 1876

A REAR VIEW OF THE THIRD STORY OF THE PRENTISS HOUSE (HOTEL) IS VISIBLE DIRECTLY BACK OF THE BOAT

appeared as the highest bidder at least three times, paying once only $30 for a lot,[32] and again $531 for four.[33] Later in the year he purchased slightly more than forty-eight acres outside the city, paying $175 for the area as it fell under the hammer.[34] In 1843 he made one small purchase in March and then secured a quitclaim for six additional lots for $305.[35]

But during the same years Prentiss allowed mortgages of an almost colossal nature to be placed against his property. At a time when he was still unmarried and responsible for only himself, save for what responsibility he assumed in Maine, he could not have had need for such exorbitant amounts of money unless he was engaged in some enterprise requiring large sums. It is probable that he borrowed chiefly to build his hotel, since it was constructed at the very time he mortgaged his property so heavily. Possibly, too, additional sums of borrowed money went into the erection of other buildings on the Commons.

Added evidence that he held title to extensive areas of ground in Vicksburg is the fact that early in 1841 he mortgaged eighteen lots to three different men, William Frazier, Thomas E. Robins, and William F. Bodley for $13,746.25.[36] Exactly one month later he mortgaged what must have been two valuable areas of land to the Planters' Bank at Natchez for $7,258, payable in twelve months.[37] As large as these amounts were, they shrink into comparative insignificance beside the fact that in the same month he mortgaged ten lots to the New Orleans Canal and Banking Company for $41,500, with the understanding that he should regain them as he paid the principal with interest at the rate of $10,000 annually.[38] Evidently, however, this was not enough money for his purposes, for the next month he negotiated a second agreement with the same New Orleans bank by mortgaging

[32] *Ibid.*, February 7, 1842.
[33] *Ibid.*, February 21, 1842.
[34] *Ibid.*, T, August 1, 1842.
[35] *Ibid.*, S, May 20, 1843.
[36] *Ibid.*, Q, March 4, 1841.
[37] *Ibid.*, April 4, 1841.
[38] *Ibid.*, April 20, 1841.

two more lots for $13,000, again agreeing to make annual payments.[39] At least two other mortgages were made in 1841. In May he encumbered two lots in favor of Stephen Stafford in order to pay notes amounting to $3,648 to Catherine Haines. This agreement allowed Prentiss to hold the lots, but provided that they could be sold at auction if he should default.[40] And in September he allowed Belmont (then Cub-Castle) to be encumbered to the Commercial Bank of Natchez for $11,547.95. His payments were stipulated as due on the first day of each March from 1842 to 1845.[41] This last mortgage has peculiar significance, for he would hardly have jeopardized his home except as a last resort.

The most unhappy and despairing letters which Prentiss ever sent to Maine were those in 1842 in which he viewed the state of affairs—for the first time with apprehension. Seemingly his finances took a turn for the worse that year. His marriage was followed by a trip to Washington, after which he came back to Vicksburg and proceeded to build Belmont by enlarging Cub-Castle. No sooner did he return than he set about the painful task of borrowing money. The very day of his arrival, May 14, he came near mortgaging to the limit. Twice in 1841 he had mortgaged property to the New Orleans Canal and Banking Company, one portion, as has been seen, for $41,500, and another for $13,000. Evidently it was necessary for him to protect these mortgages by encumbering five more pieces of property to the same institution.[42] As distasteful as this was, it must have been far more alarming to have to place a chattel mortgage upon his household belongings, and to encumber Belmont further for as much as he could borrow on it. The chattel mortgage was for money advanced to him by his law partner, Smedes, in the amount of $3,040.20, to be repaid between 1844 and 1846. Besides naming the lots which constituted about an

39 *Ibid.*, May 14, 1841.   40 *Ibid.*, May 13, 1841.
41 *Ibid.*, September 15, 1841.   42 *Ibid.*, R, May 14, 1842.

Above. CHILDHOOD HOME OF PRENTISS

From William Henry Milburn, "The Lance, Cross and Canoe"

Below. SIDE VIEW OF BELMONT

After it was purchased and enlarged by William C. Smedes

Courtesy of John Brunini and Mrs. David Porterfield

The loss of Belmont must have been the climax of ill fortune. The place was deeded to Prentiss' law partner, Smedes, for $8,000.[54] In the possession of Smedes it was enlarged and further beautified year by year until it was captured by the Federal soldiers during the Civil War and was used as a hospital before being destroyed.

Prentiss' beloved Belmont is one more example of how he bought dear and sold cheap. As has been mentioned, he paid $12,000 for it in 1839 when it consisted of but one acre and the small house he called Cub-Castle. But not only did he enlarge Cub-Castle into Belmont; he seemingly added grounds surrounding it, for the survey for the deed to Smedes indicates that it measured "about five acres more or less." [55] Thus Prentiss sold Belmont for $4,000 less than he paid for it after building a larger house and adding four acres to the grounds. According to the Inventory Book of Smedes there were at least two mortgages against it. One was held by the Commercial Bank of Natchez, and a second by the Canal Bank of New Orleans. Smedes probably made a good purchase. What he spent in clearing the title was to be deducted from the original cost, and he paid for it in bonds worth seventy cents on the dollar.[56]

One other aspect of Prentiss' financial grief, the extent to which he had signed notes for others who were unable to meet their obligations, virtually defies interpretation. One example is worth noting. Never did a man have stronger support from a newspaper than Prentiss had in the Vicksburg *Whig*. There is a story with financial implications back of this relationship. The editor of the *Whig* was William H. McCardle, and his fellow publisher was Marmiduke Shannon. McCardle had been engaged in news-

[54] Deed Book T, Chancery Court, Warren County, Vicksburg, December 1, 1846.

[55] *Ibid.*

[56] Inventory Book of William C. Smedes for 1848–1849, in possession of Mrs. David Porterfield, Vicksburg, Mississippi. This information was made available to the writer, May 10, 1943, by V. Blaine Russell of Vicksburg.

paper work in Maysville, Kentucky, in the early 1830's, and
when he came to Vicksburg he carried with him a letter
from Henry Clay to Prentiss. The letter recommended him
as "a young gentleman of high character, of good abilities
and of good principles." It mentioned, also, that he was
considering "transferring to some point in Mississippi
where he . . . might be able to render more service to
the cause which he . . . had espoused.[57] The cause was
the Whig party. Prentiss was evidently one who came to
his financial aid in getting started. When the Vicksburg
Register became the Vicksburg *Whig* in 1839, it was owned
and edited by Shannon and McCardle. Some of Prentiss'
money helped to back the enterprise, evidently, for in 1841,
when $10,000 owed to Shannon and Prentiss fell due, the
actual ownership was transferred to Isaac H. Hays and John
H. Martin, while McCardle and Shannon were retained as
editors.[58] Prentiss may have lost no money this time, but
the transaction illustrates the manner in which, for a time
at least, he assumed obligations and tied up goodly quantities of money.

Debt-ridden, Prentiss remained at Belmont during the
summer of 1845. Besides attending court, he told George
Prentiss, "I am busy studying Civil Law, and preparing myself for New Orleans." [59] With all his own financial worries,
he still found it possible to send four hundred dollars to
his mother, and promised to send more.[60]

Prentiss' financial debacle would have been lessened had
he been able to leave Vicksburg even with the world. This
could not be, however, and his creditors hounded him to

[57] Clay to Prentiss, Ashland, September 8, 1838, in Whittemore Collection.
[58] Deed Book Q, Chancery Court, Warren County, Vicksburg, January 1,
1841.
[59] Prentiss to George Prentiss, Vicksburg, April 21, 1845, in Whittemore
Collection; quoted also, in *Memoir of S. S. Prentiss*, II, 360.
[60] *Ibid.*, except that the matter of money is omitted in the letter as
recorded in *Memoir of S. S. Prentiss*.

the end of his days. One example is illustrative of this. In July, 1845, Prentiss induced a Vicksburg citizen, George L. Record, to lend him $1,500. He signed two notes, one for $800, to be paid in January, 1846, and one for $700, to be paid in February, 1846. In November of 1848 these notes were still unpaid and the interest had increased the total to $1,770. Record was determined to collect. He made a trip to New Orleans, interviewed Prentiss, and then wrote him a letter in which he made four propositions, giving Prentiss little more than an hour to decide what he would do. In the interview, Prentiss evidently declared his inability to pay the whole amount, and asked for six or eight weeks of additional time, so that court fees could become available, making it possible to pay fifty cents on the dollar. Record seemingly recognized the hopelessness of ever collecting all, and made his four propositions accordingly. One was: "That I will take for the notes two good acceptances, one for 60 days the other for 4 months 400 Dollars each, $800." The second one stated, "Or I will take an accepted Draft on any wholesale grocery or Drygood store in the City payable in goods or groceries at Sight for $800." By the third alternative Prentiss could save $50 if he could find "good endorsers" for two notes, "payable at one of the Solvent Banks in the City, one at 60 days the Other at 4 months, for 375 Dollars each." In the final alternative, Record showed some slight confidence in Prentiss by stating that he would allow a renewal of the notes at their face value for six and twelve months. In addition, Record castigated Prentiss rather severely for his long neglect, telling him: "I fear you have not fixed your mind upon a settlement of the notes as a thing that must be done at the time you specify." Finally, Record told him, "I am prompted to say to you that if One of the Propositions herein contained is not acceded to, I shall be compelled to leave it in the hands of an atty. to be used as Circumstances shall dictate." [61] Truly Prentiss was compelled to drink a bitter cup. At the same time, he did not appear embittered as might have been expected. Seemingly he did not blame others for his personal misfortune. To his credit it must be said that he bore his financial ordeals with the fortitude becoming a man.

[61] George L. Record to Prentiss, New Orleans, November 30, 1848, in George L. Record Papers in Merritt M. Shilg Collection, Department of Archives, Louisiana State University. The two original notes bearing Prentiss' signature are with the letter.

Chapter XI

THE CITIZEN ORATOR OF NEW ORLEANS

MISSISSIPPI'S repudiation of her bonded indebtedness, together with the decision of the United States Supreme Court on the Vick case, called forth from Prentiss the severest invective: "I consider this State as disgraced and degraded, and I have sworn that I will not bring up my children within reach of its infamous doctrines."[1] Prentiss was not the man to make declarations and then retract them. He decided to locate elsewhere.

He was actually older than his thirty-seven years. The demands of incessant court appearances, the political exertions he had been obliged to put forth in the Mississippi legislature, the disputed Mississippi election, the term in Congress, the two national political campaigns, the Mississippi bond repudiation episode, and his own financial anxieties and reverses had all taken their toll of physical energy. Moreover, strong drink had made its inroads on his constitution. Yet Prentiss was to sustain the loss of personal fortune, start afresh, and try to win again. Having full confidence in his inherent talents, he staked everything on one item—his health.

After considering various cities in which to locate, chiefly New York and Baltimore, he decided to go to New Orleans. He wound up his business in Mississippi as best he could. The difficulties he encountered on this score may be surmised from his statement: "My property seems to be useless in the payment of debts, and, as I have no lamp of Aladdin,

[1] Prentiss to George Prentiss, Vicksburg, January 22, 1845, in *Memoir of S. S. Prentiss*, II, 358.

some of my debts will have to wait a little my conven-
ience." [2] Though now more a pauper than a prince, he still
had friends in Mississippi. It was but natural that they
should wish to express their farewells. A dinner was held
in his honor in Vicksburg, at which William A. Lake presided and gave expression to appropriate sentiments. Prentiss responded and spoke once more to his fellow townsmen.
Doubtless the Vicksburg *Whig* was never more sincere than
when it stated: "his countenance and voice gave full expression to the feelings, which the address of the President
on the occasion, and other manifestations on the part of the
company had excited in his bosom." Certainly emotions
other than contempt for Mississippi were in his heart. "He
returned his thanks for the compliment paid him by his
personal friends . . . and dwelt for some moments upon
the . . . friendships formed and the social ties severed
by his removal." Emotions ran still higher as he "spoke
of his natal home—his school-boy haunts—his emigration
here, his residence here with all his associations, and his
departure for his new home." [3]

While Prentiss did not leave Vicksburg until November
of 1845 (never to visit it again, although he did return often
to Natchez and Longwood), he laid his final plans the last
of September. "I start to-day for New Orleans to make final
arrangements for removing," he told his mother. "From
New Orleans I shall go up to Alexandria, which is on Red
River, in Louisiana, to attend the Supreme Court. I expect
to get back here about the middle of October. We shall then
pack up immediately and be off." [4]

[2] *Ibid.*
[3] Vicksburg *Daily Whig*, November 3, 1845. Another significant notice
of the dinner is the following: "Hon. S. S. Prentiss—This gentleman, who is
now one of our fellow citizens, was complimented with a public dinner at
Vicksburg on the 30th ult., as a parting compliment, and in token of the
regard felt for him by his old and former friends." New Orleans *Daily
Picayune*, November 7, 1845.
[4] Prentiss to his mother, Vicksburg, September 26, 1845, in *Memoir of
S. S. Prentiss*, II, 360–61.

One aspect of his final arrangements for residence in New Orleans may have been taken care of on this trip. Prentiss needed a legal associate, and found one. As early as October 8, the Vicksburg *Whig* announced: "The Hon. S. S. Prentiss and John Finney have entered into partnership in the practice of law, in the city of New Orleans." [5] As Prentiss became established in New Orleans, beginning as early as December 20, the partnership advertised, "Prentiss and Finney, Attorneys and Counsellors at Law, New Orleans, La.—Office No. 56, Canal street, up stairs." [6]

New Orleans and Prentiss were no strangers, his public and business appearances there having been frequent. He was happy to be situated in the Crescent City where his professional talents could be exercised. New Orleans as a commercial city, located strategically for shipping and financial transactions of all kinds, supplied many a lawyer with a lucrative practice. Prentiss had reason to believe that his clientele would be sufficient to enable him to pay his Mississippi debts, and to achieve in addition a competence of his own. He expressed his optimism in an annual New Year's letter to his mother in 1846: "We have at length got fairly settled down in New Orleans, and begin to feel at home. I am much pleased with the change, and like New Orleans a great deal better than Vicksburg. We are quite pleasantly situated, and have a nice house. I am gratified with my prospects here, and do not doubt I shall succeed very well. I have already considerable business, and if my health is spared, do not fear for the future." [7]

But taking residence in New Orleans with the intent to practice law presented one hazard and an immediate challenge. To practice before the bar in Louisiana, it was necessary for him to master the Louisiana code, based upon

[5] Vicksburg *Daily Whig*, October 8, 1845. This same announcement was carried in the New Orleans *Daily Picayune*, October 7, 1845.

[6] New Orleans *Daily Picayune*, December 20, 1845.

[7] Prentiss to his mother, New Orleans, January 1, 1846, in *Memoir of S. S. Prentiss*, II, 395.

French civil law, which contrasts sharply with the British common law upon which Mississippi law is based. But with one political campaign two years behind him, and another two years in the offing, he was free during the interim to master the Louisiana code and to devote himself almost entirely to law, except when there came one of the frequent demands on him for public addresses as a citizen of New Orleans.

And New Orleans was not the city to deprive herself of the radiance of his oratorical eloquence or of his influence as a public-spirited and cultured person. He became so identified with the civic life of the city that time after time Seargent S. Prentiss was the orator of the day. He must go down in history as a skilled occasional or demonstrative orator, as well as a forensic and deliberative one. While he was not untried in this variety of oratory before he lived in New Orleans, his fame in this field grew as more opportunities and calls came to him. Prentiss was accepted into the civic life of New Orleans; soon he became almost a celebrity, and certainly one of the city's leading spokesmen.

What must be considered the first highly significant occasion in which Prentiss, as the orator of the day, delivered a demonstrative speech deserving a place in the history of American public address, came very shortly after his going to New Orleans. On December 22, 1845, he delivered the annual address on the anniversary of the landing of the Pilgrims. It was not his greatest speech, but certain factors operated to set it apart from most of his public addresses. Probably no speaker since the organization of the New England Society in New Orleans in 1842 was better qualified to speak,[8] since his life had been lived both in New England and in the South. In one respect, however, the speech was not characteristic of him. For some reason he deviated from his usual mode of extemporaneous delivery and gave the address from manuscript exactly as he had

[8] New Orleans *Daily Picayune*, December 23, 1842.

written it. Consequently, "being unused to this style, it is said that he seemed to be cramped by the manuscript, and did not, therefore, deliver it with the same unction as those speeches bursting from him in his usual mode." [9]

Still the speech is worthy of Prentiss. If the manuscript prevented his usual freedom, it did not diminish the high acclaim which the orator and the speech received by all the New Orleans papers. Unquestionably Prentiss spoke from the depths of feeling on this subject and occasion, at a time when, because of antislavery and abolition sentiments, many southerners were not kindly disposed to hear eulogies on northern virtues. Prentiss saw his opportunity once more, and above all else, to plead the cause of the Union.

The speech proper was delivered in the church of the Reverend Theodore Clapp. Following the address, the New England Society assembled at the St. Charles Hotel for a dinner. The audience at the church was large, the *Delta* saying it was "filled from gallery to desk," [10] and the *Picayune* reporting that it "was thronged to its utmost capacity with a most respectable and fashionable auditory." [11] In addition, the speech as a whole was published, the *Picayune* announcing that in spite of an extra large edition already printed, "Our next weekly edition will contain the truly eloquent and stirring address." [12] The printing of the speech made it immediately available far and wide to reprint, so that it was read by thousands of Americans.[13] Since it was read from manuscript, and was, quite naturally, available for the exact printing of what was delivered, the record of this speech is far more authentic than that of most of Prentiss' speeches.

[9] Shields, *Seargent Smith Prentiss*, 375.
[10] New Orleans *Daily Delta*, December 23, 1845.
[11] New Orleans *Daily Picayune*, December 23, 1845.
[12] *Ibid.*, December 26, 1845.
[13] As an example of this, the Boston *Daily Advertiser* gave extensive space to the meeting of the New Orleans Society and carried the full speech in its issues of January 12, 13, 1846.

Much of the speech was an expression of Prentiss' New England background. While he opened with appropriate remarks about the high significance of the day, and though he traced the story of the Mayflower's crossing, calling it "a little tempest-tost, weather-beaten bark," he stated early, "It is not my purpose to enter into the history of the pilgrims."

Other objectives ran through the speech. One was to treat of "some of the traits that distinguished the enterprise of the Pilgrims from all others, and which are well worthy of remembrance." This was an old story, but Prentiss tried to revive its significance by concrete comparisons and contrasts. For example, he asked the question: "How did the Spanish colonize?" His answer was: "Let Mexico, Peru and Hispaniola answer." Since the Pilgrims, though they had their faults, were not tempted by gold, his great rhetorical question was: "Who would not rather be of the Pilgrim stock than claim descent from the proudest Norman that ever planted his robber blood in the halls of the Saxon, or the noblest paladin that quaffed wine at the table of Charlemagne?"

Prentiss lingered on the noble traits of the Pilgrims and on their ideals and purposes. He praised earnestly and at length the American system of free education, which he designated as one safeguard of democracy. He could not think of it as originating with the Pilgrim fathers without recalling his own schooling. Out of this reminiscence came a unique word picture of his early district school in Maine. Without warning his hearers specifically, Prentiss for a moment returned to Maine. "Behold yon simple building near the crossing of the village road. It is small and of rude construction, but stands in a pleasant and quiet spot. A magnificent old elm spreads its broad arms above and seems to lean towards it, as a strong man bends to shelter and protect a child. A brook runs through the meadow near, and hard by there is an orchard—but the trees have suffered much and bear no fruit, except upon the most remote and inaccessible branches. From within its walls comes a busy hum, such as you may hear in a disturbed bee-hive. Now peep through yonder window and you will see a hundred children, with rosy cheeks, mischievous eyes and demure faces, all engaged, or pretending to be so, in their little lessons. It is the public school—the free, the common school—provided by law: open to all: claimed from the community as a right, not accepted as a bounty." From this greatest of Pilgrim institutions redounded tangible manifestations of good. Prentiss tried to portray them: "Here the children of the rich and poor, high and low, meet upon perfect equality, and commence under the same auspices the race of life. Here the sustenance of the mind is served up to all alike, as the Spartans served their food upon the public table. Here young Ambition climbs his little ladder, and boyish Genius plumes his half-fledged wings." There was a message for the South in all of this. Prentiss knew how his educational heritage in New England surpassed that afforded southern children—those such as he himself had tried to teach at Rokeby and Dunbarton —who had to depend primarily on family plantation tutors, or none at all. The South needed in 1845 to hear him say: "The Common village school is New England's fairest boast—the brightest jewel that adorns her brow. The principle that society is bound to provide for its member's education as well as protection, so that none need be ignorant except from choice, is the most important that belongs to modern philosophy. It is essential to a republican government. Universal education is not only the best and surest, but the only sure foundation for free institutions. True liberty is the child of knowledge; she pines away and dies in the arms of ignorance."

The speaker could not devote all his time to the one theme of education, however. Many of his hearers, certainly the members of the New England Society, were able to appreciate the significance of his ideas on education, for many of them, like himself, had their roots in New England. Other virtues, such as enterprise and bold determination, had caused many of the sons of New England to wander. "Bold and restless as the old Northern Vikings," said Prentiss, "they go forth to seek their fortunes. . . . Had they been the companions of Columbus, the great mariner would not have been urged to return, though he had sailed westward to his dying day." Prentiss knew what decisions he had made in leaving Maine as a youth, and he remembered what struggles he had experienced to overcome longings to return home. His frequent declarations that he was going to return to Maine had become only occasional as years went by. Finally they had ceased entirely. Probably the explanation he gave in this speech applied to many in his audience as well as to himself. "But while we devote this day to the remembrance of our native land, we forget not that in which our happy lot is cast. . . . We are no exiles meeting upon the banks of a foreign river, to swell its waters with our home-sick tears. Here floats the same banner which rustled above our boyish heads, except that its mighty folds are wider and its glittering stars increased in number."

Prentiss did not forget that he was speaking to a New Orleans audience. Although his specific listeners were, like himself, imbued with Pilgrim traditions, many others, particularly a very large reading audience, had other feelings toward New England in 1845. They resented the abolitionists, whom they considered to have originated in New England. Accordingly, Prentiss conceived it his great task as he moved to his peroration, to plead the cause of the Union and of national understanding. His transition was this: "The sons of New England are found in every State of the broad Republic. In the East, the South, and in the unbounded West, their blood mingles freely with every kindred current. We have but changed our chamber in the paternal mansion; in all its rooms we are at home, and all who inhabit it are our brothers. To us the Union has but one domestic hearth; its household gods are all the same. Upon us, then, peculiarly devolves the duty of feeding the fires upon that kindly hearth; of guarding with pious care those sacred household gods." Since Prentiss had sung the song of Unionism so often, he was happy to do it again. Now he was saying in New Orleans in slightly different words what he had said in Boston's Faneuil Hall in 1839: "We cannot do with less than the whole Union; to us it admits of no division. . . . Accursed, then, be the hand put forth to loosen the golden cords of Union; thrice accursed the traitorous lips, whether of Northern fanatic or Southern Demagogue, which shall propose its severance."

The very closing of the speech was a further embellishment of this theme with words of prophetic significance for New Orleans. Prentiss saw the great port city in which he was speaking as playing an ever greater role in the life of the nation, provided the Union be left undisturbed. Commerce and culture would be on the march. "And when, a century hence," he closed, "this Crescent City shall have filled her golden horns; when within her broad-armed port shall be gathered the products of the industry of a hundred millions of freemen; when galleries of art and halls of learning shall have made classic this mart of trade; then may the sons of the Pilgrims, still wandering from the bleak hills of the North, stand upon the banks of the Great River, and exclaim with mingled pride and wonder, Lo! this is our country: when did the world ever witness so rich and magnificent a City—so great and glorious Republic!" [14]

Praise accompanied and followed the speech. The New Orleans *Delta* said it was "Like a well laid out parterre [abounding] in the choicest flowers—like a tiara on the

[14] For standard versions of this speech, see *ibid.*; *Memoir of S. S. Prentiss*, II, 397–408; Shields, *Seargent Smith Prentiss*, 376–83; New Orleans *Daily Picayune*, December 23, 1845.

forehead of beauty, it sparkled with brilliant diamonds. To attempt to give an idea of it as a whole by any summary or synopsis, would be like endeavoring to impress one with the harmony of a well-tuned organ by striking a single key." [15] Since Prentiss was a newly arrived resident, a part of the praise he received was combined with a welcome to him. Toasts were drunk at the dinner of the Society following the speech, the last one being to Prentiss for his speech, "so replete . . . with beauty and eloquence." Thus the Society greeted "him as a citizen of New Orleans." [16]

Calls on Prentiss for public utterances became constantly more frequent as he became increasingly identified with the southern city. For example, early in March, 1846, in the Armory Hall, he "delivered the tenth in a series of free lectures" on the People's Lyceum. "It was a crowded auditory," according to the *Daily Delta*, that listened to his lecture "on the subject of the 'Liberal Arts and the importance of their cultivation in the country.'" Ironically enough, "After the lecture a beautiful banner was presented to the Lady Franklin Total Abstinence Society." [17]

Nearly one year later, in February, 1847, Prentiss gave one of the greatest occasional speeches of his life. The situation was ideal for the orator to express profound pathos, and to arouse sympathy for peoples less fortunate than those to whom he was speaking.

The destitute conditions of the people of Ireland resultant from the potato famine of 1845–1846 received nation-wide sympathy in the United States. Early in 1847 a movement got under way to solicit contributions in food, clothing, and money to send to Ireland. Cities, organizations, and groups responded at once. The Baltimore and Ohio Railroad Company offered its facilities for the free transport of all commodities designated for Ireland.[18] Min-

15 New Orleans *Daily Delta*, December 23, 1845.
16 New Orleans *Daily Picayune*, December 23, 1845.
17 New Orleans *Daily Delta*, March 3, 1846.
18 *Niles' National Register*, LXXI (1846–1847), 404.

isters gave their benediction to the movement, and public-spirited citizens set out to obtain contributions. Mass meetings were held far and wide, and newspapers gave graciously of their space to announce what was being done at home and in other centers. By February 20, New York City had raised as much as $25,000 and had chartered a ship to carry provisions.[19] Other cities such as Baltimore, Providence, and Boston made their offerings. Like New York, Boston chartered a ship to carry her cargo.[20]

Not the least energetic support was manifested in New Orleans. As a result, there emanated from Prentiss, the chief orator of the day, his Irish Famine speech. Also, the occasion in New Orleans provided a platform for Henry Clay to speak on the same subject. Thus the two orators and devoted friends came before the same civic gathering at the same time.

The New Orleans meeting was held February 4 in the Commercial Exchange with Governor Isaac Johnson presiding. Clay spoke first. After "he briefly but forcibly addressed the meeting upon the distressing conditions of affairs in Ireland," [21] and Governor Johnson "in a brief but exceedingly happy, zealous, and taking speech" addressed the gathering, "the audience with a single voice, called for Prentiss." [22]

This Prentiss speech is a model of mid-century oratorical eloquence of the demonstrative type, wherein the lofty and ennobling reach the sublime, as it was understood in the 1840's. Prentiss embellished his speech by filling it with brilliant figures and metaphors, and by diffusing it with poetic and historical allusions. Its delivery occupied less than an hour, a shorter period than was common with him.

After two or three opening sentences Prentiss proceeded to bring his cause before the people of New Orleans in a

19 Boston *Daily Advertiser,* February 20, 1847.
20 *Ibid.,* April 13, 1847.
21 New Orleans *Daily Picayune,* February 5, 1847.
22 New Orleans *Daily Delta,* February 5, 1847.

singularly beautiful word picture of Irish history and struggle. *Niles' National Register* quoted it, saying by way of
introduction, "The Tenor of his remarks may be judged
of by the following extract: [23] 'There lies upon the other
side of the Atlantic a beautiful island, famous in story and
song. Its area is not so great as that of the state of Louisiana,
while its population is almost half that of the Union. It has
given to the world more than its share of genius and greatness. It has been prolific in statesmen, warriors and poets.
Its brave and generous sons have fought successfully all
battles but their own. In wit and humor it has no equal;
while its harp, like its history, moves to tears by its sweet
but melancholy pathos. Into this fair region, God has seen
fit to send the most terrible of all those fearful ministers
who fulfill his inscrutable decrees. The earth has failed to
give her increase; the common mother has forgotten her
offspring, and her breast no longer affords them their accustomed nourishment. Famine, gaunt and ghastly famine,
has seized a nation with its struggling grasp; and unhappy
Ireland, in the sad woes of the present, forgets for a moment the gloomy history of the past.' "

This part of the speech set the tenor for all that followed; the force of his language on this plane was continuous. But as Prentiss analyzed his audience, he recognized the difficulty of portraying to people in New Orleans,
living in the rich valley of the Mississippi, the dire consequences of famine. "You who have never been beyond the
precincts of our own favored country; you, more especially,
who have always lived in this great valley of the Mississippi—this cornucopia of the world—who see each day
poured into the lap of your city, food sufficient to assuage
the hunger of a nation, can form but an imperfect idea of
the horrors of famine; of the terror which strikes men's souls
when they cry in vain for food."

To meet the problem of making famine real to his well-

[23] *Niles' National Register*, LXXI (1846–1847), 404.

fed audience, Prentiss chose the analogy of war with its consequences, and proceeded to depict famine as an even deadlier enemy. "In battle, in the fullness of his pride and strength," he said, "little recks the soldier whether the hissing bullet sing his sudden requiem, or the cords of life are severed by the sharp steel." In famine-stricken Ireland men died differently. "But he who dies of hunger wrestles alone, day after day, with his grim and unrelenting enemy. . . . He has not the hot blood of the soldier to maintain him; for his foe, vampire-like, has exhausted his veins. Famine comes not up like a brave enemy, storming, by a sudden onset, the fortress that resists. Famine besieges. He draws his lines around the doomed garrison; he cuts off supplies; he never summons to surrender, for he gives no quarter." Prentiss' end picture was vivid, not to say lurid: "Day by day the blood recedes; the flesh departs; the muscles relax, and the sinews grow powerless. At last the mind, which at first had bravely nerved itself for the contest, gives way under the mysterious influences that govern its union with the body. Then he begins to doubt the existence of an overruling Providence; he hates his fellow-men, and glares upon them with the longings of a cannibal, and, it may be, dies blaspheming!"

All this served as a basis for Prentiss' plea for gifts. "Who will hesitate to give his mite," he asked, "to avert such awful results? Surely not you, citizens of New Orleans, ever famed for your deeds of benevolence and charity." He reminded the people specifically of their former contributions "to oppressed Greece and struggling Poland," and then drove home his appeal: "Within Erin's borders is an enemy more cruel than the Turk; more tyrannical than the Russian. Bread is the only weapon that can conquer him. Let us, then, load ships with this glorious munition, and, in the name of our common humanity, wage war against this despot Famine."

His appeal was not yet complete, however. To make

doubly sure that city-wide contributions would be forth-
coming, Prentiss next supplied two motives, a lower and a
higher, which might actuate his hearers. First, because famine conditions abroad had raised the price of our commodities: "We cannot do less, in common honesty," he
insisted, "than to divide among the starving poor of Ireland a portion of the gains we are making out of their mis-
fortunes." To some, then, he pleaded: "Let us in God's
name, 'cast our bread upon the waters,' and if we are selfish
enough to desire it, we may recollect the promise, that it
shall return after many days." But there was in Prentiss'
mind a higher motive, and this he employed as he reached
his climax. "We ought to thank our Maker that he has
permitted us to exercise equally with himself that noblest
of the Divine attributes, benevolence." Perhaps no finer opportunity ever came Prentiss' way in all his extensive oratorical career to draw upon his favorite of all poets, Shakespeare, than at this emotionalized instant. "Go home and
look at your family, smiling in rosy health, and then think
of the pale, famine-pinched cheeks of the poor children of
Ireland; and I know you will give according to your store,
even as a bountiful Providence has given to you—not
grudgingly, but with an open hand; for the quality of
benevolence, like that of mercy

> 'Is not strained,
> It droppeth as the gentle rain from Heaven
> Upon the place beneath: it is twice blessed,
> It blesses him that gives, and him that takes.' " [24]

Prentiss was at his best in this dazzling and brilliant kind
of utterance. The effects of the address and the heights it

[24] In the versions of the speech supplied by Shields, *Seargent Smith
Prentiss*, 385–87, and in *Memoir of S. S. Prentiss*, II, 412–15, the address is
concluded at this point. Some additional closing sentences, including two
poetic interweavings, are presented in the New Orleans *Daily Delta*, February 7, 1847. George Prentiss states: "I omit the closing, and, as it was
delivered, most beautiful portions of the address, as it is entirely spoilt by
the reporter, who, Mr. P. naively observed to me 'doubtless knew much
better than himself what he meant to say.'" *Memoir of S. S. Prentiss*, II, 415.

ascended were described by one New Orleans paper in a colorful account: "Before you have so far recovered from the glare of one brilliant conceit, as to be able to report it, you are hurried with the admiration of one still more brilliant; and thus hastening from one to the other, like a butterfly hovering over a beautiful parterre of rich and fragrant flowers, you are left in a maze of indistinct and mingled brilliancy, unwilling and unable to determine upon which you will light, as the most striking and beautiful." [25]

The Irish Famine speech was delivered under circumstances trying for Prentiss because he was daily expecting a message of death from Maine. After his first years in Mississippi it was not only his privilege to return to Maine for periodic visits, but he also enjoyed visits from his brothers and sisters. He saw Samuel now and then when the latter's boat stopped at Vicksburg on trips up and down the Mississippi. George was with him for several weeks on two different occasions, once before his European voyage and once following. Likewise, Anna came to Mississippi at least once and was present for his wedding, remaining some weeks longer. Also, late in 1845, before he left Vicksburg and following his early residence in New Orleans in 1846, Abby came to visit, and, it would seem, to search for health. In one of Prentiss' letters to his mother at that time, he mentioned the cold and inclement weather, adding: "It is astonishing how Abby has stood it. I think she has continued to improve ever since she came out, . . . and I have no doubt if she continues to hold on till the warm spring days, she will then improve rapidly. You cannot imagine what a comfort it is to have her with us." [26] Abby did not regain her health, however, either in the South or after her return home. In just a year after her visit, and following the birth of his third child, Seargent Smith, January 5,

[25] New Orleans *Daily Delta*, February 5, 1847.
[26] Prentiss to his mother, New Orleans, January 1, 1846, in *Memoir of S. S. Prentiss*, II, 396.

1847, Prentiss was distressed by letters from relatives in Maine to the effect that Abby was nearing her death. She died of pulmonary ailments January 30, 1847, just six days before he delivered the Irish Famine speech, her death being the first in the family who survived infancy. Prentiss received the news about February 11, and wrote his mother touchingly. He said it "was the severest blow I have ever experienced." [27] Abby's death may have set up remorse in Prentiss for certain of his own imperfections, such as his surrender of his strong physique to drink. At any rate, he wrote: "she was so good, that we know she is now in Heaven, and freed from all care, unless it be that her affectionate heart is still troubled for us, whom she loved so well." [28] In an equally touching letter to Anna he said, among other things, "We shall soon travel the same road; would to God, we were all so well prepared." [29]

Very soon the orator was called upon again to address his fellow citizens. Prentiss' removal to New Orleans and establishment there was contemporary with the events of the Mexican War. He did not espouse the course of the United States in declaring war on Mexico, his Whig principles being contrary to the policies of President Polk. However,

[27] *Id.* to *id.*, New Orleans, March 16, 1847, *ibid.*, 418. The death of Abby was by no means unexpected. Prentiss doubtless wrote too optimistically of her improvement. The condition of Abby's health had been a family concern for many months before her death. In 1844 Prentiss was warned of her serious condition. In December of that year William Prentiss wrote that he had seen Abby during the summer and expressed the idea that a trip south would have been beneficial had it been made earlier but considered it too late then. William Prentiss to Prentiss, New York, December 23, 1844, in collection of Mrs. E. H. Redfield, New York. In October of 1844 Anna wrote that a trip south was out of the question, that Abby was "*very* unwell," that her cough "seems now to have seated," and that she had "*raised Blood*" on frequent occasions. Anna Prentiss to *id.*, Newbury Port, Conn., October 7, 1844, Redfield Collection.

[28] Prentiss to his mother, New Orleans, February 11, 1847, in *Memoir of S. S. Prentiss*, II, 416. In George L. Prentiss (ed.), *The Life and Letters of Elizabeth Prentiss* (New York, 1882), 104, the same letter is quoted with one additional sentence: "With the exception of yourself, dear mother, she was, of all our family circle, the best prepared to enter her Father's house."

[29] Prentiss to Anna Prentiss, New Orleans, February 12, 1847, in *Memoir of S. S. Prentiss*, II, 418.

with the declaration of war, he did not hesitate to employ his oratorical powers toward arousing public fervor to achieve victory. On more than one occasion he appeared before New Orleans gatherings during the war to keep alive the fires of patriotism and to express approbation for General Zachary Taylor and his feats in Mexico.[30]

But not until hostilities neared their end did Prentiss again rise to one of his pinnacles of eloquence. The specific occasion was an address of welcome for the city of New Orleans to two groups of volunteers in the war, the First Mississippi Rifles under Jefferson Davis, who was by then a colonel, and the Second Kentucky Infantry, whose term of service had expired after Monterey and Buena Vista. Along with the returning volunteers came the remains of several soldiers and officers who had been killed.

The speech, delivered June 11, 1847, was an address of welcome with all that the name implies and more. Prentiss did not feel bound by limits of time, but spoke at length in terms of praise to the soldiers, of those who went but did not return, and of scenes of happiness in families reunited at their firesides.

The exordium of the speech expressed the desire of Prentiss to meet the responsibility resting upon him as the spokesman for the people of New Orleans. "I am their honored organ on the occasion," he said, "and most warmly do I sympathise with their feelings, and participate in their wishes." He felt he could do no better than to say for New Orleans: "Welcome, then, gallant volunteers! ye war-worn soldiers, welcome home! The heart of Louisiana warms toward you. Welcome, thrice welcome from your glorious battle-fields! In the name of the citizens of New Orleans, I greet and embrace you all."

Again, analogies, metaphors, and other figures were his *forte*. He interspersed and saturated his speech with them.

[30] New Orleans *Daily Delta*, May 21, 1846; February 18, 1847; New Orleans *Daily Bee*, February 18, 1847.

Following his initial greeting of welcome, he declared: "No longer do you tread upon hostile shores, nor gaze upon foreign skies. Useless now are your sharp swords and unerring rifles. No lurking foe waylays you in the impenetrable chaparral, or among the gloomy gorges of the mountain. Henceforth your path will be ambushed only by friends." Prentiss traced the course of activity of the volunteers since he had seen them leave New Orleans a year before, reminded the audience and the soldiers of the deeds of valor at Monterey and Buena Vista as he described the events of the war, and then brought the men back in victory to New Orleans, reiterating, "Welcome, then, thrice welcome, victors of Monterey!"

But Prentiss soon exceeded the bounds of a strict speech of welcome and offered words in memoriam of those who did not return from the battlefields. "But alas!" he said, "the joys of our greeting are mingled with sorrow. We gaze upon your thinned ranks and seek in vain for many beloved and familiar faces. Why come they not from the battle-field? . . . Ah! I see it all—your laurel wreaths are thickly entwined with cypress—the dead cannot come to the banquet! Alas! alas, for the noble dead. If we cannot welcome, we will weep for them."

Prentiss did not limit his remarks to those who died in battle; he remembered as well the many who died in Mexico from disease. These, he felt, deserved equally high tribute, even higher, because, "It is easy to die in battle. The spirit is stirred to a courageous madness by the rushing squadron, the roaring cannon, and the clashing steel. All the fierce instincts of our nature are aroused, and the soldier seeks for death as the bridegroom seeks his bride. Besides

'Fame is there to tell who bleeds,
And honor's eye on daring deeds.' "

This was all in great contrast to the fate of those who died in battle, for "to waste away with sickness—to be crushed by the blows of an unseen enemy, with whom you cannot grapple; to know death is approaching slowly but surely; to feel your name will occupy no place on the brightest scroll of fame—thus, without any of the pride and rapture of the strife, to meet bravely the inevitable tyrant, is the highest test of the soldier's courage, the noblest proof of the patriot's devotion." For these, then, Prentiss pleaded. "Honor, then, immortal honor, to the brave who fell, not on the battle-field, but before the shafts of disease."

The peroration of the speech was brief. Prentiss envisioned the happy reunion of the soldiers with their families, saying in part: "The bonfires are already kindling upon the hills. In every grove and pleasant arbor the feast is spread. Thousands of sparkling eyes are watching eagerly for your return." [31]

Seldom have returning armies been more lavishly or grandly welcomed. The effect of the speech was such as to arouse significant commendation. The report of it by the *Picayune* was copied, for example, by the Boston *Advertiser*. This account said, among other things: "Often as we have listened to him never did he appear to us more eloquent. As he described the glorious deeds of the men he was welcoming, their faces were lit with an expression of joy, but when he came to speak of the cypress being mingled with the laurel—when he spoke of the men who fell at Monterey and Buena Vista, and of those who died without the satisfaction of sharing in the glories of the battle-field —the head fell and a universal grief pervaded the assemblage." [32] This speech was long remembered by those who heard it. A. De Puy Van Buren stated: "I have seen soldiers who heard it and spoke of it as having the thrilling effect of

[31] For versions of the speech, see New Orleans *Daily Picayune*, June 12, 1847; *Memoir of S. S. Prentiss*, II, 421–28; Shields, *Seargent Smith Prentiss*, 390–95.

[32] New Orleans *Daily Picayune*, June 11, 1847; Boston *Daily Advertiser*, June 21, 1847. Following the speech Jefferson Davis was called for and spoke briefly.

martial music on the audience. The address was clothed
with all the beauty and brilliancy of a Clay or Choate, and
the deep pathos and patriotism and natural pride of a
Webster." [33]

Prentiss was a tired man as the hot New Orleans summer
months of 1847 approached. He desired very much, especially because of the death of his sister, to take his family
for a visit to Maine. But the pressure of his profession, and
the need of extricating himself from debts contracted in
Mississippi, led him to forgo the pleasure of a vacation and
to remain in New Orleans. However, a siege of yellow fever
swept New Orleans that summer, forcing him for the safety
of himself and his family to leave the city. He took leave to
go to Longwood, where with his family, he enjoyed for a
time a much-needed rest. "Longwood is a sweet, quiet
place," he wrote in this period of relaxation, "and we
are all enjoying excellent health. . . . Seargy looks like a
young prince. Geordie puts me in mind every day of grandfather Lewis, and has the same vivacity and quickness for
which he was so remarkable. . . . Natchez is as dull as
a deserted village. Most of the fashionables are at the
North." [34] By November, or earlier, Prentiss was again in
New Orleans, his family returning in December. [35]

The Shakespeare which Prentiss had learned to love in
his student days at Bowdoin and which remained a lifelong asset to his oratory, occupied a vital place in his cultural life during the years he lived in New Orleans. Undoubtedly, one reason why he enjoyed New Orleans more
than Vicksburg was because of the opportunities he had of
hearing and seeing certain Shakespearean actors and other
celebrities as they visited the city.

[33] A. De Puy Van Buren, *Jottings of a Year's Sojourn in the South* (Battle
Creek, Mich., 1859), 289.
[34] Prentiss to Anna Prentiss, Longwood, September 5, 1847, in *Memoir of
S. S. Prentiss*, II, 430.
[35] *Id.* to George Prentiss, New Orleans, November 6, December 8, 1847,
ibid., 431–33.

Early in 1847, James E. Murdoch, actor, reader, and teacher of elocution, appeared on circuit in New Orleans. After Murdoch's rendition of several Shakespearean plays, Prentiss, with other eminent individuals, tendered him a complimentary dinner at the St. Charles Hotel. More than one hundred people were present. Governor Johnson was the official chairman at the banquet, while Prentiss presided at one of the six smaller tables. Toasts were drunk throughout the evening, and complimentary remarks were made by the Governor, followed by a response from Murdoch. On this occasion Prentiss was again the central oratorical figure, concluding the banquet festivities in "a long and eloquent address eulogistic of the drama and dramatic poetry, embodying delicate compliments to Mr. Murdoch. . . . He concluded by giving a toast to the drama." [36] "S. S. Prentiss—the unfailing and ever-eloquent Prentiss—," commented the Daily Delta, "also made one of his poetic and eloquent off-hand speeches, replete with just and beautiful sentiments and rich and ingenious metaphor." [37] Something of the high esteem Prentiss felt for Murdoch, as well as his interest in the career of Murdoch as an actor and interpretative reader, is further shown when again in 1850 Murdoch was in New Orleans, probably on circuit just prior to a European tour. Prentiss headed the list of ninety-four signers of a letter to Murdoch expressing their appreciation of his career, wishing him a happy professional tour abroad, and stating further, "your farewell benefit will take place on Saturday evening of this week, and we shall take great pleasure in striving to render it as gratifying to yourself as it should be worthy of the high stand you hold in your profession." Prentiss was probably the author of the letter, for Murdoch's reply was addressed to him.[38]

New Orleans was always strongly French in population

---

36 New Orleans Daily Picayune, March 3, 1847.

37 New Orleans Daily Delta, March 3, 1847.

38 New Orleans Daily Crescent, February 2, 1850; New Orleans Daily True Delta, February 1, 1850.

and interest. In this connection, it is interesting to note another occasional appearance of Prentiss in 1848. At a mass meeting in the St. Louis Rotunda, Prentiss participated in an expression of "joy over the success of the Republicans in France, and their sympathy in the cause of liberty, equality and fraternity all over the world." A succession of speakers took part, and then Prentiss, recorded the *Delta,* "appropriately concluded the meeting, with one of those glowing, poetical, and beautiful extempore speeches, in which he excels all other men of the age. Mingling pathos and wit, poetry and scriptural allusion, historical incidents and political reflection, all blended harmoniously together in a sparkling and glowing style, this speech . . . was equal to his best efforts and as the strongest evidence of its merits, it held entranced an audience which had already been listening for four hours to speeches of great merit." [39]

Another meeting similar to that held for Murdoch was a complimentary dinner tendered to William C. Macready in 1849. Macready came in February, and continued his programs well into March, reading Shakespearean plays. At the conclusion of these programs, his patrons, including Prentiss, wrote him a highly congratulatory letter and invited him to a dinner to be held at the Verandah Hotel. Macready accepted the invitation in an equally laudatory letter. The dinner occasion was much like that when Murdoch was the guest. After the usual number of toasts and remarks, "Mr. Prentiss was called on to respond to the sentiments of the distinguished guest, which he did in his usual vein." [40]

Two other like events, occurring in January and Febru-

[39] New Orleans *Daily Delta,* April 12, 1848.

[40] New Orleans *Daily Picayune,* March 21, 1849. For further notices of Macready's appearances, requests for additional readings, the letters to and from him, and the final dinner, see *ibid.,* March 17, 18, 1849; New Orleans *Daily Bee,* February 12, March 13, 1849; New Orleans *Daily Crescent,* March 13, 1849.

ary, 1850, deserve mention, inasmuch as Prentiss was again a participant. One had to do with requests of more than a hundred signers petitioning William M. Fleming, another Shakespearean reader, to present for a second time the *Merchant of Venice*.[41] In February another reader, Miss E. Kimberly, came to New Orleans. Her stay was brief, apparently, and she was requested in a letter signed by Prentiss and numerous other citizens to read at least one more play. Her response was an agreement to read *The Tempest*.[42]

If Prentiss was not to live a long life, the range of his activities is the best evidence that he lived intensely. For him there was always too much to do and enjoy in the present to surrender when fate robbed him of an independently wealthy position. There was a place for esthetics and culture in his life, else his name would hardly have been linked so often with civic occasions and causes.

In the midst of his legal and civic labors, another political campaign was soon to put additional obligations upon him in order to ensure a Whig victory.

41 New Orleans *Daily Picayune*, January 18, 1850; New Orleans *Daily True Delta*, January 18, 1850; New Orleans *Daily Bee*, January 18, 1850; New Orleans *Daily Crescent*, January 24, 1850.

42 New Orleans *Daily Delta*, February 5, 1850; New Orleans *Daily True Delta*, February 8, 1850; New Orleans *Daily Bee*, February 9, 1850.

Chapter XII

CAMPAIGN OF 1848

THE campaign of 1848 challenged Prentiss to plead again for Whig unity and victory. Notwithstanding that the state of his health (now more precarious than he realized) gave him ample justification for refraining from political exertions, it was not his disposition to forsake the Whigs in 1848 any more than in the campaigns of 1840 and 1844. And, as in 1840, Prentiss subordinated his personal preference for available candidates; although he was anxious that Clay become the standard-bearer, he accepted Zachary Taylor. Contrary to his practice in 1840 and 1844, however, when Prentiss toured the nation as well as his resident state of Mississippi, in 1848 he confined his efforts to Louisiana.

As evidenced by the campaign of 1844, Clay was probably not the man to solidify the Whig vote to ensure victory. In contrast, Taylor, with recent military glory to his credit, was a rising political hero, particularly in Louisiana, where, in Baton Rouge, he maintained a home. Taylor was, to be sure, an unorthodox type of candidate. He was not trained in statecraft, and took little interest or part in political affairs. But the Whigs had perceived the vote-getting power of a military hero in 1840. Now in 1848 they conceived a widespread enthusiasm for "Old Rough and Ready."

The lack of common party principles and platform was a constantly perplexing difficulty of the Whigs. Hence there was a tendency for some elements within to strike out individually along certain avenues. The Louisiana Whigs were guilty of this independence of party action, and

came near nipping Taylor's political ascendancy in the
bud. They might easily have caused the defeat of the Whigs
once more, had matters not been adjusted. Louisiana had
its chance to name the presidential nominee. But if Taylor
proved not to be sufficiently popular nationally, he would
not win. Consequently, there developed in Louisiana an
attempt, which Taylor himself aided and abetted, to run Old
Zach independent of party. The Louisianians hoped that
they could promote Taylor's general popularity, and they
hoped, too, that Democrats, especially those in the South,
would be willing to forget party affiliations and support
Taylor. Throughout 1847, the Baton Rouge *Democratic
Advocate,* in its support of Taylor as an independent candidate, argued: "such is the iron strength of the fetters imposed by party on the understanding and actions of its
followers, that the appropriation of his name by the political press, on one side, checked the warm impulses of gratitude which had been manifested on the other." Since Taylor was hardly of either party, really, but belonged rather
to the nation and would be hurt by identification with a
party, the *Advocate* appealed: "It is a consummation de-
voutly to be wished, that party spirit would sleep for one
presidential term; that the poison which has infused its
bitterness and bane, in the bosom of society, separating
kindred, and too often converting the pleasantness of the
social compact into wrangling and discord, should be neu-
tralised and rendered in[n]oc[u]ous for a time. If such an
event be destined to follow the election of General Taylor,
as the candidate of the people, we think that there are not
many of the rational and sensible of either party who would
refuse to offer a heartfelt 'God speed,' him to the brave old
Chieftain, or would not band together to effect a purpose
so exalted." [1] This attempt to popularize Taylor in a non-
partisan fashion obviously could not remain a neutral matter; it would either gain momentum or lose it.

[1] Baton Rouge *Democratic Weekly Advocate,* July 7, 1847.

Prentiss was one of those who saw the danger of this movement, and he did his share to counteract it. In January, 1848, Louisianians, "irrespective of party," anxious to elevate Old Zach to the presidency, met in the Commercial Exchange in New Orleans. There is significance in the account that while the crowd was large, and that resolutions were drafted, Prentiss, though called upon for a speech, "did not appear." [2] He was probably present, but may have refused to speak because the time was not opportune to express his negative sentiment. Randall Hunt could not or would not speak either, but Peyton gave the movement his blessing. Since this was a more or less unofficial meeting, a committee, consisting of William Christy, Ralph King, and Peyton were designated to make plans for another convention on February 22. [3]

The February convention was held on schedule. It had rather rough sailing, and resolutions favoring the running of Taylor as an Independent were so amended and altered that a motion was finally carried tabling all resolutions until the various districts of the state could be heard from. [4] It was made clear, however, that Taylor was the choice of the meeting, and electors were chosen. [5]

But the opposite kind of movement was under way as well. If Prentiss could not be found to speak in January, he was readily available when what may be called the third meeting of Taylorites gathered in New Orleans to reach a final decision on whether they could act independently or send delegates to the national convention. This meeting began the night of March 14 and the matter of sending "Delegates to attend the Whig National Convention— Delegates who would go there untrammelled in their choice

[2] New Orleans Daily Picayune, January 23, 1848; New Orleans Daily Delta, January 23, 1848.

[3] New Orleans Daily Delta, January 23, 1848.

[4] Ibid., February 22, 1848.

[5] Ibid.; New Orleans Daily Bee, February 22, 1848; Leslie M. Norton, "A History of the Whig Party in Louisiana" (Ph.D. dissertation, Louisiana State University, 1940), 287–89.

of a candidate for President and Vice President of the United States, and who would be prepared to act in a manner the most conducive to the interest and harmony of the Whig party," [6] was placed before the assembly. This was Prentiss' opportunity, and he made the most of it. He struck out against the rash efforts to bolt the party and urged the necessity of party regularity among Louisiana Whigs. In December, after Taylor's election, the New Orleans *Delta* alluded to the speech of Prentiss, "by whose timely intervention, the crazy *nolens volensities* were thwarted in their purpose of running General Taylor independent of parties and conventions. This act was the very crisis of General Taylor's Presidential fortunes." [7] Hunt joined Prentiss as another spokesman in this common effort.

In this very significant address to a divided and discordant convention, Prentiss made clear two things: first, that Clay was his own personal choice, but that if the Whig party preferred Taylor, then he would support him; and second, that the national Whig party was far more important than the interests and ambitions of any individual or minor group within the party.

The specific utterances of Prentiss on this occasion are worthy of close observation. His was the mission of correcting a dangerous tide of affairs; he used his oratorical voice and prestige against it most successfully. This is perhaps the best speech of Prentiss as a pacifier. His opening remarks freed him of any ulterior political motives, for he assured the convention that he came "as a private citizen," who, though he had fought many political battles, was now immersed in private duties. "It is only now as one who has no aspirations beyond the position of a mere private in the ranks that I appear among you to-night." Another personal position and attitude he expressed, too, and in so doing he hoped to engender a like frame of mind and emotion. "I

6 New Orleans *Daily Picayune,* March 15, 1848.
7 New Orleans *Daily Delta,* December 30, 1848.

am still a warm, devoted, enthusiastic Whig," he asserted, "such as I have ever been since I learned to distinguish between right and wrong, and such as I expect to be when the grave shall demand my mortal frame." He reminded the audience immediately that he considered "the object of this meeting to be, to secure harmony and union in our party—to secure a representation in the National Convention, which is to determine to whom the great Whig banner shall be confided in the coming contest." If this were true, his appeal followed logically. "We must sink all personal preferences and predilections in the great good of our party. We came together to offer up the affections and partialities of our hearts upon the alter of Whig harmony." For this purpose and reason, "As a staunch veteran Whig," he continued, "who has never swerved from his duty and devotion, or turned his back upon the enemy, I come to give my counsel, humble as it may be, in furtherance of this meeting." To those who held that Taylor should be run independently, and who depreciated the idea of waiting upon the endorsement of a national convention, he had his appropriate answer. "What is mere personal, individual action in great political contests, but the folly of the soldier who at Buena Vista would have shouldered his musket and proceeded alone against the bristling bayonets and serried ranks of the Mexican host! It is only by keeping together— by, in military phrase, preserving the touch of the elbow, that success is achieved in military operations; and so it is in party contests, which are mere civil battles between large masses." The climax of this contention and appeal was phrased for the minds of men to think about. "If the State of Louisiana could elect the President, I acknowledge there would be no necessity for such consultation; but our sister States have something to say in this matter, and their will and counsel must be heard—their might and influence acknowledged."

Prentiss had up to this point insisted it was the obligation

of each to subordinate his individual desires for the good
of the greater whole. Now it was his turn to subordinate
personal preferences. He stated publicly what he was willing to surrender, and in a manner causing "a tremendous
outburst from the crowd, which shook the building and
made the name of Clay reverberate through the immense
room in tones of thunder." To Prentiss, Clay was still the
ideal choice. His seventy years were no more a handicap
than the weight that time had placed on the aging Taylor.
Thus he said: "Had I the choice of a President—I should
cling to my first love—I should shout aloud the name of
that veteran statesman who has attained the very highest
eminence on the pedestal of fame,—under whose banner I
have so often been proud to fight—whose white plume I
have so often followed in battle." This was what Prentiss
was sacrificing in the way of personal preference.

Thus the issue was clear in his mind. To preserve the
Whig party it was necessary to send delegates who would
support the majority opinion of the national convention.
Since Prentiss had eulogized Clay, he was duty bound in
New Orleans, where the enthusiasm for Taylor was immense, to pass judgment on him as well. He tried to be enthusiastic about Taylor, and declared that in his opinion
he would be elected if nominated. He promised his support
of Taylor, saying he "should be proud to fight under the
banner of that gallant old chief, the prestige of whose vic-
tories over a foreign enemy would give him irresistible
strength before the people in a civil contest." This was
based upon one premise, however: Taylor must be the
choice of the national convention. "I have no confidence in
the independent no-partyism, which has lately exploded
in this city. I trust not to the gifts of the enemy." It was
difficult for Prentiss to be soaringly eulogistic. The most he
could promise if Taylor should be nominated was that his
military service of forty years would stand him in good
stead in civil duties, and that "He would call around him a

cabinet of the first whigs—the soundest, wisest, and safest counsellors of the union."

Prentiss gave up Clay with great reluctance. Even after he had done so, it was with far greater eloquence of language that he spoke of Clay than of Taylor. "Should Henry Clay be the candidate, I should again, scarred and worn soldier as I am, seize my crutch and go forth to battle." Prentiss was in the position that, while he did love Clay more, he did not love Taylor less. In any instance, he would support Taylor if he were nominated in the national convention. Again Prentiss returned to his condemnation of the movement in Louisiana to run Taylor irrespective of party. This time he said, "I don't believe that we have reached a political millenium—that the lion will lie down with the lamb, and the little child may play with the asp." He came closer home. "We have already seen . . . this independent no-partyism cool off in two weeks. Some of our friends were too quick off the trigger, but they have seen their error and are rapidly retracing their steps." The *Delta* observed that all of Prentiss' remarks on Clay "were very perceptibly more earnest and impassioned than his references to Gen. Taylor." His preference, very evident in the written account of the speech, must have been infinitely more so to his listeners in 1848. Yet he never departed from the premise that the party was bigger than the man.

Prentiss concluded "as his voice began to fail him." "We are like the fair lady who looks into her box of jewels and is sorely puzzled to determine which brilliant stone or glittering diamond shall glitter on her lovely brow," he said, and Louisianians should "not be guilty of the folly of quarrelling about individuals when we have great principles to guard—to contend, to fight for." [8] Randall Hunt followed

<hr />

[8] *Ibid.*, March 15, 1848, contains a lengthy account of the meeting, including a full résumé of Prentiss' speech. For other accounts, see New Orleans *Daily Picayune*, March 15, 1848; New Orleans *Daily Crescent*, March 15, 1848; New Orleans *Daily Bee*, March 15, 1848; *Semi-Weekly Natchez Courier*, March 21, 1848; Baton Rouge *Weekly Gazette*, March 18, 1848; Boston *Daily Advertiser*, March 27, 1848.

Prentiss, and then came the balloting on the resolution to select delegates to the Philadelphia convention.

In this "short and animated" [9] speech, Prentiss gained extensive commendation. His eulogy on Clay was interrupted by so much frequent and vigorous cheering that the *Delta* reporter was unable to capture many of his references and allusions.[10] The *Picayune* stated that he "spoke in his usual happy strain of eloquence," [11] and the *Crescent* called his speech "appropriate to the occasion, and in parts truly eloquence." [12] Certainly the movement in Louisiana to run Taylor as an independent was sidetracked. Moreover, Prentiss was selected as one of the delegates to the Philadelphia convention, but he was unable to attend. One of the very interesting and revealing letters which Prentiss sent to Maine was written a few weeks later. He first stated: "I take very little part in politics; indeed the only speech I have made since I removed to the city, was the one of which you saw an imperfect report. I did it to produce harmony among the Whigs here. It is perfectly ridiculous for a respectable party to make its success dependent upon any one man." Unequivocally he stated his comparison of the candidates. "That Henry Clay is a thousand times better than Gen. Taylor, for the first office of the nation, no man of sense and observation can deny. Clay is a statesman, well acquainted with our institutions, our political history, our relations, both foreign and domestic. He understands polity, and is every way fitted to guide the councils of the country. General Taylor is a brave, honest, simple man; wholly ignorant of politics. To him all matters of State will be Gordian knots, and as he cannot solve them with his sword, he will be compelled to call in others to untie them; in other words, he must be guided by his Cabinet." Yet he admitted that the choice of Taylor would not be too unfor-

9 New Orleans *Daily Crescent*, March 15, 1848.
10 New Orleans *Daily Delta*, March 15, 1848.
11 New Orleans *Daily Picayune*, March 15, 1848.
12 New Orleans *Daily Crescent*, March 15, 1848.

tunate. His administration would be, he prophesied, "if not brilliant, at least a safe and good one." Nevertheless, "If Clay can be elected, the Whigs ought not to hesitate a moment in preferring him to General Taylor; but if he cannot, then General T. is infinitely preferable to any Democrat." At heart, Prentiss found it difficult to accept Taylor. "I have met him several times in private," he said further, "and am delighted with the old man's modesty and simplicity; he is, without doubt, a good man, of sterling qualities; but he is certainly weak, and ignorant in matters out of his profession." [13]

The Democrats held their convention in Baltimore in May. Theirs was not the bright outlook of four years before; spirits were not high, and trouble bedogged the proceedings of the convention. New York was represented by two delegations: the "Hunkers," close adherents to party principles, and the "Barnburners," antislaveryites, each seeking to be seated. Compromise was impossible of acceptance to either group, and the Barnburners withdrew and later joined with "Free-Soil Democrats" and "Conscience Whigs" to nominate Van Buren. Although Polk's administration had brought in vast new territories as a result of the Mexican War and the Oregon settlement, this action of the groups in nominating Van Buren, with Charles Francis Adams for Vice President, divided the party.

Nevertheless, the Democrats, probably anticipating the choice of the Whigs, proceeded to offer a military personage to the country as their candidate. Lewis Cass of Michigan, considered a northern man with southern principles, and who, also, antedated Stephen A. Douglas in developing the concept of squatter sovereignty, became the choice, with William O. Butler for the vice-presidency. The platform dodged the question of slavery in an effort to hold both northerners and southerners, and Cass was accepted as an

[13] Prentiss to George Prentiss, New Orleans, May 22, 1848, in *Memoir of S. S. Prentiss*, II, 452-53.

opponent of the Wilmot Proviso. The campaign of Cass
was doomed from the start, however. His military career in
the War of 1812 did not match Taylor's in the Mexican
War. He was hampered by the Van Buren nomination,
which received strong support in the East and North, and
was also opposed by another minor party, the Native Americans, who threw their support to Taylor. Besides, Cass could
not obtain the unqualified support of southern slave advocates, especially when Taylor, the Louisianian, was considered safer.

The Whigs gathered in Philadelphia in June. Super-
ficially they seemed no better united than their opponents.
Taylor led on the first ballot by 111 to 97 for Clay, with
Winfield Scott, John McLean, and John M. Clayton getting
enough votes to prevent a majority. New England did not
support Taylor at first; the old general was most strongly
the favorite of the southern delegates. He was finally nominated, however, and Millard Fillmore was assigned the
second place on the ticket after two ballotings. Taylor received his notification of nomination "while standing upon
the levee at Baton Rouge." [14]

The role of Prentiss in the campaign is clearly defined.
He made good his declaration to support the choice of the
national convention. Also, because the slavery issue was
injected so strongly into the campaign, the conclusion seems
justified that Prentiss fell not far short of being one of its
protagonists. He condemned the Wilmot Proviso and revealed in certain of his speeches ideas and attitudes which
he had never dreamed years earlier he would utter. He
accepted Fillmore as a capable candidate and did not hesitate to meet the objections of southerners that he was un-
sound on their institutions.

The first opportunity offered Prentiss to carry out his
promise to support the Whig party regardless of its nominee
came in the same month Taylor was named. The occasion

14 New Orleans *Daily Bee,* June 15, 1848.

was a huge Whig gathering in New Orleans to ratify the proceedings of the Philadelphia convention. Along with Hunt, Preston W. Farrar, Peyton and others,[15] Prentiss spoke from a lavishly draped speakers' platform erected in Canal Street.[16] The speech did not receive adequate coverage by the New Orleans press, probably because the space was needed for the resolutions which were adopted following his address. One paper stated it would not "attempt even a sketch of the masterly speech of Mr. Prentiss," but thought his "analysis of Whig principles was one of the most felicitous expositions . . . ever listened to," and maintained that "His wit, his playful irony, his vigorous logic, his splendid imagery, carried the audience with him through a prolonged and exhausting effort, and he retired as he was welcomed, with deafening acclamations." [17]

The body of resolutions, five in number, was presented immediately after Prentiss' speech. The first one was an immediate approval of Taylor and Fillmore as the candidates. The second was an expression of commendation to the delegates of the Philadelphia convention, who, as "faithful agents for the judicious," deserve the "affections of the people." The third resolution was a further acceptance of the candidates as "men of tried integrity, of high practical ability, of known patriotism, and pure republican principles," which made them "alike equal to the various duties of those high offices, and to the momentous times in which they are called to act." In the fourth resolution there was, as would be expected, a condemnation of the Polk administration and the Democratic party. The final resolution was a pledge to "use all industry, honest and effective power, and open but just means, to accomplish at the ballot-box the filial adoption of these distinguished nominations, and for that purpose recommend a speedy and harmonizing

[15] Washington *National Intelligencer,* July 4, 1848
[16] *Semi-Weekly Natchez Courier,* June 30, 1848.
[17] New Orleans *Daily Bee,* June 26, 1848.

organization of our friends, and a bold and candid appeal to the patriotism of our country." [18]

An interesting aspect of this New Orleans meeting and Prentiss' address is that it attracted the attention of the *Campaign,* official Democratic organ, which thanked him for making a genuine Democratic speech. Attempting to turn the tables, it took the position that, "Mr. Prentiss, the celebrated whig orator of New Orleans, has confessed, in his speech at the ratification meeting, that the democratic machinery has been productive of the most successful results." Prentiss may have been quoted out of context, but he was represented as saying "this nation had never been so prosperous as at the present time"; and "that the whigs, adhering to conservative principles, were perfectly content to allow the country to remain in the flourishing and happy condition in which it was found, and acknowledged to be at this very period." Also, it insisted that he said "all the old issues had been laid aside, and become obsolete." "No higher compliment could have been paid to . . . the present administration," it continued. "If the nation is prosperous, what party has contributed to make it so? Of course, the party which has been in power." It referred to the country's prosperity without a National Bank, to the "brilliant achievements in two years" in the war with Mexico, to "admirable commercial treaties, . . . thus increasing the facilities of our commerce in distant seas," and then added: "Thanks, then, for the frankness of the orator! we might have suspected that our too practical judgments had overrated the value of the present administration; but here comes a professional political opponent, who offers the same tribute to its merits." The *Campaign* could only conclude: "Then, we ask Mr. Prentiss, why change the party or the principles in power? . . . So successful have our avowed principles proven, that even Mr. Prentiss admits they have no cause of complaint; and the whigs are hard put to it

[18] Washington *National Intelligencer,* July 4, 1848.

for objections, that they have laid aside all their old issues." [19]

Prentiss was ordinarily the recipient of introductions;
seldom did he present the speaker of the occasion. But in
July he made one brief and rather unique speech of introduction which the New Orleans *Bee* reported in full. Taylor had agreed to meet the shipmasters of New Orleans, and
Prentiss was engaged to present him to the body which met
in the St. Charles Hotel. Consequently, on their behalf he
addressed Taylor: " 'General.—I am requested by the shipmasters of the port of New Orleans to act as their speaking-
trumpet on this occasion, and as I have more *brass* than any
one else, perhaps it is appropriate I should do so. They are
accustomed to use that instrument, and in its loudest tones
desire to express their admiration of yourself, sir. They
love the stars and stripes, sir, and they have carried them
over many seas, and the more they see of them the more they
love them. They know General, that you have sustained
them nobly upon the land, and when they go abroad again
they desire to say that they have seen and taken by the hand
that great general whose name is now associated with that
of Washington. Permit me, gentlemen, at your request, to
introduce you to Gen. Zachary Taylor.' " [20]

Not until August did Prentiss begin his more intensive
campaign efforts. The *Delta* published an article on August
18 entitled "Our Orators Awake." It mentioned that Democrat John C. Larue was then in Texas "taking the stump,"
that Judah P. Benjamin "is close upon Larue's heels, battling powerfully for 'Rough and Ready,' " and that he was
being counteracted by Pierre Soule, "the great orator of the
Democrats." Chiefly it emphasized that "Mr. Prentiss, the
incomparable wit, orator and jurist, will leave in a few days
on a tour . . . through the Florida Parishes." One of his

[19] Washington *Campaign*, July 19, 1848.
[20] New Orleans *Daily Bee*, July 10, 1848.

stops would be at Clinton, where the *Delta* announced he would probably be replied to "by his old confrere and friend of his youth, the gallant and able Gen. Felix Huston." The *Delta* added enthusiastically: "We need not inform our readers who S. S. Prentiss is. When in the true vein and thoroughly aroused," it declared, "he can say more happy things than any half dozen orators we ever heard. He is the Sheridan of this country." [21] Prentiss explained his doings and his further plans, when in the midst of his tour he wrote: "I am making some personal excursions in favor of Taylor, and shall continue to do so till the election. Last week I went to Clinton, in the northern part of Louisiana, and addressed the people there; and on the 2d prox. I am to be in Baton Rouge, by appointment to participate in a public discussion which is to take place between the two parties." He also reflected on the prospects of Taylor. He believed Louisiana safe for him, "But it is by no means certain; and while I have much hope, I am not over-sanguine as to the general result." Sources of hope were present in his mind, however. One was that "the dissensions in the Democratic ranks are favorable; and I hope Van Buren will kill off Cass in the Northern States." Another was: "We have just received the news that Polk has signed the Oregon bill, with the *Wilmot proviso*. This is a heavy blow to the Southern Democracy, who have made that the leading question; and I am of opinion it will result to the decided advantage of the Whigs." [22]

The Clinton occasion was a ratification meeting of the nominations of the national Whig convention. Prentiss was one of several speakers, others being Benjamin and Peyton.[23] One other point where he appeared before the great debate in Baton Rouge was at Plaquemine. This was de-

21 New Orleans *Daily Delta*, August 18, 1848.

22 Prentiss to William Prentiss, Pass Christian, August 25, 1848, in *Memoir of S. S. Prentiss*, II, 457.

23 Baton Rouge *Weekly Gazette*, August 12, 1848.

scribed as the largest gathering of the campaign in Louisiana with the exception of the New Orleans ratification meeting. The two chief speakers were Peyton and Prentiss, who together spoke for five hours.[24]

In 1840 and 1844 the Whigs of Baton Rouge had announced the likelihood of Prentiss' presence for political rallies. Each time they were compelled to state his inability to be present. In 1848 he did appear, in an interesting company of colleagues and opponents in what the New Orleans *Crescent* called "the grand 'model' debate of the campaign." [25] The speakers were described as follows: "[Isaac T.] Preston was there, with his sledge-hammer arguments, demolishing the fabric of whigism; Prentiss, with his flowery rhetoric and beautiful sentences, was there to aid in the discomfiture of democracy; Larue, logical, reasoning, calculating and reflecting, and [Lourent J.] Sigur for the democrats; and Benjamin and Peyton for the Whigs, were present." The order of speaking was reported, "Prentiss, Sigur, Peyton, Preston, Benjamin, Larue, and Prentiss concluding." The spot where the debate occurred was "in the street adjoining the Statehouse square, beneath the shade of some beautiful China-Trees." [26]

The Baton Rouge *Gazette,* a Whig paper, quite naturally covered the debate. While it gave attention to each speaker, it gave Prentiss the most. It mentioned that in his opening speech he passed some high compliments on the ladies present and then approached the importance of the contest by stating that, of the three nominees, the people of Louisiana should vote for Taylor. His reason was that Taylor was safe on the slavery issue, whereas Cass was not. He denied the charges that the Whigs of the South were abolitionists, as asserted by "locofoco orators," and instead maintained that "Cass is opposed not only to the extension of slavery and

24 *Ibid.*, September 2, 1848.
25 New Orleans *Daily Crescent,* September 5, 1848.   26 *Ibid.*

[has] prayed for its abolition everywhere, and again that he was in favor of the Wilmot Proviso until 1847, but that his views and sentiments had suddenly changed before the bright allurements of the Presidency." The only other item of Prentiss' opening speech noted was that he also defended Fillmore as having been unfairly charged on the same issue.

The remarks of the other speakers were noted also. Sigur argued that what was called the locofoco party "stood on the platform founded by Jefferson, and then eulogized Mr. Cass for past services and tried to place him in a favorable attitude towards the South." Peyton spoke for an hour. He answered Sigur, defended Fillmore, "exposed the shuffling and unsoundness of Cass on the subject of slavery and proved on the other hand the soundness and consistency of Gen. Taylor on the subject." Preston received little attention, but Benjamin, among other things, "portrayed clearly the dangerous position of Mr. Cass up to 1847 on the subject of slavery, and his change on this subject, since then, and appealed to the audience to vote for Taylor in preference to 'a Northern man with Southern principles.'"

What Larue argued was not stated specifically. The *Gazette* said: "His speech . . . was characterized by nothing in particular, but denunciation of the whig party and their candidates." Moreover, it added of Larue: "He is a man of talents, but a little more moderation in political strife, would be by far more acceptable to those whom [sic], if they differ with him in opinion, or politics consider themselves as patriotic and as good citizens as any of his creed." This observation on Larue is significant in that Prentiss probably bore the brunt of some personal attacks. Prentiss, as has been observed, closed the speaking. Evidently he refuted Larue, as well as Preston, and vindicated himself "by saying that he was an American, descendant of revolutionary parents, that he was no abolitionist nor would he support any one knowing him to be so, and that he considered him-

self as patriotic as any of the gentlemen who had spoken on
the democratic side or any other locofoco." [27] It was hardly
a coincidence that the *Gazette* should have criticized Larue
for questioning the patriotism of others, in view of the space
it gave to Prentiss' refutation. Again in 1848, as in other
years, Prentiss was impugned as being too much at heart a
northerner, an enemy of slavery, even an abolitionist.

Throughout September and October Prentiss fulfilled
several additional speaking obligations for Taylor. One of
his speeches, the most fully reported of the campaign, was
late in September at Carrollton. It attracted wide attention
and is a further index to the kind of political argument he
used in 1848. Prentiss asserted at the outset that he appeared
only from a sense of duty as election time drew nearer; as
he put it, "in the waning of another moon." Hence it was
time for the voters to be making their choices. He quite
naturally saw the advantages in favor of Taylor, especially
in slaveholding Louisiana. The case against Cass he approached with a rhetorical question: "Would you go, for
your leader, to the cold North, and choose one who has shed
no lustre on Louisiana, who knows not your interests, and
has no sympathies in your feelings, your hopes and your
pursuits, one too,—who . . . thanked his God that he had
ever been opposed to slavery, that he never owned a slave?"
The reasons for this kind of speaking were obvious; it was
the safer qualities of Taylor, particularly for southern interests, which he emphasized.

Prentiss tried to show, too, that there were other practical reasons for supporting Taylor. He capitalized upon
Taylor's military record, and contended that if political
considerations were not allowed to interfere, Louisiana
"would ring with one loud acclaim for noble old Zach."
Democrats were inclined to admit this themselves, and so
he asserted: "We all know that if they could have got ahead
of the Whigs they would [have] monopolized him long ago.

[27] Baton Rouge *Weekly Gazette,* September 9, 1848.

. . No! if old Zach had only received the *imprimatur,* the endorsement of the Baltimore Convention, the eulogies which the Whigs now sing to him would have been cuckoo notes to the loud shouts—the welkin ringing paeans of the strong-lunged democracy." But, as Prentiss went on to say, the Democrats were opposed to Taylor because the Whigs nominated him. His answer was almost a denial that Taylor was a Whig. "He does not belong to us Whigs. We have given no bribe," he asserted, "no price for him. He has started without any pledges or promises to us." Rather, Taylor belonged to the nation, for "He had only declared, that if the people will choose him as their President, he will perform the duties of the station with an honest heart, and with such talents as God has vouchsafed him. He will be the President as he has been the leader of our armies—not of a party or class, but of the whole people." This made Taylor the sensible choice. In view of these reasons, Prentiss could only say: "Would you exchange such a man for Lewis Cass? It would be like an exchange of a fifteen-shilling pinchbeck galvanized watch for one of those old-fashioned turnips, all true gold, and worth a hundred dollars. Why can't the Democrats take Old Zach? If we can stand him without any pledges or platform from him, why can't they; we only desired him to stand where he does—on the platform of the Constitution—the only platform wide enough for an honest man. We do not build up any temporary bridges across creeks, so hastily and clumsily erected that every day they require mending, and ask him to pass over them, instead of over the massive solid, granite-built, iron-fastened bridge of the Constitution."

But Prentiss desired to do more than make Louisiana safe for Taylor by pleading that Old Zach scarcely belonged to the Whigs any more than to the Democrats. Southern interests necessitated stronger inducements, and so Prentiss had to reveal his own southernized sentiments. He could not dodge the slavery question in 1848. Admittedly Fillmore was not an asset to Taylor in Louisiana. Prentiss recognized this as he moved to the issue: "It is alledged that Old Zach, your neighbor and fellow citizen, is placed in an attitude of hostility to slave institutions, by virtue of his association with Fillmore, a Northern man." Prentiss had his answer to this. He first tried to minimize the problem by saying: "This subject of slavery and abolition has been most improperly and imprudently dragged into this contest, and made an issue when it never should have been referred to." Since it had been, Prentiss saw what the southern attitude should be. He stated candidly the northern point of view: "Any man, at all acquainted with the views of the Northern people, knows that ninety-nine out of every hundred of them are free soil men—opposed to the extension of slavery. There is no respectable Northern man who is in favor of Congress interfering with slavery in the States where it exists." If this was a safe assertion, he was equally sure of himself in affirming that Fillmore was as safe as Cass. "Indeed," he declared, "upon the whole subject of slavery, he is fully as sound as Cass, who has resorted to hypocrisy, to doubtful oracles and ambiguous givings-forth, calculated to mislead and deceive all parties." Moreover, he asserted, "If I had time, I could show that Lewis Cass, who is now amusing the people with such doubtful sphinx like oracles, apparently in favor of the rights of the South, was in truth the father and originator of free soil agitation in the Northwestern Territory." This charge made, he followed it up. His contention was that instead of Fillmore, the real enemy of southern interests was Cass, "the great head and front of the present anti-slavery movement." Instead of being honestly a northern man of southern principles, he was, Prentiss declared, an "apostate . . . among the mongrel host of free-soilers, abolitionists, amalgamationists, and vote-yourself-a-farm men." This situation was a challenge to the South. Prentiss envisioned the slavery cause in jeopardy when, at the same time, there was no difference of opinion in the South regardless of party allegiances. Thus he emphasized: "The time will soon come when Whig and Democrat will have to stand together on this subject. It behooves us, then, to eschew all premature agitations and divisions on a matter of such primary and fundamental importance to our peace and happiness."

One other minor point, the charge that Taylor was opposed to the veto power, was taken up and refuted. Prentiss' answer was that Taylor did not consider the executive to be the legislative organ of the government, and that "he will exercise it [the veto] under such restrictions and provisos as will leave untrammelled the legislative powers of the government."

The remainder of the speech was a further comparison of Taylor and Cass. His severest attacks on Cass followed when he indicted him as having "swallowed the whole Baltimore platform, old planks and new, pins, joists, supporters and all; a platform the best portions of which are stolen from other people's lumber yards, and which has required so much mending, that none of the old timbers now remain in its patched and rotten frame." One of the "rotten planks" was the Wilmot Proviso, which he said "was stolen from the Buffalo Lumber Yard." Since the Whigs in 1848, as always, were without a very concrete platform, the temptation was strong to chide the Democrats for having so many planks in theirs, especially with the party divided and two candidates in the race. His attitude was that formerly the Democrats were not so much concerned about planks, "But now the banks have caved in, some of the pins have rotted out, the stream has swollen considerably, and new planks have to be added, and the underworks must be strengthened by additional timbers." This caused "an interesting question of multiplication" to arise. "If it took seven planks for a Van Buren platform, and eleven for Cass, how many will it take for the next Democratic candidate?" Further, he charged: "These bridges are not permanent works, erected for posterity, but they are temporary structures, built in a single night, like those which a frantic man throws up for his own purpose, to get over a stream in his path, and cares not whether any body else will ever be able to follow him." Moreover, he indicted, "Now this is a presumption and tyranny which no Whig Convention would dare to assume."

Prentiss paid certain additional compliments to Taylor. Before closing, he set forth again the qualities of the Whig candidate. He exploited Taylor's military record in Mexico for all it was worth. Also, he emphasized the attributes of honest sagaciousness in the assertion, "There will be no trading politicians around him." The assurance of domestic tranquillity as well as improved foreign relations was assumed.

In the peroration of the speech Prentiss cleared himself of any ulterior motives in defending Taylor. He stated that he had no personal interest in the election "other than my concern of honor, the peace, the happiness of my country." Prentiss could assume from the knowledge his hearers had of his own life that they would believe him: "I seek no office—I desire none—I would have none. It has been my destiny, at which I do not repine to car[v]e my fortune with my own hand." If his hearers would believe this, they would doubtless accept as true his further personal declaration: "If I could be prompted by a desire to share the spoils of office, the rewards of successful partisanship, I should long since have abandoned the Whig party and sought some relief and comfort in the warm embraces of Democracy. Without vanity I think I might calculate on an eager welcome to the Democratic ranks, and if my repentence was very bold and zealous I might, peradventure, receive at their hands some little sop to console me for my long wandering in the cold and dreary regions of Whigdom whilst they have been enjoying exclusive possession of the flesh-pots of office." [28]

[28] New Orleans *Daily Delta*, September 23, 1848; *Semi-Weekly Natchez Courier*, October 3, 1848.

During October Prentiss continued to speak for Taylor and Fillmore. Early in the month he appeared with other speakers at a "Rough and Ready Barbecue at Trinity, Louisiana," where oratory prevailed for six hours.[29] He was the last speaker of the day, and the Natchez *Courier* said of his efforts: "For two hours he held the audience as by a magic spell. . . . Time, place, and differences of opinion, all seemed to be forgotten." [30] A few days later he was before a mass meeting of the New Orleans Whigs, held at the St. Louis Exchange. Again Prentiss was preceded by several speakers, and concluded the oratory of the occasion, defending Taylor and repudiating the charge of the Democrats that Old Zach was unsafe because he stood on no political platform. As always, the New Orleans papers complimented him. The *Delta*, after mentioning several of the speakers, asserted that Prentiss "made the speech of the evening." [31] The *Bee* considered his exordium one of "unrivalled felicity," and his speech as a whole a series of "sparkling thoughts and brilliant conceptions, and profound truths." It stressed, too, how he portrayed the debt Louisiana owed Taylor, and how he "examined the various objections to Gen. Taylor started by Locofocoism, and swept them away like cobwebs." [32] The *Crescent* approved the address as "a masterly effort—a speech of strong argument, keen invective, and pungent wit." It emphasized also that "Several hits were made during the speech that made the democrats present feel as if they had come in contact with an electric eel." [33]

Two of Prentiss' children were born in the midst of his speech-making in presidential campaigns, George in 1844, and Eunice, at Natchez, in 1848. Writing to George Prentiss, Seargent told of the exertions he was making for Taylor along with the announcement of the birth of his fourth

29 *Semi-Weekly Natchez Courier*, October 10, 1848.
30 *Ibid.*, October 17, 1848.
31 New Orleans *Daily Delta*, October 19, 1848.
32 New Orleans *Daily Bee*, October 19, 1848.
33 New Orleans *Daily Crescent*, October 19, 1848.

child: "I have worn myself down, and can scarcely speak above a whisper. Indeed, I never was so thoroughly used up in my life. My breast is a good deal inflamed, and my throat sore. . . . But I have something more interesting to tell you than politics—at least more so to me. This morning I got a note from Mrs. Williams, informing me that on Saturday morning I became the father of a fine, bouncing girl, and that both daughter and mother were doing most excellently well." [34]

One more speech from Prentiss concluded his work for Taylor. The occasion was unique, an open-air meeting sponsored "by the Fillmore Rangers and Boatmen Club, on the Levee" at New Orleans.[35] "Prentiss the unapproachable," stated the *Delta,* "launched out into one of those bold and highly metaphorical speeches, for which he is so remarkable." His adaptation to his audience may be inferred from the words: "He spoke particularly to the boatmen—to those engaged in directing steamboats and vessels; and the fecundity of his imagination was never more strongly displayed than in his inimical figures and metaphors, drawn from the avocation of those to whom his remarks seemed to be chiefly directed." [36] A heavy rain fell while he was speaking, "but the orator, using the occasion for a fine simile, kept on in his impassioned and energetic style." The reporter for the *Delta* found the rain too drenching to remain, but the one for the *Crescent* followed the meeting to some near-by buildings where the speaking was continued.[37]

Though he did not know it, Prentiss' political speaking was virtually over. With the exception of some slight efforts in the Louisiana elections of 1849, in which it was noted he "was laboring under great hoarseness," [38] the Whig

---

[34] Prentiss to George Prentiss, New Orleans, October 24, 1848, in *Memoir of S. S. Prentiss,* II, 460.   [35] New Orleans *Daily Delta,* November 4, 1848.   [36] *Ibid.*   [37] New Orleans *Daily Crescent,* November 4, 1848.   [38] New Orleans *Daily Bee,* October 17, 30, 1849; New Orleans *Daily Picayune,* October 30, 1849.

party, in its own last years, was not to have his services.

Prentiss naturally rejoiced in Taylor's election. Again he asked but one favor, the right to resume his law practice unmolested. Although he was named by the New York *Herald* as its choice for attorney general in Taylor's cabinet, the New Orleans *Delta* knew that such an offer could not attract him. "We think it hardly probable that Mr. Prentiss would give up his lucrative practice in this city for even the office of Attorney-General, which, to a good lawyer, is the most profitable of the Cabinet offices." [39] The *Delta* was correct. Prentiss, as soon as the election results were safely in, declared: "I have nothing to ask for. I would not take any office within the gift of the President, even if it were tendered to me. I return from the political struggle to my professional pursuits with renewed pleasure." [40]

[39] New Orleans *Daily Delta*, December 30, 1848.
[40] Prentiss to George Prentiss, New Orleans, November 25, 1848, in *Memoir of S. S. Prentiss*, II, 463.

Chapter XIII

PRENTISS THE ORATOR

In 1853, three years after Prentiss' death and burial near the Mississippi River at Natchez, Joseph G. Baldwin wrote: "And long will that noble river flow out its tide into the gulf, ere the roar of its current shall mingle with the tones of such eloquence again—eloquence as full and majestic, as resistless and sublime, and as wild in its sweep as its own sea-like flood,

—the mightiest river
Rolls mingling with his fame forever." [1]

If Prentiss, because of his fatal addiction to alcohol and to reckless gambling, exhibited traits not worthy of imitation, and if his speaking, by twentieth-century standards of conversational communicativeness, was overflorid, his fame and success in his own times may well inspire the would-be orator. By antebellum standards, he was a deliberative, forensic, and occasional orator *par excellence,* and his influence was resistless, brilliant, magnetic, and dazzling. As expressed by Reuben Davis: "Those who heard him can never forget the strange charm of this wonderful speaker. It was like music and poetry, and flame and fire, and love and hate, and memory and inspiration, all bearing away in one swift torrent the soul given up to its enchantment." [2]

Irresistible and enchanting, electric in general public address, Prentiss' genius was so enduring that all who ever

[1] Joseph G. Baldwin, *The Flush Times of Alabama and Mississippi* (Americus, Ga., 1853), 221–22.
[2] Davis, *Recollections of Mississippi and Mississippians,* 81.

heard him remembered his power. Long after his death, the *Ouachita Telegraph* recorded: "For fifteen years, no matter with whom he spoke at the hustings, the cries of 'Prentiss! Prentiss!' displayed the popular enthusiasm in his behalf, and its impatience of any intervening orator." [3] Multiple instances of testimony might be cited, comparable to that of Horace S. Fulkerson, who frequently experienced Prentiss' oratorical enchantment, and once said, "It was gold dust that covered his garments," [4] and continued: "I often heard Mr. Prentiss at the bar and on the political rostrum. . . . I believe the enthusiasm he excited in the minds and hearts of those who heard him has survived longer than that aroused by any speaker of modern times. I can truthfully say that even while I am penning these lines I am under the magic spell of his oratory, so vivid is the recollection of his weird supernatural eloquence of speech and manner." [5] Many years later still, another man who often saw him "stand on the platform in the open air, under the shining stars, and improvise by the hours," declared: "When he spoke it was as if he unwound a thread of gold. As he proceeded he seemed to hang upon it precious jewel after jewel of thought and of imagination." [6]

In these characterizations, as well as in his speeches, which indicate what his language habits were, we have the clue to the kind of orator Prentiss was. His was the florid style, then most acceptable to the people of the South, and for that matter, to people everywhere. For it should be emphasized that Prentiss was not a local southern orator. His national reputation began when for three days he defended his right to a seat in Congress and was listened to by an enraptured body including Webster, Clay, and Calhoun. His Faneuil Hall appearance followed, and then his speeches

---

[3] Monroe *Ouachita Telegraph,* December 2, 1868.
[4] Fulkerson, *Random Recollections of Early Days in Mississippi,* 102.
[5] *Ibid.,* 106–107.
[6] Address of Carleton Hunt, *Fifty Years' Experience in Practice at the Bar,* delivered before the Louisiana Bar Association (New Orleans, 1908), 64.

of national significance in the campaigns of 1840 and 1844. For a man whose period of office holding was so brief, it was an unusual distinction to attain so quickly a national reputation. Moreover, he was less than thirty years of age at the time. One who knew him declared: "I will say, however, that I believe that *Alexander Hamilton* and *S. S. Prentiss* head the list of all men in the United States who have achieved greatness in early life. Prentiss's oratory burst on the people like a meteor athwart the sky, and ended as suddenly with his early death." [7]

Prentiss belongs to the golden age of American eloquence. His active years from 1830 to 1850 coincide with those of Webster, Clay, Calhoun, John Quincy Adams, Thomas A. Corwin, and scores of others whose speeches are considered monumental in the annals of American public address. America has in no period produced greater orators than in the years of Prentiss' life. In sheer eloquence, it is doubtful whether any surpassed him. If eloquence alone were the criterion for evaluating speakers, Prentiss would rank at the top. That he was eloquent needs no proof but the reading of his speeches and the comments of those who heard him. One man who saw and heard men by the hundreds as they came and went from Washington recorded: "Seargent Smith Prentiss, who came to Washington during the Van Buren Administration to claim a seat in Congress as the Representative from Mississippi, was the most eloquent speaker that I have ever heard." [8] The naming of Prentiss as the orator of "Purple Patches" by Edgar DeWitt Jones in his book *Lords of Speech*,[9] reveals quite clearly how men have thought of him. If Prentiss is almost forgotten in the twentieth century, at least by the nation as a whole, he was, nevertheless, no local Mississippi spokesman

[7] Samuel G. French, *Two Wars: An Autobiography* . . . (Nashville, 1901), 90.

[8] Ben: Perley Poore, *Perley's Reminiscences of Sixty Years in the National Metropolis* (Philadelphia, 1886), 214.

[9] Edgar D. Jones, *Lords of Speech* (Chicago, 1937), 81–92.

in his day. The name of Prentiss was linked inseparably with the Whig party, north and south. He was thought of primarily as an orator, and enjoyed the prestige of that title whenever his name was mentioned or appeared in print. Not only would the New Orleans *Picayune* say, as it did once, "The Hon. S. S. Prentiss, the great Mississippi orator, arrived in town yesterday from Vicksburg," [10] but other papers in far distant corners of the United States would use the word "orator" when they carried notices concerning him. In truth, George Prentiss, as a minister, lived in reflected glory and had his own prestige enhanced more than once by the fact that he was Seargent's brother. In 1845 when he was chosen for a pulpit in New Bedford, Massachusetts, there appeared the notice: "The Rev. Geo. L. Prentiss, of Portland, Me. has accepted the invitation of the South Trinitarian Church in this town to become their preacher. . . . Mr. P. is a brother of the distinguished Mississippi orator of that name." [11]

But it is not germane to the present purpose to belabor the point of Prentiss' reputation. What were his sources of power and what were his shortcomings? To what extent was Prentiss a great orator? In his public address there were undoubtedly unique elements of perfection, and there were, likewise, deficiences, especially if he is judged in the light of modern standards of oratorical criticism.

Prentiss succeeded through both native endowment and diligence. Nature gave him a mental brilliance and alertness, a natural and easy flow of speech in conversation and public utterance, a splendid diction and a superb voice quality. All these he cultivated. Declamations at Gorham and the opportunities afforded in the Peucinian Literary Society, together with those in Spouteroi at Bowdoin College, gave him speaking experiences from his early youth.

---

10 New Orleans, *Daily Picayune*, December 22, 1840.
11 New Bedford *Bulletin*, quoted in Boston *Daily Advertiser*, January 22, 1845.

Capacity and inclination combined with such opportunities as were available to start him off oratorically.

Along with these obvious oratorical advantages must be considered the benefits of a thoroughly good classical education. He preferred to read, not too studiously perhaps, but for the sheer pleasure he derived from history, fiction, and poetry. His mind retained and repeated. He memorized with ease, and what he absorbed stayed with him. Shakespeare was his favorite author, and his speeches are accordingly full of allusions and quotations from the great dramatist, as well as from other fine literature. What he read in childhood and later at Bowdoin was not for so much school credit to be put aside. Instead, his readings became a part of his private and public personality. As a consequence, his vast literacy colored and permeated every public address, while allusion after allusion, and quotation after quotation, were intermingled with his own beautiful, at times almost poetic, phraseology.

In addition, Prentiss labored to perfect nature's gifts. His oratory was scarcely a mere magical power which he possessed by accident. Writing of the inability of the public to fathom the sources of his oratorical genius, George Prentiss stated: "Much of this popular wonder arose, no doubt, from simple ignorance or misconception of the facts of his early life." [12] George Prentiss knew and observed his brother's intensive application at Gorham and Bowdoin College, and others perceived it during the heyday of his career in Mississippi. "True," Baldwin testifies, "he labored more than most men; but he labored as he frolicked—because his mind could not be idle, but burst into work as by the irrepressible instinct which sought occupation as an outlet to intellectual excitement. . . . He studied more than he seemed to study,—more probably, than he cared to have it believed he studied." [13]

[12] *Memoir of S. S. Prentiss*, II, 467.
[13] Baldwin, *Flush Times of Alabama and Mississippi*, 219.

It is trite to say that Prentiss loved to speak and reveled in the process. He was seldom too exhausted to fulfill requests for remarks, and when once started, he continued with ease and delight. Enraptured by the process, he so revealed his exquisite delight that those who heard him shared his joy in the speaking situation. "I have thought in those transporting moments when the golden words were dropping from his lips," wrote Fulkerson, "when with head erect and his shoulders working like the wings of a bird in flight, he was as happy as mortal can well be; that in such moments the beautiful images which his fancy created were entrancing his soul and lifting him far above and beyond his earthly surroundings, 'as far as the stars of heaven are above the clods of the valley,' as I once heard him say." [14]

Since Prentiss loved to speak, he cultivated the art until it became highly effective. He once told his brother that "although he could not enter a drawing-room and accost a lady, without trembling and mental embarrassment, he was utterly unconscious of any such feelings in appearing before a public assembly, however large or grave." He was fully aware of this confidence in the presence of hearers. "If I were, of a sudden, to be transported to Old England, and let down, through the roof, into the assembled House of Lords, I doubt not, the instant I found myself on my legs, I could begin a speech to their Lordships on any subject, *which I understood,* without the slightest hesitation or embarrassment." [15] This enthusiasm and ease in speaking, combined with incessant demands for performance, caused him to think about, and strive for, the qualities of good oral style. Possibly, more than he should have, Prentiss conceived of speaking situations as opportunities for exhibition, with the result that his addresses were too much "show-pieces." Yet those who heard him were impressed as well with what may be called the "natural manner." For

[14] Fulkerson, *Random Recollections of Early Days in Mississippi,* 107.
[15] *Memoir of S. S. Prentiss,* II, 476.

a man who earned his living by speaking constantly in the courtroom, as well as on numerous political and demonstrative occasions, the artificial, the exhibitory, the pompous, would have been fatal. George Prentiss listed Prentiss' absolute sincerity, depth and fervor of his personal convictions," [16] as the first attributes which impressed his hearers, and then hastened to add: "Closely allied to this deep earnestness was his perfectly natural manner of speaking. It would have been as impossible to associate with him rhetorical tricks and affectation, as to associate them with daylight, or with the vivid flash of lightening. They were utterly alien from his nature; although a passage occurs, now and then, in his reported speeches, which might lead to a contrary impression." [17] This same conclusion concerning Prentiss has been expressed by Dunbar Rowland. "One of his greatest powers was his impressive demeanor, . . . free from the pose that is so common where mediocrity seeks to hide itself behind pompous affectation. His style in the delivery of his speeches was impressively deliberate, but he would often indulge in passionate outbursts in which his words flowed from him like some mighty torrent." [18] It is something of a paradox that such overdecorative words and sentences as Prentiss used should have been thought of as unaffected and natural. Other commentators speak of his torrential emotions, especially in passages of invective. Perhaps we should keep in mind that the comments we read are from men of Prentiss' own period, whose ideas of oratorical style were much the same as his own. Such men would not regard exaggerated diction or overornamental phraseology as necessarily artificial or unnatural. Moreover, it is possible to deliver even the most "purple" of passages naturally and sincerely. Prentiss apparently was able to do so.

---

[16] *Ibid.,* 469.   [17] *Ibid.,* 470.
[18] Dunbar Rowland, "Political and Parliamentary Orators and Oratory of Mississippi," in *Mississippi Historical Society Publications,* IV (1901), 365.

More accurately, Prentiss may be thought of as a highly dramatic type of orator. This is the reason why, regardless of whether he spoke one hour or three, Rowland could say of him: "A remarkable feature of his oratory was that it never wearied the hearer." [19] The enchanting effect which men felt is explained on this basis. The dramatic is made up primarily of language effects. Prentiss was a student of language, and strove to perfect his usage of it. Many who knew him remarked on his conversational brilliancy. "In conversation he was irresistible," said Reuben Davis. "I have sat at the wine table with him for hours, every one present so captivated by his delightful talk that even the wine, of which there was no stint, seemed less intoxicating than his presence." [20] It was the easiest thing for him then, since assemblies caused no fear but rather inspiration, to transfer to larger groups his language faculties. In contrast, Prentiss did not write with the ease with which he spoke. In matters of punctuation he was somewhat unorthodox, inaccurate even for his day, as his letters indicate. On this point George Prentiss stated: "In 1844 he told me that it almost pained him to write a common letter, he had become so scrupulous and particular in the choice of words. . . . His few manuscripts which remain, indicate slow composition; they contain numerous erasures, not merely of words, but of whole sentences." [21]

In his language habits Prentiss thought in terms of the figurative and illustrative. Abstractness was not a part of him. The extent to which he cultivated the habit of finding illustrations for his arguments and points may be inferred from a conversation he once had with Edward Wilkinson. To the question of Wilkinson, "did [he] not think his speeches too imaginative, as he had heard said of them?" Prentiss is purported to have replied: "The natural bent

[19] *Ibid.*
[20] Davis, *Recollections of Mississippi and Mississippians*, 83.
[21] *Memoir of S. S. Prentiss*, II, 474.

of my mind is to dry and pure ratiocination, but finding
early that mankind, from a petit jury to the highest deliberative assembly are more influenced by illustration than
by argument, I have cultivated my imagination in aid of
my reason." [22] It may be doubted that Prentiss, imaginative
as he was, possessed a purely argumentative or logical cast
of mind. It is not to be doubted, though, that he knew the
universal power of an illustration. Regardless of the audience, irrespective of the type of address, Prentiss' speeches
are permeated with the figurative. Analogies were not reserved for either the intelligentsia or the frontiersmen. "He
gave the unlettered back-woodsmen more credit for appre-
ciating these rarer beauties of speech than is generally
done." [23]

Since Prentiss found writing far more difficult than
speaking, another attribute of his oratory becomes evident.
He was essentially an extempore speaker, sometimes seemingly impromptu. His eulogy on Lafayette and his New Orleans address on the anniversary of the landing of the Pilgrims appear to be the only occasions when he relied on
written manuscripts. This does not mean that his speeches
were unprepared. George Prentiss stated emphatically: "It
can hardly be doubted that his more important speeches
were carefully premeditated; but not one of them was ever
written. . . . A few leading points and landmarks were
fixed in his memory: all the rest—language, style, imagery
—were left to the excitement of the occasion." [24] Probably
no more certain evidence of Prentiss' preference for the extempore method may be ascertained than from the letter
(quoted earlier) which he wrote to his sister following the
delivery of his Sub-Treasury speech in Congress. "I don't
know whether I shall take the trouble to write out my
speech. I had rather make ten than write one; and as I am

[22] Van Buren, *Jottings of a Year's Sojourn in the South*, 285.
[23] *Ibid.*, 282.   [24] *Memoir of S. S. Prentiss*, II, 474-75.

determined to quit political life, I see no reason for putting myself to much trouble." [25] Prentiss did write certain of his speeches for publication, but his decided preference for the extempore method is the chief explanation for the inadequate texts of his speeches.

Since Prentiss was so highly extempore, having only a few landmarks in mind, and not even using notes before his audiences, another attribute of his speaking comes to the fore. Prentiss spoke at length, not briefly, as a rule. A three-hour speech was not uncommon; a one-hour speech was unusual. Since figures, illustrations, and allusions were so much a part of all he said, we must conclude that through his imaginative tendencies he was adept at improvising as he went along. The extempore method, rightly conceived, sets no limitations on preparation. All language and materials of any speech may well be pondered and organized in advance. Neither is embellishment restricted to the written discourse; the ornate may be premeditated. But it is highly doubtful that Prentiss did overmuch premeditation. Rather, figures, images, and colorful descriptions flashed upon his mind as he went. Out of his readings, memories, and imaginings, language forms flooded upon him. In testimony, we have what is purported to be Prentiss' own explanation in this regard. To the question of his friend, Judge George Winchester, as to how he was able to express so many figures of speech and flights of fancy, Prentiss replied: "When I get to speaking and become excited, I am like a little boy walking through a meadow when he sees a beautiful butterfly, with its fancy wings of gold and starts in pursuit eager to capture his glittering prize, then in the race, up jumps another and still another until the whole sky is filled with beautiful Butterflies, each a new one, capable of attracting the boy's attention, so with me, each fancy

25 Prentiss to Anna Prentiss, House of Representatives, June 26, 1838, *ibid.,* I, 346; Whittemore Collection.

starts a new one till in the pursuit my whole mind is filled with beautiful Butterflies." [26]

An interesting but unanswerable question about Prentiss is the extent to which he was under the influence of alcohol when he spoke. William C. Smedes, who knew him most intimately, is said to have expressed himself to the effect that Prentiss was never so eloquent as when drunk.[27] Be this as it may, those who knew him saw other sources of power. Reuben Davis wrote: "I have heard him say that he had committed so much poetry to memory that he often spoke without being conscious whether he uttered his own words or those of some favorite poet." [28] Another added: "His imagination was unsurpassed, and the rich stores of his mind supplied him with never-ending material, quoted and original. The slightest allusion to anything gave the key to all its peculiarities. If he had occasion to speak of the diamond, its bed in the Galconda, its discovery by some poor native, its being associated with commerce, its polish by the lapidary, its adorning the neck of beauty, its rays brilliant and serene, its birth, its life, its history, all flashed upon him. So with every idea in the vast storehouse of his mind; he seemed to know all things in mass and in particulars, never confused, never at a loss; the hearer listened, wondered, and dreamed." [29] If Prentiss spoke thus, it is not to be wondered at that he was quoted as saying: "I am as much astonished at my own conceptions as any of my auditors; and when the excitement is over, I could no more reproduce them than I could make a world." [30]

But a speech is no mere series of metaphors and similes. Figurative language is useful only as it embellishes and en-

[26] George W. Shackelford to Shields, Fayette, Miss., July 8, 1881, in Shields Collection, Department of Archives, Louisiana State University.

[27] Information given the writer, June 4, 1943, at Vicksburg, in interview with Mrs. David Porterfield, daughter of Smedes.

[28] Davis, *Recollections of Mississippi and Mississippians*, 82.

[29] Thorpe, "Reminiscences of Seargent S. Prentiss," *loc. cit.*, 243.

[30] W. H. Milburn, *The Lance, Cross and Canoe . . . in the Valley of the Mississippi . . .* (New York, 1892), 619.

hances an idea. The arguments and truths undergirding the speaker's language are more essential. Since Prentiss' speaking divides itself into three categories of public address—forensic, deliberative, and demonstrative—it is important to remember that he possessed the capacity to speak on themes and issues appropriate to the respective modes. How profound Prentiss was politically may be open to question. His deliberative speaking consisted heavily of tributes to the Whig party and its leaders, and denunciations of the Democratic party and its spokesmen. Closely knit arguments were not characteristic of him in campaigns. Nevertheless, in the Mississippi state legislature and again in Congress, it is evident that he could build a case and that he could bolster it by lines of reasoning, evidence, and citation of precedents. When Prentiss debated constitutional issues, he was at his best argumentatively. But even in these speeches, the tendency to embellish was too strong to be averted. In 1840 and 1844 it was not so much argument as popular party enthusiasm that counted. In rousing enthusiasm Prentiss was at home. In a certain sense his political campaign speeches became demonstrative in type.

In the legal realm Prentiss could not avoid argument or the necessity of handling facts and evidence. Unfortunately, his forensic speeches, the kind he gave oftenest, are not available for analysis. However, the one or two which have been preserved, as well as his many legal briefs before high courts, show issues, evidence, and citations of law and precedents. Just as his constitutional speeches were the most argumentative and analytical among his deliberative address, his legal briefs, when examined, are impressive with what may be considered pure logic. Main issues and partitions are evident; lines of reasoning are presented and followed up. A reading of his legal briefs establishes the fact that Prentiss, though imaginative, was also capable of logical argument.

But it is probably true that Prentiss was more an orator

than a debater or systematic speaker. When Jefferson Davis debated the bond question with him in 1843, he noted Prentiss' inability to confine his arguments to brief fifteen-minute intervals of speaking. Prentiss preferred to elaborate, hence the tendency to utter sublime sentiments and to paint word pictures rather than to unfold matter-of-fact arguments. As successful as he was at the bar, he was not the speaker to rely solely, or chiefly, on pure probative force. This, then, probably explains his success as an occasional orator. A eulogy on Lafayette, an anniversary of the landing of the Pilgrims, the famine scenes in Ireland, soldiers returning home from Mexico—these constituted themes upon which he could be pathetic and lofty. The beauty and pathos of the Irish Famine speech will grip the reader today and must have impressed profoundly those who heard it.

It must not be said, however, that Prentiss was devoid of intellectual qualifications. Without these very endowments he could not have used the emotional weapons so appropriately. His brilliant mind explains to a great extent the high level of his utterances. Prentiss had been classically trained and was an educated man. "Such were his intellectual features," said Lynch, "which constantly asserted themselves, whether he stood before a jury of the backwoods or before the bar of the High Court; on the flower-decked rostrum surrounded by thousands of eager listeners, or in the halls of Congress, the same halo of genius clustered around his brow. Calm and self-possessed, he was never at a loss for either subject-matter or a happy manner of expression." [31]

Audiences served to stimulate Prentiss; to their stimulation he fulfilled his obligations with high emotional fervor. Fulkerson declared: "He drew his audience up with him, making them partakers of his own felicity." [32] At the same time, under all circumstances, he was, apparently, as Lynch

[31] Lynch, Bench and Bar of Mississippi, 219.
[32] Fulkerson, Random Recollections of Early Days in Mississippi, 107.

commented, "calm and self-possessed." When he became absorbed in his theme, his animation radiated to his audience, inevitably causing feeling to run high. Preparation and readiness explain, in a great measure at least, his self-possession. His brother said: "This absolute command of his mental forces never appeared more surprising than in the ease with which he could frame images, or institute comparison for the illustration of his subject. . . . However high he might attempt to soar, he always . . . descended at his pleasure." [33]

Further on the positive side, it can be said that Prentiss was equipped to speak. His ideas, the content of his speeches, did not fall far short of his eloquent delivery. What he possessed in the way of native gifts of mind and manner was aided by intellectual qualifications. In summary of Prentiss as a speaker, the comments of Lynch may be as valuable as those of any who ever sought to appraise him. "There was no subject which he could not clothe with interest. . . . He was more than an orator; he was the living personification of human speech in its splendor and in its majesty. In him all was eloquent—the tone, gesture, attitude, and look, as well as the inspiration. Yet beneath all this glitter flowed the deep, strong current of knowledge. His eloquence never assumed the character of mere superficiality, but was the sparkling ebullition of the caldron of thought that seethed beneath, the aroma of the flowers of his mind. While he possessed an almost inimitable command of language, it was not the mere result of memory, but his words were the natural and well-fitting garments of his thoughts. His memory was one vast storehouse of facts, so orderly arranged, so stratified and laminated, that he could at any time pluck whatever he desired from its copious vaults. . . . He had but to will, and all presented their sparkling goblets to his lips." [34] This may be an overdrawn

[33] *Memoir of S. S. Prentiss*, II, 476.
[34] Lynch, *Bench and Bar of Mississippi*, 219.

portrayal of Prentiss the orator, but at least one man saw him in that light.

Notwithstanding all that was ever written about the eloquence of Prentiss, little is on record as to what may be called the special traits of his delivery. His voice quality was evidently splendid, for it is commented on by numerous auditors. He must have had good volume, for before large groups, whether indoors or in the open air, he could be heard distinctly. Certainly he was a rapid speaker, his rate being such that reporters were unable to keep up with him. One defect of his utterance was a slight lisp, which gave certain of his words a hissing sound.

Other questions are more difficult to answer. Did he gesture? Also, was he a speaker of little or much platform movement? Since his lameness necessitated the constant use of a cane, the inquiry as to his bodily activity and movement is interesting. Almost none who heard him mentioned these matters. True, Fulkerson did comment on his "shoulders working like the wings of a bird in flight." Almost the only statement of Shields in this regard is that when he once heard him on the bond question at Fayette, Mississippi, "He walked the narrow rostrum like a caged tiger." [35] But movement was not easy for him; besides, he was always sensitive regarding the handicap. The observation of Sparks is probably quite accurate that his lameness "was a serious obstacle to his locomotion, and in speaking compelled a sameness of position, injurious to the effect of his oratory." [36]

Uncomplimentary remarks on Prentiss' oratory are in general few. The Democratic newspapers in Mississippi which attacked his Whig principles mercilessly, such as the Natchez *Free Trader,* the Columbus *Democrat,* the Vicksburg *Sentinel,* and the Jackson *Mississippian,* and all his political opponents conceded him the oratorical advantage.

[35] Shields, *Seargent Smith Prentiss,* 323.
[36] Sparks, *Memories of Fifty Years,* 351.

They criticized him primarily for the weakness and un-soundness of his political logic and premises, and not as a speaker. Likewise, his legal opponents dreaded his persua-sive powers before juries. Occasionally, however, intima-tions were made that his style was overdone and that he was too much flattered as an orator. Once in 1842 the Baton Rouge *Gazette,* a Whig paper, thought there was too much "protection of Mississippi's favorite son." It alluded to one of his appearances, concluding: "The subject on this occasion admitted of no extended effort. The production, it would be supposed, would glow with ardent feeling and eloquent and impressive language. And such indeed, it was; but we have seen, (and that recently—on the same good theme too,) efforts far superior, by men whose names are en-tirely unknown on the records of oratorical fame." [37] This type of criticism, in which the implication is clear that Pren-tiss overelaborated on ordinary themes and then might be surpassed in ideas by men without oratorical prestige, re-sembles the criticism of another great American speaker, Robert G. Ingersoll, who in evaluating Prentiss said that the trouble with him, though he "was a very great talker," [38] was that he "said profound and beautiful things, but . . . lacked application. He was uneven, disproportioned—say-ing ordinary things on great occasions, and now and then, without the slightest provocation, uttering the sublimest and most beautiful thoughts." [39]

To state the times and places when Prentiss overembel-lished an ordinary theme and then failed to do justice to a larger one would be a difficult task. Since all his speaking was of the eloquent variety, the idea that he was often in-clined to soar out of bounds, even to the extent of causing his friends and supporters to suggest moderation, is of sig-nificance.

[37] Baton Rouge *Weekly Gazette,* March 4, 1842.
[38] *The Works of Robert G. Ingersoll* (Dresden Memorial Edition, New York, 1929), VIII, 541.
[39] *Ibid.,* 598.

When Prentiss died, the tributes to him and his oratory found their way into print in great numbers. At that time one New Orleans paper dared to say: "It is no disparagement of the fame of Mr. Prentiss to say, that the style of his oratory was not popular at the bar of this city, where the public taste is regulated by a severe standard, yet, it cannot be denied that he had great natural gifts and a wonderful command of words. His address was exceedingly captivating, his expression pleasing, his language copious, flowery, and seductive, more calculated however to sway the passions than the judgments of mind, yet evidencing a high order of talent and stamping him no ordinary man." [40]

The greatest criticism is yet to be leveled against Prentiss as a speaker. His eloquence may go undisputed, but it cannot be said that he spoke with the power or influence to direct much or any of the course of American history. Webster was eloquent, but he obtained decisions before the United States Supreme Court which charted events. Likewise, in Webster's deliberative oratory, historical trends were set. Calhoun was not eloquent in the sense ascribed to Prentiss, but he argued premises and issues so definitively as to direct the thinking and conduct of great groups. Another Mississippi speaker, Lucius Q. C. Lamar, doubtless outranks Prentiss, because public opinion was shaped and the welfare of peoples influenced by his spoken word. Never has the purely ornate and eloquent been a substitute for ideas or for more profound factors of influence. Hence Prentiss cannot be included by critics in the first tier of American speakers. The modern student of oratorical criticism does not ask "How eloquent?" but "With what effect?" [41]

Various explanations may be offered for the fact that the

[40] New Orleans *Daily True Delta*, July 6, 1850.

[41] For a treatment of this point of view, see William Norwood Brigance, "The Twenty-Eight Foremost Orators," in *Quarterly Journal of Speech* (Detroit), XXIX (1938), 376–80; *id.* (ed.), *A History and Criticism of American Public Address* (New York, 1943), I–II, *passim*.

oratorical influence of Prentiss lived scarcely longer than his own life span. It may be true that he lacked great capacity to deal with issues profoundly, and that he substituted powers of eloquence only. But more important, it should be borne in mind that in politics and law he was not in a position to influence events as much as it might seem. Prentiss was primarily a jury lawyer. He had the chance in but one case before the United States Supreme Court to have handed down a decision in his favor. His cases before the Mississippi and Louisiana State Supreme Courts, though important, were yet of local or regional significance. To evaluate properly the influence of a jury lawyer is most difficult.

It must be remembered, too, that Prentiss had but a brief career as a public official, and that as a very young man. He might well have been in public office during a great portion of his life, but he honestly preferred his law practice. Moreover, his early death cut short what might have been years of influential leadership. Also, while Prentiss was an ardent Whig, he was satisfied to be the aider and abettor to the ambitions and aspirations of other men of the party. Prentiss made a good start as a deliberative speaker in the Mississippi state legislature and later in Congress. Moreover, his efforts for the Whig party in campaigns did not go unappreciated. Nevertheless, Prentiss with all his eloquence, lost as often as he won. He was on the winning side in the elections of Harrison and Taylor, but he lost when he tried the hardest, as in 1844, to elect Clay. He lost also when over a four-year period he fought bond repudiation in Mississippi.

As an occasional orator Prentiss may deserve a greater glory than has been shown him. But in spite of American fondness for anniversary and cornerstone occasions, where both noble, and sometimes ignoble, sentiments have been uttered, history has been made by the words of statesmen in different situations and by lawyers before high courts, as well as by ministers and reformers. Prentiss was hardly one of these.

But if Prentiss lacked certain elements of greatness, if his life was lived too recklessly, and if he leaned too far in the direction of emotionalized speaking, he was no mere "spread-eagle" orator. He was a speaker who immersed himself in an immediate theme, fortified himself by reading, became experienced in multiple and successive audience situations, and did sustained speaking for hours, weaving figures, images, and allusions into the warp and woof of his own thoughts. In Prentiss there was too much classic lore, historical appreciation, legal precedent, and too much analytical power in his unaffected mind and manner to permit him to be indicted as "sound and fury, signifying nothing." If less successful as a parliamentary or deliberative speaker, he was an ideal occasional orator, and a preeminently able forensic pleader. His name and fame are well established in the oratorical firmament.

Chapter XIV

PRENTISS THE LAWYER

PRENTISS exercised splendid foresight when he determined early in life to become a lawyer. In the legal realm his talents found their maximum expression and development. He disliked public office, and, after every political contest in which he figured, he shunned all opportunities for political reward and returned at once to his law office and the courtroom. Prentiss was above all else a lawyer. As such he was remarkably able, and in a short span of years acquired a far-flung reputation. His powers of memory, analysis, and oratory were joined time after time in the unraveling of legal intricacies and in lucid exposition before judge and jury. These specific talents were in the mind of James D. Lynch when he wrote of Prentiss: "He possessed in an eminent degree those powers of analysis which could enter into the very gist and heart of a proposition and wind it off upon a thousand spindles, and a masterly synthesis that could then gather up such threads as suited his purpose, and weave them back into one compact and unbroken cable." [1]

Within a short time after Prentiss was admitted to the Mississippi bar, he acquired a flourishing law practice. Moreover, though his rise was sudden, it was not fleeting. His practice grew as his name spread. To a great extent he was an itinerant lawyer. His cases, criminal and civil, were argued in many a Mississippi courthouse. The records of one such court will show something of the number of his

[1] Lynch, *Bench and Bar of Mississippi*, 218.

cases. As he became established with Guion in Vicksburg, he was identified with forty cases in the Civil Circuit Court of Warren County in 1834. In 1835 the number of his cases in this same court doubled.[2] Besides these eighty cases, he had numerous criminal cases in Warren and in other counties. Actually, the great majority of Prentiss' cases in Mississippi were in the inferior courts. Nevertheless, a goodly number were appealed to higher courts, so that he appeared before the State Supreme Court no less than twenty-four times.[3] The chief reason for his moving to New Orleans in 1845 was to reap the benefits of a more lucrative practice. He was not disappointed in the amount of business which fell into his hands there. Aside from all his practice in lower Louisiana courts, he was counsel in as many as forty-four cases before the State Supreme Court between 1845 and his death in 1850.[4]

[2] Records of the Civil Circuit Court, Warren County, Vicksburg.

[3] Chawning v. Cox, 1 Howard (Miss.) 130 (1834); Marsh et al., Appellants, v. Williams, 1 Howard (Miss.) 132 (1834); Penrice, Appellant v. Cooks, 1 Howard (Miss.) 227 (1835); Byrd v. The State, 1 Howard (Miss.) 247 (1835); Hageman v. Sharkey, 1 Howard (Miss.) 277 (1836); Ex parte Brown, 1 Howard (Miss.) 303 (1836); Vick v. Mayor and Aldermen of Vicksburg, 1 Howard (Miss.) 379 (1837); Patterson and Tyler v. Phillips, 1 Howard (Miss.) 572 (1837); Maulding v. Rigby, 1 Howard (Miss.) 579 (1837); Longacre v. The State, 2 Howard (Miss.) 637 (1837); Strong v. Runnels, 2 Howard (Miss.) 667 (1837); Reeves v. Burnham, 3 Howard (Miss.) 25 (1838); Planters' Bank v. Snodgrass, 4 Howard (Miss.) 573 (1840); Doss v. Jones, 5 Howard (Miss.) 158 (1840); Ross v. Verterner, 5 Howard (Miss.) 305 (1840); Fulton, Robb, et al., Appellants v. Doe ex dem. McAfee, 5 Howard (Miss.) 751 (1841); Amos and Roe v. Edward R. J. Allnut, 2 Smedes and Marshall 215 (1844); Samuel Garland, Executor of John A. Rowan, Deceased v. Susan A. Rowan, 2 Smedes and Marshall 617 (1844); Payne, Green and Wood v. Baldwin, Vail and Hufty, 5 Smedes and Marshall 661 (1844); Philip Coleman v. John Doe, ex dem. Tish-Ho-Mah, 4 Smedes and Marshall 40 (1844); Richard T. Archer and James Watson v. Volney Stamps, 4 Smedes and Marshall 353 (1845); The Commercial Bank of Rodney v. The State of Mississippi, The Commercial Bank of Manchester v. The State of Mississippi, The State of Mississippi v. The Bank of Port Gibson, The State of Mississippi v. The Grand Gulf Bank, 4 Smedes and Marshall 439 (1845).

[4] Hefferman v. Brenham, 1 La. Ann. 146 (1846); Thorn v. Besmon et al., 1 La. Ann. 270 (1846); Penny v. Parham et al., 1 La. Ann. 274 (1846); Conrey et al v. Brenham et al., 1 La. Ann. 397 (1846); Gilmore et al. v. Brenham et al., 1 La. Ann. 414 (1846); Lyon v. Fisk, 1 La. Ann. 444 (1846); Fisk v. Fisk et al., Executors, 2 La. Ann. 71 (1847); City of New Orleans v. Fisk

The range and scope of Prentiss' legal cases bear testimony to the fact that he was master of more than one phase
or aspect of the law. Chiefly, he was a jury lawyer. Not infrequently, especially in his earlier legal career, he was involved in numerous criminal cases. However, most of his
cases indicate clearly that his civil practice exceeded his
criminal practice. But regardless of the kind of case Prentiss took to court, examination shows his briefs to be the
product of research, analysis, and synthesis. Inevitably, too,
his oratorical gifts were brought to bear for persuasive effects.

Just as Prentiss was not chiefly an advocate before judges,
but rather a jury lawyer, he was also not a lawyer to build
his fame before the United States Supreme Court. Nevertheless, in a random sampling, i. e., the arbitrary selection
of certain of Prentiss' cases to illustrate his methods and the

----

et al., Executors, 2 La. Ann. 78 (1847); Urquhart et al. v. Sargent, 2 La. Ann.
196 (1847); Ledbetter v. Ledbetter, 2 La. Ann. 215 (1847); Boyd v. Brown,
2 La. Ann. 218 (1847); Benton v. Roberts, 2 La. Ann. 243 (1847); The Union
Bank of Louisiana v. Guice, Executor, 2 La. Ann. 249 (1847); Atchison et al.
v. Parks, Administrator, et al., 2 La. Ann. 306 (1847); Goodloe v. Holmes
et al., 2 La. Ann. 400 (1847); The Planters' Bank v. Bass, 2 La. Ann. 430
(1847); Davis v. Hood, 2 La. Ann. 453 (1847); McCullough et al. v. Minor,
Executor, 2 La. Ann. 466 (1847); Dennistoun et al. v. Nutt et al., 2 La.
Ann. 483 (1847); Cavelier et al. v. Moss, 2 La. Ann. 584 (1847); Newman v.
Goza, 2 La. Ann. 642 (1847); Jacobs et al. v. Sartorius et al., 3 La. Ann. 9
(1848); The State v. Jones, 2 La. Ann. 9 (1848); Smith v. Ward et al., 3 La.
Ann. 76 (1848); Oliver v. Lake, 3 La. Ann. 78 (1848); Morton et al. v.
Packwood, 3 La. Ann. 167 (1848); Union Bank of Mississippi v. Ellis et al.,
3 La. Ann. 188 (1848); Scott v. Duke, 3 La. Ann. 253 (1848); Oates v. Coffin,
3 La. Ann. 339 (1848); Sargent et al. v. Davis, 3 La. Ann. 353 (1848); The New
Orleans Canal and Banking Company v. Morgan, 3 La. Ann. 356 (1848);
Morancy v. Dumesnil et al., 3 La. Ann. 363 (1848); McDowell et al. v. Read
et al., 3 La. Ann. 391 (1848); Tufts et al. v. Carradine et al., 3 La. Ann. 430
(1848); Ward et al. v. Warfield et al., 3 La. Ann. 468 (1848); Farr v. Byles,
3 La. Ann. 669 (1848); Cobb et al. v. Parham et al., 4 La. Ann. 148 (1849);
McGill v. McGill, 4 La. Ann. 262 (1849); Brown for the use of &c. v. Routh
et ux., 4 La. Ann. 270 (1849); Jones v. Lawrence, 4 La. Ann. 279 (1849);
Wilts et al. v. Peters et al., 4 La. Ann. 339 (1849); McMaster v. Mather,
4 La. Ann. 418 (1849); G. W. Denton v. J. Erwin et al., 5 La. Ann. 18 (1850);
Wm. Seawell v. Payne & Harrison, 5 La. Ann. 255 (1850); R. D. Blosman v.
Thomas Mather, 5 La. Ann. 335 (1850); Heirs of Stephen Henderson v.
P. A. Rost et al., Executors, 5 La. Ann. 441 (1850); William J. Frierson v.
Charles J. Brenham, 5 La. Ann. 540 (1850).

types of cases with which he was identified, his one and only appearance before the nation's highest tribunal comes up for special notice.

In 1833, as a mere youth, Prentiss went to Washington to argue before John Marshall and his associate justices. Pitted against Attorney General Roger B. Taney, Prentiss presented the claims of one Joseph Stewart of Arkansas, whose title to certain lands had been contested.[5] The circumstances surrounding the case were involved, and as the law and facts were against him, Prentiss labored at a disadvantage.

Sometime before the United States negotiated the Louisiana Purchase, the Spanish government, it was alleged, had confirmed one Sampeyreac in a grant of ten arpents of land in front of the Strawberry River, within the district of Arkansas.[6] As the territory embraced in the Louisiana Purchase came to be subdivided, the land allegedly Sampeyreac's was partly in Missouri and partly in Arkansas. In 1828 the land was purchased by John Bowie, and in the same year Bowie transferred the title to Stewart. Two years later, 1830, the Supreme Court of Arkansas, upon the petition of the district attorney, handed down a decision which declared that Sampeyreac was a fictitious individual and that the title by Stewart was consequently fraudulent.[7]

Prentiss was engaged by Stewart in an effort to secure from the Supreme Court of the United States a reversal of the decision of the Arkansas court. In representing Stewart at Washington, Prentiss based his contentions on fourteen points. In essence, he argued that the Arkansas court had no jurisdiction over titles acquired during the time of the Spanish and French possession of the territory, that the time had elapsed which would allow a bill of review, that no new evidence had been brought to light which would allow such

[5] Bernard Sampeyreac and Joseph Stewart, Appellants v. United States, Appellees, 7 Peters 222 (1833). See also, Shields, Seargent Smith Prentiss, 56–58.
[6] 7 Peters 222 (1833).   [7] Ibid.

a review, and that, though Sampeyreac was a fictitious person and the original grant of land to him was done fraudulently, Stewart was "an innocent purchaser." Specifically, Prentiss contended for Stewart: "He holds the land under the decree of confirmation, and not under a patent. His purchase was made in good faith, and he should not be disturbed, however fraudulent the acts of those who presented the claims for confirmation. He could know nothing but the recorded acts of the Court of Arkansas, proceeding under and according to the provisions of the laws of congress, in a matter specifically intrusted to that court. As the United States ought not to seek from him the restoration of the property taken from them by the frauds of those to whom he as well as the government was a stranger, so this court should not sanction such a claim." [8]

The contentions advanced by Taney countered Prentiss' precisely. He argued that the Arkansas court was justified in verifying all titles to land acquired before the United States assumed ownership of the territory and that the land claimed by Stewart, acquired as it was through fraud, was without clear title.

Obviously, Prentiss was handicapped by the fact that Sampeyreac was a fictitious individual. Fraud admittedly existed in the original title, and it was more than could be expected that the Supreme Court would overlook that fact in arriving at a decision. As a result, Prentiss lost.

Doubtless the most interesting and sensational trial in which Prentiss was engaged was in 1839 while he was in Congress. It was the trial of Edward C. Wilkinson at Harrodsburg, Kentucky. Prentiss was the counsel for the defense and was this time highly successful. Wilkinson had gone from Mississippi to Louisville, preparatory to his marriage there, and had taken with him his brother, Dr. Benjamin R. Wilkinson, and John Murdaugh. The three Mississippians registered at the Galt House in Louisville, and

8 *Ibid.*

then went to the tailor establishment of John W. Redding, where Benjamin ordered a suit of clothes. Some time later the Wilkinsons and Murdaugh returned to Redding's tailor shop to get the suit and found that the coat was ill-fitting. When Edward advised his brother to refuse payment Redding became angered. In a short time a fight occurred, and apparently Edward Wilkinson struck Redding with a poker. That night Redding, his brother-in-law, named John Rothwell, and others went to the Galt House to seek further revenge on the Wilkinson brothers and Murdaugh. The story goes that Redding accosted Edward in the barroom and threatened to kill him for the poker incident. Wilkinson evidently tried to avoid conflict, but more angry words ensued; other friends of Redding intervened, one John Meeks in particular, and a genuine fight took place. The Wilkinsons and Murdaugh were seemingly compelled to fight in self-defense and came out best, as both Meeks and Rothwell were killed. The Mississippians were placed in jail pending trial. Because of the intense feeling in Louisville, the state legislature granted a change of venue to Harrodsburg, where the trial was held in March, 1839.[9]

When Prentiss learned of the Louisville affray, he wrote to Edward Wilkinson from Washington, offering his aid in the defense of the prisoners. The offer was accepted, and as soon as Congress adjourned, Prentiss went to Kentucky to join the other members of the defense counsel, chief of whom was John Rowan, against the venerable Benjamin Hardin, who had been retained by the state in the prosecution. Prentiss reached Harrodsburg March 11, a few days after the trial had commenced. When all the testimony had been concluded and various members of the counsel on respective sides had spoken to the jury, Prentiss concluded the arguments for the defense. Hardin followed Prentiss in

[9] Shields, *Seargent Smith Prentiss*, 254–57; Lucius P. Little, *Ben Hardin— His Times and Contemporaries—With Selections from His Speeches* (Louisville, 1887), 289–90.

a five-hour speech in an effort to offset the powerful impression which Prentiss had made on the jury. Prentiss and Hardin by their masterly speeches made the Wilkinson trial one of the most famous in Kentucky history. "The arguments of Seargent S. Prentiss for the defense, and Benjamin Hardin for the prosecution," wrote L. F. Johnson, "were the leading features of the trial. These two arguments have caused the Wilkinson trial to be designated the greatest criminal trial in the history of the State." Johnson declared further: "Prentiss made the finest argument and most eloquent appeal to the jury that was ever heard in a court of justice in Kentucky. During its delivery he was frequently interrupted by applause from the vast assembly of people who crowded in the court room; and when he closed his argument he was greeted with loud cheers and prolonged applause." Hardin, too, was at his best. "For five hours the logic and eloquence of the eccentric Hardin held the attention of the jury and the large assembly of people. Hardly, if ever, has such another argument been made. The wonderful argument of Prentiss seemed to have brought out the best that was in the able advocate who opposed him." [10]

Prentiss was well aware that he was defending men who had committed murder, albeit in self-defense. Extended prefatory remarks were felt essential to the ultimate defense. He expressed regret that it was his duty to defend his honored friends but congratulated them upon the fact that they were being tried before a just tribunal free from passion and prejudice. He expressed his own confidence that justice would prevail, made it known that the prosecution was headed by one of Kentucky's greatest lawyers, and then challenged the court and jury to render justice. "Here in the heart of Kentucky, my clients have sought and obtained an unprejudiced, impartial jury. You hold in your

[10] L. F. Johnson, *Famous Kentucky Tragedies and Trials* (Louisville, 1916), 77–78.

hands the balance of justice; and I ask and expect that you will not permit the prosecution to cast extraneous and improper weights into the scale, against the lives of the defendants. You constitute the mirror, whose office is to reflect, in your verdict, the law and the evidence which have been submitted to you. Let no foul breath dim its pure surface, and cause it to render back a broken and distorted image. Through you now flows the stream of public justice; let it not become turbid by the trampling of unholy feet." [11]

The first basic position taken by Prentiss in his appeal to the jury was that circumstantial evidence proved the existence of a conspiracy by Redding, Rothwell, and others to take the lives of the Mississippians. To substantiate this, he examined minutely the testimony of a large number of witnesses. After untangling the oral evidence of the various witnesses, he concluded thus: "Gentlemen of the jury—I have now performed my task, which embraced the circumstantial evidence. Out of the mouths of fifteen different witnesses, most of them gentlemen of high character and undoubted veracity, I have exhibited to you an almost countless variety of circumstances, the occurrence of which, or any great portion of them, is absolutely incompatible with any other hypothesis than that of the existence of a conspiracy, which I proposed at the outset to prove. Upon this hypothesis, all these circumstances are easily explicable, and in perfect accordance with the ordinary principles of human action. I have combined the scattered strands of evidence: I have finished the cable which I promised; and now challenge the opposing counsel to try their strength upon it."

Second, Prentiss defended his clients on the ground that they were compelled to act in self-defense. He pointed out

11 Shields, *Seargent Smith Prentiss*, 266; *Memoir of S. S. Prentiss*, II, 76. What were probably the remarks of Prentiss in the trial were taken by T. Egerton Browne, who sent the speech as he took it to Prentiss for further revision. *Memoir of S. S. Prentiss*, II, 69–70.

that Meeks began the actual fight when he struck Murdaugh with a cowhide, that Dr. Wilkinson made little actual resistance though struck repeatedly by Rothwell, and that Edward Wilkinson was provoked to attack Rothwell, fatally, as it turned out, in defense of his brother.

These circumstances brought Prentiss to the position of claiming a praiseworthy and justifiable self-defense for the prisoners. He commented that the law of self-defense, emanating from British common law, deserves even wider application in the United States, that it pervades all human nature and conduct, and that it is not only natural but honorable. On this point he declared to the jury: "Kentucky has no law which precludes a man from defending himself, his brother, or his friend. Better for Judge Wilkinson had he never been born, than that he should have failed in his duty on this occasion. Had he acted otherwise than he did, he would have been ruined in his own estimation, and blasted in the opinion of the world. And young Murdaugh, too, he has a mother who is looking even now from her window, anxiously watching for her son's return; but better both for her and him that he should have been borne a bloody corpse to her arms than that he should have carried to her unavenged the degrading marks of the accursed whip!"

Contending further that his clients were compelled to defend themselves because their lives were in danger, Prentiss drew his appeal to a close, imploring the jury: "As you shall do unto them, so, under like circumstances, may it be done unto you."

Five hours of pleading by Hardin for the prosecution did not undo the determination of the jury to render a verdict of acquittal. Prentiss had won by keen legal analysis and synthesis, but perhaps most of all, by overwhelming oratory.

In 1840, Prentiss was associated with a most significant

slave case in Mississippi, Jane B. Ross *v.* Verterner.[12] Jane's
father, Isaac Ross, provided in his will of 1834 that upon
his death his slaves were to be manumitted and allowed to
go to Liberia under the supervision of the American Colonization Society, if a majority of them so voted. But, if a
majority of them chose to remain in the United States, they
were all to be sold along with his estate and the money
turned over to the Colonization Society to be invested at
6 per cent interest for the founding of a seminary of learning in Liberia. Ross stipulated further that the seminary
was to be controlled by the Colonization Society for one
hundred years, after which it should become the property
of the government there. If no government existed, then
the seminary was to be owned by the state of Mississippi.
A codicil added a short time before Ross's death provided
that the majority decision should not bind the minority;
but it retained the provision that the proceeds from the sale
of those who elected to remain in America should go to the
Colonization Society.

Ross died in 1836, and his heirs, first in Chancery Court,
and then before the Mississippi State Supreme Court in
1840, attempted to have the will declared void on the
ground that it violated the laws of Mississippi relative to
the manumission of slaves. Attorneys T. B. Thrasher and
Joseph Holt were retained by the heirs. Prentiss represented the executors, David Verterner being the first named
in the will.

Thrasher and Holt argued three points: first, that the
will was contrary to the laws and policies of the state; second, that the American Colonization Society had no right
to accept proceeds from the sale of the slaves to establish
the Liberia Seminary of Learning; and, third, that since
the two foregoing contentions were true, the slaves must
necessarily become the property of the heirs. Prentiss coun-

[12] Jane B. Ross *et al.,* Appellants *v.* Verterner *et al.,* 5 Howard (Miss.)
305 (1840).

tered these three issues by advancing two other issues: first, that the provisions made by Ross in his will were for the manumission of his slaves and were entirely legal; and second, that the bequests to the American Colonization Society were also legal.

To the arguments of his opponents that Mississippi had prescribed certain rules for freeing slaves which the will of Ross violated, Prentiss contended that the state had no law which would prevent a slaveowner from permitting his slaves to go to a foreign country. He maintained, pointedly, that if Ross in his lifetime had a perfect right to carry his slaves to Liberia and grant them freedom, he had the right to make such provisions in his will. Moreover, Prentiss argued that Mississippi's laws on manumission were merely police regulations applicable within the bounds of the state.

Against the objection of Thrasher and Holt that the American Colonization Society had no right to receive bequests of the nature provided by Ross, Prentiss pointed out that as a corporation it could be designated as a trustee. He showed that previous court decisions had established the right of corporations to accept estates and that this was merely another such occasion. He concluded by stating that the bequest was not only legal, but a noble act which should receive commendation.

Prentiss won this case, and the decision as delivered by James E. Trotter followed closely the lines of reasoning which he had maintained.[13]

The last public appearance of Prentiss was fittingly enough in the courtroom. In June, 1850, he defended the Cuban revolutionist Narcisso Lopez, whom the United States government charged with violating its neutrality laws in an effort to incite the Cubans to revolt against Spanish rule.

[13] For additional references to this case, see Helen T. Catterall (ed.), *Judicial Cases concerning American Slavery and the Negro* (Washington, 1926–1937), III, 280, 290, 305n, 309, 361.

Lopez, born in Venezuela in 1799, and having served in the Spanish army there, had settled in Cuba about 1822.[14] In 1848 he went to New York, and there endeavored to organize two bands of Americans to go to Cuba to free the natives. One group was to sail from New York, the other from New Orleans, and both were to meet in Cuba.[15] Prevented from securing aid in New York, Lopez went to New Orleans in the early spring of 1850 [16] and enlisted the aid of various individuals, including John A. Quitman and as many as six hundred others, "composed of the very best of our Mexican volunteers." [17] Lopez sailed from New Orleans to Cuba May 8 [18] but failed completely in his aim. Agitation against the expedition caused the President to issue a proclamation that it violated the United States neutrality laws, and the Spanish consul at New Orleans issued a warrant for the arrest of Lopez.

As a result, Lopez was brought to New Orleans for a preliminary hearing. His trial began early in June, 1850, and continued for some days. The task assumed by Lopez's attorneys, Prentiss, John Henderson, and E. Warren Moise, was to show that the affidavit for the arrest of Lopez contained no genuine charges against him. If this point could be established, then there would be no reason for referring the case to any higher court than that of the United States District Court in New Orleans.

On June 7, Prentiss made the last speech of his life.[19] In a weakened condition, he spoke at length, trying to show that an affidavit for the arrest of anyone must state specifically the grounds upon which it is issued. He declared that the affidavit for the arrest of Lopez merely stated the opinion or belief of the Spanish consul that the prisoner was

[14] Anderson C. Quisenberry, *Lopez's Expedition to Cuba, 1850–1851* (Louisville, 1906), 28–29.

[15] *Ibid.,* 30.   [16] *Ibid.,* 33.

[17] New Orleans *Daily Crescent,* May 31, 1850.

[18] Quisenberry, *Lopez's Expedition to Cuba,* 47.

[19] This speech was reported by the New Orleans *Daily Delta,* June 8, 1850.

guilty of inciting insurrection in Cuba, but that no actual charges were set forth. In his effort to show this Prentiss asked: "The question here is, upon what ground you may arrest and detain a man in the custody of the officers of the court? Can you do this upon your simple dictum, upon the mere suggestion of some other person,—or from your mere caprice and suspicion? Can you arrest me now for murder because you choose to do so,—because I may look like a murderer, or because somebody else may have whispered into your ears that I had committed murder? Is this the law of the United States? Have Judges and District Attorneys this enormous power of issuing warrants, upon any grounds that may please them, for the arrest and detention of prisoners? . . . The affidavit must swear to some facts or circumstances of the alleged offense. . . . If persons may be arrested on such affidavits as this, alleging no facts or circumstances of the offense charged, on the simple belief of a party that an offense has been committed somewhere; if this were the law, I would rather live on that poor, miserable, afflicted Island of Cuba, which certain gallant young men of our country have lately visited, for the purpose of aiding the oppressed people to achieve their liberties, than reside in a country where the law is carried out in the manner and form of this proceeding." [20]

Prentiss was unable to clear Lopez, and the filibusterer was bound over to United States Commissioner Joshua Baldwin,[21] who with other court officials, deliberated on the Lopez case long after Prentiss was dead.

Some of Prentiss' many hundreds of cases were of little importance; many were as significant as the four just treated. Prentiss was certainly more than an ordinary lawyer. Despite the loss of such conspicuous cases as the Stewart and Lopez cases, he had a wide reputation as a winner. He succeeded through native brilliance, ambition, and labor. In these respects, the Wilkinson case presents an excellent

20 *Ibid.*   21 *Ibid.,* June 9, 1850.

example. More than a half century after his death the memory of his legal powers was recalled by one Louisiana lawyer, Carleton Hunt, who told his fellow members of the bar assembled in New Orleans: "Let the young lawyer, ambitious to be an orator, not despair, but setting the example of Prentiss before him, let him imitate it by going hard to work. If, as is not unlikely, he should fall far short of the consummate pattern before him, he will at least, providing he perseveres, have left many of the faults of his beginning behind him." [22]

[22] Hunt, *Fifty Years' Experience in Practice at the Bar*, 63.

Chapter XV

PRENTISS THE MAN

SOME years after the death of Prentiss, a contributor to the New Orleans *Crescent* related an interesting incident observed in crossing the Mississippi River by ferry at New Orleans: "Among the passengers on this boat were two bright and handsome looking boys, about thirteen and eleven years of age, respectively, and a pretty little girl of eight or nine in a blue hood, . . . all with their satchels and books, evidently returning to Algiers from a school on this side of the river." The writer was particularly interested in the boys and girl when he "heard they were the children of the late Seargent S. Prentiss," and remarked: "It seems that wherever these children go, the renown of their father hangs upon them and people look upon them and admire them with a feeling which may be easily understood by all who knew what the father was." [1]

The renowned father of these children, brilliant in mind, fiery in temperament, alternately melancholic and exuberant in spirit, and poetically imaginative in thought and speech, is universally depicted by those who knew him as a striking and commanding personage. His contemporaries describe him as slightly less than medium in height, about five feet, six inches.[2] He was rather stoutly built, and his "chest was one of uncommon expansiveness." [3] His head

[1] New Orleans *Daily Crescent*, February 3, 1860.
[2] Foote, *Bench and Bar of the South and Southwest*, 33; Reminiscences of Balie Peyton to George Prentiss, in *Memoir of S. S. Prentiss*, II, 273; Sparks, *Memories of Fifty Years*, 369; Rowland, "Political and Parliamentary Orators and Oratory of Mississippi," *loc. cit.*, 362.
[3] Foote, *Bench and Bar of the South and Southwest*, 33.

was large for his body,[4] with a high forehead. His eyes "were gray, deep set, and brilliant," [5] and his eyebrows, which "were full, but not bushy, . . . were gently arched." [6] The observation of Sparks that "his mouth was the most striking feature of his face—large and flexible," [7] is graphically attested to by the comment of Foote that "his upper lip was a little shorter than is customary, and of a flexibility I have never seen equalled. Often was he seen to curl it up, and both in mirth and anger, displaying to view a row of strong well-set and beautiful white teeth." [8]

Favored by nature with a strong physique which was marred only by a lifelong lameness of the right leg and endowed with an intellect of superior quality, Prentiss was a man among men. Classically trained at Gorham and Bowdoin, he continued his intellectual growth to the end of his life. He fed early and throughout life on the Bible, Shakespeare, Milton, Bacon, Scott, Cooper, Irving, Byron, Fielding, Thackeray, and Dickens. These, as George Prentiss said, "imparted a richness, strength, and felicity to his diction, as well as a dignity to his sentiments, that could hardly be attained by any other process." [9] The value which Prentiss set upon his extensive reading of literature can be ascertained from his statement "that a classical allusion, a quotation from the poets, or an illustration from Scott, was as good in the backwoods of Mississippi as in the halls of Congress." [10]

Two authors in particular were his favorites. Shakespeare and Byron best satisfied his literary tastes. In the gamut of Shakespeare he found passages to fit every mood. In Byron he found solace and companionship of another and more specific variety. There was much of the melancholy in Pren-

4 *Ibid.;* Sparks, *Memories of Fifty Years,* 369.
5 Sparks, *Memories of Fifty Years,* 369.
6 Foote, *Bench and Bar of the South and Southwest,* 33.
7 Sparks, *Memories of Fifty Years,* 369.
8 Foote, *Bench and Bar of the South and Southwest,* 33.
9 *Memoir of S. S. Prentiss,* II, 477.
10 *Ibid.,* 478.

Courtesy of William D. McCain

SEARGENT S. PRENTISS

FROM A PORTRAIT IN THE MISSISSIPPI HALL OF FAME

tiss. Shields, who knew him intimately, says: "While at Rokeby he would have deep fits of gloom lasting for weeks. Wrapt in the solitude of his own feelings, I have known him to walk for hours, at night, back and forth upon the gallery." [11] Numerous analogies have been drawn between the temperaments of Prentiss and Byron. Shields stated that "Byron was his chief favorite; in fact, the case of his genius was not unlike that of the poet's: the same brilliant imagination, the same capacious memory, the same exquisite diction, the same classic culture; if we add to this a similar physical infirmity, the likeness is still more complete; this misfortune warped Byron into misanthropy and colored the life of Prentiss with a faint tinge of jocular cynicism." [12] These same resemblances were observed by A. De Puy Van Buren, who wrote: "There was much about him to remind you of Byron: the cast of his head, the classic features, the fiery and restive nature, the moral and personal daring, the imaginative and poetical temperament, the scorn and deep passion, the deformity of which I have spoken, the satiric wit, the craving for excitement, and the air of melancholy he sometimes wore, . . . the collisions, mental and physical, which he had with others, his brilliant and sudden reputation, and the romantic interests which invested him, make up a list of correspondences, still further increased, alas! by his untimely death." [13]

Prentiss' genuine familiarity with the best British poets of the centuries led him to foster a strong admiration for England. According to George Prentiss: "He cherished a hearty affection for Old England, loved to speak of her as the Mother Country, and though not insensible to her faults, was fully aware of the vast debt we owe her for no small portion of what is good or stable in our social system, our laws, and our political institutions." [14] Prentiss gleaned

[11] Shields, *Seargent Smith Prentiss*, 28.
[12] *Ibid.*, 42.
[13] Van Buren, *Jottings of a Year's Sojourn in the South*, 278.
[14] *Memoir of S. S. Prentiss*, II, 536.

the best from the past but lived intensely in the present, as his brother knew when he observed that "His reading, too, embraced a great deal of periodical literature." His critical and selective faculties led him to choose as his favorite a leading British periodical of the day, *Blackwood's Magazine.*[15]

Probably no clearer index to Prentiss' sensibilities can be found than his letters, written over a period of years to his relatives in Maine. His powers of discrimination are revealed particularly in his letters to George Prentiss, whom he endeavored to advise and guide from time to time. George, like Seargent, went to Bowdoin College. When George was a student there, Seargent once wrote him: "You could read nothing more advantageous to you than history. It would be well to read some biography—more especially, the lives of the great men of our country—Washington, Franklin, &c. It will raise your ambition, and show you what can be done through industry and exertion, by those whose advantages have not been as good as your own."[16]

Seven years after his own graduation Seargent was in a position to reflect soberly on the benefits he derived from his college experiences. He did not overlook his membership in the Peucinian society, where training in public speaking was cultivated in the development of the fuller man. Disclosing his ideas at length on the subject to George, then in college, he counseled him: "Let me particularly recommend to you to cultivate, as much as possible, your powers of elocution, for which the society you belong to, will afford ample opportunity. By this, I mean the faculty of debating; of expressing your own ideas in the best and most effective manner." Prentiss' reasons for stressing the importance of training in public address are interesting. "This attainment is to every man of the utmost importance," he

[15] *Ibid.*
[16] Prentiss to George Prentiss, Natchez, September 22, 1830, in *Memoir of S. S. Prentiss,* I, 105.

asserted. "It is no less than the power of *using* his other attainments, for to what advantage is information, unless one is able to convey it and show the world one possesses it? Indeed, my observation of mankind has convinced me, that success in life depends not so much upon the actual *quantity* of knowledge, which a man possesses, as upon the skill and facility with which he is enabled to bring it to bear upon the affairs in which he may be engaged." Prentiss had himself not proved his best when he wrote these lines, but he was on his way and had encountered men of abilities in the legal realm at least. Thus he could say further: "This is particularly true with regard to great men. Their greatness consists less in the extent of their knowledge than in the way in which they use it. There are hundreds, perhaps thousands, of men in the United States, who exceed Henry Clay in information on all subjects; but his superiority consists in the power and adroitness with which he brings his information to bear." Accordingly Seargent concluded to his college brother: "I would again press before any other acquisition, that of expressing forcibly and with ease any idea, which the mind may entertain. This faculty is attained with difficulty in after life, but with ease in youth, at College, and nowhere so well as in the Debating Societies of such institutions." [17]

George Prentiss chose the ministry as his profession. As has been stated before, Seargent aided him in his desire for European study by no small measure of financial assistance. During George's four years of study and travel in Europe, the brothers kept up a chain of correspondence which mirrors the lives of both men.[18] In 1839, shortly after George arrived in England, and before he began his theological and philosophical studies in Germany, one of his letters, descriptive of his impressions of the British Parliament,

[17] *Id.* to *id.*, Vicksburg, August 9, 1833, *ibid.*, 125.
[18] *Memoir of S. S. Prentiss*, I–II, *passim*; Prentiss, *Bright Side of Life*, I, *passim*.

brought a most interesting reply from Seargent. Among the Britishers whom George heard speak was Henry Brougham. Concerning his reaction to this parliamentary speaker, Seargent replied: "I am inclined to agree with you in relation to Brougham. He has too much versatility of talent for my idea of a man who is to become the land-mark of his age. This may seem paradoxical, but the chronicles of the past will show that most men who have made an indelible impression upon the race, have concentrated their energies, and confined them in a single channel. Diffusion weakens no less in mental than in physical power. 'The Admirable Crichton' could not have become a Napoleon, a Milton, or a Shakespeare. Lord Brougham is too much of an Admirable Crichton for my taste." [19] This quotation may be taken as good evidence that Prentiss knew something of the men in the European as well as the American spotlight.

Two years later George was immersed in philosophical study in Germany. Seargent evidently feared that his brother was pursuing abstract learning at the expense of the more practical, and so he sent him another letter full of interesting and significant counsel. "Well, my dear boy," he wrote, "I mean no offense against 'divine philosophy,' and ask pardon of Plato, Aristotle, Thomas Aquinas, Duns Scotus, and yourself. But, in sober truth, are you not devoting too much time to this study? Have you made yourself sufficiently acquainted with history and biography, especially the former?" Again he supplied arguments for his point of view. "These are the great storehouses, from whence to draw, not only lessons of practical knowledge, but also the food for philosophy herself—the subjects for reflection. It is useless to have a mill without corn to grind; equally so to have philosophy without knowledge. The reason why I make these suggestions is, that in accounts you have given me of your studies, I do not remember that you

[19] Prentiss to George Prentiss, Vicksburg, September 25, 1839, in *Memoir of S. S. Prentiss*, II, 146.

have ever mentioned history, biography, or general politics—by which I mean the philosophy and science of government as it actually exists in the world." Seargent was trying
to think in terms of George's future usefulness as he concluded: "Not that I suppose you ignorant of any of these
points, I know the contrary; but I wish you to become much
more than a subtle metaphysician. I wish to see you a wise,
practical man, acquainted with the past history of the
world, and able to make such knowledge subservient to its
happiness. I wish to see you possess those general stores of
information on all subjects which, if ten years younger, I
would myself strive to obtain." [20]

Such instances of advice in the letters of Prentiss to his
relatives are not numerous. Still less frequently was he inclined to be critical. Yet in one of his letters to Anna Prentiss he dared to remind her of a weakness in her style of
letter writing. "By-the-by, though you excel anyone I know
in the kind and gentle art of letter-writing, your epistles are
not always exempt from criticism. I do not mean in sentiment or ideas, but in words. So I will turn pedagogue again,
my dear, and give you a lesson. You use too often the adverb
'very;' it precedes almost every adjective used. Such frequent repetition is not only objectionable for its monotony,
but actually weakens the idea it is intended to strengthen.
To use 'very' so often is a *very* bad habit. Well now, am I
not an impertinent boy to criticise those who write so much
better than myself?" [21]

The intellectual traits of Prentiss are shown by these instances of gracious and sensitive qualities of mind and temper. As he admonished George Prentiss to be a practical
man, he endeavored to be such himself. As a man, he lived
intensely in the present, enjoying much and meeting with
his share of joy and sorrow. As a man among men, he revealed certain traits of mind which his contemporaries

---

[20] *Id.* to *id.*, Vicksburg, January 5, 1841, *ibid.*, 187–89.
[21] *Id.* to Anna Prentiss, Jackson, January 31, 1841, *ibid.*, 190–91.

never failed to notice. All agree that his power of memory was unusual. Likewise, they were invariably impressed with his endowment of imagination and quickness of repartee. Shields, who knew him well, has given incidents illustrative of these traits. As a member of a hunting expedition in the Yazoo Valley, Prentiss once gave one of the most singular speeches of his life. Concerning the expedition Shields related how, after the party had started, "they discovered, upon overhauling their commissary stores, that a very important *condiment* was lacking; a squad was immediately sent out for the missing article." While the remainder of the party was compelled to wait until the others returned, Prentiss climbed a near-by Indian mound. While he was on the mound, "Some of the loiterers at its base raised the cry 'Prentiss, give us a speech.' 'A speech!' 'A speech!' was echoed and reechoed by the party. 'Upon what subject?' asked Prentiss. 'The rostrum upon which you stand,' was the reply." In response, "Like an Italian *Improvisatore*," Shields stated, "he began with a playful sally of wit, warming as he spoke. His imagination peopled the forest with the lost tribe, that mysterious race, the 'mound-builders,' who in ages past inhabited the country, before even the birth of the aboriginal trees which stand above the tops of the huge piles. He introduced every variety of character, kings, princes, courtiers, and warriors. He marshalled armies in battle array and fought battles. Going on thus for more than an hour in a vein of philosophical reflection and poetical invention, he imparted a thrilling, almost real, interest to the imaginery scene." [22]

Prentiss' quick flashes of mind made him exceptionally apt in repartee. From an incident of his own memory, Shields related how when he was a small boy he observed this trait in Prentiss. "Prentiss was playing billiards with a young man of perfect form; straight as an Indian, he was tall, graceful and athletic; just as he had made a lucky hit

[22] Shields, *Seargent Smith Prentiss*, 314.

and was walking around the table to follow up the blow, he remarked sarcastically, 'No man on such a pair of legs as you've got can beat me at billiards.' Without a moment's hesitation Prentiss retorted, as he limped around the table, 'It is a marvel to me, sir, why God Almighty should put *a head with so little brains on such a good pair of legs* as you've got.' " [23]

The capacity to reply and retort so marked Prentiss that years after his death the New Orleans *Crescent* chanced to print an example. Commenting upon the enmity between Prentiss and Governor McNutt of Mississippi, the *Crescent* related how Prentiss on one occasion suddenly came to McNutt's defense. Traveling by steamboat on the Mississippi, a group of individuals in the presence of Prentiss denounced the Governor for certain of his official acts. One critic, going beyond the limits of propriety, called McNutt a dog. "This brought Prentiss to his feet, and with a flushed cheek and flashing eye he eloquently defended his absent fellow citizen and Chief Magistrate . . . and concluded by making the man who styled him a 'dog' to make ample apology for the expression, on the ground that if he did not that he (Prentiss) would consider it a personal matter. Then said Prentiss, in conclusion, if 'McNutt is a dog, he is our dog, and no curs from a distance shall bark at him in my presence while he is absent.' " [24]

One other story is illustrative of Prentiss' repartee. This narrative, told by John B. Coleman of Port Gibson, pertains to Prentiss at Brandywine Springs, en route from Natchez to Vicksburg. In a card game, Prentiss lost all the money he had with him. Refusing to accept a loan, he remained in town until funds could reach him from Vicksburg. The next night, without a cent, he entered the hotel room where cards were being played. After going from table to table and watching the games for a time, he "de-

[23] *Ibid.,* 61–62.
[24] New Orleans *Daily Crescent,* April 16, 1859.

livered a glowing, eloquent, and powerful lecture or sermon on the evils of gambling. . . . Coleman saw and heard
all this, but had never made the personal acquaintance of
Prentiss. The next morning Coleman was on his way to
get his before breakfast glass of water, when he met Prentiss in company with Mr. 'A' returning to the hotel. A and
Coleman greeted each other, and A seeing that P and C were
not acquainted introduced them in the following words:
having allusion as you will note to Prentiss' determination
not to play any more while at the Spring, and to his sermon
of the night before—

" 'Mr. Coleman permit me to introduce to you my *friend*
Mr. Prentiss—a reformed scoundrel.'

"Prentiss, quick as a flash, and with a gracious bow at
once responded.

" 'Mr. Coleman I now introduce to you my *former friend*
Mr. A.—— a confirmed scoundrel.' " [25]

The account of Prentiss' rise and fall financially has been
told. Nevertheless, his financial generosity is another trait of
Prentiss the man. Certainly Prentiss never hoarded money.
On the contrary, he spent lavishly, even to the point of
improvidence. Not all of his money was spent for ill, however. His mother, sisters, and brother had occasion more
than once to thank him for his financial assistance. Exam-
ples, touching and illustrative, revealed particularly by
George Prentiss, exemplify this side of his life.

Before and after his four years in Europe, George spent
some months with Seargent in Mississippi. He stated that
he early thought of joining his brother there and, to get a
start, of becoming a family tutor. Seargent advised against
this and, George says, offered "me whatever funds I might
need to complete my professional studies. He desired that I
should devote myself to the law, and made me a most gen-

[25] W. J. William to Joseph D. Shields, New Orleans, November 16, 1883,
in Shields Collection. This letter was written after William had read Shields,
Seargent Smith Prentiss. The Mr. A. referred to was probably Mr. Archer,
but William is not sure.

erous, or rather a most extravagant proposition in case I would do so and become his partner." [26]

By 1837 Prentiss was able to make very substantial financial contributions toward the welfare of his family in Maine. A letter written to him by George Prentiss in November of that year acknowledged the receipt of two thousand dollars, which George told him was "seven hundred more than we expected, but as your generosity foresaw, not more than we needed." [27]

Prior to this time, the Prentiss family in Maine had received a still more significant gift from its Mississippi son and brother. Shortly before the summer of 1837, the family had purchased a house in Portland and moved thither from Gorham. Seargent arrived home for a visit in June of that year, "and not liking the situation of this house or the house itself, purchased another one on Danforth Street, in the upper part of the city. It was large, convenient, shaded by magnificent elms, and at that time was one of the most attractive in Portland." [28]

One other example of family generosity is noteworthy. It is as difficult to say how much money was sent to Maine over a period of years as it is to say how much was sent to George in Europe. Once, without designating the amount received, George wrote Seargent: "A thousand thanks for your long letter and for the remittance of which it was the harbinger. God bless you, my dear brother, for all your goodness." [29]

A most striking incident illustrative of Prentiss' financial generosity and integrity relates to James Hazlett, long a citizen of Vicksburg. Coming from Pennsylvania penniless in 1829, he settled in Vicksburg, and in a few years saved $450. Borrowing a like sum, he purchased for $900 a flatboat loaded with corn, which was moored at Vicks-

[26] Prentiss, *Bright Side of Life*, I, 25–26.
[27] George Prentiss to Prentiss, Portland, November 30, 1837, *ibid.*, 55.
[28] *Ibid.*, 45.
[29] George Prentiss to Prentiss, Oxford, England, August 31, 1842, *ibid.*, 290.

burg. The boat and corn being worth twice the amount Hazlett paid, he hoped to sell the corn at a substantial profit and retain the boat. With a servant, Hazlett proceeded to sleep on the boat the night following the purchase in order to guard it. Near midnight the boat was struck by a heavy millstone which had been allowed to roll down the hill. The boat was splintered, and sank with the corn, Hazlett and his servant barely escaping with their lives. Shortly Hazlett's misfortune became known with regret to many citizens of the town. A few days later Hazlett was invited into a certain place of business and given a check for $1,900 by the proprietor. "Ten years elapsed before young Hazlett discovered . . . that his loss had been repaired by S. S. Prentiss and a sense of moral and honorable obligation growing out of the fact, that he was one of the mob, which had precipitated the mill stone, which unintentionally it is true, and yet somewhat wantonly had struck the bark upon which had been freighted young Hazlett's hopes, had inspired Prentiss with the commendable plan of reparation." [30]

Probably no finer example can be found of how Prentiss was willing to give to others what he possessed than the incident related by Balie Peyton, while the latter was United States Minister to Chile. Peyton told how in the summer of 1835, while returning from Washington to Tennessee, he had registered with his wife and two children at the Galt House in Louisville. The two children, Emily and Balie, aged five and three years, were running up and down the corridor of the hotel. They suddenly returned to their parents "exclaiming, *'Look! What a gentleman has given Balie!'* who had a handsome diamond breastpin in his bosom." The mother of the children demanded that it should be returned, but the children came back "stating that the gentleman insisted on Balie's keeping it as a present. Shortly thereafter I received a card," Peyton wrote,

[30] Undated and unsigned manuscript in the Shields Collection.

"with the compliments of Mr. Prentiss, who invited me to his room. I found him surrounded by a party of friends, to whom he introduced me, apologizing, at the same time, for what he was pleased to term the liberty he had taken, in a manner peculiarly bland and courteous." [31]

Another aspect of Prentiss' character was his love of outdoor life and its recreational advantages. In spite of being a cripple and unable to move about without a cane, he did not neglect this side of his life. Horseback riding was necessary in his circuit court duties, keeping him in the saddle often for weeks at a time. Such rides may have been exhausting, but they had their tonic effects as well. Shields stated that "he was an untiring rider, and fairly revelled in it." [32] Doubtless the enthusiasm of Prentiss for horses and riding explains the fact that at one time his name headed the list of sixteen signers of an announcement of a meeting to be held at the Vicksburg Courthouse to organize a Jockey Club.[33]

Likewise hunting and fishing were favorite diversions with him. In childhood and in young manhood he spent hours in the woods with a gun or along streams with a rod. Accounts of all his visits to Maine after coming south are replete with mention of fishing excursions. In a description of his Maine home, George Prentiss included the remarks: "There were two trout streams in the vicinity . . . the Branch and the Great Brook; the latter,—including Jordan's Brook,—was Seargent's favorite resort. He pronounced it 'the most classic stream in North America.' " [34]

In contrast to George Prentiss, who chose the ministry as his profession, Seargent was little under the influence of the church. All in all, the pattern of his outward life was hardly in accordance with orthodox standards of church

[31] Balie Peyton to George Prentiss, Legation of the United States, Santiago de Chile, September 25, 1852, in *Memoir of S. S. Prentiss*, II, 272.
[32] Shields, *Seargent Smith Prentiss*, 60.
[33] Vicksburg *Daily Whig*, March 1, 1843.
[34] *Memoir of S. S. Prentiss*, I, 25.

adherents. He had drifted a long way from the devout teachings of his early youth, as is shown in his habits and conduct. It may be doubted, however, that the early influences were forgotten. The term "unconverted" was applied to him by George Prentiss, who, at the same time, insisted he was not "an unbeliever; far from it. He cherished a deep reverence for Christianity and for the Bible." [35] Possibly the feelings of Prentiss on religion can best be seen in a letter he once wrote his mother, who had inquired concerning his "sentiments on the subject of religion." Prentiss stated that he had not "experienced any change on the subject since he left home," but that instead, "In all its great principles, I also trust, I have implicit belief." He could only say, however: "I confess that with regard to what is called *conversion*, I never well understood it. So far as religion teaches us to do good, and to abstain from evil, I acknowledge its excellence, and hope I am not entirely without its influences; but the distinctions of sects, and the necessity of belonging to any one of them as well as a great many of the abstract principles of belief—considered essential by some denominations, by others not—are all beyond my comprehension. If I am wrong, it is from want of understanding and not from willfulness." [36] This letter, doubtless an epitome of his creed, embodied the reasons why he was not able to identify himself with any church. Of this matter Shields said, "He did not profess to be pious and only occasionally attended church, sometimes the Presbyterian and sometimes the Episcopal." [37]

Prentiss was a man who possessed many friends. His conversational brilliance and personal enjoyments in the excitement of the group were invariably noted by those who have written down their impressions of him. He had his

[35] Prentiss, *Bright Side of Life*, I, 24.

[36] Prentiss to his mother, Vicksburg, August 27, 1833, in *Memoir of S. S. Prentiss*, I, 127.

[37] Shields, *Seargent Smith Prentiss*, 42.

enemies, too, and these brought him to the verge of death several times. Just as Prentiss could engage in the choicest of pleasantries, he was equally severe in impulsive scorn, invective, and sarcasm. Most of his enmities were the result of conflicts in politics and law, so that what was said and done resulted in challenges to duels either from Prentiss or to him.

The story of his two duels with Henry S. Foote has been told. These were the only ones he ever actually fought. He came so close to fighting others, however, that these episodes make up a part of his life in the South.

Prentiss must have been in a white heat of anger once when he challenged Governor Tucker to a duel. The Vicksburg *Sentinel* had poured out its political wrath on Prentiss so often that he looked with suspicion upon anyone who might show the slightest favoritism toward it. During 1842 a dinner was held in honor of the editor, James Hagan. Tucker attended and as Prentiss said to him, "you were present and joined in the expression of that regard and approval." Prentiss told Tucker that the "impunity" which Hagan "enjoys does not however extend to others," and asked him: "I wish to know whether in attending the dinner given to him (you intended to approve unconditionally of his editorial course and particularly whether) you intend directly or indirectly in any manner or form to sustain, endorse or approve any portion of his personal abuse referred to or to sustain him as a gentleman in reference to such course towards myself." The day before he sent this letter he had written another which was an outright challenge, and had designated John A. Quitman not only to carry the challenge, but to act as his second and make all arrangements.

The attitude of Tucker was that he was under no responsibility to defend his presence at the dinner, but that if Prentiss would ask him for an explanation in a proper manner, he would have no objection to telling why he attended. Because Tucker had made a speech at the dinner, thus indicating his endorsement of Hagan, Prentiss insisted on holding Tucker personally responsible. After the first two letters from Prentiss to Tucker, conveyed by Quitman, the remainder of the correspondence was between Tucker and Quitman direct. Quitman held that Tucker had been disrespectful of him personally, as he had been designated to convey Tucker's reply to Prentiss. As Tucker had insisted on giving all explanations directly to Prentiss, Quitman sent him repeated protests. Finally Tucker withdrew his note stating he would not explain through Quitman. Thereafter the whole matter was dropped and no duel fought.[38]

In 1843 Prentiss issued another challenge, this time to John F. H. Claiborne. Prentiss clashed with few men more strenuously than with Claiborne, the first time during the disputed election controversy, and then very personally in 1843.

At one time Prentiss was retained as an attorney for certain land speculators in the Choctaw Indian problem. In May, 1830, there was drawn up with the Choctaw Indians, and ratified in February, 1831, the Treaty of Dancing Rabit. It provided that the Choctaw lands east of the Mississippi River in Mississippi be ceded to the United States and that the Indians were to be removed to reservations in Arkansas. By one provision of the treaty, however, any Choctaw head of a family who chose to remain in Mississippi and become a citizen could do so by signifying his intention to the agent within six months after the ratification of the treaty. In that case he would be given 640 acres for himself, half that amount for each unmarried child over ten years of age, and a quarter section for each child under ten. If the Indian should then reside on the land for five

years after the ratification of the treaty, it would be granted
to him in fee simple.[39]

The first agent appointed was William Ward, who seemingly failed in his assignment. He had no specific instructions but to register the names of the Indians who applied
to him. These instructions really did not reach him until
May, 1831, so that he had but three months to register all
the Indians who might come to him. With time short, instructions vague, and Ward "a man of intemperate and
careless habits," he registered no more than sixty-nine heads
of families, though hundreds had applied.[40]

In 1833 George W. Martin was appointed to locate the
reservations made and was asked to secure from Ward the
reservations as designated. Many more Indians claimed sur-
veys than had been registered. The treaty was unpopular
with the Indians, and white settlers were waiting to purchase the lands offered for sale. Land companies naturally
developed, notably the Choctaw Land Company.

As early as 1836 the Mississippi State Legislature appointed a commission to investigate the instances of fraud
in the Choctaw area. Congress had become interested in
the problem even earlier (1834), because of the influence of
George Poindexter in the Senate. Claiborne in the House
pushed into notice the petitions of many Mississippians,
who said that the Indians were being defrauded. Slowly
attention was drawn to the problem, and the House of Representatives approved a bill to appoint a commission to look
into it. This was of little consequence, inasmuch as a Senate amendment limited the work of the commission to the
first day of March, 1838. The matter did not die, however.
In view of constant petitions and pressure a second commission was set up in 1842.[41]

[39] *American State Papers, Public Lands*, VII, 557; Franklin L. Riley,
"Choctaw Land Claims," in *Mississippi Historical Society Publications*, VIII
(1904), 345.

[40] Riley, "Choctaw Land Claims," *loc. cit.*, 346.   [41] *Ibid.*, 365.

The establishment of the second commission brought Prentiss and Claiborne into conflict. Claiborne was named chairman of the commission, with Colonel Ralph Graves and William Tyler, brother of John Tyler, as the other members. Another Prentiss friend, Thomas J. Word, was employed by the commission to examine records and gather testimony. Owing to Word's preliminary findings, Claiborne took steps to stop the further sale of lands. Since Prentiss had been employed, it was said, by land companies on a "contingent fee of $100,000.00 to protect their interests," [42] he and Claiborne became natural opponents.

The entire work of the commission and the Choctaw problem itself involved Prentiss to only a slight degree, apparently. However, as the commission appeared in Mississippi and held meetings, first at Hopahka, at Yazoo Village, and then at Hillsboro, trouble developed. If Prentiss was looking for an excuse for a clash with Claiborne, he found it in the Choctaw situation.

Claiborne had become convinced that the land companies and speculators were seeking to undermine the work of the commission. In one or more articles in the Vicksburg *Sentinel,* for which he took the credit of authorship, the charges against the speculators were set forth. When the commission met in Hillsboro, Prentiss, attorney for the speculators, raised the question of Claiborne's competency to sit on the commission, contending that the articles in the *Sentinel* prejudiced his case. Claiborne replied the next day against Prentiss' accusations, and declared he was only one member of the commission, and that he had acted out of duty. After a strong defense of himself, Claiborne is said to have left the room. Prentiss is then reported to have made a "scathing denunciation of Mr. Claiborne, stating that he would impeach him, and that if he was allowed to sit as a member of the commission he would not appear before it." [43] The tension was so great that Claiborne was told his life was in danger. In the end there came a challenge from Prentiss to Claiborne.

Had Claiborne been willing to fight, another Prentiss duel would have been fought. Claiborne had his reasons for feeling he could refuse a duel and still keep his honor. To Prentiss he first stated: "Whether you choose to be regarded as attorney or speculator, I deny the slightest accountability to you, or any one else, for any steps I may choose to take to protect the public interest, in the legitimate discharge of my duties." He was even more emphatic in the further stand which he took. "And, in resisting a combination so formidable, I feel perfectly justifiable in invoking to my aid, and in the aid of the country, the moral influence of the *Press,* so far as the *power* and *threats* of your associates have left the *Press* free to act. A thousand frowns, and a thousand challenges will not deter me from my duty, if I am permitted to discharge it. My blood will not acquit the parties implicated of the charge, nor wash out the suspicions that rest upon their transactions. Investigations, deep, broad, searching and uninterrupted, can alone settle the point. Bullying, and dragooning, and even assassination will not do it." [44]

These were strong words directed to Prentiss, who doubtless knew that his role as attorney for the land speculators was none too praiseworthy. In any case, the duel was averted by Claiborne's refusal to fight. Prentiss did not, and could not, under the circumstances, present additional challenges if Claiborne was willing to believe his own honor could be sustained without designating a second or choosing weapons.

After Prentiss moved to New Orleans he came near fighting again, this time with Henry Clay Erwin, twenty-year-old grandson of Henry Clay. The challenge, to Prentiss this time, resulted from certain highly abusive language which Prentiss used in court against James Erwin, the father of

44 *Ibid.,* 380.

the boy. A case of fraud involved Erwin in some transactions in New Orleans. Prentiss was secured to prosecute him. In his court speech Prentiss was terribly severe as he "gave the history of every remarkable villain from Cataline, Judas Iscariot, down to Benedict Arnold, and then exclaimed: 'With all their iniquities, not one of them was altogether a villain. Cataline was brave, Arnold resented wrongs, and Judas hung himself. But he, . . . [Erwin] was a coward, resented no wrongs, would not hang himself, and stood alone in the catalogue of villains, mantled all over with crime and sin, without one redeeming virtue upon which to rest a claim for heaven's mercy.' " [45]

Almost at once Erwin's son, Henry Clay Erwin, came from Kentucky and challenged Prentiss on the grounds of his abusive language. He said that "his father was unable to attend to matters of that sort, and that he had a right to assume his quarrel." [46]

Prentiss was placed in a difficult position. Young Erwin was but twenty years of age and the grandson of Henry Clay. Prentiss admired the young man, saying of him, "and a very clever fellow he turned out to be." [47] After considering what he should do, Prentiss accepted the challenge because, as he said, "I was also convinced that, if I declined the challenge, a street fight would probably ensue, as well as other difficulties, in which my friends would be involved; and I believed that it was the cheapest mode of disposing of the affair, to accept the call." [48]

But the duel was averted. Friends, including Balie Peyton and Alexander C. Bullitt, interceded to persuade Prentiss to postpone for two weeks the duel in order to allow time for amicable settlement of the quarrel. In that time Prentiss retracted his harsh words, writing Erwin to that

[45] William H. Sparks, in *Philadelphia Weekly Times*, June 11, 1881.
[46] Prentiss to George Prentiss, New Orleans, February 29, 1848, in *Memoir of S. S. Prentiss*, II, 436.
[47] *Ibid.*   [48] *Ibid.*

effect. The retraction was accepted, much to the joy of all concerned.[49]

But more than anything else, Prentiss' life, noble and sublime in numerous manly qualities, was marred by a fatal and vicious influence. As expressed by the *Ouachita Telegraph* years after his death: "In his moral development he had all the infirmities of a child of genius. . . . To his infirmities of a social character, . . . Mr. Prentiss succumbed, and one of the most splendid intellectual lights that was ever produced was suddenly extinguished in the midst of its blaze of illumination." [50] There is no doubt that Prentiss drank to great excess and in consequence went to an early grave. "Indulgence was his fatal habit," asserted Sparks, "and it was soon apparent that the power of wine was mastering his will and threatening ruin." [51]

[49] *Ibid.*, 437; Sparks, *Memories of Fifty Years*, 366–67; Lynch, *Bench and Bar of Mississippi*, 232–33.

[50] Monroe *Ouachita Telegraph*, December 2, 1868.

[51] Sparks, in *Philadelphia Weekly Times*, June 11, 1881. This aspect of the life of Prentiss is implied, but little more than mentioned, in *Memoir of S. S. Prentiss* and in Shields, *Seargent Smith Prentiss*. The explanation for George Prentiss' deliberate omission of this phase of his brother's life in *Memoir of S. S. Prentiss* is found in a letter written by him to Shields in which he says: "No one knows better than I do that there were such things in my brother's life; nor did I try to conceal the fact in writing his memoirs. I have not a shadow of doubt but that the omission of any detailed account of these things in your work will if it is published, meet with the hearty approval of all right minded, judicious friends, and admirers of my brother. His real character was very beautiful, as well as very remarkable; and at this late day especially it seems to me perfectly right, and no violation of truth, to give a picture of its beauty and its remarkable truth without dwelling upon its shadows. These should not be ignored, but they need not be described." George Prentiss to Shields, New York, January 20, 1883, in Shields Collection. In another equally interesting letter urging Shields to minimize in his biography of Prentiss the influence of drink on her husband, Mary Prentiss stated to Shields: "I never saw Mr. Prentiss seriously affected by wine except on two occasions. The first was soon after my marriage, and the second was on the occasion of his meeting and addressing the returned Mexican volunteers. He died of Chronic Dysentery, a disease inherited from his father, who also died of it, and who was an exceedingly temperate man. I know you will excuse my warmth in speaking on these things, as you can enter into my feelings on the subject." Mary J. Prentiss to Shields, New Orleans, June 19, 1881, in Shields Collection.

Prentiss became addicted to drink very early, it would seem. He was accused of "loose habits," as has been noted, as early as 1837 when he was first a candidate for Congress. By 1840, as has been observed also, his alcoholic habits were given clear emphasis by the Democratic press in his home city of Portland when he spoke there. Certainly drink secured a hold on him which he could not throw off. If one account by Sparks is to be taken seriously, Prentiss had his regrets. Prentiss once told Sparks that there were "two great errors in his life: leaving his native home to find one in the South, and not marrying when he first commenced the practice of law. My constitution was strong and suited to a northern clime, and there home-influences would have restrained propensities that have grown with indulgence, and are threatening in their consequences." [52] Sparks also related his last conversation with Prentiss, in which their ways of life were viewed together. They stood upon the portico of the St. Charles Hotel in New Orleans as Prentiss was about to leave for his last visit to Maine. Prentiss took from Sparks a cane which he had given him years earlier, and said: " 'Oh, were I . . . to-day, what I was the day I gave you this! . . . We were both young then, and how light our hearts were! We have gathered about us household gods, and we worship them; how sad to think we shall have to leave them! You married long before I did. Your children will grow up while yet you live; I shall never see mine other than children.' " Sparks stated that he protested and encouraged Prentiss to believe he would see his children grown. To this Prentiss replied: " 'I know what you mean, and I know what I will; but, like Laocoon in the folds of the snake, the serpent of habit coils around me, and I fear its strength is too powerful for mine. Perhaps, had my angel of to-day been my angel when first a man, I had never wooed the scorpion which is stinging me to death; but all I can do I will. This is all I can promise.' " [53]

[52] Sparks, *Memories of Fifty Years*, 370.   [53] *Ibid.*, 367.

But perhaps Prentiss would never have been so great a coiner of eloquent oratorical epigrams and figures had he not been partially inspired by the stimulating effects of alcohol. If another account of Sparks is to be accepted, it may be that, in earlier days at least, Prentiss did not view so pathetically the effects of alcohol on his life. Sparks told the story of how, in 1837, when Prentiss was a candidate for Congress, he met McNutt in public debate. McNutt tried to capitalize upon Prentiss' habits of drink and urged the people to vote against him because of his dissipation, declaring "that his slavery to the bottle was rendering useless despite his genius, learning and eloquence." Prentiss made his reply. After indicting McNutt with inability to appreciate fine wines and with addiction to cheap corn whiskey which he drank in seclusion, Prentiss went on to say: "Now I will admit, fellow-citizens, that sometimes when in the enjoyment of social communion with gentlemen I am made merry with them and the rich wine of France. It is then I enjoy the romance of life. Imagination, stimulated by the juice of the grape, gave to the world the song of Solomon and the psalm of that old poet of the Lord, glorious old David. The immortal verse of the wandering Old Homer, the blind son of Scio's Isle, was the inspiration of Samian wines, and good old Noah, too, could have sung good and merry songs from the vines he planted, but having to wait so long his thirst, like the Democratic nominees here, became so great that he was tempted to drink too deeply and got so drunk he could not sing." This analogy was good enough to follow up. "And this, I fancy," Prentiss continued, "is the reason why this distinguished gentleman never sings. Perhaps there is no music in his soul. The *glug, glug, glug* of the jug as he tilts and pours from its reluctant mouth the corn so loved of his soul is all the music dear to his ears unless it is the *glug, glug, glug* as it disappears down his capacious throat. Now, fellow-citizens, during this ardent campaign which has been so fatiguing, I have been drunk once. Over in Simpson county, where the people are poor and honest, I was compelled to sleep in the same bed with this distinguished nominee; this delight of the Democracy; this wonderful exponent of the principles and practices of the unwashed Democracy, and in the morning I found myself drunk on white corn whiskey. I had lain too close to this soaked mass of Democracy and was drunk from absorption." [54]

Along with drink, card playing and gambling were frequent diversions in the life of Prentiss. Nights with cards varied the monotony of circuit court duties and aroused excitement in this fiery and restless individual. Shields stated: "It need not be disguised that in early life Prentiss became a victim of this mysterious and singular infatuation; it was not from the love of lucre, but the wild excitement of the hazard and the pleasure of exhibiting great skill in the game." [55]

One story on record typifies the excitement which Prentiss derived from gambling. It was told by Coleman and passed on to Shields. Coleman was in attendance at court in Jackson, Mississippi, and lodged at the same hotel where Prentiss was registered. During the evening Prentiss became involved in cards and gambling. After Coleman had retired and was asleep, a messenger brought a note from Prentiss asking him to send all the money he could spare. Coleman acceded to the request and went to sleep again. The messenger returned in a short time with a second request from Prentiss for money. Coleman went through his pockets another time and sent Prentiss all he had. After another interval of sleep, Coleman was awakened a third time by a request from Prentiss that he send him his watch. Out of friendship, Coleman granted this favor and slept uninterrupted. The next morning, going down the street past a saloon, Coleman was attracted by sounds of hilarity

[54] Sparks, in *Philadelphia Weekly Times,* June 11, 1881.
[55] Shields, *Seargent Smith Prentiss,* 22.

inside, and looked in to see Prentiss, "glass in hand, surrounded by a set of rollicking companions, recounting with
boisterous mirth the adventures of the previous night."
What happened was that early in the evening Prentiss lost
heavily. "With a change of luck in his favor, he had broken
the bank, and not only won all the money the gamblers
had, but a large amount besides of valuable jewelry, consisting of watches, and diamond rings and breastpins. These
articles he was exhibiting triumphantly to the crowd."
Coleman entered the saloon, and as Prentiss saw him he
called " 'hello John—come in—here's your money and your
watch—look here,' pointing to a confused heap of jewelry
lying in his handkerchief on the counter—'look there and
pick out your watch. I've got lots and cords of them, and
other valuables. I'm going to open a jewelry store, and
undersell the town.' " Prentiss remembered the loan of
money, too, and added: " 'And by the way here's your $400
you loaned me last night.' " Coleman then protested that he
had lent him but $100, to which Prentiss responded " 'Oh
well . . . if I didn't borrow it from you, I did from somebody else. Yes! I remember now, it was that damned fellow
from Grand Gulf that let me have the other $300. It don't
matter though. I bursted the bank, swept all the deposits,
and have got money enough to pay off everybody and set
up a jewelry store besides.' " [56]

The rollicking times which Prentiss had on occasion
with men of various sorts have tended to live in Mississippi
history. Old men continue to report stories which they
heard in youth from their elders who knew Prentiss personally. The most frequent story, one which no biographer
would dare omit, is that of the Prentiss bedbug speech.

Somewhere in Mississippi (the town is not certain) while
Prentiss was on circuit, he was lodged in the same room
in a hotel with a fellow attorney. In the night the bedbugs

[56] J. S. Johnston to Shields, Auburn Hall, January 11. 1883, in Shields
Collection.

began to bite so ferociously that sleep was impossible. Some-time in the early hours of the morning, Prentiss was able by lighting a lamp to catch one of the bedbugs. He pinned it to the wall, and the two lawyers decided to hold the trial of the bedbug. A jury was necessary, and so the owner of the hotel and his sons were awakened and empaneled. Then the trial began. Some say Prentiss defended, and others that he prosecuted. Legend has it that Prentiss made one of the most striking speeches of his life. For hours, it is said, he developed his case, elaborated on the theme, and spoke as eloquently as men ever heard him.

Another story widely circulated and remembered is that of how Prentiss spoke from the top of a lion's cage. In one of his political campaigns he was followed by a traveling circus, much to his annoyance. Just as Prentiss was in the midst of a speech, the circus, with its elephants, lions, and other animals, would be seen approaching. Their atten-tion distracted, many of the crowd would leave to view the circus on the march, causing Prentiss to feel that his cam-paign was being injured. Finally he went to the circus man-ager and registered a complaint. The man replied that by following Prentiss he could get his best crowds. An agree-ment was worked out whereby they traveled together, the proprietor allowing Prentiss to finish his speech before he opened the circus to the crowd. In addition, he permitted Prentiss to use as a speaker's platform one of the circus wagons with a lion's cage on it. Sometimes for a better posi-tion from which to harangue the crowd, Prentiss would climb on top of the cage. This novel and elevated position added fire to his speaking. When he wished for added com-motion, especially when attacking his opponents, he would prod the lion into roaring by pushing his cane through the bars of the cage.

Even after all such incidents and traits of character in Prentiss are related, it is still difficult to know very precisely the kind of man he was. He seemingly embodied much of

nobility and of the admirable, but many flaws and weaknesses, too. The best in his life was set forth by his eulogistic
biographer, Shields, as well as by George Prentiss in *A
Memoir of S. S. Prentiss*. The tendency of George to glorify
Seargent irked J. F. H. Claiborne no end. Claiborne admired Prentiss in many respects though they had been enemies for years. But of *A Memoir of S. S. Prentiss* he could
only hold "that it was full of error . . . and a mere travesty
of his [Prentiss'] career, personal and political." Claiborne's
charge was that George Prentiss presented Seargent "as a
semi-saint and somewhat of a Puritan to please New England tastes, when all knew he was the farthest possible removed from saintliness and Puritanism." [57] To the credit
of both Claiborne and Prentiss, there was effected a recon-
ciliation of the two men in New Orleans shortly before
Prentiss' death.

True, Prentiss was no saint. Nevertheless, his life was in
essence above all forms of hypocrisy. Friends and foes alike
knew how he lived. His affections ran deep for his immediate loved ones, and his sense of obligation to those he
loved made him beloved by them in spite of his faults.
Prentiss was withal in certain respects a romantic figure,
so much so that he has been the subject of at least one book
of fiction.[58] Prentiss had his share of tributes and honors,
but it is doubtful if any were ever more sincere or genuine
than that recorded in the diary of the Natchez free Negro,
Johnson, when he wrote: "I sold Mr SS. Prentiss a Cannary
Bird To-day for Five Dollars. and I sold him a Cage for 2.
dollars which Sum he paid like a gentleman." [59] Johnson
had his ideas of what constituted a gentleman, ideas which
Prentiss evidently fulfilled in the highest manner.

[57] Quoted in Riley, "Life of Col. J. F. H. Claiborne," *loc. cit.*, 231.
[58] Norvelle Richardson, *The Lead of Honor* (Boston, 1910).
[59] Diary of William T. Johnson, March 12, 1845.

Chapter XVI

LAST DAYS

PRENTISS' creative days were near an end when at the close of the campaign of 1848 he expressed the hope of returning to his "professional duties with renewed pleasure." His splendid physical constitution had been too definitely undermined by labor and drink to be rebuilt. Rest and relaxation might have restored his depleted energies, but neither his temperament nor his financial condition allowed him to cease activity. Earlier acute signs of physical breakdown had become definitely chronic by the late months of 1848, and when in December of that year a scourge of cholera swept New Orleans, Prentiss became a victim.[1] Recovering somewhat, he was left in a greatly weakened condition and was afflicted with chronic dysentery for the remaining time he was permitted to live.

By June, 1849, Prentiss had regained his health sufficiently to anticipate a vacation from New Orleans which he hoped would restore him entirely. Early in the month he went with his family to Longwood. From there he wrote to his relatives in Maine that he would soon start by steamer for a visit, bringing all his family except Seargent, who was to remain with his grandmother at Natchez.[2] In this, his last visit to Maine (and the first one for his wife and children) Prentiss looked again upon the haunts of his childhood and gave himself over to recuperative endeavors as he

[1] Memoir of S. S. Prentiss, II, 524; Shields, Seargent Smith Prentiss, 413.
[2] Prentiss to George Prentiss, Longwood, June 27, 1849, in Memoir of S. S. Prentiss, II, 527.

went on fishing excursions and visited with relatives and friends, not the least of whom were Daniel Webster, at Boston, and Henry Clay, who was residing that summer at Newport.[3]

Late in September Prentiss bade Maine and his loved ones what proved to be a final farewell and returned to New Orleans, literally to die. What physical regeneration he may have gained on vacation he appears to have lost by October, when he wrote to his mother that in spite of "delightful weather" and "prospects of a pleasant winter," he "was ill with a cold." [4] Feeling the absolute necessity of laboring professionally to support his family and to extricate himself from debt, he assumed obligations far in excess of his strength. In December, a sick man, he went to Morehouse Parish in Louisiana to engage in a trial, which exacted a great toll of energy, as may be inferred from a letter to his relatives in Maine. "The weather was very inclement and the roads horrible, some thirty or forty miles being through the worst swamp I ever saw in my life. I suffered a great deal from cold and wet, and have had, in consequence, a slight return of my old malady." [5]

More evident signs of the approaching end appeared early in 1850. Notwithstanding his being "so feeble that he could with difficulty eat or sleep; yet," stated his brother George, "he scarcely ever worked so hard." [6] Very likely his too strenuous exertions in these days of illness hastened his death. For instance, in this period one of his legal cases in New Orleans demanded his close attention and his appearance at court for three weeks.[7] Continued illness, accompanied by fainting spells and "terrible restlessness and nervous irritability," [8] convinced him that he must lay

---

[3] *Ibid.*, 530–31; Shields, *Seargent Smith Prentiss*, 414.

[4] Prentiss to his mother, New Orleans, October 31, 1849, in *Memoir of S. S. Prentiss*, II, 539.

[5] *Id.* to undesignated relatives in Maine, New Orleans, December 10, 1849, *ibid.*, 540.

[6] *Ibid.*, 542.   [7] *Ibid.*   [8] *Ibid.*

plans for another rest period if he were to remain alive. He made such plans, though he was not to be permitted to carry them out, and wrote to his mother: "I have taken a beautiful cottage on the sea-shore for the summer. It is at Pass Christian. There is a fine fruit-orchard and a garden attached, and a splendid grapery." [9]

In the midst of these days of illness in the spring of 1850, Prentiss was the recipient of an honor to which, if it had come in an hour of health, he would have responded with all the enthusiasm and talent which resided within him. In April he was invited to deliver at Harvard University the first inaugural address of the Story Law Association.[10] His health would not allow him to accept the invitation, and as Shields stated: "Sadly and mournfully Prentiss had to decline this honor." [11]

Prentiss was fighting a losing struggle to enjoy once again the health that would sustain him in his profession. Warm summer days in New Orleans failed to restore him, and he was compelled to tell his mother: "I have been prostrated for three weeks by a severe attack of my old disease. For ten days I have been lying on my back, unable to sit, or scarcely to move. I attribute my attack to over-exertion in Court and exposure to the weather. I had been more or less affected by the disease all winter, but it was not so violent as to prevent my attention to business. Some very important cases, however, compelled me, during inclement weather, to attend Court many days in succession, which, doubtless, aggravated the malady, and brought on the bad spell from which I am just recovering." Still anxious to improve his physical condition, he announced: "At the earnest solicitation of her mother, Mary has concluded to give up our notion of spending the summer on the sea-shore, and will spend it at Longwood. In that event, I shall probably, in

---

[9] *Id.* to his mother, New Orleans, March 9, 1850, *ibid.*, 545.
[10] *Ibid.*, 546; Shields, *Seargent Smith Prentiss*, 417.
[11] Shields, *Seargent Smith Prentiss*, 417.

July, make a rapid trip to the Virginia Springs, and try the waters for a short time." [12]

Though his family did go to Longwood in the summer, Prentiss never reached the Virginia Springs. More ill than he realized but hopeful of recovery, and trying desperately to face the world once again free from financial worries, he wrote pathetically to George Prentiss on June 2: "I am—still thanks to a Kind Providence—improving rapidly in health, though more slowly than I could wish in strength. One feels perfectly well, when the slightest imprudence throws everything aback, and one has to get well again from the beginning. I am dieting with great care; I eat nothing but tea and dry toast, with occasionally a little bit of lamb or mutton. Pastry, fruit, especially apples, are *mala prohibita*. For several days I have been entirely free from the disease, but am very weak and feeble; I shall not recover my strength until I get away from this enervating climate. I am staying at the St. Charles Hotel. Mary and the children went up to Longwood ten days ago; and, notwithstanding my weakness, my business in Court has kept me so busy during the time, that I have not been able to write to you before." The remainder of the letter is pathetic, written, as it was, by a dying man. "I have broken up housekeeping, and am going in for a general curtailment of expenses, to see if I cannot work out of debt. What a jubilee I would have if I could once again stand forth and say, I owe no man a cent. Well, I am going to strive for it. The rapid growth of our four beautiful children warns me that I must make some provision for their education. When Mary comes down in the winter to stay a month or so, I will take rooms. This arrangement will save from two thousand five hundred to three thousand dollars a year. One or two years will be something handsome." [13]

[12] Prentiss to his mother, New Orleans, May 9, 1850, in *Memoir of S. S. Prentiss*, II, 548.

[13] *Id.* to George Prentiss, New Orleans, June 2, 1850, *ibid.*, 549.

It was futile for Prentiss to dream of the future. His decline was too much accelerated in June of 1850. The defense which he agreed to make for Lopez demanded more strength than he had to give. But having undertaken the defense on June 7, he spoke for the prisoner in a speech "which for nearly an hour commanded the attention of a large audience." [14] Reporting the speech in full, the New Orleans *Delta* stated: "We were pained to observe the debilitated and weakened condition of this estimable gentleman and unequaled orator, who, for some time past, has been laboring under a severe and prostrating disease. His remarkable intellect, however, still retains its native vigor and brilliancy, despite great physical weakness." [15]

The Lopez speech was the last effort of the expiring genius. He fainted as he concluded and did so repeatedly in the next few days. On June 17 he attempted a trip to his office, but fainted on the way and was taken back to his hotel.[16] The next day he was carried to a boat bound for Natchez. The Natchez *Courier,* announcing his arrival, said: "Much anxiety is felt by his friends, (and who are they not) and it is hoped that the pure air of the City of the Hills may renew his strength and invigorate his system." [17]

Prentiss had but a very few days to live. He lingered until July 1. The day following, his remains were placed near those of Winthrop Sargent, early territorial Governor of Mississippi, in the Sargent family cemetery. The graveyard is across the road from Gloucester, home of Sargent, and but a short distance from Longwood. On the simple tombstone are the words, "I am the resurrection and the life; he that believeth on me, though he were dead, yet shall he live." Near Prentiss are buried his wife who died in 1891, having been his widow for more than forty years;

14 New Orleans *Daily Crescent,* June 8, 1850.

15 New Orleans *Daily Delta,* June 8, 1850.

16 *Memoir of S. S. Prentiss,* II, 1850.

17 Natchez *Daily Courier,* quoted in New Orleans *Daily Crescent,* June 24, 1850.

Eunice, in 1901; Jane, in 1902; and Seargent Smith, New Orleans lawyer, in 1907. A fourth spot is marked by a stone in memory of Prentiss' first son, George, who died of camp fever in the Confederate Army at Tullahoma, Tennessee, December 7, 1862.

Still a young man, only forty-two years old, Prentiss had lived intensively, abundantly, and with love of life. His passing was deeply mourned in Mississippi, Louisiana, and the South generally. The New Orleans *Crescent* declared that the announcement of his death "will be received with the deepest sensibility through the valley of the West." [18] The New Orleans *Bee* stated: "Seldom have we witnessed so universal an expression of sorrow as that which the death of Sargent [sic] S. Prentiss has elicited from our community." [19] In the Baton Rouge *Gazette* appeared the words, "May the sod lay light upon his breast, for the green turf never pressed upon a nobler heart than that which lately throbbed in the bosom of Sargeant [sic] S. Prentiss." [20] Memorial services were held by the bar associations at Natchez, Vicksburg, and New Orleans. With Judah P. Benjamin presiding at the New Orleans commemorative occasion, Judge Henry A. Bullard pronounced a beautiful eulogy in which he said of Prentiss: "He had more of the talents of the Italian *Improvisatori* than any man living, or perhaps, than any man dead." [21]

Prentiss probably gave no thought to what memorials might ever be raised in his memory. In the quiet rural burial ground his unpretentious grave can be found among tangled vines and moss-hung oaks. When as a young man he had delivered a eulogy on the beloved Lafayette of France and suggested the most fitting last resting place for the friend of America, he came near to describing what has proved to be his own. "Let no cunning sculpture, no monu-

18 New Orleans *Daily Crescent*, July 4, 1850.
19 New Orleans *Daily Bee*, July 8, 1850.
20 Baton Rouge *Weekly Gazette*, July 6, 1850.
21 New Orleans *Daily Delta*, July 7, 1850.

mental marble, deface with its mock dignity the patriot's grave, but, rather, let the unpruned vine, the wild-flower, and the free song of the uncaged bird, all that speaks of freedom and peace, be gathered around it." Prentiss has not been altogether forgotten, however. A county in northern Mississippi bears his name, as does a town in the southern part. In subsequent years Mississippi has also been proud to include him in her official hall of fame. One other tribute to his memory is significant. His alma mater, Bowdoin College, perpetuates a tradition each commencement of honoring her most distinguished alumnus of a hundred years before. This honor was bestowed on Prentiss in 1926, just as it was jointly bestowed on Longfellow and Hawthorne in 1925, on Franklin Pierce in 1924, on William Pitt Fessenden in 1923, and on other sons of Bowdoin in preceding and succeeding years.

CRITICAL ESSAY ON AUTHORITIES

Manuscript Collections

The search for the private correspondence and papers of Seargent S. Prentiss has been disappointing in results. Almost the only letters to a public figure of his day now available are those in the John J. Crittenden Papers in the Manuscripts Division of the Library of Congress. There are two private collections, one in the possession of Mrs. John B. Whittemore of Portland, Maine, and the other belonging to Mrs. Elizabeth Redfield of New York City. These contain a number of letters of a family nature by and to him between the years 1828 and 1845. In the Whittemore Collection there is one valuable letter from Henry Clay to Prentiss. Access to one other private collection, in which it is said there are numerous important letters and documents, was denied to the writer by the owner of the collection, Mr. E. Bryan Dabney of Vicksburg. It can only be hoped that there are no materials in it which would alter the the conclusions arrived at in this work.

The most valuable manuscript papers throwing light on certain aspects of Prentiss' life are those in the Joseph D. Shields Collection in the Department of Archives, Louisiana State University. It contains various letters of reminiscence by contemporaries of Prentiss. In this same collection there are also letters from Prentiss' wife, his son Seargent, Jr., and his brother George.

The search for correspondence between Prentiss and Clay has not yielded what was hoped for in view of their close personal and political friendship, although the Clay Papers in the Manuscripts Division of the Library of Congress are valuable for general information on the political affairs of the time. However, in addition to the one Clay letter in the Whittemore Collection, another exists in the Southern Historical Collection at the University of North Carolina, and one in the Manuscripts Division of the New York Public Library.

A few other letters have been found. One from Prentiss to Governor Charles Lynch is in the Department of History and Archives at Jackson, Mississippi. In the G. L. Record Papers of the Merritt M. Shilg Collection, in the Department of Archives, Louisiana State University, is one from George L. Record of Vicksburg to Prentiss. The late Seargent Prentiss Nutt of Washington, D. C., permitted the use of a letter concerning Prentiss from Alvarez Fisk of Natchez to Dr. Rush Nutt of the same city.

Other materials of a manuscript nature have proved most useful. The Records of the Peucinian Literary Society, in the Library, Bowdoin College, particularly those for Prentiss' college years of 1825–1826, were most helpful. Equally so was the Scrapbook of the Class of 1826, Bowdoin College, likewise in the Library, Bowdoin College. Here were found highly interesting miscellaneous materials.

There are four sources of great significance in understanding the tangled financial transactions of Prentiss in Vicksburg: (1) the Deed Books of the Chancery Court; (2) the Minute Books of the Civil Circuit Court; (3) the Will Book (1818–1823) of the Chancery Court; (4) the papers of John Lane in the Vick Case (Box 147) in the Probate Court Records.

Finally, it should be mentioned that the Diary of William T. Johnson, a free Negro of Natchez, in the Department of Archives, Louisiana State University, has yielded most interesting observations on Prentiss, on other Mississippi persons, and on Natchez life generally.

Published Correspondence

While relatively few unpublished letters of Prentiss seem available, the opposite is true in regard to those which have been published. A standard source, containing invaluable letters, is [George L. Prentiss (ed.)], *A Memoir of S. S. Prentiss,* 2 vols. (New York, 1855). A great portion of this work is given to the quotation of Prentiss' many letters to his immediate family as well as to various public men of his day, from his first years in Mississippi until his death. These volumes have been of more assistance than any other source. Likewise, in an exceedingly rare work, George L. Prentiss, *The Bright Side of Life,* 2 vols. (Asbury Park, N. J., 1901), there are additional letters of value. In still another work, George L. Prentiss (ed.), *The Life and Letters of Elizabeth Prentiss* (New York, 1882), there are some important letters. Of considerable significance, too, is Virginia Q. McNealus (comp.), *Code Duello, Letters Concerning the Prentiss-Tucker Duel of 1842* (Dallas, 1931).

There is certain other published correspondence of general

rather than specific value. Some sources are John S. Bassett (ed.), *Correspondence of Andrew Jackson,* 7 vols. (Washington, 1926–1935); Calvin Colton (ed.), *The Life, Correspondence, and Speeches of Henry Clay,* 6 vols. (New York, 1864); Dunbar Rowland, *Jefferson Davis, Constitutionalist, His Letters, Papers and Speeches,* 10 vols. (Jackson, 1923); Fletcher Webster (ed.), *The Private Correspondence of Daniel Webster,* 2 vols. (Boston, 1857).

Governmental Publications and Other Documentary Collections

Of very direct assistance in studying Prentiss' congressional career have been two sources: *Register of Debates in Congress,* 14 vols. (Washington, 1824–1837), and the *Congressional Globe,* 1833–1873, 46 vols. (Washington, 1834–1873). Through these it has been possible to understand and trace the events of the disputed Mississippi election of 1837–1838, as well as Prentiss' congressional activities, and hence to utilize better the newspaper items of that time in which were recorded aspects of the same events. Repeatedly, too, it has been necessary to turn to the *Biographical Directory of the American Congress, 1774–1927* (Washington, 1928), for help in identifying accurately other persons during Prentiss' period in Congress. For Presidential messages to Congress, James D. Richardson (ed.), *A Compilation of the Messages and Papers of the Presidents, 1789–1902,* 10 vols. (Washington, 1897–1905), has been useful. In the attempt to understand Prentiss' role in the Mississippi State Legislature, the Mississippi *House Journal,* 1836–1837 (Jackson, 1817—), served primarily.

Some valuable help was derived from consulting *American State Papers. Documents, Legislative and Executive, of the Congress of the United States,* 38 vols. (Washington, 1832–1861). Of distinct aid has been Francis N. Thorpe (comp.), *The Federal and State Constitutions . . . and Other Organic Laws . . . of the United States . . . ,* 7 vols. (Washington, 1909). Of equal help has been Clarence E. Carter (comp. and ed.), *The Territorial Papers of the United States* (Washington, 1934—), particularly Vols. V and VI, *The Territory of Mississippi, 1798–1817,* which bear on Mississippi history. Another work, Helen T. Catterall (ed.), *Judicial Cases concerning American Slavery and the Negro,* 5 vols. (Washington, 1926–1937), aided materially.

The records of the State Supreme Courts of Mississippi and Louisiana were of invaluable assistance in tracing the appearances of Prentiss before the high courts of the two states. The Mississippi records consulted were those from 1 Howard (Miss., 1834), to 5 Howard (Miss., 1844), and from 2 Smedes and Marshall (1844), to 4 Smedes and Marshall (1845). The Louisiana records used were from 1 La. Ann. (1846), to 4 La. Ann. (1849). For Prentiss' one appearance before the United States Supreme Court, 7 Peters 222 (1833), was used.

Newspapers and Periodicals

Newspapers and periodicals have proved of more than usual value in tracing the events in the career of Prentiss. It has been possible to find nearly every aspect of his life, and especially of his oratory, sketched in these sources, particularly in the newspapers.

The Mississippi papers, chiefly those of Natchez and Vicksburg, were the most valuable. The paper of the earliest date which yielded items of interest was the Natchez *Southern Galaxy*, 1829–1830, a weekly publication which was followed by the Natchez *Courier*. The *Courier*, at times published daily and at other times semiweekly, proved of great assistance from the beginning of Prentiss' public career in 1836 to his death. It was an ardent Whig organ, from which he received unqualified support. The Democratic opposition paper in Natchez was the *Mississippi Free Trader*, established in 1835. It appeared first as a weekly, but from 1838 to 1858 it was a semiweekly, known as the *Mississippi Free Trader and Natchez Gazette*. Since it was often at loggerheads with the *Courier*, its files from 1836 to 1844 were of distinct value. The Mississippi paper most eulogistic of Prentiss was the Vicksburg *Whig*. It emerged from the Vicksburg *Register*, which had run from 1829 to 1839. The *Whig* was most of the time issued daily, but frequently as a triweekly. Extensive use of the files of the *Whig* as well as those of the *Register* has helped immeasurably in securing a complete review in favorable terms of Prentiss' political activities. Exactly opposite in political attitude was a weekly publication from 1836 to 1838, known as the Vicksburg *Sentinel and Expositor*, which became a daily from 1838 to 1860, called the Vicksburg *Sentinel*. For commendation of Prentiss, the Vicksburg *Whig* exceeded all others; in denunciation of him, particularly after 1840, the *Sentinel* knew no bounds.

The New Orleans newspapers proved of great assistance, especially for those years while Prentiss lived there. The leading papers were published daily and were as a group laudatory toward him, personally and politically. The New Orleans *Picayune,* founded in 1837, proved of value even for the period before 1840 and particularly from 1845 to 1850. Likewise, other papers, namely, the New Orleans *Crescent,* 1848–1850; the New Orleans *Delta,* 1845–1850; and the New Orleans *Bee,* 1845–1850, all virtually competed with each other in according his activities ample space. One other Louisiana paper, the Baton Rouge *Gazette,* 1840–1850, a weekly publication, was of decided help.

Prentiss received widespread notice in many national and metropolitan newspapers. First among those to record events of his career was the Washington *National Intelligencer.* From the time of his advent into public life in 1836, it never failed to give him a goodly portion of acclaim. While the *Intelligencer* originated in 1803 as a Jeffersonian organ, it repudiated Jackson, and was a supporter of the Whigs during Prentiss' period. An example of a large metropolitan paper revealing items of interest concerning Prentiss is the Boston *Daily Advertiser,* particularly from 1840 to 1844. As a Whig paper, it reported his activities quite fully in two presidential campaigns, especially his appearances in New England and eastern cities. Two Maine newspapers, the Portland *Daily Advertiser,* 1837–1844, a champion of Whig tenets, and the Portland *Daily Argus,* 1840–1844, a Democratic organ, were most useful in describing Prentiss' several appearances in his native city.

Many other newspapers were consulted. Some were examined through successive years; others for specific events. The Washington *Madisonian,* 1839, proved helpful for Prentiss' congressional activities. The Washington *Campaign,* 1848, a Democratic campaign paper, was used advantageously. A Louisiana weekly, Democratic in tenets, the Baton Rouge *Advocate,* 1847–1848, was useful in illustrating the support Zachary Taylor received from both Whigs and Democrats in Louisiana in 1848. A Democratic Mississippi paper, the Jackson *Mississippian,* 1836–1845, proved of value for the periodic references it made to Prentiss. Two daily Tennessee papers, the Nashville *Whig,* 1844, and the Nashville *Banner,* 1844, abound with information concerning Prentiss in connection with the Whig conclave there in August, 1844.

Additional Mississippi papers proved helpful, such as the

Conservative Holly Springs Banner, 1840, and the Liberty *Weekly Advocate*, 1844. Items from the columns of still other Mississippi newspapers were often reprinted in such leading papers as the Natchez *Courier*, the Vicksburg *Whig*, the Vicksburg *Sentinel*, as well as in New Orleans papers and others of even greater circulation.

A further list of papers used is as follows: Portland (Me.) *Express*, 1925; Boston *Herald*, 1899; Philadelphia *Weekly Times*, 1868; Newark (N. J.) *Daily Advertiser*, 1844; Exeter (N. H.) *Weekly News-Letter*, 1837–1839; Monroe (La.) *Ouachita Telegraph*, 1868.

The most important periodical used was *Niles' National Register*, 76 vols. (Baltimore, 1811–1849). In this periodical it has been possible to find not only valuable notices pertaining to Prentiss himself, but numerous items of interest about Mississippi. For instance, much information was derived from this source relative to the problem of bond repudiation. Other periodicals most helpful are as follows: *Mississippi Historical Society Publications*, 14 vols. (Oxford, 1898–1913); the *American Whig Review*, 16 vols. (New York, 1845–1852); the *Journal of Mississippi History* (Jackson, 1939—); the *Journal of Southern History* (Baton Rouge, 1935–1941; Nashville, 1941—); the *Quarterly Journal of Speech* (Detroit, 1915—); the *Mississippi Law Journal* (Oxford, 1929—).

Reminiscent Works and Autobiographies

A great many of Prentiss' contemporaries who prepared reminiscent works and autobiographies of one kind or another have left pen portraits and accounts of him. Prentiss was a man who evidently impressed those who knew him. As a result, many wrote their impressions. To a remarkable degree, the memories and opinions of any one individual are supported by the others.

Of first importance are the writings of certain Mississippians, as well as other southerners. In Henry S. Foote, *The Bench and Bar of the South and Southwest* (St. Louis, 1876), and *Casket of Reminiscences* (Washington, 1874), are presented the intimate comments of one of Prentiss' most frequent legal opponents, but also one of his admirers. From an even more astute observer of men and events in Mississippi, Horace S. Fulkerson, *Random Recollections of Early Days in Mississippi* (Vicksburg, 1885), there are given characterizations of Prentiss of a most interesting nature. Additional insight is to be gained from Reuben

Davis, *Recollections of Mississippi and Mississippians* (Boston, 1891). In James D. Lynch, *The Bench and Bar of Mississippi* (New York, 1881), are accounts in a similar vein. Another writer, William H. Sparks, *The Memories of Fifty Years* (Philadelphia, 1870), has left personal memories of Prentiss, but he was probably less concerned than others about adhering to the truth. In a highly readable work, Joseph G. Baldwin, *The Flush Times of Alabama and Mississippi* (Americus, Ga., 1853), have been preserved impressions of genuine worth. Of very distinct value has been [Mrs. Jefferson Davis], *Jefferson Davis, Ex-President of the Confederacy: A Memoir*, 2 vols. (New York, 1890). An analytic tribute is the address of Carleton Hunt, *Fifty Years Experience in Practice at the Bar,* delivered before the Louisiana Bar Association (New Orleans, 1908).

Prentiss was observed, too, by numerous individuals outside the South. Sources of great value in this category are Charles F. Adams (ed.), *Memoirs of John Quincy Adams,* 10 vols. (Philadelphia, 1876); Thomas H. Benton, *Thirty Years' View; or, A History of the Working of the American Government for Thirty Years, from 1820 to 1850,* 2 vols. (New York, 1854–1856); Samuel G. French, *Two Wars: An Autobiography* . . . (Nashville, 1901); Ben: Perley Poore, *Perley's Reminiscences of Sixty Years in the National Metropolis* (Philadelphia, 1886); John F. Darby, *Personal Recollections of Many Prominent People I Have Known, and of Events—Especially of those Relating to the History of St. Louis—During the First Half of the Present Century* (St. Louis, 1880); William Henry Milburn, *The Lance, Cross and Canoe . . . in the Valley of the Mississippi . . .* (New York, 1892). Two other helpful works written by travelers and sojourners in the South are: [Joseph Holt Ingraham], *The South-West,* 2 vols. (New York, 1835), and A. De Puy Van Buren, *Jottings of a Year's Sojourn in the South* (Battle Creek, Mich., 1859).

Biographies

Aside from [George L. Prentiss (ed.)], *A Memoir of S. S. Prentiss,* which contains letters as well as ordinary biographical material, only one other biographical study of Prentiss has ever been published. It is that of Joseph D. Shields, *The Life and Times of Seargent Smith Prentiss* (Philadelphia, 1883). The chief merit of this work is the author's accuracy in respect to the facts of Prentiss' life. But as a pupil, friend, and admirer of

Prentiss, he was unable to be sufficiently objective in treatment, and is, therefore, overeulogistic. Moreover, he did not handle the organization and arrangement of his data so as to present Prentiss in relation to the major events of the day. Since there is no index, no table of contents, and no chapter headings, it is often difficult for the reader to find the treatment of any one item. However, since the author was careful in factual matters, this biography has served to give readers a valuable account of Prentiss.

Biographies of many other persons of the day have proved indispensable. For Prentiss' early life in Mississippi, certain works have been particularly contributive: Charles S. Sydnor, *A Gentleman of the Old Natchez Region: Benjamin L. C. Wailes* (Durham, 1938); James B. Ranck, *Albert Gallatin Brown, Radical Southern Nationalist* (New York, 1937); Mack Swearingen, *The Early Life of George Poindexter, A Story of the First Southwest* (New Orleans, 1934); Wendell H. Stephenson, *Isaac Franklin, Slave Trader and Planter of the Old South* (University, La., 1938). All of these works have aided materially in giving a background understanding of the men and environment with which Prentiss identified himself.

For Prentiss' later period in public and political life, biographies of other men have been helpful. The best have been Bernard Mayo, *Henry Clay, Spokesman of the New West* (Boston, 1937); George R. Poage, *Henry Clay and the Whig Party* (Chapel Hill, 1936); Denis T. Lynch, *An Epoch and a Man, Martin Van Buren and His Times* (New York, 1929); Eugene I. McCormac, *James K. Polk, A Political Biography* (Berkeley, 1922); George F. Milton, *The Eve of Conflict, Steven A. Douglas and the Needless War* (New York, 1934); William E. Dodd, *Jefferson Davis* (Philadelphia, 1907); H. J. Eckenrode, *Jefferson Davis, President of the South* (New York, 1923); Robert McElroy, *Jefferson Davis; the Unreal and the Real,* 2 vols. (New York, 1937).

Certain other biographical studies, though not scholarly in nature, have proved useful: J. F. H. Claiborne, *Life and Times of Gen. Sam. Dale, The Mississippi Partisan* (New York, 1860); id., *Life and Correspondence of John A. Quitman,* 2 vols. (New York, 1860); Lucius P. Little, *Ben Hardin—His Times and Contemporaries—With Selections from His Speeches* (Louisville, 1887); James P. Hambleton, *A Biographical Sketch of Henry A. Wise* . . . (Richmond, 1856); Baxter H. Wise, *The Life of Henry A. Wise* (New York, 1899).

Special Articles

Certain special articles of decided help have been T. B. Thorpe, "Reminiscences of Seargent S. Prentiss," in the *American Whig Review* (New York), XIV (1851), 236–50; Dunbar Rowland, "Political and Parliamentary Orators and Oratory of Mississippi," in the *Mississippi Historical Society Publications* (Oxford), IV (1901), 357–400; Cleo Hearon, "Nullification in Mississippi,"*ibid.*, XII (1912), 37–72; Franklin L. Riley, "Life of Col. J. F. H. Claiborne," *ibid.*, VII (1903), 217–44; R. M. Jones, "Some Facts Concerning the Settlement and Early History of Mississippi," *ibid.*, I (1898), 85–89; Charles H. Brough, "The History of Banking in Mississippi," *ibid.*, III (1900), 317–40; James E. Walmsley, "The Presidential Campaign of 1844 in Mississippi," *ibid.*, IX (1906), 179–97; Buford Rowland, "William Wordsworth and Mississippi Bonds," in the *Journal of Southern History* (Baton Rouge), I (1935), 501–507; W. H. Watkins, "Biographical Sketch: Sargeant [*sic*] S. Prentiss as a Lawyer," in the *Mississippi Law Journal* (Oxford), XIII (1940), 125–36; Dallas C. Dickey, "Disputed Mississippi Election of 1837–1838," in the *Journal of Mississippi History* (Jackson), I (1939), 217–35; *id.*, "The Oratorical Career of Seargent S. Prentiss," in the *Quarterly Journal of Speech* (Ann Arbor), XXVI (1940), 221–29, reprinted in the *Journal of Mississippi History*, II (1940), 63–71; William Norwood Brigance, "The Twenty-Eight Foremost Orators," in the *Quarterly Journal of Speech*, XXVI (1938), 376–81.

General and Special Histories

Reliance has been placed upon a number of indispensable general and special works. For Prentiss' early life three have been of value: Nehemiah Cleaveland and Alpheus S. Packard, *History of Bowdoin College* (Boston, 1882); Louis C. Hatch, *The History of Bowdoin College* (Portland, 1927); Walter L. Fleming, *Louisiana State University, 1860–1896* (Baton Rouge, 1936).

For the years in which Prentiss was active in public and political life, certain other works have served at many turns. Of genuine significance have been Arthur C. Cole, *The Whig Party in the South* (Washington, 1914); William O. Lynch, *Fifty Years of Party Warfare* (Indianapolis, 1931); E. Malcolm Carroll, *Origins of the Whig Party* (Durham, 1925); Charles S.

Sydnor, *Slavery in Mississippi* (New York, 1933); Reginald C. McGrane, *Foreign Bondholders and American State Debts* (New York, 1935); Edward Stanwood, *A History of the Presidency*, 2 vols. (Boston, 1928); Frederick J. Turner, *The United States, 1830–1850* (New York, 1935); Oscar D. Lambert, *Presidential Politics in the United States, 1841–1844* (Durham, 1936); William E. Dodd, *Statesmen of the Old South, or From Radicalism to Conservative Revolt* (New York, 1911); Leslie M. Norton, "A History of the Whig Party in Louisiana" (Ph.D. dissertation, Louisiana State University, 1940); J. F. H. Claiborne, *Mississippi, as a Province, Territory and State, with Biographical Notes of Eminent Citizens* (Jackson, 1880); Dunbar Rowland, *History of Mississippi, The Heart of the South*, 2 vols. (Chicago, Jackson, 1925); *id., Mississippi . . .* , 4 vols. (Atlanta, 1907); Robert Lowry and William McCardle, *A History of Mississippi* (Jackson, 1891); Anderson C. Quisenberry, *Lopez's Expedition to Cuba, 1850–1851* (Louisville, 1906); L. F. Johnson, *Famous Kentucky Tragedies and Trials* (Louisville, 1916); Edgar D. Jones, *Lords of Speech* (Chicago, 1937); William N. Brigance (ed.), *A History and Criticism of American Public Address*, 2 vols. (New York, 1943).

INDEX